Swan Songs

Akhmatova and Gumilev

By

Frances Laird

*To Mary Anne,
With love & best wishes.
Frannie*

© 1999, 2002 by Frances Laird. All rights reserved.

No part of this book may be reproduced, stored in a retrieval system, or transmitted by any means, electronic, mechanical, photocopying, recording, or otherwise, without written permission from the author.

ISBN: 1-4033-2418-2 (e-book)
ISBN: 1-4033-2419-0 (Paperback)

This book is printed on acid free paper.

Cover photograph by Margarette Beckwith

This book is lovingly dedicated to the memory of my parents,

Sidney and Harriet Beckwith.

A Note on the Translations

However bitter adversaries they were in matters of style in the literary world of Petrograd, 1921, Nikolai Gumilev and Alexander Blok found themselves most irrevocably opposed over the matter of the translation of poetry. Blok believed that it was the translator's job to find words to somehow convey the "spirit" of the poem into the new language. It was not the poem's formal qualities that mattered, but some ineffable inner meaning or essence that was vital for the translator to impart. Gumilev, on the other hand, maintained that every feature of a poem, including rhyme, metre, number of syllables, length of line as well as the literal meaning of its words were intrinsically necessary to the poem and must be retained when the translator transformed it into another tongue.

Most translators of today fall into the Blokian camp. All poems, irrespective of the formal characteristics of the original, generally end up translated into the free verse form. There is little attempt to retain the musical qualities of rhythm and rhyme that characterized the original poem, what makes up that indefinable aural dimension of poetic significance so treasured in Russian poetry.

I count myself a follower of Gumilev's way. It is, of course, an impossible task to preserve every aspect of a poem in its new language. The translator of poetry must accept the fact that he or she is inevitably doomed to failure. At its best, the translation of poetry can only be more or less successful. Yet I have found that if the translator makes a scrupulous and honest attempt to retain the formal qualities as well as the literal meaning of the original, a Russian poem can suddenly spring into life in English and the echoes of the poet's voice can still be faintly heard.

My goal in translating the work of Anna Akhmatova and Nikolai Gumilev is to attempt to recreate the poems in a new language, as close as possible to the original, yet as fresh and vital as if they had been written in English. I am neither an academic nor a native speaker of Russian, so errors are bound to be present in *Swan Songs*. But I hope that they will be minor ones and will be forgiven. As to whether in these translations I have succeeded in making two poets and their poems come to life, it is for you, the reader, to make the final judgement.

Frances Laird

Table of Contents

Introduction   The Swans of Tsarskoe Selo 1

Chapter I   Under the Lime Trees 21

Chapter II   The Rusalka 36

Chapter III   Rejection 69

Chapter IV   Ballad 94

Chapter V   At the Fireside 121

Chapter VI   Poisoned 148

Chapter VII   Evening 176

Chapter VIII   At the Stray Dog 199

Chapter IX   The Real Twentieth Century Begins 234

Chapter X   Love and War 256

Chapter XI   Revolutions 286

Chapter XII   Dying Petersburg 315

Chapter XIII   The Lost Streetcar 337

Chapter XIV   The Silver Age Tarnishes 369

Chapter XV   Terror and Grief 396

Chapter XVI   An Unwed Widow 422

Chapter XVII   The Banks of the Neva 439

Conclusion   The Absent Hero 457

Swan Songs
Akhmatova and Gumilev

Introduction
The Swans of Tsarskoe Selo

At the end of the nineteenth century, a traveller from St. Petersburg stepping down from the train at Tsarskoe Selo might have thought he had arrived at a small, provincial backwater. A welcome relief from the wide avenues and granite squares of the bustling capital city, the streets were shaded by rustling limes and black ravens croaked from a perch atop the cross of the onion-domed church on the central square. There was little to attract the tourist here, no museums, concert halls or spas, so the only guest house in the town was often empty.

Nor was Tsarskoe Selo a mecca of pedagogy and learning; the lone bookshop opened its doors only in August, the week before the school year began. But for the young men eager to make their way as officers in the imperial guards, Tsarskoe Selo provided a training center for regiments of Tsar Nicholas II's army. Ranks of young hussars, lined up like toy soldiers, marched across the parade grounds, the wind catching the plumes of their helmets, the sun glinting on the silver buttons and gold braid of their fairy-tale uniforms. After hours, birch switches tucked under their arms, the recruits could be seen crossing the empty square to the public baths.

On a market day, the streets would grow livelier, the marketplace jammed with rough wooden tables piled high with ironware, bolts of fabric and bast sandals and farmers' carts heaped with potatoes, onions and cabbages. Beyond the town center stretched dusty streets with one-storied wooden houses surrounded by plank fences and narrow lanes edged by ditches choked with nettles and burdock.

This was the everyday face of Tsarskoe Selo. But the real identity of the little town that lay in the low country about twenty miles south of St. Petersburg was rich and many-layered. It was here in "the Tsar's Village," at a healthy distance from the swampy surrounds of St. Petersburg, that the tsars of Russia had built their sumptuous and ornate summer palaces that nestled into spacious, leafy parks. As we shall see, Tsarskoe Selo was a place peculiarly suited to the nurturing of poets, including the two who feature as the central figures in this book.

Nikolai Stepanovich Gumilev and Anna Andreevna Gorenko (Akhmatova) were born in the penultimate decade of the nineteenth century. In many ways their backgrounds were similar. Their families, if not distinguished by wealth and high social position, were of the *dvoryanin* class, the Russian landed gentry. Both enjoyed comfortable, if modest, lifestyles in the waning years of the nineteenth century. And both families had their roots in the service and traditions of the imperial Russian navy. But more importantly, both Anna Gorenko and Nikolai Gumilev grew up, attended school and spent many years of their lives in the town of Tsarskoe Selo.

Close friends during their days at the Gymnasium, Anna and Nikolai were separated when Anna's parents divorced and she moved away. But after a lengthy and problematic courtship, their marriage and a wedding trip to Paris, they returned to live in the Gumilev home in Tsarskoe Selo. Throughout these years and even after they were divorced, Anna Akhmatova and Nikolai Gumilev wrote poems to and about one another. These poems, newly-translated and set into the chronology of their lives, will cast new light upon the passionate, complicated and tragic love that bound them to one another.

In her memoirs, Akhmatova lists the poems that Gumilev wrote about her. From a close reading of these, Gumilev's ardent, obsessive, ever-changing view of Anna emerges. We cannot identify with certainty the poems of Akhmatova which were inspired by her relationship with Gumilev, as, though perhaps more numerous, they are not specifically identified by her. In selecting these I have relied upon their dates and their placement within the context of the poets' personal histories. I have supplemented this poetic core with additional poems by these and other poets, memoirs, literary reviews, letters, journal entries, and reminiscences of friends and acquaintances to create a fuller picture of the unusual love from which much of the poetic *oeuvre* of Anna Akhmatova and Nikolai Gumilev springs.

The site of Tsarskoe Selo had been chosen in the eighteenth century by Catherine, wife of Peter the Great, for a country retreat. Earlier the location of Saritsa, an ancient Russian settlement which had fallen to the Swedes, it was re-named Saari with the coming of Finnish settlers. Under Peter the collection of wooden houses became Sarskoe Selo (Sarsky Village), then in 1808, Tsarskoe Selo (the

Tsar's Village). After the 1917 revolution, the Bolsheviks attempted to erase any reminders of its tsarist past with a name more politically correct, Detskoe Selo (Children's Village). Today the town is called Pushkin after the poet, Alexander Pushkin, who had happily spent his school-days there nearly two centuries ago.

Catherine's country house was subsequently redesigned under Empress Elizabeth by the Italian architect Carlo Bartolomeo Rastrelli, who transformed it into an enormous and opulent palace executed in the Russian Baroque style. The Catherine Palace was painted robin's-egg blue and its facade, elaborately decorated with white columns, caryatids, cornices, pilasters and pediments, seemed to run on forever through verdant parkland. The five golden domes of the palace chapel, poking high through a leafy crown of trees, gleamed in the sun. For two centuries the Russian imperial family had passed the summer here, far from the fetid, fever-laden miasma of St. Petersburg.

When Anna Gorenko and Nikolai Gumilev were growing up in Tsarskoe Selo, Tsar Nicholas II and his family occupied the Alexander Palace, elegant but smaller and more suitable as a residence. The grandiose Catherine Palace was reserved for formal receptions, balls and banquets so dazzling in their splendour, pomp and ceremony that foreign visitors were stunned with the showy opulence. Nicholas II, a reluctant emperor, was most comfortable in his role as the Victorian paterfamilias, with Alexandra and their daughters, Olga, Tatyana, Marie and Anastasia, and son, Alexei, surrounded with a complicated hierarchy of court functionaries and retinues of servants.

An electric air of excitement energized the sleepy town when the imperial family was in residence behind the high walls of the Alexander Palace. The usually quiet streets would rumble with gleaming carriages marked with the Romanov's double-headed eagle and carrying members of the imperial family, courtiers and official visitors. Elegant landaus made their way among the troikas, wagons, farm carts and hansom cabs, bearing ladies of the nobility out to take the air, driven by their liveried coachmen. Minor artistocrats mixed easily in the streets with peasants, merchants, policemen, young guardsmen in training, servant girls and children on their way to school. A housewife hurrying to the market would not have been surprised to round a corner and come face to face with the Tsar himself out for a morning stroll among his "children."

But Tsarskoe Selo was distinguished by more than the glitter and pageantry of tsarist splendour. For as its present name, Pushkin, suggests, poets and poetry had been a salient feature of its cultural landscape for nearly a century. From 1812 to 1817, Russia's most beloved poet, Alexander Pushkin, had been a student in the Imperial Lycée at Tsarskoe Selo. The young Pushkin, ardent, impetuous, with dusky skin and a mop of dark, curly hair, had not only made his first amorous forays into the plush parlors of Tsarskoe Selo. It was here that he had written his early poems and formed friendships that had struck deep and lasting roots. On January 8, 1815, the youthful poet

Frances Laird

tasted his first public triumph when, upon graduating to the upper level of the lycée, he read "Recollections in Tsarskoe Selo." The elder poet, G. R. Derzhavin, listened, ecstatic, as the fifteen year-old Pushkin recited his poem celebrating the defeat of "the universal lash," Napoleon, and his "rapacious Galls" at the hands of the Russians. Three years later, with "Tsarskoe Selo," Pushkin paid nostalgic tribute to the town he had barely left.[1]

<u>Tsarskoe Selo</u>

Preserver of sweet feeling and past delights,
Oh, you, genius long known to the singer of groves,
Recollection, if before me you could paint
The enchanted places where in spirit I still live,
The woods where once I loved, where feeling was developed,
Where my childhood flowed and then merged into youth,
Where cherished and brought up by nature and by dreams,
I knew poetry and merriment and peace.

Lead, lead me under the broad canopies of limes,
That always had obliged me in free and lazy times,
To the lake shore, to the quiet slopes of hills!…
Again the carpet of thick meadows I will see,
A decrepit bunch of trees and the bright valley,
And the familiar picture of the fertile shores,

> And on the quiet lake among the twinkling waves
> The proud flock of serene and tranquil swans.
>
> —Alexander Pushkin
> 1817[2]

Tsarskoe Selo could cast an enchanting spell over some who lived there. Innokenty Annensky, a poet and Gumilev's headmaster at the Nikolaevsky Gymnasium, frequently warned: "'You will be poisoned by Tsarskoe.' Annensky's son wrote: The charm of this enchanting garden-city, whose *allées* are filled with history become legend and legend become history, literally enters your blood and poisons you..."[3] Since Pushkin's time, a host of Russian poets—Tyuchev, Lermontov, Zhukovsky, Komarovsky, Annensky himself—had found inspiration in its landscapes. It is not surprising that Tsarskoe Selo was called "the City of the Muses."

For Anna Gorenko, the gravel paths of the imperial gardens, its willow-edged ponds and avenues lined with lime trees, were haunted by the shades of poets, especially the lingering spiritual presence of Pushkin. Later she would write:

> Down the *allées* the dark lad had wandered,
> He had stood, yearning, at the lake's edge,
> And for more than a century we've cherished
> The still barely heard swish of his step.

Frances Laird

> There the needles of pines now cover,
> Thick and prickly, the stumps of the trees…
> It was here lay his hat with three-corners
> And his dog-eared book of Parny.
>
> —Anna Akhmatova
> (from "In Tsarskoe Selo")[4]

But Tsarskoe Selo might just as easily have been called "the City of Swans," for the reed-fringed ponds of the imperial gardens, their dark, mirror-like surfaces dotted with water lilies and brushed with trailing branches of silvery willows, were home to swans. Pure white or ebony, poised and regal, they glided slowly over the glassy waters. Although these patricians of the animal world might have been seen as a living symbol of the Russian aristocracy living near-by, the swans of Tsarskoe Selo had assumed a special significance—as the symbol of its poets.

The idea of the poet as swan did not originate in Tsarskoe Selo, but had classical precedents in Horatian odes and the myth of Orpheus, whose soul took the form of a swan. The swan's purity of color, silence, and erect elegance conveyed a nobility that set it apart from ordinary waterfowl. Not caught up in the mindless swoop and jabber of the flock, the swan, like the poet, retained its solitary, free spirit and unpredictability.

But the most powerful link between poet and swan is rooted in the legend of the heart-piercing song the swan utters as it senses the approach of death. With this haunting call the swan sings its sorrow at leaving this world, while celebrating the culmination of its earthly life on a triumphant note. The swan, like the poet, demonstrates in this ultimate expression the transcendent power of poetic song over death.

The particular linking of the swan with the poets of Tsarskoe Selo was solidified by the repeated images of the swan in the poems of Pushkin, Derzhavin, Zhukovsky, and other poets associated with the town. As we follow the lives of Anna Akhmatova and Nikolai Gumilev, we will see how they came to join the ranks of those poets, famous and obscure, known as the "swans of Tsarskoe Selo."

Despite its legendary past, imperial glitter and poetic associations, Tsarskoe Selo retained its small town atmosphere. Because minor aristocrats, former courtiers and government officials tended to retire there, Tsarskoe Selo was socially and politically conservative, even stuffy. Growing into adolescence there, Anna Gorenko and Nikolai Gumilev, with their rare talents, passionate ideas about life and art, hunger for beauty and high poetic aspirations, would struggle against the ruling social conventions.

Nikolai Gumilev in his teens was already determined to live the exalted and adventurous life he imagined of a poet. Although tall and well-built, his appearance was somewhat less than heroic. In an attempt to compensate for his physical imperfections, a slight lisp and a wandering eye, he adopted a proud, even arrogant manner and the extravagant and impeccable dress of a dandy. All this made him the inevitable target of teasing for his schoolmates.

Frances Laird

Anna fit no more easily than Nikolai into Tsarskoe Selo society. But in 1905, her family's move to Crimea: "…saved her from the more or less open persecution on the part of the brutalized Tsarskoe Selo residents that Gumilev was forced to endure. In this terrifying place everything that was above a certain level was subject to annihilation."[5] Yet it was in the very ordinariness of Tsarskoe Selo that Akhmatova found a rich vein of poetic imagery and inspiration that nourished her poetry until the end of her life.

The writer's biography is invaluable in orienting the reader to the geography of his/her poetic universe, deepening an understanding and appreciation of the poems. Reversing this process, I will use the poems of Akhmatova and Gumilev to illuminate the intertwined lives of these two poets. Apart from his poems and a handful of letters, Gumilev wrote nothing of his life with Akhmatova. For the mass of biographical archives that provide raw material for the life of a writer did not exist for Nikolai Gumilev. He was killed without warning at the age of thirty-five, with no time to gather his papers, to look back over his life with the relative objectivity of old age, to write the memoirs which would have illuminated his relationship with Anna Akhmatova. When he was arrested by the secret police, everything in his possession—notes, bills, official papers, letters and manuscripts—fell into their hands. His papers, scrutinized for evidence of his "crime," were scattered over the floor and left to be cleared out by the building manager of the House of the Arts where he lived. Those hauled away by the Cheka agents were left to yellow in the files of some vast depository until incinerated in a bureaucratic ash pit.

Since Gumilev had been officially labeled an "enemy of the people," a designation which remained unchanged until the Communist government crumbled, his friends and acquaintances, fearful of being incriminated and falling victim to the purges, would have felt compelled to destroy any trace of their association with him. As the night raids of the Cheka (the Extraordinary Commission in the Struggle Against Counter-Revolution and Sabotage) became more frequent, all over Petersburg his letters would have been hastily crammed into smokey woodstoves. Poets and writers who recorded their memories of Gumilev did so after emigrating from Russia, when they were well beyond the reach of the Cheka. These hitherto untranslated memoirs have provided much valuable information about Gumilev.

Akhmatova, whom we might have expected to write with special insight about this seminal relationship in her life as woman and poet, remained mysteriously reticent about it. Lydia Chukovskaya remembered that Akhmatova spoke of Nikolai in a positive, even affectionate manner. Yet she revealed little in conversations about the emotional turmoil of their years together, speaking only in a general way about what had gone wrong in their marriage. Why did Akhmatova shy away from this subject? The strange, ineluctable attraction that drew the two together at an early age, the conviction that their marriage was destined by fate, the relentless struggle of each for autonomy—all charged their love with a special drama that went well beyond erotic excitement or even the mutual affection and commitment of married love. In her memoirs Akhmatova avoided discussing this, writing "...I am not touching upon that special, exceptional relationship, that incomprehensible union which has nothing to do with being in love or marital relations...The time has truly not yet come for a discussion of this kind of relationship."[6] She implies that the nature of their union was beyond the ordinary understanding of love, that however that emotion manifested itself in their lives, its true significance was inaccessible to the outsider. It was as if in Akhmatova's mind the love of these two poets existed on some rare, indefinable, spiritual plane. We can never be certain exactly what happened between the two, because Akhmatova and Gumilev left only a few suggestive clues to the real nature of their relationship. So we are left to take what does remain—both historical and literary—and join them in a careful, reasonable, and creditable way in the attempt to uncover their story.

When Anna Akhmatova, with her striking beauty and her inimitable poetic voice, first appeared in literary St. Petersburg, a stir of curiosity and admiration arose among the bourgeoisie as well as those in the artistic world. Eager to know more about her, Akhmatova's first readers were only too ready to read her poetry as autobiography in verse. With "He loved three things..." they might conclude that it was Gumilev who hated howling children and raspberry jam with his tea.[7] Or judging from "My husband beat me with a patterned strap..." that Gumilev must have been violent and abusive.[8] But poetic truth, however convincing in its essential verity, must not be confused with fact. As in "Song of a Final Meeting," Akhmatova's poems opened a window into the private spaces of a woman's heart. But it is the confusion, disillusionment and emotional abandonment that strike us as real, whatever the actual situation from which these feelings arose.

Song of a Final Meeting

How helplessly my breast grew colder,
But my footsteps still were light.
The glove that was meant for my left hand
I was pulling onto my right.

It then seemed there were so many stairsteps,
Though I knew there were only three!
From the maple came autumn's whisper,
It was begging, "Die with me!

I am tricked and deceived by my cheerless,
Malevolent, changeable fate."
And I answered: "Dear one, dear one,
I'll die with you...for me it's the same."

Frances Laird

> It's the song of a final meeting.
> At the darkened house I gazed.
> And in only the bedroom burned candles
> With indifferently-yellow flames.
>
> > Anna Akhmatova
> > 29 September 1911, Tsarskoe Selo[9]

A love affair had ended and a woman stumbles down the stairs of her lover's house, her consternation betrayed by her clumsy attempt to pull on the wrong glove. The dry rustling of the maple tree heralds the coming death of the year, just as it signals the end of her love affair. Moaning over the tricks and deceptions of fate, the tree invites her to join it in finding escape from her pain in death. Looking back, she sees the house plunged in darkness, except for the bedroom window where the candles burn, not with the red-hot blaze of passion, but with a dull, cold, yellow flame.

While Akhmatova strips away the sentiment to bare the pain of love's deceptions and betrayals, hers is not the gritty, unvarnished truth-telling of the confessional poet. Her experience, whether actual or imaginary, is distanced and objectified by the imagery of the poem, loosening it from close association with the poet/speaker. Akhmatova accomplishes this in three ways. First, she diverts our attention from the "I" of the speaker onto external objects, a glove, three stairsteps, a tree, a candle-lit window through which the woman's emotions are expressed. She brings into the poem the eerie whispering of the maple leaves, an intensely experienced, but imaginary voice from the natural world. Lastly, she organizes these images into a highly formal structure, four rhyming quatrains in a musical, anapestic (~~') metrical pattern. This poem, as its title indicates, is a song, not a page torn from a diary.

These are literary techniques that Akhmatova used to mask and protect herself. For while she may have enjoyed her role as a celebrated poetess of St. Petersburg, she fiercely guarded the privacy of her emotional life. When her first poems were published, she even hid the journal containing them under the sofa cushions, embarrassed at seeing bared on the printed page her hidden thoughts and feelings. Not surprisingly, it is often difficult to make out Gumilev's presence in Akhmatova's poems. The lover is often barely seen, a shadowy presence just off-stage, hidden behind the curtain in a candlelit bedroom or betrayed by a glove and a riding crop left on the table. He may have been objectified in the wasp sting on a ring finger, a familiar silhouette, or a cool, penetrating but disembodied gaze or transformed into the shepherd or the tsarevich of a young girl's daydreams. As the source of the poet's melancholy, pain or exultation, rarely did her lover appear with the solidity and actuality of a real person.

But Akhmatova does provide clues to the meaning of her poems in the dates she gives them. Akhmatova had an exceptionally tenacious memory for the dates of significant events in her life and in the world around her, never failing to remember anniversaries. The precise date of a poem was not accidental, but the key that unlocked the source of its inspiration and insight into its meaning. When the poems selected here are set into the history of Akhmatova's life, found in the biographies by Amanda Haight and Rosemary Reeder, new and unsuspected meanings are discovered that illuminate the Akhmatova-Gumilev relationship. The poems by Gumilev, although dated only by the year, are equally revealing when fitted into the context of his life. Gumilev's early poems are so self-consciously and artfully crafted that it is may be difficult to sense the person and passion that lay behind them. As the critic Zhirmunsky observed: "…He avoids the lyricism of love and of nature, as well as overly personal confessions and too deep self-absorption. To express his mood he creates an objective world of visual images, intense and clear, and he introduces into his verse a narrative element, giving it a semi-epic character…Gumilev is drawn to the depiction of exotic lands where his vision finds a visual, objective embodiment in the colors and varied sights."[10] Some critics denigrated his poems for their artifice and aestheticism, citing the influence of the French Parnassan poet, Lecomte de Lisle. Scornfully rejecting this, Akhmatova recognized the deep and ardent feelings embedded in the poems Gumilev wrote about her: "…these poems are vital and terrifying, it is from them that a great and splendid poet arose. The *terrifying* and burning love of those years is made out to be Lecomte de Lisleism…[the italics are hers]"[11] To Akhmatova, the poems of this "still unread poet," were fueled by intense passion. "The tragedy of love permeated all of Gumilev's early poetry," she writes.[12] She saw that, as well as their strange and haunting beauty, they possessed a frightening visionary and prophetic power.

The early poems of Akhmatova were often variations on the bitter-sweet exultations and tribulations of love. But Gumilev's significance for her went beyond merely inspiring these. It was with his encouragement that she had begun to write the poems collected and published in her first book, *Evening*. He was the first to recognize Anna as a poet, her first teacher, critic, and publisher (in *Sirius*, a literary journal he edited as a student in Paris). And even after they had separated, he remained the warmest admirer of her work. In the days following Gumilev's arrest and execution in 1921, grief-stricken poems poured from Akhmatova's pen and his presence haunted her memory and imagination. In the decades to come, Gumilev's ghost would linger in the background of Akhmatova's poetic universe to make a final shadowy appearance, or non-appearance, in *Poem Without a Hero*, her last great work which she was writing and re-writing up until her death in 1966.

As Russia underwent the wrenching and catastrophic upheavals of war and revolution, Anna Akhmatova and Nikolai Gumilev struggled to carry on their lives and their work, to remain true to their ideals as poets and human beings amidst political chaos, cultural disruption and social disintegration. It was in this vast, pitiless meatgrinder of history that Gumilev was caught up and destroyed. Miraculously, Akhmatova survived the civil war, two world wars, the extremes of poverty and deprivation, and years of the Stalinist terror. After Gumilev's execution, as the rising tide of political terror threatened to engulf Akhmatova and her son, Lev, she was determined to preserve his poetry and protect his posthumous reputation. She understood the role that his ardent and compelling love for her had played in the development of his poetry as well as her own. And she was moved by the expressive power of Gumilev's last poems.

This motivated Akhmatova to collect and preserve his few, scattered papers and the manuscripts of his poems. Gumilev had appeared to her three times in her dreams asking for her help and "...a feeling, precisely of this sort, compelled me over the course of several years (1925-30) to devote myself to the collection and organization of materials related to Gumilev's legacy."[13] If Akhmatova could not muster the emotional and psychic strength to explore the painful years of her life with Gumilev, she knew her moral responsibility to preserve his memory and his work. Akhmatova was certain that, had he lived, he would have won wide recognition as a poet. "His best book is *The Fiery Pillar*. He did not live to see fame. It was just around the corner."[14] If he had lived out his rightful span of years on this earth, something few Russian writers did in those terrible times, he may have taken his place beside Osip Mandelstam, Boris Pasternak, Marina Tsvetaeva and Akhmatova herself in the pantheon of great modern Russian poets.

Aside from his poetry, the biographical information about Nikolai Gumilev is sparse—a few letters, fragments of journals of his African experiences, his newspaper accounts from the World War I battlefields, memoirs written by his friends. No comprehensive biography of him has yet been published in English. For Akhmatova we have the two biographies, her memoirs and critical articles on Pushkin, the recollections of her friends and acquaintances, and a sprinkling of correspondence. And the poems which we search eagerly for clues about the poet, but which still will hold back their secrets. A poet's life is a thing of impenetrable mystery, as Akhmatova herself recognized when she asked almost plaintively of Nikolai Gumilev: "What did he live for, where was he going?"

The time has come to explore that "incomprehensible union" with Nikolai Gumilev that Akhmatova herself was so hesitant to scrutinize. Though she might discourage us from reading her poems as autobiography, poetry as rich in imagery, as lyrical and many-layered as that of these two poets will stand whatever its relation to reality. That we are given a point of entry into the fascinating and formative relationship of Anna Akhmatova and Nikolai Gumilev, one that shaped the directions of their creative lives and brings us to a deeper understanding of both as artists and as human beings, is ample justification for a careful and sensitive biographical reading of the poems.

How did each poet depict himself or herself within the confines of the poem? How did each perceive and depict the other? How did these images reflect the truth of their relationship? How for each did the perception of the other change and develop over time? How did these changing images in the poems parallel the changes in their relationship to one another? How did this relationship end for both poets? And finally, how was it remembered and redeemed in the work of Akhmatova in the months and years following Gumilev's death? These are some of the questions that I will attempt to answer.

The love of Anna Akhmatova and Nikolai Gumilev was profound, stormy, complex, emotionally tangled and vividly embodied in the verse they wrote. These poems reveal the hidden workings of this most unusual of relationships, the mutual love of two highly gifted and imaginative poets. Each poet, allowing us to gaze into the deepest nature of him/herself as well as into his/her understanding of the other, offers views at once revelatory and self-revelatory. In a careful reading of these poems within the context of the poets' histories and their time, we can begin to fill the empty spaces in the biographies of Anna Akhmatova and Nikolai Gumilev.

Chapter I

Under the Lime Trees

It was in December of 1903, on a wintry street in St. Petersburg that Anna Gorenko and Nikolai Gumilev first met, as Anna's friend, Valeriya Sreznevskaya, remembered. The Christmas holidays were approaching and the snow-packed sidewalks of the city were bustling with crowds of people. Horse-drawn trams rumbled and bumped over the ice-rutted streets. Brightly painted sleighs, harnesses jingling, slid past, their shaggy horses snorting clouds of crystalline droplets as they scrambled over the bridges arching the ice-choked canals. Ringing in the frigid air were the sing-song cries of hawkers of greenery, sugared buns and tinware. In the shadow of St. Isaacs Cathedral, mountains of blackish-green spruce trees were heaped for sale, ready for the glass ornaments and candles that would light the faces of children. Flocks of pigeons burst up into the grey sky, then wheeled in widening circles before sinking to peck busily through the street litter. Along the Neva, like bare trunks of a floating forest the masts of ships were clustered at the granite embankments. The palaces off Nevsky Prospekt glowed in shades of crimson, lime and rose, set off with ornately-carved, white trim. And floating over the low city, shining like a blessing in the thin, pale northern light, were the rounded vaults and golden onion domes of churches and the gleaming spires of the Admiralty and the Church of St. Peter and St. Paul.

Valeriya, her brother Seriozha, and Anna had taken the train from Tsarskoe Selo to buy decorations for their Christmas trees. As they approached Gostiny Dvor, the shopping arcade on Nevsky Prospekt, Valya spotted two familiar faces—Dmitri and Nikolai Gumilev. Back in Tsarskoe Selo, Mitya and Kolya took music lessons from the same teacher as she did. The jostling crowds of people, bundled to the eyes in furs and heavy layers of woolens, eddied around them as Valya stopped to greet the boys and to introduce her friend, Anna.

The moment of their meeting, when Anna Gorenko drew a gloved hand from her fur muff and offered it to Nikolai, lifting her dark-lashed, luminous grey eyes to acknowledge his greeting, was a fateful one. But as many such moments, it passed unnoticed and only took on its true significance in retrospect. The Gumilev brothers joined the three friends in their shopping expedition and they all returned together on the train to Tsarskoe Selo.[1] Stiff, silent young Kolya, with his rather haughty manner and plain looks, did not make a significant impression upon Anna at their first meeting. But for Nikolai Gumilev, this chance encounter on a St. Petersburg street marked the beginning of a passion that would haunt him for the rest of his life.

Valeriya soon noticed that Kolya Gumilev would materialize suddenly in the street outside the house on Shirnaya Street that she and her family shared with the Gorenkos. When the Nikolaevsky Gymnasium for Boys had let out its students for the day, she would see Kolya lingering expectantly near-by, waiting for Anna. It was her opinion that: "Anna didn't care for him…But even then Nikolai was not one to give up easily. He was not a handsome young man, being somewhat stiff, outwardly arrogant, and inwardly unsure of himself. But he was well-read and loved the French Symbolists. Though he wasn't very fluent in French, he could read it well enough without having to resort to translation. He was tall and thin with beautiful hands and a pale, rather elongated face. In my opinion, he didn't cut a striking figure, but he was not totally lacking in elegance."[2]

Valya and Anna passed the after-school hours in the usual ways of schoolgirls. "We took long walks together. Frequently, especially when we walked home from the gymnasium, Nikolai would be lurking around a corner somewhere and suddenly join us. We didn't like his company and, I must confess, naughty girls that we were, that we often set about to tease him. We knew that he detested German, so we would begin to recite aloud a long German poem. The rhythmic, florid verses, which we never forgot, lasted until we reached our house. Poor Nikolai would patiently endure our recitation the whole way."[3] But Nikolai would put up with teasing, mockery, and even German poetry if he could catch a glimpse of Anna walking home from the Mariinsky Gymnasium for Girls or exchange a few words before she disappeared into the house. Perhaps to ingratiate himself with her family, Kolya struck up a friendship with Anna's brother, Andrei. Anna's resistance was softened and soon she was strolling with her new friend along the town's lime-shaded streets and the gravel paths and *allées* of the imperial gardens.

Frances Laird

In the near-by Alexander Palace, Tsar Nicholas II and the Romanov family lived on in a luxurious and self-enclosed world. But the acres of imperial gardens which lay beyond the palaces were open to the public. The vast landscapes had been sculpted, planted and ornamented in the English Romantic style in the time of Catherine the Great. She had sent her architects to study 18th century English parks and had hired an English gardener, John Bush, to lay out her gardens in the "natural" style of Capability Brown. The gravel pathways meandered about ponds clotted with lemon yellow waterlilys and onto promontories planted with weeping willows. The ever-changing vistas took in a Chinese bridge and pagoda, a Turkish pavillion, and neo-classical grottoes that rose and sank back into the greenery as the visitor strolled along. Obelisks memorializing imperial triumphs pointed sharp, stone fingers to the sky. Tucked into niches of manicured shrubbery, white marble figures in the classical style posed and gestured remotely. There was just one fountain in the park, a milkmaid holding a broken pitcher, from a story of Lafontaine. This image from the work of the sculptor Sokolov found its way into more than one Russian poem.

Akhmatova's earliest memories were of Tsarskoe Selo: "...the lush, verdant splendor of the parks, the common where my nanny took me, the hippodrome, where little dappled ponies galloped, the old station..."[4] But it wasn't just the formal, manipulated nature of the imperial gardens that fed her imagination. The dusty, vigorous tangles of plant life burgeoning in the ditches along the back streets of

Tsarskoe Selo also emerged in her poetry. When Lydia Chukovskaya noticed how she loved goosefoot, Akhmatova replied: "'Yes, very much. Nettles too and also burdock. Since childhood. When I was small, we lived in Tsarskoe, in a little side street, and burdock and goosefoot used to grow in a ditch there. I was small and they were large, with broad leaves, scented, warmed by the sun—I've loved them ever since then.'"[5]

But to return to her beginning, Anna Andreevna Gorenko was born in a tiny dacha in Bolshaya Fontana, a village on the Black Sea, on June 23, 1889 (June 11, Old Style). This was St. John's Eve, or Midsummer's Night, the celebration of the summer solstice. The peasant customs of ensuring good fortune by leaping over blazing bonfires and bathing in the river by moonlight were linked to legends of Ivan Kupala and rooted in ancient pagan fertility rites. Akhmatova believed that her birth at this auspicious time accounted for her near magical powers of intuition, her love of the water and the powerful effect that the moon exerted upon her.

The third of six children, she was named after her grandmother, Anna Yegorovna Motovililova. Her birth followed that of her brother, Andrei, and sister, Inna. The younger children were two sisters, Iya and Irina (who died of tuberculosis as the age of four), and brother, Viktor. When Anna was two, her father retired from his post in the Russian navy, took one in the civil service in St. Petersburg, and moved the family to near-by Tsarskoe Selo. It was in their hundred-year-old house near the train station, on the corner of

Bezymyanny Lane and Shirokaya Street, that, banished to her yellow bedroom, little Anna peeled off layers of wallpaper until she reached the last, bright red layer of the original wall, once that of a tavern. It was to this house that she would return in her dreams.[6] Anna described her bedroom with its window overlooking Bezymyanny Lane, "…which in winter was covered in deep snow and in summer was magnificently overgrown with weeds: thistle, sumptuous nettles, and a giant burdock. A bed, a small table for preparing lessons, a bookshelf. A candle in a bronze candlestick…An icon in the corner. No attempt was made to relieve the severity of the decor with knick-knacks, needlework, picture postcards."[7] From there she could look upon the unfolding spectacle of funeral processions that would pass to and from the train station: "A boys' choir would sing with angelic voices, and you couldn't see the coffin for all the fresh greenery and flowers, which were dying from the frost. People carried lanterns, the priests burned incense, the blinkered horses stepped slowly and solemnly. Behind the coffin walked the guardsmen…and then the gentlemen in their top hats. The carriages with formidable old women and their dependents followed the catafalque as if they were awaiting their turn…"[8]

Inna Gorenko employed a nanny to help care for the children, an old woman from Kaluga, the source of folk wisdom expressed in such enigmatic and strangely prophetic sayings as: "'She will be spicy'; 'Our affairs are up in smoke,' and 'Looking backward, you'll never see enough.'" Anna remembered: "Up in the Tsarskoe Selo garden I found a pin shaped like a lyre. My governess told me, 'It means you will be a poet.' But the most important thing happened…in Gungenberg when we were living in the Krabau dacha. I found a Tsar-mushroom."[9] This was seen by her nanny as a rare sign of good fortune.

The Gorenkos summered on the Black Sea, in the Tur's dacha on Strelets Bay near Sevastopol, not far from ancient city of Khersones. There Anna could happily revert from a well brought-up young lady to a child of nature, a "wild girl." "I was about thirteen at the time. I used to wear shoes on bare feet and a dress on my naked body with a tear here, all the way down the thigh…right down to the knee, and, to hide it, I used to hold my dress with my hand like this…I used to throw myself into the sea off anything—off a rock, off a boat, off a boulder, off a beam…" A disapproving aunt once scolded her, saying that if Anna were her daughter, she wouldn't stop crying for sorrow. Anna replied cheekily: "It is better for us both that you are not my mama."[10] Akhmatova continued: "My mama often used to send us children to the market in Khersones for melons and watermelons. Actually it was a risky thing to do; we had to go out into the open sea. So once, on the way back, the children insisted that I should row too. But I was very lazy and didn't want to row. I refused. First they scolded me, then they started to make fun of me, saying to each other: 'We are transporting watermelons and Anya.' I took offence. I stood on the side and jumped into the sea…But I managed to swim back, although all this happened very far from the shore…"[11]

Frances Laird

The pleasures of her Tsarskoe Selo life were more sedate, like the concerts in near-by Pavlovsk, where the ancient train brought visitors to the *salon de musique* in the station. Her memories of the brilliant scarlet strawberries on display in the station store, the cool, moist boutonniéres of roses and mignonette for sale in the flower stall, the greasy dishes served in the station restaurant and the clinging smell of cigars were vivid and long-lasting.

Anna Gorenko's early life differed little from those of other girls of her class. She learned to read from Leo Tolstoy's primer for children and began learning French at the age of five. "In Tsarskoe Selo [I] did everything expected at the time of a well brought-up young lady. [I] knew how to fold [my] hands, curtsey, answer an old woman's questions politely and concisely in French, and fasted in the school church during Holy Week."[12] The love of the written word was neither cultivated nor particularly valued at home or school. Akhmatova remembered: "...I took *Poems on the Beautiful Lady* [a well-known collection by Alexander Blok] to school and the pupil who was top of the class said to me: 'Gorenko, how can you read this nonsense all the way through!' A chubby, blond, little girl, with a little white collar and a huge bow in her hair—her whole future mapped out...There was no way of getting through to her. And that's what all of them were like." School was a burden for Anna; she had few friends and, at least in the lower grades, was not an outstanding student. "...I didn't like secondary school...And they didn't like me particularly either."[13]

A visit to St. Petersburg, in the 1890's still the Petersburg of Dostoevsky, was always exciting: "I took it in particularly freshly and keenly after the quiet and fragrance of Tsarskoe Selo. Inside the arcade there were clouds of pigeons and large icons in golden frames with lamps that were never extinguished in the corner recesses of the passageways. The Neva was covered with boats…Many of the houses were painted red (like the Winter Palace), crimson and rose…There were still a lot of magnificent wooden buildings…On the other hand, there was almost no greenery in Petersburg…In the nineteenth century there was nothing but granite and water."[14] Her father took Anna, dressed in her school uniform, to the opera in the Mariinsky Theatre in St. Petersburg. And there were visits to the Russian Museum with her mother. Even then she had formed her own opinions on art. "What I couldn't stand were the exhibitions of the *Peredvizhniki* [*The Wanderers,* a school of naturalistic painters attracted to social themes]. Everything was lilac. I used to go up the stairs thinking: How much better these old paintings hanging on the staircase are."[15]

Andrei Gorenko, Anna's father, was a naval engineer who, in his white uniform laden with gold buttons and braid, invariably caught the eye of the ladies. Valeriya described him as: "Handsome, tall, slender, always immaculately dressed, his top hat slightly tilted, as worn in Napoleon III's time."[16] Unfortunately, he could not resist a pretty woman and at least one of his love affairs resulted in an illegitimate child.[17] Anna's maternal grandfather, who had also served in the Russian navy, was a fur trader in Siberia before returning to Kiev where he grew quite wealthy raising sugar beets. Anna's mother, Inna Stogova, had taken courses at the Bestuzhev Institute and had been politically active in revolutionary circles in those times of growing political ferment. She had even been a member of The People's Will, a Socialist Revolutionary group which had taken part in political assassination plots and encouraged the overthrow of the Romanov dynasty. Andrei Gorenko was her second husband. The first, an older man whom she had been forced against her will to wed, shot himself soon after the marriage. Valeriya described her as: "...a small woman, rosy, with an exceptional complexion, fair-haired, with exceptional hands..[and] a marvelous command of French...her pince-nez continually falling down, and she wasn't able to do anything, not a thing..."[18]

Although previously acquainted, Valeriya and Anna became friends when they both spent a summer holiday in the resort town of Gungenburg: "Anna [then fourteen years old] was a slender young girl with cropped hair. She was altogether unremarkable, rather quiet and reserved. I was very gay, mischievous and outgoing. We didn't become close friends then, but we saw each other often and chatted amicably."[19] But the friendship became closer when a fire destroyed the home of the Tulpanovs (Valeriya's maiden name) and they moved into the lower floor of the house on Shirokaya street where the Gorenkos lived. "The house had a wonderful, large garden where the children could play the entire day without supervision, and this was one less worry for our parents and governesses…[Anna] was writing poetry and reading many books, some of which were banned. And she had changed a great deal, inwardly and outwardly. She was now tall and slender with the lovely, delicate figure of a girl on the threshold of womanhood. Her long, black hair was thick and straight as seaweed, her arms and legs were white and shapely. She had large grey eyes that contrasted strikingly with her dark hair, eyebrows, and lashes."[20]

The Gorenko family, who spoke French among themselves, was close and not as strict as Valeriya's. "True, Anna's handsome father often raised his voice," Valeriya remembered. "But at the same time he could be very witty and unexpectedly jovial…It seemed to me that Anna was allowed great freedom."[21] The family was not bookish; Anna remembered only a thick volume of Nekrasov's poetry, a gift to her mother from her first husband. Nekrasov, with his long, gloomy narrative poems of peasants and humble folk sunk in poverty and despair, was a "realist" whose poetry was admired by those who wanted to bring social change to Russia. Yet Nekrasov could convey the breathtaking natural beauty of the Russian countryside. The sad history of this volume may have cast a mournfully romantic aura over Nekrasov's poetry which Anna was allowed to read only on feast days and holidays.

Anna and Nikolai had in common the fact that both of their fathers had made their careers in the Russian navy. Nikolai had been born in 1886 at a naval base on the island of Kronstadt in the Gulf of

Finland, where his father, Stepan Yakovlevich Gumilev, was serving as a doctor. His mother, Anna Ivanovna, had been the sister of an admiral. In 1886, when Kolya was one year old, the Gumilevs moved to Tsarskoe Selo. Nikolai was a shy child, sensitive and imaginative. He was happiest rambling the woods and meadows of his family's modest estate at Slepnevo, in the province of Tversk, where they spent their summers. In 1896, the Gumilevs moved to St. Petersburg, then to Tiflis, the capital of Georgia, for Mitya was suffering from tuberculosis and it was thought that he would recover in the dry climate. There Kolya was caught up in the writings of Marx and the excitement of revolutionary politics, a brief fascination that never recurred. More importantly, in Tiflis Gumilev began to write and on a page of the local newspaper, the *Tiflisky Listok*, his first poem appeared in print. Soon he was determined to dedicate his life to the art of poetry, a single-minded purpose that would never be shaken. When the Gumilevs moved back to Tsarskoe Selo in 1903, Kolya was happy to discover kindred spirits in a small group of budding poets at the Nikolaevsky Gymnasium.

A glimpse of the teen-aged Kolya comes through the eyes of Nikolai Otsup, then six years old and the brother of a classmate of Gumilev's. Upon Otsup, who would one day become a close friend of the poet, Gumilev's appearance had made a powerful impression: "a head strongly elongated, as if drawn upward, slanted eyes, heavy, slow movements and a difficult pronunciation." His brother had told him that this student was the poet Gumilev, whose poems had appeared not long before in the school magazine.[22]

When the Gymnasium had been dismissed and Kolya and Anna were free to go for walks, their conversations would have touched on many things. But it was a lively and engrossing passion for poetry that would have drawn them into their most animated discussions. Kolya Gumilev was intellectually precocious, having read widely in the classics of Russian and European literature. He was especially drawn to the writings of Nietzsche with his ideas of the supremacy of the will and the life-transforming power of art. Though he knew the work of the French Symbolist poets, Baudelaire, Mallarmé, Verlaine, and Rimbaud, he was most interested in the poetry of the Russian Symbolists.

Anna had had a love for poetry since childhood and, despite the lack of a library at home, had found the books she needed. "At the age of thirteen," she recalled, "I already knew Baudelaire, Voltaire and all the *poetes maudits* in French."[23] By then Anna was fluent in the French language and could read poetry with ease. Her disdain for the birch groves and harvest scenes of "The Wanderers" may have stemmed from a desire to be *au courant* with the new artistic trends. At the end of the 19th century, *Mir Iskusstva*, or World of Art, a circle of artists, musicians and writers, had formed in St. Petersburg with the aim of educating the Russian people in the art of the past and drawing them into a renaissance of Russian culture in the twentieth century. The World of Art presented public lectures, art exhibitions, concerts, and poetry readings and published a literary journal edited by its leader, Sergei Diaghilev. With his darting black eyes, sensual mouth and brush of black hair accented with a tuft of white at one temple, Diaghilev was a compelling figure. The artist, he wrote, must turn away from the depiction of the real world and its social problems to express with his unique and individual genius themes with metaphysical and spiritual significance. The novel and exciting ideas of the World of Art surely enlivened the conversations of Anna and Nikolai as they walked for hours beneath the rustling lindens.

As a student in the Nikolaevsky Gymnasium, Nikolai Gumilev was already writing the poems that would make up his first volume, *The Path of the Conquistadors.* The title indicates a poetic persona he had imagined for himself—the adventurous knight and heroic warrior. In this guise he would journey through strange, unknown lands, following his destined path, to be put to the test in body and spirit. Another heroic persona was the cruel young tsar, clad in scarlet tunic, armed with a gleaming steel sword and astride his black steed. The poor, wandering singer was one that more closely suggested the poet himself. Or Nikolai might cast himself as a master of the universe, arrogant, all-powerful, whose passion was set fire by a pale, silent maiden. The wild places of his poems were peopled with the gnomes, trolls and dryads of fairy-tales. Marble palaces stood on high cliffs below crimson moons, swirling mists, diamond-like stars and blood-red sunsets.

Invariably one bright star would draw the poet/hero on through impenetrable mists and the blackest night, where he would find his Beloved waiting for him at his path's end. The incarnation of his ideal of Woman, she would be the ultimate blessing and reward for his unflagging strength, manliness, courage and fidelity. Gumilev's poetic ideal of Woman undoubtedly grew from Vladimir Soloviev's concept of the Eternal Feminine. Soloviev believed that this divine feminine principle, which he called Sophia, would reconcile human beings through love and bring about a world transfigured by a universal harmony. The mystical metaphysics of Soloviev were a seminal influence upon the Russian Symbolist poets.

Gumilev's poetic imagery was fed by his experience of the soaring Caucasus mountains of Georgia, the wild, craggy mountaintops, dangerous precipices and rocky, bottomless abysses. His world of heroic feats and fantasy offered an escape from the monotonous schoolboy's life in a provincial Russian town. In his poems, Kolya could envision himself as the Nietzschean hero, active, virile, powerful and heroic, qualities eagerly sought by an intense, awkward, homely and diffident young man.

Chapter II
The Rusalka

One person who took Nikolai Gumilev's aspirations to become a poet seriously was Innokenty Annensky, the headmaster of the Nikolaevsky Gymnasium. Annensky was an erudite teacher of Greek and Latin and a gifted translator of the plays of Euripides into Russian who had penned his own tragedies based on themes from classical myths. But it was Annensky's lyric poetry, with it refined, piercing and desolate beauty, that remained his most enduring literary work.

However, Annensky's gifts were not those of a headmaster, for he failed abysmally in the practical matters of running a school. One student remembered filthy classrooms and the broken-down desks, carved up with students names. The older students, already sporting mustaches, loafed about or behaved outrageously. Discipline was no better among the teachers. The principal came to class drunk in the morning and snored away comfortably at his desk, while a half-crazy mathematics teacher would glower silently at his students from beneath beetling grey brows like a sick bird.

Annensky himself would make his grand appearance only two or three times a week. Slowly, ceremoniously he would proceed down the hall, his head thrown back, his right hand laid affectedly on the lapel of his frock coat. Under his other arm he held his briefcase and the folios of Greek texts that he used in his classes. Clustered about him, a dense, noisy crowd of students moved en masse along with him. Above the hubbub, with vacant gaze and Olympian calm, Annensky strode majestically along the grimy corridor, only to disappear once more into his director's apartment.[1] With Annensky as his mentor, Gumilev soon was well-known in the tiny circle of poetry-lovers in Tsarskoe Selo.

Annensky's influence upon Anna Akhmatova would be every bit as important as that upon Nikolai Gumilev. For it was after reading Annensky's collection of poems, *The Cypress Chest*, in 1910, that Akhmatova began to find her own poetic voice. But even before this, Anna and Valeriya had loved to read together the poems of Annensky. They had made a search of an overgrown part of the imperial gardens for the statue called *Peace*, the subject of one of their favorite Annensky poems. When they found it, Valeriya recalled:

For a long time we looked at its face, wounded by rain, white with dark spots...and in a horrible and strange way we repeated...the last exclamation of this amazing poem, 'Give me eternity and I will give back eternity for indifference to insults and the years.' And how strange, almost children, adolescents, young girls, how we loved to observe from afar the tall figure of the poet walking along, and behind him always his old valet carrying a small folding chair—he was suffering at that time from chest pains.[2]

Annensky must have caught sight of young Anna somewhere, on the street or in the company of her older sister, Inna. For when he heard in 1904 that Sergei von Shtein, a professor at St. Petersburg University, was going to marry Inna Gorenko, Annensky reportedly

Frances Laird

replied: "I would marry the younger one." It was a compliment that Anna would never forget.[3]

Some sense of the impact of Annensky and his poetry upon Kolya during those sessions in the poet's study, beneath the bust of a brooding Euripides, are conveyed in his poem, "Memories of Annensky," written after his headmaster's sudden death from a heart attack in 1911.

<u>Memories of Annensky</u>

To such melodious, unexpected ravings
    Calling people's minds with his own,
Innokenty Annensky was the last of
    The swans of Tsarskoe Selo.

I recall the days: I, shy and hurried,
    Entered his high study's door,
Where, calm and courteous, waiting for me
    Was the poet with the graying hair.

Those sentences, so strange and captivating,
    As if by chance he let them fall.
He hurled into the dark and empty spaces
    Of nameless dreams—me, weak and frail.

Swan Songs
Akhmatova and Gumilev

Into the twilight of receding things and
    A perfume which is barely sensed,
Oh, that voice, sinister and tender,
    As it reads verse sounds out again!

In it sobs out some kind of resentment,
    Copper ringing, thunder's stride,
Euripides' profile above the dresser
    Was dazzling to my burning eyes.

In the park I know a bench; they tell me
    That he had loved to sit alone,
Looking pensively on the blue distance
    Down *allées* turned to purest gold.

Evening there is wonderful and awful,
    In mist the marble flagstones shine.
A woman, like a shy gazelle, is hurrying
    In shadows toward a passer-by.

She gazes, she is singing and then weeping,
    Again she weeps and sings and sighs,
Not understanding what all this is meaning,
    But only feeling—it's not right.

Frances Laird

> The waters murmur, lingering at the sluices,
> The shadows smell like moistened grass,
> And pitiful the lonely muse's voice is
> Of Tsarskoe Selo—the last.
>
> Nikolai Gumilev
1911[4]

Anna, like Nikolai, had known early in her life that she would become a poet. When she was ten years old, she fell ill with a mysterious fever. For a week she was delirious but, miraculously and against everyone's expectations, she recovered. It was after this close brush with death that she began to write poetry. Akhmatova remembered: "I wrote my first poem when I was eleven years old (it was terrible) but even before that my father for some reason called me a 'decadent poet.'"[5]

Though Anna may have dreamed of becoming a famous poet, her mother could be exasperated by what she considered her daughter's conceited attitude. When she was fifteen, they happened to be traveling near Bolshaya Fontana and stopped to look at the dacha where Anna had been born. Akhmatova remembers: "At the hut's entrance I said, 'Some day they'll put up a memorial plate here.' I wasn't being vain. It was just a silly joke. My mother was distressed. 'My God,' she said, 'how badly I've brought you up.'"[6]

Andrei Gorenko opposed his daughter's professed vocation, which he considered a highly dubious pursuit for a well brought-up young woman. To dream up lines of sentimental verse for a friend's autograph album was one thing, but to devote oneself seriously to poetry was quite another. When asked who had chosen her pen-name, Akhmatova answered: "'Nobody, of course. In those days no one was interested in me. I was a sheep without a shepherd. And only a crazy 17-year-old girl would choose a Tatar surname for a Russian poetess. That's the surname of the last Tatar princes of the Horde. Taking a pseudonym occurred to me because, having found out about my poems, my father had told me:"Don't bring shame upon my name." "I can do without your name then!" I said.'" [7] Her pen-name, Akhmatova, was that of her great-grandmother on her mother's side, an 18th century Tatar princess who had descended from the Khan Akhmat, in his turn a descendant of Genghis Khan. She cites a single poetic forebearer: "…You will find no one in my family who wrote poetry, except for the first Russian poetess, Anna Bunina, who was the aunt of my grandfather, Erazm Ivanovich Stogov."[8]

Soon after she and Nikolai Gumilev met, the image of Anna began to appear in Gumilev's poetry. Hers may be the cold, marble-white corpse of a young woman lying at the bottom of an abyss in "The Song of the Singer and the King." She was the Moon Maiden with dishevelled braids, sorrowful eyes and a voice like the quiet trembling of strings to whom the hero gives a gold and ruby ring ("Lucifer gave me five mighty steeds…"). In 1904, a year after she

Frances Laird

and Nikolai had met on the street in St. Petersburg, he wrote "The Rusalka" with the dedication on the original copy, "To A. A. Gorenko."

The Rusalka

A necklace burns on the rusalka
And its rubies are sinfully red.
These are dreams that are strangely sad
Of a drunkeness, painful and worldly.
A necklace burns on the rusalka
And its rubies are sinfully red.

The rusalka's glimmering gaze
Is the dying out gaze of midnight.
It gleams at first briefly, then longer,
When the winds from the sea start to wail.
It enchants, the rusalka's gaze.
The rusalka has eyes that are mournful.

I adore her, this wench-water spirit,
All lit up by the night's mystery
And I love her bright, glowing gaze
And the rubies, burning and blissful…
For I, too, have come from those abysses,

Swan Songs
Akhmatova and Gumilev

From the bottomless depths of the sea.

Nikolai Gumilev

1904[9]

Akhmatova takes care to warn us about mistaking the image in Gumilev's poems for an actual person: "The heroine, like the landscape, is encoded—it could not have been any other way."[10] Such "encoding" suggests that there can be no direct identification of the poetic image with the actual subject. Akhmatova insisted: "I know Gumilev's main themes. And the main thing is his cryptographic writing."[11] The phrase, "it could not have been any other way" implies that for the poet an exact depiction of his subject in the poem was not his goal, that the poetic image was suggestive of the qualities the poet saw in the person who inspired the poem.

"The Rusalka," with its exotic, dream-like imagery and almost hypnotic anapestic (~~') rhythms, clearly falls within the Russian Symbolist tradition. The water sprite fascinated Russian poets, including Pushkin and Lermontov, and Konstantin Balmont, a Symbolist admired by Gumilev, had recently published a poem entitled "She is Like a Rusalka." But Gumilev needed no poetic precedents to envision Anna Gorenko as a rusalka. For he had heard her tell of summers on the Black Sea, where she would swim for hours in a torn dress. The gravel paths they walked in the park skirted the willow-edged lake, the haunt of the rusalka. It was on a bench there, as the dragonflies dipped over the glassy waters, that Kolya first confessed his love to Anna and they exchanged their first kiss.[12] Kolya even went so far as to ask an artist friend to paint a mural on his bedroom wall of Anna Gorenko as a rusalka.

In Slavic folklore, the rusalka was a water nymph who had been transformed from her human shape as a young woman. Betrayed in love, she had thrown herself into the river, but was saved from death and granted life in a form half human, half fish. A young man happens upon the rusalka and, enchanted by her grace and wild beauty, falls in love with her. Trusting his vows of eternal love, the rusalka abandons the weedy currents of the stream to follow him. But setting foot on dry land, she immediately loses her ability to speak. Inevitably the young man's ardor wanes and, rejecting the rusalka for her fishy coldness, he finds love with an earthly woman. The rusalka, who can only look on in mute and tormented despair, rushes back to the stream where she had once lived so happily and finally succeeds in drowning herself. Among the southern Slavs of the Danube and Dnieper rivers, the rusalka was a gay and charming creature. But in the folk tales of the northern Slavs, the Russians, she is more closely associated with death. Her face is gaunt, pale and corpse-like, her hair wild and tangled and her luminous eyes give off an eerie greenish light.

In Gumilev's intoxicated, dream-like vision, the rusalka fascinates the poet with her glowing eyes and penetrating gaze. Yet she remains silent, aloof, and strangely passive. Her ruby necklace heightens the white nakedness of the her body, lending a strange eroticism to this cold, pale creature. The rubies shine "sinfully red," a favorite Symbolist color suggesting the fire of passion and lust, while the pale grey of the rusalka's eyes, captivating the poet with their sadness, glows like a midsummer "white night." In a surprising reversal, the poet sees himself not as alien to her world, but as a fellow creature of the rusalka's watery realm. For he, too, feels a stranger on the earth and longs for the underwater "abysses," a frequent image in Gumilev's early poems that conveys danger and the extreme and perilous displacement of the hero into another reality. The poet and the rusalka, both out of place in the ordinary world, share a common provenance and spiritual home.

In Moscow, Valery Bryusov was the undisputed leader of Russian Symbolist poets and was strongly influenced by the French Symbolist poets, Baudelaire, Mallarmé, Rimbaud and Verlaine. The French Symbolists, rejecting the clear diction, formalized style and impersonal subject matter of the Parnassian school, had discovered that subtle, complex and indefinable meanings could arise out of the dynamic interplay of words and images. Words could be chosen for their connotative power of suggestion as well as their denotative function. From sounds and repetitions of words, in metre and in rhyme, a pure musicality alone could engender meaning. Using these techniques, the poet could break through the shell of this world into another, hidden, mystical, resonant with significance, that lay beyond it. Although the French Symbolists had an undeniable impact on the poetic sense and vocabulary of Russians, Russian poets had already begun to turn away from realistic subject matter expressing social and political truths. And there were clear Russian precedents for this more musical, individual and self-revelatory style of expression in the work of earlier 19th-century Russian poets, like Tyuchev and Fet.

In "The Rusalka" two images with strong Symbolist associations dominate—the rusalka's ruby necklace and her shining eyes. In the semi-hallucinatory world of the poet, both give off a strange and unsettling emanation. The rubies burn with a fiery glow that is "sinfully" red, while the rusalka's sad eyes that enchant the poet gaze out in gleaming grey. The rubies convey the flagrant sexuality of the wench, while the mournful gaze of the rusalka, "the dying-out gaze of midnight," projects the cold, fish-like asexuality of the water sprite, virginal and pure, untouched by warm, human hands. These two images play against one another to evoke a creature who projects a disembodied, almost abstract carnality combined with a cold and distant purity. The rusalka, trapped in a limbo between the human and the animal worlds, possesses the amphibian's ability to live on land and in water and shares the cold-bloodedness and inactivity of these creatures. The eerie otherworldliness of the poem is intensified by its musicality, with the running anapestic metre, the alternating feminine and masculine rhymes and the repetitions of lines and phrases, to create an hypnotic, incantatory quality.

Although her physical body remains virtually invisible in the poem, Gumilev's Anna/rusalka exerts a potent erotic pull, with her sexual power residing, not in the body of an innocent young girl, but in the jewels that adorn it. With the absence of sexual experience, her femaleness has assumed power in this symbolic form. The rusalka's eyes, the pale grey of Anna Gorenko's eyes, exerted a magnetic fascination over the poet, as if her physical presence were centered and concentrated there. They are enchanting, hypnotic, a natural illumination like the ghostly light of a northern "white night." But she remains in a physical sense insubstantial, elusive and unattainable. Even at this early age Gumilev could see two opposing and contradictory sides of Anna Gorenko—the virginal purity of the child of nature and the incipient sexuality of the experienced woman.

In Gumilev's poems, a powerful and unsettling strain of prophetic foresight, an uncanny gift of prevision, can be discerned, one that Akhmatova saw running throughout his entire poetic work. Already in fifteen-year old Anna Gorenko, Gumilev had sensed the two contraposed qualities of innocence and worldliness that would emerge years later in her own poetry. This perceived dichotomy in Akhmatova's poetry would be carried over and used to undermine not only her work, but her character, culminating in Zhdanov's vicious denunciation of her in 1946, as "half nun, half harlot."

Yet another prescient theme, seen obliquely in the Anna/rusalka's silence, but more directly in the folk tales, is that of the power of the poet's voice. When the ability to speak is sacrificed, willingly or unwillingly, what results is the torment of muteness. The silencing of the voice is the ultimate sacrifice, a kind of living death for both the rusalka and the poet. With the Bolshevik revolution, the silencing of the poet, whether by censorship or by death, would become only too real for Akhmatova and for Gumilev.

Also couched in the subtext of the rusalka tale was the impossibility of a lasting love between two creatures at home in different worlds. A fateful love, the inevitable cooling of passion, betrayal, separation and death—the whole rusalka story laid out the path their own lives would follow in the years ahead. Gumilev's imagination came to be shadowed by an increasingly dark and ominous prevision of his future, so strangely prescient in his poetic vision as to reveal the details of his own death. The themes taken up by Gumilev in this first poem about Anna as a water sprite would resonate down the decades of that terrible century.

The quiet, bourgeois existence of the Gorenkos ended in 1905 when her parents divorced. Anna's father, now retired from his government post, had decided to leave his wife and make his home with his long-time mistress, Yelena Strannolybskaya, an admiral's widow. Inna Gorenko moved with her children to Evpatoriya on the Black Sea, where the costs of food and housing could be covered with the small amount of money that must support them. Anna, who was aware of her father's failings, was sanguine about his departure. But she could not have been happy to leave her home on Shirokaya Street, Valeriya and her other friends, the Mariinsky Gymnasium and Kolya Gumilev.

For the Gorenkos in Evpatoriya, the political tumult of the outside world broke suddenly into their lives with the news of January 22,

1905, "Bloody Sunday." The demands of the Russian people for freedom and a more representative government had grown ever more insistent, even strident. But Nicholas II wavered between ineffectual attempts at conciliation and draconian repression of all dissent. When hundreds of thousands of his faithful subjects, bearing holy icons and his portrait and singing the national anthem, gathered in the square before the Winter Palace to protest the harsh conditions under which they were forced to labor and live, Nicholas' response was brutal. Troops of mounted police opened fire without warning on the unarmed crowds, pursuing them over the vast, stone-paved square and down narrow side streets. A hundred and thirty demonstrators were killed and hundreds more were wounded. The Tsar was not even present to hear their appeal, for he had taken his family to the safety of Tsarskoe Selo. With this deadly response to their grievances, the Russian people began to lose their loving respect for their Tsar "Father" and for imperial rule.

Meanwhile, Nicholas II was pursuing an aggressive, but futile, military course in the Russo-Japanese War. On February 8, 1904, the Japanese made a sudden, devastating attack upon the Russian navy anchored in Port Arthur, on the coast of China. The remnants of the Russian fleet, a few antiquated ships that had sailed from the Baltic Sea, were destroyed in a sea battle in the Tsushima Straits separating Korea and Japan. This catastrophic defeat of the Russian imperial navy deeply affected the Gorenko family. Akhmatova looked back on Tsushima as a precursor of the evils in store for the twentieth century, devastating wars, revolutions, totalitarian oppression and political murder on a scale never seen before in human history.

Kolya Gumilev was finishing his last year at the Nikolaevsky Gymnasium when Eric Gollerbakh first heard of this rather odd young man who was always writing poetry and reading. He recalled: "…He supported the famous traditions of the lyceé Gymnasium students. First of all, he zealously pursued the young ladies. I vividly remember Gumilev standing at the exit of the Mariinsky Girls Gymnasium, where a crowd of pink-cheeked, laughing girls run out at half past two. He was singing out in his unusual voice: 'Let's go to the park, let's take a stroll, let's wander about.'"[13] Gumilev's voice struck Gollerbakh as "deep, somehow thick and intoxicating, springing from a low, baritone to high, almost squeaky notes. His way of speaking was measured, almost cadenced, tasteful, intelligent, without haste."[14]

To his appearance Kolya paid the exacting attention of the dandy. Young Dmitri Klenovsky viewed his school-mate with a certain awe. "I remember that he was always especially immaculately, even smartly dressed. In the school newspaper was a caricature of him: he stood preening before a mirror, in a tightly-fitting full dress uniform with stirrup trousers and glossy black boots."[15] Outwardly, Gumilev cultivated the image of a fashionable young man about town, perhaps to counter his intense inner life of intellectual and creative pursuits. Yet, shy, sensitive and full of self-doubt, he lived half inside, half outside the fantasy world he had created for himself. Although he pursued other young women, his obsessive love for Anna Gorenko, inflamed by his poetic imagination, was very real. Around Easter of 1905, Anna was horrified to learn that Kolya, in despair when she had refused to take his protestations of love seriously, had attempted to kill himself.

Till then, despite his fervent declarations of love, Anna had looked upon Kolya less as a lover than as a good friend and kindred spirit with whom she could talk about poets and poetry. Suddenly all that was changed. Had he put a rope around his neck in a moment of deep despair? Was it a calculated, histrionic gesture made for melodramatic effect? Or was it a deliberate attempt to pressure Anna to agree to go away with him? Certainly this close encounter with death bestowed a romantic allure upon a young poet who, for the sake of a woman's love, had nearly sacrificed his life. Whatever lay behind Kolya's suicide attempt, Anna was shocked and frightened. They quarreled over this and stopped writing to one another.

Nikolai turned his attention to his poetry and in February, 1906, he wrote Valery Bryusov asking for guidance as he set out upon his literary career, the first of many letters between the budding poet and his mentor.[16] He battered Bryusov with questions. What are his opinions of Gumilev's poems? To which journals should he submit them? What should he do if he submits work and hears nothing? The young poet put himself in Bryusov's hands with a touching confidence in his advice and instruction. Bryusov's direction of his young "disciple," as Gumilev called himself, can be traced in their eight year correpondence. In his review of Gumilev's *Path of the Conquistadors* in the Symbolist journal *Vesy (The Scales)*, Bryusov had severely criticized the poems as imitative and overly influenced by the Decadents. But he'd discovered a few wonderful poems among them with genuinely successful images. Gumilev thanked him effusively for resurrecting his lost self-confidence and for the invitation to submit poems to *Vesy*.

Meanwhile, Anna had moved in with her aunt's family in an apartment on Meringovskaya street in Kiev and enrolled in the Fundukleyevskaya Gymnasium. Far from her family in Evpatoriya and friends in Tsarskoe Selo, she was overwhelmed by feelings of loneliness and isolation. Not only had she fallen into a hopeless and completely unreciprocated infatuation with V.G. Kutuzov, a St. Petersburg University student, her sister, Inna, had recently died of tuberculosis. She wrote of her life in Kiev and her secret crush to her bereaved brother-in-law Sergei von Shtein:

…The only good moments are when everyone goes out to dinner to a tavern or goes to the theater, and I listen to the silence in the dark living room. I always think about the past, it's so large and bright. Everyone here is very nice to me, but I don't like them…I am always silent or crying, crying or silent…Since August I have been dreaming day and night of going to Tsarskoe, to Valya, for Christmas, even if it's just for 3 days…My dear Shtein, if you knew how stupid and naive I am! I am even ashamed to admit it to you. I still love V.G. Kutuzov. And there is nothing in my life, nothing except this feeling…Do you want to make me happy? If so, then send me his picture…[17]

Anna confided in her brother-in-law, as she may have in Inna, had she been living. She felt alien in her aunt's family, where nobody made a pet of her or indulged her delicate sensibilities and mercurial moods. Her only escape was in moony memories of the past or dreams of Christmas with Valya in Tsarskoe Selo, perhaps even a heart-stopping glimpse of the adored Kutuzov.

In another letter to von Shtein, Anna begged to know if Kutuzov would be in Petersburg for Christmas. "I fell ill from the thought that my trip might not take place (a marvelous means of achieving something), I have a fever, heart palpitations and unbearable headaches. You have never seen me so terrible..." When she had fainted on the rug, there had been no one to help her to her room. Monstrous faces emerged out of the designs of her bedroom wallpaper. Then she confessed to her own bungled try at suicide. "Did Andrei tell you how in Evpatoriya I attempted to hang myself and the nail pulled out of the plaster wall? Mama cried, I was ashamed—in general it was awful!" Yet she was not completely without admirers: "Last summer Fyodorov [a minor poet] kissed me again, swore that he loved me and again smelled like dinner." She asked her brother-in-law to answer quickly her request for the photograph of Kutuzov.[18]

Anna spent Christmas, not in Petersburg, but in Kiev where Aunt Vakar, she was sure, could not stand her. "Everyone mocked me as much as they could; Uncle knows how to shout quite as well as Papa, and if I closed my eyes, the illusion was complete...Perhaps you would send me a picture of Kutuzov in a registered letter? I'll just make a little copy of it for a locket and send it back to you at once." Her hopes that von Shtein would invite her to St. Petersburg were in vain: "Why didn't you telegraph me as we agreed? I waited for a telegram day and night, I got my money and my dresses together and nearly bought a ticket."[19]

In her letter of January, 1907, she is still impatiently expecting the photograph. "Is it really so difficult to send me a picture and a few words? I am so tired of waiting! Why, I have been waiting more that five months now. Things are very bad with my heart, and as soon as it begins to hurt, my left arm goes completely numb…Send me a picture of V.G.K. I beg you for the last time."[20]

But before Anna could acquire the photograph, her infatuation had cooled. In the summer of 1906, Kolya Gumilev had visited her in Evpatoriya and they had come to some understanding. Kolya travelled on to Paris for study at the Sorbonne, while Anna, with the help of a love-struck tutor, set out to complete her final year at the Gymnasium in Kiev. With Kolya's visit and their resumed correspondence, Anna wrote to von Shtein of her new romantic interest:

Don't be surprised; with a stubbornness worthy of better direction, I decided to inform you about an event which must fundamentally alter my life, but this turned out to be so difficult that until this evening I couldn't bring myself to send this letter. I am going to marry my childhood friend, Nikolai Stepanovich Gumilev. He has loved me for three years now, and I believe that it is my fate to be his wife. Whether or not I love him, I do not know, but it seems to me that I do. Do you remember Bryusov's

Swan Songs
Akhmatova and Gumilev

> 'Crucified together for torment,
> My ancient enemy and my sister!
> Give me your hand! Give me your hand!
> The sword has been thrust! Hurry! It's time!'
>
> And I gave him my hand, but what was in my soul, only God and you, my faithful, dear Seryozha, know...
> ...I'm not writing anything, and never will. I have murdered my soul, and my eyes are created for tears, as Iolanthe says. Or do you remember Schiller's prophetic Cassandra? One facet of my soul adjoins the dark image of this prophetess, so great in her suffering. But I am far from greatness.
> Don't say anything about our marriage to anyone. We still haven't decided where or when it will take place. *It is a secret*; I haven't written even to Valya.[21]

In the breathy excitement of this girlish letter, with its wild and sentimental occilations, most striking now is Anna's comparison of herself to the Trojan princess, Cassandra. Apollo gave the daughter of Priam the power to foretell the future. But when she refused his amorous attentions, he left her power to predict intact, but destroyed her ability to persuade others of the truth of her prophecies. In the decades ahead, Akhmatova would take on that prophetic mantle and be celebrated as the Cassandra of her age in a poem by Osip Mandelstam.

In a postscript to her letter, Anna asks a rather surprising question: "Do you have anything new by N.S.Gumilev? I have no idea what and how he is writing now, and I don't want to ask."[22] Anna, too, began to write more poetry, including poems she wrote addressed to Gumilev as her "brother," but none of these early poems survive. Far from Tsarskoe Selo and buffeted by events great and small, Anna must have found solace in expressing her deepest feelings in poetry.

For Kolya, enrolled in a course in French literature at the Sorbonne, his correspondence with Bryusov, the only poet to take an interest in his work, was more vital to him than ever. Bryusov advised him on metre and rhyme and suggested topics for articles. Kolya wrote furiously in his first weeks in Paris, though he admitted to Bryusov that much of it was rubbish. He was working on a dramatic piece and, with the high expectations of youth, already planned to offer it for staging at the Vashkevich Theatre. In a letter dated 11 November, 1906, Bryusov questions him about the effect of Paris on his inner life and the direction his poetry would take. Nikolai had begun to question an aesthetic based on mystical visions, dreams and magic. He wrote: "It [Paris] gave me the sense of the depth and seriousness of the most trifling things, the briefest moods. When I left Russia, I thought I'd occupy myself with occultism. Now I see that a necktie conceived of with originality or a successfully written poem can give the spirit the same tremor as dead people summoned up..."[23]

He sent off his latest poems for the older poet's scrutiny, hoping that he would publish them in *Vesy*. But when Bryusov asks him to review Diaghilev's exhibition of Russian art, he refused, believing it beyond the scope of his capabilities. "Russian art is presented from its very beginning, from a time when it, perhaps, didn't even exist. I speak of a few icons. I can't write about it in the style of Sologub; I am no mystic. I can't write in the style of Max Voloshin; I am no artist. I could write in my own style only about two or three paintings..."[24]

Gumilev, alone in that huge, bustling, self-important foreign capitol, felt cut off from the life swirling around him. Some days the only creatures he spoke to were the maid or the lions in the zoo. Yet there were other Russian poets in Paris, drawn there by its irresistable attractions. Konstantin Balmont resided near-by on a quiet street near the Luxembourg Gardens. Gumilev wrote to Bruysov: "Having arrived in Paris, I sent a letter to Balmont, as his true reader, and somewhat of a past disciple, asking him if we might meet, but I haven't received an answer..." This snub clearly bothered him. "A famous poet who doesn't consider it necessary to answer a beginning poet has certainly fallen as a man in my opinion."[25]

But Gumilev did hold a letter of introduction to Zinaida Nikolaevna Gippius, a well-known poetess and wife of the writer, Dmitri Merezhkovsky. The pair had been forced into exile in Paris for their opposition to the tsarist government during the 1905 revolution. Before their flight abroad, the Merezhkovskys' weekly literary salon in their St. Petersburg apartment had been at the heart of the Symbolist literary world.

Zinaida Gippius was an exotic figure, "..slender, fragile, with a mass of copper hair, green eyes and thickly powdered face, she wore an ebony cross and rings on her fingers, smoked fragrant cigarettes and played with a glittering lorgnette."[26] Gippius would receive her guests in a flowing, snow-white gown, lying recumbent upon a chaise longue. Despite her theatrical appearance, Gippius had a keen intellect and a deep interest in esoteric philosophical and religious questions. Her piercing gaze through the lorgnette and her exacting, often cruel judgements inspired fear, even hatred, in those she skewered on her epigrammatic barbs.

Sometime late in the fall of 1906, Nikolai learned the Merezhkovsky's Paris address and, clutching his letter of introduction, he approached their door. There are three different accounts of this visit: one by the poet, Andrei Bely, who was present, one by Gippius, and one by Gumilev himself (the latter two in letters to Bryusov).

According to Bely, when Gumilev rang the doorbell, Gippius was drinking tea with her husband, Dmitri Merezhkovsky, Bely and Boris Filosofov. Bely opened the door to find a pale youth, snub-nosed, with starting eyes and half-opened mouth. The obviously nervous Gumilev was led into the sitting-room, clutching his top hat in his shaking hands. Bely asked:

Swan Songs
Akhmatova and Gumilev

"Who do you want?"
"You," he trembled with fear, "are Bely?"
"Yes."
"I recognized you," he narrows his eyes.
"To whom have you come?"
"To Merezhkovsky," he flung this out with pride, even as a challenge.
Gippius appeared here. Putting aside his top hat, he clicked his heels and deeply, rather nasally, he said:
"Gumilev."
"But—what do you want?"
"I," he mumbled, "Me...Letter for me...He gave you..." he stumbled. And with strength he threw out, "Bryusov."
The top hat, clutched with a black glove under his clean-shaven chin, trembled from nervousness.
"Who are you?"
"A poet from *Vesy.*"
Bely had not the faintest idea who Gumilev was, having left Moscow before his poems had appeared in *Vesy*. Dmitri Merezhkovsky then walked into the sitting-room.
"You're not at the right address. We aren't interested in poems here...An empty thing—poems."
"Why?" the youth blurted out, with the stupidity of incomprehension. He put up a good show. "Actually you have wonderful ones of your own." And he quoted some lines...
Gippius broke in. "What do you write about? Well? About billy goats?"
"About parrots."
She mocked the poor boy who stood awkwardly before her...With a glance Gippius invited me to amuse myself with the "billy goat" sent to her, then pointed with her lorgnette to the door.
"Go now."
Her husband sighed, "What is this for, Zina?" and went out, shuffling into his study...
[Gumilev] sat on the divan, squeezing his top hat in his hands, his walking stick exactly upright, gazing at the wall and deciding whether or not they were laughing at him. Suddenly, having grasped the

situation, he rose, ceremoniously put on his top hat, dryly said good-bye and left...[27]

This was a humilating and deeply painful encounter which Gumilev never forgot. Writing to Bruysov, he introduced the subject by saying "...I have acquired a mystical horror of famous people and this is why." He set the scene essentially as Bely had described it and said that initially he was treated kindly by the assembled friends. When Filosofov began to question him about his philosophical-political convictions, he found it difficult to fully explain his views in a social conversation, but answered as well as he could.

> At first they considered me as a mystical anarchist—which turned out to be wrong. As a disciple of Vyacheslav Ivanov—also wrong. As a follower of Sologub—also wrong. Finally, they compared me with some French poet, Betenoire [obviously a joke]...
> This was the end of me. Merezhkovsky put his hands in his pockets, stood at the wall and, abruptly through his nose, he began: "You, my dear, have gone wrong! This is not the place for you! Our acquaintance with you will give nothing to you nor to us. It's shameful to talk only about trifling matters and on the serious questions we will never agree. The only thing we could do is to save you as you stand above the abyss. But really, that is..." Here he stopped.
> I added. "An interesting matter?"
> And he answered bluntly: "Yes." and turned his back on me.
> I sat there for a few minutes, then began to say good-bye. Nobody restrained me or invited me to stay. Andrei Bely accompanied me into the hall, evidently from pity.[28]

In the catty description she provides Bryusov, Zinaida Gippius' account is more revealing of herself than of Gumilev:

Oh, Valery Yakovlevich! Have you actually seen him? We absolutely died. Boris had enough strength to make fun of him, but I was absolutely paralyzed. Twenty years old, sickly and pale, full of old clichés, inhaling ether and saying that he alone could change the world. "There have been attempts before me—Buddha, Christ...but they were unsuccessful." He then put on his top hat and left. I found some issues of *Vesy* with his poems, wishing at least to justify your interest in the brilliance of his verse, but could not. Absolute nonsense...Why do you find him so fascinating?[29]

Whatever actually happened, this was a mortifying blow for the ambitious, yet hardly self-assured young poet. However, he was soon welcomed into another salon, hosted by Shukin, where Russian writers met regularly. When several Russian artists working in Paris decided to publish a journal, they invited Gumilev to edit the literary section. He eagerly accepted and gave his new "journal" the name *Sirius*.

Sirius was filled almost exlusively with Gumilev's own poems and articles whose authorship was concealed behind a variety of pen-names. Despite its limited authorial range and its modest size, Gumilev proudly sent Bryusov a copy of the first edition, while revealing one of his pseudonyms: "Anatoly Grant—that's me. What can I do if we have no suitable collaborators. I have to be clever, and the truth about Anat. Grant is a mystery even for my companions."[30]

In Anna's next letter to von Shtein, dated February, 1907, there is no word of Kutuzov:

It seems that my Kolya is planning to come to see me—I am so insanely happy, He writes me incomprehensible words, and I go to acquaintances with the letter and ask for an explanation. Every time a letter arrives from Paris, they hide it from me and deliver it with elaborate precautions. Then there is usually a fainting spell, cold compresses and general bewilderment. This is due to my passionate character, nothing else. He loves me so much that it is positively terrifying. What do you think Papa will say when he finds out about my decision? If he is against my marriage, I will run away and marry Nikolai secretly. I cannot respect my father, I have never loved him, why should I obey him? I have become wicked, capricious, and unbearable.[31]

Anna's effusive exaggerations may have concealed a germ of truth. The intensity of Gumilev's passion directed at her may indeed have been quite frightening, compelling her to deflect Kolya's persistent requests to marry him in the following three years. She also feared her parents' opposition to the marriage, as the two had no viable means of support. Anna could not treat his marriage proposals with the seriousness that Kolya offered them. But Anna's love life was still in an unsettled state when, on February 11, 1907, the longed for photograph of Kutuzov finally arrives:

I don't know how to express the boundless gratitude which I feel toward you. May God send you the fulfillment of your most burning desire, and I will *never, never* forget what you did for me. Five months I waited for his picture; in it he's exactly the way I knew, loved and madly feared him: elegant and so coldly indifferent, he looks at me with the tired, serene gaze of his near-sighted, light eyes...Why did you think I would be silent after receiving the picture? Oh, no, I am too happy to be silent...Seryozha! I can't tear my soul away from him. I am poisoned for my whole life; bitter is the poison of unrequited love! Will I be able to begin to live again?

Certainly not! But Gumilev is my Fate, and I obediently submit to it. Don't condemn me, if you can. I swear to you, by all that is holy to me, that this unhappy man will be happy with me...I am sending you one of my recent poems ["I Know How to Love"]. It rambles and is written without a spark of feeling. Don't judge me as a literary critic...[32]

Doubtless Kolya, the proud editor, had dispatched a copy of his first magazine to Anna. Although she may have viewed Kolya's latest literary project with an indulgent, almost sisterly amusement, *Sirius* did attain a certain literary significance. It was in its pages that the first poem by Anna Akhmatova, "On his hand are lots of shining rings..." appeared in print. As she wrote to von Shtein on March 13, 1907:

...Perhaps a short poem which I wrote when I was in Evpatoriya will appear in the third issue...but if it appears, write me your frank opinion of it, and also show it to one of the poets. Ignoramuses praise it—that's a bad sign. Don't be afraid to criticize my poem or convey the reactions of others, since I am not going to write anymore. It doesn't matter to me! ...Why did Gumilev get involved with *Sirius*? This surprises me and puts me in an unusually jolly mood. How many misfortunes our Nikola has had to bear, and all in vain. Have you noticed that the other contributors are nearly all as famous and respected as I? I think that the Lord clouded Gumilev's mind. It happens!...*Annushka*
P.S. When are G-Kutuzov's examinations over?[33]

In 1906, Gumilev began a four-part poem titled "To Beatrice." In her memoir, Akhmatova identifies the white rose in Gumilev's poem as a symbol of the first letter she addressed to him in Paris: "VI. My first letter to Paris." followed by lines from the poem: "What is it?

Frances Laird

Once more a threat or/Is it a prayer for mercy?"[34] In the poems of "To Beatrice" Gumilev remains within the aesthetic world of the Symbolists, using extravagant imagery and an elevated, even theatrical tone. In this poem about Anna Gorenko, the source of Gumilev's poetic inspiration, the Beatrice to his Dante, he conveys his unwavering dedication to the vocation of poet and the emotional, even spiritual power that Anna holds over him.

<u>To Beatrice</u>

I

Muses, refrain from your sobbing.
Pour out in songs all your sorrows.
Sing me a song about Dante
Or on the flute play me music.

Bothersome fauns, no more does
Music ring out in your cries!
Don't you know not long ago that
Beatrice left Paradise.

A rose that is strange and white in
The quiet coolness of evening…
What is it? Once more a threat or
Is it a prayer for mercy?

The anxious artist lived in
A world full of sly accusations—
Atheist, libertine, sinner,
But he loved Beatrice only.

Secret thoughts of the poet
In his capricious heart hidden
Turned into light-filled torrents,
Turned into noisemaking billows.

In the sonata-brilliante,
Muses, note the strange secret.
Sing me a song of Dante,
And of Gabriel Rossetti.

Nikolai Gumilev
1906-1909[35]

Gumilev creates a strangely indefinable world peopled with Beatrice, an odd mix of muses, fauns and maenads of classical Greek myth, and the poet himself—poetic license taken to extremes. The reader's mind strains to picture the poem's setting, placement in time and characters. Mythological creatures of classical antiquity associated with artistic inspiration, intoxication, music and madness co-exist with Dante Alighieri of 14th-century Italy, and the Pre-

Raphaelite artist, Dante Gabriel Rossetti, of late 19th-century England. It is in this unreal, dream-like atmosphere of literary and mythical presences that the the young poet situates himself.

The opening stanza, where rhetorical outcries are heightened by the pounding dactyllic rhythms (`~~), tells of the transformation into art of the raw suffering of life and the consolation offered to the poet by this miraculous conversion of pain into beauty. Both depend upon Beatrice, the divine inspiration and spiritual guide for this poet, as she was for Dante. The ecstatic singing of the fauns has lost its beauty, for Beatrice has abandoned her place in Paradise, perhaps to return to earth as Anna Gorenko.

The rapturous tone of the poem changes with stanzas 3 through 5, which seem less artily contrived and more genuine than the first two. The white rose, image of Anna's letter, is a traditional symbol of love. With its lush but fragile beauty and its haunting perfume, it is as transitory and quickly-fading. The virginal whiteness of the flower implies the purity and innocence of the one who had sent the rose/letter. But with its needle-sharp thorns, the rose, as love, can inflict pain and draw blood from the one who grasps it. Gumilev sees the rose, with its ghostly luminescence in the evening shadows, its cloying fragrance, its petals cool and damp as skin, as somehow "strange."

An ambiguous or confusing passage in Anna's letter that could be interpreted either as a warning of an action she might take or her plea that he mitigate his action was puzzling to Kolya. Either it was an assertion of her power over him or her acknowledgement of a need to obey. The question of how to reconcile their emotional dependence upon one another with an equally powerful need for separateness, autonomy and control would become central in the dynamics of their complicated relationship and be repeatedly expressed in the poems of Gumilev and Akhmatova. This fierce, unrelenting, sometimes silent, sometimes verbal struggle that underlay their love continued throughout their courtship, their marriage and their divorce, ending only with Gumilev's death.

But here the poet, diffident, uncertain, surrounded like Dante with a host of accusers, knows one thing—that he loves only Beatrice. Inhabiting a hostile world of little-minded men, reproached for his rejection of society's religious and moral conventions, he will find redemption through love and art. Fired with the inspiration of Beatrice's love, he can retrieve the secret thoughts of his own heart and transform them into illuminating and powerful poems.

For Anna Gorenko, Gumilev's singular focus upon her as his muse and lover must have been daunting. Perhaps it was out of self-preservation that she so stubbornly resisted his repeated proposals of marriage. For Kolya, this apparently unreciprocated love aroused a tumult of conflicting emotions. Though outwardly proud, even haughty, Gumilev was shaken and perplexed by his passionate and humiliating need for Anna. Here love and hate are locked in irreconcilable conflict—he doesn't know whether to kiss his beloved or curse her. In "To Beatrice," Gumilev struggles to subdue the violent rush of feelings. While he could not suppress the whirlwind of his passions, in imposing upon them the artifice of imagery and an ordered, poetic language, he could acquire a certain mastery over them.

Chapter III
Rejection

In the spring of 1907, Kolya Gumilev, on his way home from Paris, stopped to visit Anna in Kiev, where she was recovering from a serious lung ailment. After graduating from the Fundukleyevskaya Gymnasium, she had moved back to Sebastapol and her family. She wrote to her brother-in-law von Shtein:

I don't know if you heard about the illness that has taken away any hope of the possibility of a happy life. My lungs are affected *(this is a secret)* and there is a possible threat of tuberculosis. It seems to me that I am going through what Inna did, and now I clearly understand her spiritual condition. Since I am preparing to leave Russia soon for a very long time, I decided to bother you with a request to send me something from Inna's things in memory of her...I am sick, melancholy, and growing thin. I had pleurisy, bronchitis, and chronic catarrh of the lungs...We are living in abject poverty. We have to wash the floors, do the laundry. That's my life! ...If you could see me, you would probably say, 'Ugh, what an ugly face.'[1]

Her plans to leave Russia, which never materialized, suggest that she may have toyed with the idea of leaving for Paris with Kolya. Nikolai, spending the summer in Tsarskoe Selo, was able at last to arrange a meeting with Valery Bryusov in Moscow. Bryusov wrote in his diary: "N. Gumilev came to Moscow...He often alludes to 'the world.' He sat with me at 'Skorpion,' then I was with him at some foul hotel near the train station. We spoke about poetry and occultism. He had little information. Evidently, he is in his decadent period. He reminded me of myself in 1895."[2]

Kolya, finding it impossible to stay away from Anna for very long, traveled on to Sebastopol. She recalled: "He was so in love that he took money from a money-lender at high interest and travelled to Sebastopol in order so see my haughty profile for ten minutes."[3] Kolya rented a room next door and he and Anna spent hours walking along the shores of the Black Sea. When he again begged her to marry him, she may have seriously considered his offer, as her letter to her brother-in-law suggests. It was an escape from the suffocating domesticity and the tedium of household chores. However, perhaps hesitant to commit herself to such a scandalous adventure and uncertain how they both could live in Paris on Kolya's student allowance, she refused him. Akhmatova remembered how they had stood together looking out over a seashore strewn with the dark, shiny bodies of dolphins that had been stranded on the beach.[4] When Kolya returned to Paris in September, he wrote the following poem:

Rejection

A tsaritsa—or only, perhaps, a sad, little child,
She leaned out above a sea that was sleepily sighing.
So slender her figure appeared to be, graceful and lithe,
It mysteriously reached out to meet the silvery dawning.

The twilight ran out. Then some kind of bird gave a cry
And there in the wetness before her were glittering dolphins.
To swim to the turquoise estates of the love-struck prince,
To carry her there they offered their backs, smooth and glossy.

But her crystalline voice seemed to sound with a special ring
When stubbornly it said the fateful words: "No, I cannot…"
A tsaritsa—or only, perhaps, a capricious child,
A child who was tired, whose gaze betrayed impotent torment.

—Nikolai Gumilev
September, 1907, Paris[5]

There is an inherent contradiction in seeing Anna as both "tsaritsa" (another Symbolist image) and "child." As "tsaritsa," her superiority is exaggerated by a persona that distances her from the poet, endowing her with power and predominance over him. Yet each time Gumilev refers to her as princess, he counterposes its opposite– "or maybe just a sad [or capricious] child." These continually shifting images from the controller to the controlled, the powerful to the powerless, suggest again the persistent theme of dominance and submission in their relationahip.

As in "The Rusalka," Gumilev places his heroine beside the water. But the rusalka legend is reversed when the "love struck prince" of the sea promises her a new life if she will leave her home on dry land and descend with him to his "turquoise estates." The gleaming dolphins will carry them down into his world at the bottom of the sea. This may be read as the poet's demand that his heroine/Anna abandon her world of reason and social convention to plunge into the dark, submarinous depths of the instinctual and the irrational, that is, of sensuality and sexual experience. It was in such highly contrived poetic images that Nikolai Gumilev framed his proposal of marriage to Anna Gorenko.

But the "crystalline" voice sounds with a special ring rejecting him. Is it the tsaritsa speaking or the spoiled, tired, tormented child? Is it the voice of the ruler or the ruled? The radical disparity of these images reveals an unsettling contradiction inherent in the poet's conception of Anna.

Gumilev does not attempt to go beyond the circumscribed roles that he has assigned his heroine, to delve into the rich, complex inner life of a young woman. He manipulates his beloved as a feature in the landscape of his own poetic universe by assigning her arbitrary identities. In this way he can create out of selected and isolated facets of her personality the poetic persona that satisfies his own emotional, psychological and aesthetic needs. Perhaps Anna is not only rejecting Kolya's proposal of marriage, but his limited, superficial, highly romanticized conception of her as well.

Gumilev's depictions of Anna in his poems could not have helped her in her struggle to attain self-knowledge. For a sensitive and intelligent young woman possessing the latent gift of a poet, the creation of an identity must have been especially difficult. Anna's life had been shaken by her parents' divorce, her removal from her home in Tsarskoe Selo, her extended stay with unsympathetic relatives in Kiev as well as troubling events in the world. With her aspirations to become a poet, she saw no other women poets who could act as models or mentors. Surely Kolya's fictionalized and self-serving images of her could only have added to her confusion. In the fifth part of "Northern Elegies," Akhmatova admitted as much:

> Myself, I seemed to be from the beginning
> As if of someone's dream or fevered vision,
> Or a reflection in a mirror not my own,
> Without a name, without flesh, without reason.
>
> —Anna Akhmatova (1955)[6]

Undoubtedly the fevered visions in which she saw herself reflected were those of Nikolai Gumilev.

Anna knew even then that the path of her life would not follow the conventional route of marriage, husband, children, an unexceptional existence bounded by the close circle of the home. Whether implicitly or explicitly Kolya promised her a different life, she may have feared that what he really expected was a pliant, obliging and dutiful wife who would devote her life to caring for him. If he worshipped Anna for her poetic sensibility, vivid imagination, intelligence, proud and unusual beauty, would he respect her intentions, barely acknowleged even to herself, to become a poet? Or would he see her gift as just another captivating feminine talent, like the ability to converse prettily in French or to play Chopin nocturnes on the piano? If her poems were not too embarrassingly gauche, he might pass her verses round for the entertainment of his literary friends. But would he read her poetry with the same seriousness that he viewed his own?

However insistently these questions may have gnawed at her, Anna believed that she was fated to marry Kolya Gumilev. But if she were to become a poet, she herself must govern the direction her life would take, experiencing the world fully without the limits of another's demands. Just how she could find this necessary freedom within a supportive and enduring relationship with a man was a question she would struggle with in the years to come. Perhaps this uneasiness at relinquishing her life to the control of another also lay behind Anna's seemingly capricious responses to Kolya's protestations of love and her persistent refusals to marry him. She concealed her inner conflict from even her closest friends. Valeriya recalls that…"Anna never wrote of loving Nikolai, but she often mentioned his persistent courting and his numerous marriage proposals She described her flippant refusals and indifference to the whole idea. Her kind mother, feeling sorry for Gumilev, often mildly scolded her on this account."[7]

It was at this time that Nikolai Gumilev set out on the first of his journeys to regions far off the trodden track of the usual traveller. He had dreamed of seeing Africa, but his father, adamantly opposed to such extravagance, insisted that, until Kolya had finished university, he would receive neither his father's approval nor the money he needed for the trip. But Kolya scrimped and saved from his daily allowance until he had accumulated a small sum of money. Then he composed dated letters to his parents, which his friends were instructed to send from Paris at regular intervals so that they would not suspect his absence. The trip started badly in Trouville, when he was arrested for sneaking aboard a ship bound for Constantinople. But he had enough money to sail steerage and passed the night in the ship's hold with pilgrims, sharing their scanty meal. In Smyrna he considerably broadened his life experience in an amorous encounter with a Greek woman. On his return trip he was caught in a messy brawl with gangsters in the port of Marseilles, which must have provided Gumilev colorful tales for café conversations. This voyage gave him the chance to see a stranger, rawer, non-European world for himself as well as providing a respite from his fruitless and frustrating courtship of Anna. And with these alien and exotic sights and experiences, Kolya could enlarge his vocabulary of novel subjects and striking poetic images.

But back in Paris in the fall of 1907, without the heady distractions of foreign travel, Kolya suddenly lost his sense of direction and purpose. Whether from loneliness or distress at his failures as poet and lover, he took a train to the coast of Normandy where he leaped into the sea, intent upon drowning himself. This attempt to end his life failed when he was fished out by local lifeguards. Again death seemed to have exerted a compelling attraction for the young Gumilev. He wrote to Bryusov: "In life there are periods when the consciousness of succession and a goal are lost, when it is impossible to imagine one's 'tomorrow' and when everything seems a strange, perhaps even wearisome dream."[8] Beneath a veneer of self-confidence, the young poet was confused and uncertain of his way. As if hoping to find reassurance, he begged Bryusov for his opinions on his work. But Kolya, with the resilience of youth, shook off his gloomy mood and soon was hard at work on his next collection of poems.

Gumilev returned to Kiev in October, determined to marry Anna, who had just enrolled in the Law School of the Higher Women's Courses. Again she resisted Kolya's ardent courtship, perhaps now with illness as an excuse, for lung problems were plaguing her again. So Kolya travelled back to Paris alone. Letters flew off to Bryusov with new poems and an unending stream of questions. Gumilev had been experimenting with prose and promised to send Bryusov the three short novels, *The Joys of Earthly Love*, which he had dedicated to Anna Gorenko. Maintaining the humble demeanor of a student, he hoped that Bryusov would publish them in *Vesy*: "I know that I must still learn a lot, but I am afraid that I will not be able to find the boundary where experiments end and creative work begins."[9] At the opening of an exhibition of new Russian art that he reviewed for *Vesy*, Nikolai met several artists and poets. But by December he was clearly lonely and depressed again. He told Bryusov that he fed bread to the Tibetan bears in the Jardin des Plantes so often that they recognized him by sight.

Sometime in December of 1907, Kolya found a secluded spot in the Bois de Boulogne where he gulped down what he thought was a dose of potassium cyanide. Whatever the white powder was, he lay unconscious on the ground for twenty-four hours before coming to his senses. Alexei Tolstoy wrote of sitting in a sidewalk café beneath flowering chestnut trees while Gumilev, tall and rather woodenly erect in his chair, described in a slow, muffled voice his latest encounter with death. Kolya wore a bowler hat pulled down over his eyes and his long fingers rested languidly over the knob of a walking stick. He told how Death, appearing as figures dressed in white, approached and he could hear himself groaning. But the white figures drifted up into the sky and, lying in the grass and looking up at the sky, he suddenly realized that they were clouds. "Why did I want to die?" Gumilev asked. "I lived alone in a hotel. The idea of death attached itself to me. And besides, there was this girl..." Tolstoy saw something peacock-like in Gumilev—his pomposity, awkwardness, self-importance. Only his mouth, with its tender and caressing smile, revealed a boyish quality.[10]

But Kolya rebounded again when, in January, 1908, three hundred copies of his second volume of poems, *Romantic Flowers*, were published, dedicated to Anna Andreevna Gorenko. The book received favorable reviews in literary magazines, including one by

Innokenty Annensky in the newspaper *Rech*. He continued his correspondence with Bryusov, asking his opinion about a new poem. He had no one else to turn to for literary advice as his only other Russian reader had left Paris. But with Bryusov's next letter his spirits soared. His master liked *Romantic Flowers* and planned to review it for *Vesy*. Gumilev wrote: "Perhaps with this attention a poet will emerge from me whom you will not be ashamed to call your disciple."[11]

Gumilev had attempted to articulate his own theory of poetry inspired by the paintings of Gustav Moreau, the French Parnassian poets and occultism. But in a quote from an article by Bryusov, "everything in life is only the material for vividly-singing poems," he found an idea which he had cherished and been reluctant even to formulate for himself, the germ of what would become the Acmeist movement in poetry. "…I am as amazed at its depth as a coal-miner would have been amazed at his own son who had grown up in a prince's palace." He sent off to Bryusov news of other Russian poets in Paris. Alexei Tolstoy, a typical "Petersburg poet," had been writing for only a year but already considered himself a master. Andrei Bely had softened little since that disastrous evening at the Merezhkovsky's. "After three meetings with [him], I have taken away only a sense of shame and I sometimes reproached him (deliberately) for the unrestrained nature of his criticism."[12]

In March, 1908, Gumilev wrote another poem about Anna in the persona of the tsaritsa.

Swan Songs
Akhmatova and Gumilev

Tsaritsa

Your brow in curls is tinted bronzish,
Like steel, your eyes are sharp, keen-edged.
For you the meditating bonzes
Set bonfires burning in Tibet.

When Timur in despondent anger
Had left the people to their end,
They carried you through Gobi's deserts
Held high upon his battle shield.

You stepped into the fort of Agra,
Like ancient Lilith, bright you shone.
The hooves of your gay onagers were
Resounding with the ring of gold.

The night was quiet. Earth was silent.
Even flowers scarcely sighed.
And from the green canal were flying
Swarms of beetles, hovering high.

And I traced in a pillar's shadow
The features of a diamond face.

Frances Laird

      And on my bended knee I waited
      In robes rose-colored of a priest.

      The decorated bow was drawn out
      And, loving my old freedom best,
      I knew my muscles would not falter
      And that the point would find your breast.

      Then would the past have flared up, blazing,
      Triumphant would the princes come,
      With dancing in the aloe thickets
      And merry long days of the hunt.

      But with your mouth, cut out severely,
      Was such a mix of torments hid,
      In you I saw a god and shyly
      I let fall the bow I gripped.

      A multitude of slaves rushed toward me,
      And anxiously they thronged and cried.
      And as you caught sight of the headsman's
      Steel pole-axe lazily you smiled.

                                      Nikolai Gumilev
                                      March, 1908[13]

His grey-eyed tsaritsa is unquestionably a woman of power in this poem, in which he churns up a heady brew of exoticisms ranging as widely in ages and cultures as those of "To Beatrice." The poet compares his heroine to a bronze figure found in a Tibetan Buddhist monastery, to a goddess worshipped by Mongol warriors, to a Moghul princess with the seductiveness of Lilith, the demon-temptress. In stanza four, the poem makes a sudden shift from the desert sands into a lush, night garden with its all-pervading, earthly silence, but for the whir of a swarm of winged insects hovering above a still, green canal. The images of this intensely realized setting, oddly out of place plopped down into a desert landscape, were taken by Kolya from the Tsarskoe Selo gardens, as Akhmatova wryly noted: "This is somewhere near the Big Folly, and does not look much like the Gobi Desert." [14]

The poet/hero, in the guise of a priest, prepares to kill the woman who has captivated him and sapped his strength and will. Freed from her enchantment, he could return to his simple-minded male pursuits of hunting and dancing. But as he draws his bow taut, aiming an arrow at her heart, he glimpses the suffering betrayed in the subtle expression of her mouth. Instantly he recognizes her humanity as well as her divinity and, as he slowly lowers his bow, her slaves swarm about and sweep him away. He had pitied her and spared her life, but she will not show the same mercy to him.

Here the struggle of wills between the poet as priest and the woman as goddess is expressed in terms of physical force. Her authority is acknowleged by the slaves who carry out her orders, while his power resides in his bow and arrow. For each, the ultimate act of control is the taking the life of the other, he by the arrow, she by the axe.

In Paris, the *Salon des Independents* had opened, exhibiting provocative new directions in painting, and Bryusov encouraged Nikolai Gumilev to write a review for *Vesy*. But Gumilev was reluctant: "This doesn't come from laziness…There is too much kitch and ugliness in it, at least for me, having studied aesthetics in museums. Perhaps it is the chaos from which a star will be born, but for me the new movements in painting in their present form are completely incomprehensible and unsympathetic."[15] He may have led the avant garde of Russian poetry, but when it came to the painting of Post-Impressionists, Gumilev was surprisingly conservative.

In a letter to Bryusov dated April, 1908, Nikolai wrote: "A few words about Anna Comnenus, I have written a poem about her. Historians love to present her as an ideal, but many facts compel me to suspect otherwise."[16] Giving her the sad eyes and curved nose of Anna Gorenko, Gumilev recreates her as the daughter of a Byzantine emperor.

<u>Anna Comnenus</u>

A troubling fragment of age-old darkness,
The child of tsars long-forgotten by all,

Swan Songs
Akhmatova and Gumilev

The slipping-off course of the ships she follows
With her glimmering gaze on the Bosphorus swells.

Her wonderful lips are coarse and exciting,
Her curving nose strangely lovely and rare,
But her gazes are gloomy, like the grave's coldness,
And frightening the strewn-about dusk of her hair.

At her feet is a knight, like a bird he is haughty,
A grey eagle that soars above Pyrenees snows,
With a cry of delight he went into battle
For a woman's bed alcove open to most.

In vain were the songs sung about him by minstrels,
In the king's battles he won his reward—
Silent, trembling, he sees how waves hot and sultry
Cut through his ships as they headed for shore.

Long will he give those breasts his caresses
And catch with his gaze her slipping-off gaze.
But when morning comes, calm, handsome and slender,
He'll bow his head down to the well-aimed axe blade.

In April, once more will the reed pipes be weeping,
And crying high up in the clouds will be cranes.

> Then from western capes to the garden of cedars
> The ships will sail in well beyond sweet disgrace.
>
> Again the tsaritsa will stand like a harlot,
> Embracing her body, its power to excite,
> Only she will be trembling and sad in her bedroom:
> In her soul the dead one remains still alive.
>
> The heart of Comnenus does not know of treason.
> However, it does know the game's insane thirst.
> And the dark torment of torturing boredom,
> Binding the worlds forgotten by death.
>
> Nikolai Gumilev
1908, Paris[17]

Gumilev again has "encoded" Anna Gorenko in a royal personage, here the daughter of a Byzantine king, Alexei I, of the Comnenus dynasty, who reigned from 1081-1118. Though her reputation was that of a highly virtuous woman, a model of ideal womanhood, Gumilev conceives of Anna Comnenus as possessing a coarse and sensual beauty and a funereal gaze. Like a medieval knight, the hero swears fealty to her and goes off into battle in the hope that, by his feats of courage, he will win his way to her bed. Although the knight distinguishes himself in combat and enjoys her favors for a night, his ships are lost at sea. The gleaming axe of the executioner, only a menacing possibility in "Tsaritsa," now falls to cut off his head. Anna Comnenus senses the power of her body to excite the attentions of other men, but she cannot forget the dead hero. She is left with the torment of boredom and unsatisfied love to live on in a world "forgotten by death." Gumilev transforms his own dogged but fruitless pursuit of Anna into that of haughty, handsome young warrior's wooing of a regal, sad-eyed virgin-harlot. His heroism in battle wins him one night with her, for which he must pay with his life. But her punishment is his absence; she is left forever unsatisfied to live out an endless, boring existence, perhaps Kolya's implied warning to Anna Gorenko.

In one letter to Bruysov, Gumilev wrote of a "boyish joke" he had played on the Merezhkovskys. While he was chatting in the Café Harcourt with Mlle. Bogdanova, a regular at their evening gatherings, she got the idea of submitting a poem of Gumilev's to Zinaida Gippius for her opinion, without revealing his name. "[Gippius] liked the poem and it was returned with the inscription 'very good' and even Merezhkovsky was favorably disposed to it. They asked Mlle. Bogdanova about the author and asked her to bring him, but of course she won't succeed in doing that. So that if "Androgine" [the poem in question] won't be in *Vesy*, the "shy" talent-meteor will remain a mystery for Zinaida Nikolaevna."[18]

At the end of April, 1908, Anna saw Kolya again when he broke his journey on his return from Paris to live in Tsarskoe Selo. Anna had nearly finished her first year at the Kiev College for Women.

Nikolai Gumilev begged Anna to marry him, but once more she refused. In Tsarskoe Selo, he settled down to begin his literary career in earnest and, discouraged by Anna's latest rejection, a love affair with Lydia Arens. He spent the summer as usual at Slepnevo and only saw Anna later in the season when she was visiting friends in Tsarskoe Selo. In the autumn, intending to study law, Gumilev enrolled at St. Petersburg University, but soon transferred to the departments of history and philology. There he took courses in logic, psychology, ancient literature, Latin and Greek, Russian literature and history and ancient philology.

But Gumilev's self-assurance was wavering again. In Paris, as he wrote Bryusov, he had been so busy writing and living that he had had no time to think. But now back in Tsarskoe Selo he was full of doubts about his poetry. It was not that he had been lured away by the other Petersburg poets, such as Alexander Blok and Vyacheslav Ivanov. It was just that he was afraid that there was no foundation of ideas for his images; they were like the linking together of separate atoms and not organic bodies. This cogent self-criticism betrays Gumilev's growing dissatisfaction with the eclectic and arbitrary nature of his poetic imagery. Perhaps he had come to see that he had not mined his own ideas and experiences deeply enough to create poetry with the resonant meaning that arises out of necessity. Bryusov's criticism of *Romantic Flowers* as the work of a student, not of an accomplished poet, must have stung. Sensing the shortcomings of his poetry, he was reluctant to accept the invitations of editors to submit his poems and decided against publishing books he had earlier so eagerly planned.

One poem that Gumilev wrote that autumn was "The Lakes." Akhmatova recalled that, although he did not want to become another "Tsarskoe Selo swan," its landscapes arose inevitably in Gumilev's poetry. The setting for this poem was a pond that lay between Tsarskoe Selo and Pavlovsk. Akhmatova continued: "…I am the 'sad girl.' It was written during one of our protracted quarrels. N.S. [Nikolai Stepanovich] later pointed the place out to me. The *nenuphar*, of course, is a yellow water lily, and there really were willows."[19]

<u>The Lakes</u>

I smashed happiness, a triumphant profaner,
Without despair and without chiding.
But clearly I see every night when I'm dreaming
The great, shining lakes of the night-time.

On mourning-black waves the pale waterlilys,
Like thoughts of my own, are wordless
And sorrowful. Long forgot enchantment there is
Aroused by the silvery-white willows.

The bends of the road are lit up by the moonlight

Frances Laird

    That looks down upon empty meadows.

    In heavy anxiety how I am stifled

    And wring my hands till the pain stops me.

    Remembering, something should make its appearance,

    The dénouement of some twilight drama,

    Perhaps a white bird or a girl who is sad or

    A fairy tale, strange and tender.

    And out of the mist a new sun will start shining

    And there will be dragonfly shadows,

    And proud swans, as spoken of in ancient legends,

    Will come out upon the white stair steps.

    But I can't recall it. I, wingless and weakened,

    Look out on the lakes of the night-time

    And I hear the waves that powerlessly murmur

    The words of those fateful reproaches.

    I wake, as before my lips confident, certain.

    The night watch is far-off and alien.

    So earthly are they in their crudeness and beauty,

    These moments of peace and of trouble.

                              Nikolai Gumilev

                                November, 1908[20]

Swan Songs
Akhmatova and Gumilev

The poet's dream image of the lake at night is like a photographic negative of the sun-dappled scene in the imperial gardens where he and Anna had passed tender moments as young lovers. The poet realizes that he has destroyed the nascent happiness that had begun its blossoming there, that he has forgotten the bewitching power that place once held. The ebony waters, faded waterlilies and empty meadows lit by the cold light of the moon only bring pain to him now. This was once the setting for a magical and marvellous drama of a sad girl or a white bird (two images closely associated with Anna Gorenko). Perhaps, a fairy-tale dénouement would resolve the tangled story of their love, allowing them to live happily ever after. The lake would glow in the rising sun of a new dawn and swans would sink into its shining waters. But this happy vision fades. The poet, mute and wingless as a wounded swan, sees only the black lake and hears in its lapping waves only the sounds of reproaches. The dream ends as he wakes to the demands of his earthly life, where with renewed confidence as a poet, he can pass the hours of anxiety and moments of calm that are touched with a crude, prosaic beauty. Nikolai may have feared that his casual affairs with other women had profaned his special relationship with Anna and destroyed the promise of a love for which he had longed. For whatever reason, the evocative landscape in which they had once expressed their love now was permeated with mourning and loss.

Akhmatova understood the consolation that travel brought Kolya for disappointments in wooing and writing: "In the beginning, he was only healing his soul with travel and later he became a true traveler (1913)."[21] In the autumn of 1908, he set out on another journey, determined to penetrate into the heart of darkest Africa. He had written to Valery Bryusov, "I remember your warning about the danger of success and in the fall I think I'll leave for a half year in Abysinnia, so that in a new situation I'll find new words of which I have so few."[22] He stopped in Kiev to visit Anna before boarding his ship. Disembarking at Athens to pay homage to the ancient civilization, he climbed the Acropolis, where, standing before the temple of Athena, he prayed to the goddess. He wrote to a friend: "I felt that she was alive as in the time of Odysseus and I think of her with such joy…"[23]

While in Cairo, Gumilev often walked at night under a huge, pale blue moon in the deserted Ezbekia gardens, built in the English manner with artificial mountains and grottoes. But the diversions of travel had provided only a temporary distraction from his solitude, his turbulent inner life and his perceived failures as poet and lover. The rigors of the sea-voyage and the unfamiliar sights and sounds of Egypt, its crumbling monuments, crowded, narrow streets and colorful bazaars, could not ease his feelings of despondency at Anna's repeated rejections. But in the Ezbekia gardens, after considering suicide yet again, he seems to have undergone a transformative spiritual experience. Gumilev wrote of this in "Ezbekia," a poem he wrote in 1917, nearly ten years later.

Ezbekia

How strange it is—exactly ten years gone
Since that time I first saw Ezbekia,
The spacious Cairo garden, by full moon
Illuminated solemnly that evening.

I was tormented by a woman then
And neither blowing sea winds, fresh and salty,
Nor roaring din of colorful bazaars,
Nothing there could give me consolation.
I prayed to God that He might bring me death
And I prepared myself for its approach.

And yet the garden there in every way
Was like the sacred groves of a young world,
Those slender palm trees held up high their branches,
Like girls to whom God chooses to descend.
On hilltops, like some prophesying druids,
The old, majestic plane trees gathered round.

And in the gloom the waterfall turned white,
Appearing as a rearing unicorn.
Back and forth flew butterflies of night,
Among the blooming flowers rising high.
Or else among the stars—so low the stars
That they were like some ripened barberries.

And I recall, I cried: "Higher than grief
And deeper far than death is life! Take, Lord,
My willing promise that whatever happens,
Whatever sorrows or humiliations
Befall me as my lot, no sooner will
I contemplate an easy death than go
Again into a moonlit night like this,
Beneath the palms and plane trees of Ezbekia"…

Nikolai Gumilev
1917[24]

The landscape of a Cairo garden presented Gumilev with a paradisial world, lush, verdant, in a state of constant renewal, where the trees had become the bearers of wisdom and spiritual knowledge. There Gumilev came to the realization that the power of an enduring life energy could overcome the power of death. In his ecstatic vision the heavens descend, the earth rises, and the two intermingle. The butterflies soar among the stars and the stars seem as near at hand as ripe barberries. In this mystical experience Gumilev comes to a new understanding of the preciousness of life and the transcendent power of the life force, an ultimate, eternal value that can overcome sorrow and death. From this time on he will reject an "easy" death, that is, death by his own hand. In this moonlit park Gumilev was released at last from his obsession with self-destruction. Although he will test his masculinity and physical courage by exposing himself to danger, he will never again attempt sucide. Perhaps, Gumilev's obsession with Anna Gorenko was relieved as well, for she didn't hear from him again until January of 1909.

Although Gumilev had been frustrated in his attempt to travel into Abyssinia, when he returned to Russia in November, he wrote to Bryusov that the journey had been good for him; he had written nearly fifteen poems. And he was delighted to discover that his poems had been requested for three separate anthologies.

Frances Laird

Chapter IV
Ballad

In the literary circles of St. Petersburg frequented by Gumilev, Russian Symbolism. though weakening in its expressive power, was still the reigning movement in poetry. Vyacheslav Ivanov, whose literary salon the "Tower," named for the round, mock-medieval tower that protruded from his apartment building overlooking the Tauride Gardens, was its leading theorist. As well as his scholarly and critical work, Ivanov wrote esoteric poetry in the Symbolist style. Andrei Bely wrote: "The way of life in this prominence on the building, or "tower," was singular and unrepeatable…The apartment, swallowing up its neighbors, was a tangle of the most fantastic little corridors, rooms, doorless hallways…Stuffed into these strange spaces were dark brown carpets, endless shelves of books, statues, tipsy étageres filled with odd objects…You enter and you forget what country you are in, in what time. Everything is aslant—day becomes night, and night day. Even Ivanov's "Wednesdays" become Thursdays. They began after midnight." The host, wrapped up in a blanket, would lie on his sofa, correcting proofs and sipping black tea. In various corners, groups of writers drank wine and carried on heated discussions. Nikolai Gumilev was a frequent visitor, often staying overnight when it was too late to take the train back to Tsarskoe Selo.[1]

In the creative turmoil of the "Tower," Bryusov's influential grip on Nikolai Gumilev began to weaken. Bryusov, who in his letters to Paris had warned him to avoid Ivanov, would not have been pleased to read the following: "You probably have already heard about the lectures Vyacheslav Ivanov gives to a few young poets, me included. It seems to me that only now am I beginning to understand what poetry is."[2] As Bely described, Ivanov loved to pit one poet against another: "Vyacheslav loved comical duels, setting me off against Gumilev, who appeared at one o'clock to spend the night...in a black tailcoat he'd found somewhere, a top hat and gloves. He sat like a stick, with an arrogant, somewhat ironic but good-natured face, and countered with his look the attacks of Ivanov."[3]

It was at the "Tower" that Gumilev met the poetess Elizaveta Ivanovna Dmitrieva with whom he began his next love affair. In May, 1909, he traveled to the Black Sea coast to the summer home of the poet Maximilian Voloshin at Koktebel, a summer resort near Feodosiya, where Dmitrieva, too, was staying. Voloshin's dacha provided a perfect spot for summer dalliances, where Max would work his powers of seduction on the young poetesses who happened by. Akhmatova wrote: "...Max, like Vyacheslav, loved seducing people. That was his second occupation. Whenever a young girl came to Koktebel he used to walk her along the seashore in the evening. 'Do you hear the sound of the waves? They are singing for *you*.' And later the girl would tell everyone that Max had made her understand herself..."[4]

Frances Laird

Gumilev and Dmitrieva went boating on the sea and walking in the mountains. Alexei Tolstoy, also a guest, wrote: "…In the warm, starry night I went out onto the open veranda of Voloshin's house at the edge of the sea. In the darkness, on a carpet on the floor Dmitrieva was lying and reading poetry in a half-audible voice."[5] But the budding affair ended abruptly when Dmitrieva turned down Gumilev's proposal of marriage. The dejected Gumilev, when not locked in a garret room working on his poem, "The Captains," spent his idle hours arranging battles between the tarantulas he'd collected and stuffed into matchboxes.

After departing from Koktebel with a bruised ego, Kolya stopped in Lustdorf, a resort town near Odessa where Anna and her mother were staying. The meeting could not have been a happy one, for Anna sensed that his protestations of love lacked the ring of sincerity. When she refused to listen to him read *King Batinvol's Jester*, a play he had just finished writing, he burned the manuscript before her eyes in a theatrical gesture. When he tried to convince her to travel to Africa with him, she refused, and he left, disconsolate and defeated.

Sometime in 1909, Nikolai Gumilev wrote a lengthy poem called "Adam's Dream," in which he re-created the events of the book of Genesis. Since he envisions himself as Adam, it may be illuminating to look at his Eve.

from <u>Adam's Dream</u>

Swan Songs
Akhmatova and Gumilev

And Eve, the gods' plaything, a mild, gentle girl,
At times seems a child, at times summer lightening,
But now for him she seems to be a young tigress,
Arrayed in the ominous gleam of her pearls,
Harbinger of storms, of blood and of passion,
Of gloomy unhappiness and spiteful gladness.

Gold can entice and a glance give great joy,
But in gold the shadows of dark powers are hiding.
They keep control with a profaner's hand and
They pour out their poison in brotherly bowls,
Unable to satisfy, they laugh and torment
Instructing with furious crying and with groaning.

He struggles with her…He is sly like a snake,
With nets of temptations he snared and entrapped her,
There Eve is—a whore, she senselessly babbles,
There Eve is—a saint with a sorrowful gaze.
First moon maiden, then she is maiden of earth,
But strange, she is strange, everywhere, evermore.

Nikolai Gumilev
August, 1909[6]

Eve is gentle and childlike, yet this outwardly mild, passive nature conceals a fierce and destructive energy that she shares with the natural world, with lightening, storms, and predatory beasts. Adam must capture her as a hunter would his prey—with traps and stratagems. A creature of the moon with her dreams and visions and her inexplicable, changeable moods, Eve is a creature of the earth as well in her intense love of nature and her attraction to sensual delights.

Anna Gorenko was the inspiration for this poem, as Akhmatova has attested. Her mysterious sensitivity to lunar changes, her closeness to the natural world, her power to enchant, her abrupt and extreme mood changes from wild gaiety to depression, her strangeness—all are qualities attributed to the young Anna. Again the theme of the struggle for domination emerges. And again in the Eve/Anna there is a fusion of the saintly and the depraved. How ironic that this simplistic and ultimately destructive characterization should first appear in the poems of her most passionate lover!

With only the modest experience of *Sirius,* Gumilev tried publishing another journal, *Ostrov (The Island)*. Though he succeeded in putting out only one issue, he wasn't discouraged. A subsequent journal, *Apollon*, that he co-edited with the poet and art historian Sergei Makovsky, in time would become the most important literary and art magazine in St. Petersburg, defining the modernist movements in Russian poetry. In the first issue, published October 15, 1909, Innokenty Annensky contributed an essay on contemporary poetry. Gumilev's "Letters on Russian Poetry" and "On Contemporary Lyrics" provided seminal discussions on the new directions in poetry. Mikhail Kuzmin, called the "Abbot" as he was the oldest of the editors, wrote about contemporary fiction, while other writers contributed timely articles and reviews.

Kuzmin, with his dark-circled, heavy-lidded eyes and pointed beard, was a weirdly decadent, but familiar presence on the literary scene. He composed music for small, experimental theatres and cabarets and had been an early disciple of Diaghilev's World of Art movement and of Symbolism. Much of his poetry was written on the erotic themes of homosexual love. Akhmatova was not an admirer: "We—Kolya for example—took everything seriously, but in Kuzmin's hands everything became a game...He was friends with Kolya only at the start, but then they quckly went their separate ways. Kuzmin was a very nasty, malevolent and rancorous person."[7]

The German poet, Johannes von Gunter, wrote about a party held at a Petersburg restaurant to celebrate the launching of *Apollon:*

> The first speech about *Apollon* and its high priest, Makovsky, was given by Annensky. After him appeared two well-known professors. Our dear Gumilev spoke fourth in the name of the young poets. But as before this we had knocked back a large glass, it followed that his speech turned out to be a bit disconnected...[8]

The festivities at the Kyuba Restaurant continued into the small hours, when von Gunter and Gumilev ended up at the Riga Hotel where they attempted to revive themselves with black coffee, seltzer water and aspirin.

Frances Laird

Innokenty Annensky was viewed with affection and respect as a father figure by the young poets of Petersburg, who often gathered in his home in Tsarskoe Selo. In the late fall of 1909, Anna Gorenko must have returned for a visit, for Georgy Adamovich described an evening at Annensky's when Anna first plays a role, albeit a very small one, in the literary life of Petersburg. Adamovich and his friend had caught one of the last trains to Tsarskoe Selo and arrived in a snowfall that had transformed the town into a composition in black and white. Adamovich was struck by the sudden, deep quietness that pervaded Tsarskoe Selo and the damp, sweet air that seemed so pure and clean after the murk of St. Petersburg. The driver of the horse cab was in no hurry as they trotted along the darkened streets of a city already half asleep. "...More mysterious than in the daytime was the proximity of the palace: something that was not good, something unpleasant was taking place in it—or was still only being readied—and the city was not deceived, guarding its premonitions as long as it was possible from the rest of happy-go-lucky Russia." The effects of Rasputin's pernicious influence over the Romanovs were beginning to be felt.

As they were taking off their coats in the front hall of Annensky's house, all was silent in the poet's study. But when he opened the door, Adamovich realized that all the guests had already assembled there. Gumilev quickly stood up to greet them as Annensky, in his reticent, somewhat artificial but polite manner, extended his hand. Adamovich recalled: "He was no longer young...I remembered his smooth hair, shining dully in the light of a low lamp…It was stifling hot and smelled of lilies and dust."

Suddenly Adamovich realized that Annensky had just finished reading a new poem and, in the awkward silence that followed, his guests were trying to think of appropriate remarks.

From the divan in the half-light, someone had just risen, some flowery compliment hung in the air, the poet was squinting favorably, giving to understand that he appreciated it and was surprised and disarmed by the depth of analysis. Then suddenly Gumilev broke in.

"Innokenty Fedorovich, to whom are these poems addressed?"

Annensky, still rather absent, smiled.

"You are asking a question to which we all want an answer…We're listening."

Gumilev said, "You are right. I do have a theory on this score. I asked you for whom you write poems, not knowing whether you thought about that…But it seems to me that you write them for your ownself. But it's still possible to write poems to other people or to God. Like a letter."

Annensky watched him attentively.

"I never thought about it."

"It's an important distinction. It begins from style and later moves away into some kind of depths and heights. If to yourself, then essentially you set out only conditional signs, hieroglyphs that you yourself interpret and understand, you see, as if in a notebook. Perhaps, and to God himself, too…But if you address yourself to people, you want them to understand you and then you must sacrifice much of what is personally precious."

"And you, Nikolai Stepanovich, to whom are you speaking in your poems?"

"To people, of course," Gumilev quickly answered.

Annensky fell silent. "But is it possible to write poems to God, according to your terminology, with the polite request to return them? They always return and they are more magical then than the others. What do you think, Anna Andreevna?"

Suddenly animated, he turned toward a woman seated at a distance in a deep armchair, who was slowly leafing through some old album. She trembled as if frightened by something. A mocking, sad smile was on her face. The woman became even more pale than before, helplessly raised her eyebrows, straightened the full silk dress falling from her shoulders.

"I don't know."

Annensky shook his head. "Yes, yes, 'there is wisdom in silence,' as they say. But it is better for it to be in words. And it will be."

The conversation came to a sudden stop.

"Well, let's ask someone else to read us poems." With his earlier indifferent affability, the poet continued to speak.[9]

Already Annensky seemed to understand the depth and capability of this quiet young woman, doubtless brought along by Gumilev and sitting unobtrusively in a corner.

But a scandal was brewing in the office of *Apollon*, an affair that Von Gunter saw as symptomatic of those pre-war years, the excitability and the inclination toward spiritual masquerade which "created the fertile soil for the growing of especially poisonous orchids."[10] As editor of *Apollon,* Sergei Makovsky had received on elegant, black-bordered notepaper a letter and the poems of a mysterious lady who signed herself "Cherubina de Gabriac." There was no return address. Soon he received others containing poems Makovsky considered quite interesting. Then came a telephone call from the woman, who spoke with a low, enticing, slightly lisping voice. Makovsky discovered that she was a Spanish aristocrat, sensitive, alone, a strict Jesuit, and thirsting for life. A host of young poets promptly fell in love with her, sight unseen, including Nikolai

Gumilev, who swore that he would win the exotic poetess. Von Gunter wrote: "The whole editorial staff burned with the desire to get a glimpse of this fairy-tale being. Her voice was such that it penetrated directly into the blood. Where three people gathered, the talk was only of her."[11] But Cherubina de Gabriac refused any meeting and remained elusive and unattainable.

Soon after, Von Gunter happened to visit the "Tower," where several women poets had gathered, among whom was Gumilev's late lamented lover, Elizaveta Ivanovna Dmitrieva. Von Gunter described her as, while not beautiful—her mouth was a bit too big and her teeth protruded—small, plump, well-proportioned and radiating sexuality. Dmitrieva caustically remarked that the mysterious Cherubina de Gabriac was probably ugly or she would have shown herself to her admirers. Von Gunter, staying to listen to the poetry, found Dmitrieva's poems to show a genuine talent. When he accompanied her home, to his astonishment Dmitrieva revealed that she herself was Cherubina de Gabriac, that she and Voloshin had collaborated in this elaborate hoax upon the editors of *Apollon*.[12]

However amusing it may have been, this affair was to bring serious consequences. Akhmatova believed that Annensky's life had been cut short by it, for instead of publishing his poems in the forthcoming issue of *Apollon*, Makovsky substituted those of Cherubina da Gabriac. "Annensky was stunned and dejected...Later on I saw his letter to Makovsky; it contained the line: 'Better not to think about it.' And one of his terrifying poems about anguish is dated the very same month...And a few days later he fell and died at Tsarskoe Selo railway station." Akhmatova was convinced that Annensky's heart attack had been brought on by this disappointment, that he had been "murdered.. by the enemies of art, who refused to print his poems on time."[13]

Makovsky attempted to save face by pretending that he had known all along that Dmitrieva was the enigmatic Spanish poetess. But Gumilev was outraged to discover that Dmitrieva had not only rejected his marriage proposal but had made a fool and a laughing-stock of him among his friends. When he was rumored to have described his former lover in explicit and unflattering terms, Maximilian Voloshin, with the permission of Dmitrieva's husband, took it upon himself to defend the lady's honor in a duel. Voloshin wrote of the circumstances:

He [Gumilev] and I met at Golovin's studio in the Mariinsky Theatre during a performance of *Faust*. Golovin at that time was painting the portraits of the poets who were collaborators at *Apollon*. That evening I was posing. In the studio were a lot of people, one of whom was Gumilev. According to the rules of the art of dueling that Gumilev, a great expert, had taught me the previous year, I decided to give him a slap in the face—powerfully, sharply and unexpectedly...

On the floor in the huge studio was the scenary taken down from *Orpheus*. All of them had already assembled. Gumilev stood with Blok at the other end of the hall. Chaliapin was singing "The Invocation of Flowers" down below. I decided to let him finish. When he finished, I walked up to Gumilev, who was talking with Tolstoy, and gave him a slap in the face.

At that moment, I was terribly taken aback. But when I recovered my wits, I heard Annensky say: "Dostoevsky is right. A slap in the face does sound wet." Gumilev recoiled from me and said: "You

[Gumilev uses the intimate form] will answer to me for this."...I wanted to say: "Nikolai Stepanovich, this is not Bruderschaft." But I now understood that this had nothing to do with the rules of the art of the duel and suddenly the question burst out of me: "Do you understand?" (That is, do you understand why?) He answered: "I understand."[14]

Following hallowed poetic precedent, the duel was fought just outside St. Petersburg on the spot where, in 1837, Alexander Pushkin had been mortally wounded in his duel with the Count d'Anthès. Fortunately, this confrontation did not have the same tragic outcome, but was a bungled and laughable affair from start to finish. On the way to the duel, Voloshin's car got stuck in a snowdrift and as he and his second, Prince Shervashidze, struggled through thigh-deep drifts to the appointed place, Voloshin lost his boot in the snow. The requisite fifteen paces separating the two duellers were measured out by Shervashidze and the pistols, which Voloshin described as "...if not the same pair which Pushkin duelled with, then contemporary with it," were examined.[15] Alexei Tolstoy, who was handing out the pistols, fell into a hole filled with icy water. Mikhail Kuzmin, Gumilev's second, was too frightened to watch and huddled behind a box of medical supplies. Gumilev shot first, then stood, his tall figure outlined darkly against the snow, a perfect target in his black top hat and frock coat. He waited for Voloshin to fire. Voloshin attempted to shoot his gun, but it kept misfiring. Finally, Tolstoy tore the pistol out of his hand and shot it into the snow. No one was injured and somehow honor was satisfied.[16]

Frances Laird

No doubt this new scandal gave rise to stories highly entertaining to the Petersburg literary set. What Anna knew of Gumilev's affair with Dmitrieva or when she heard of his duel with Voloshin is unclear. Since Gumilev's amorous adventures were the subject of much literary gossip, she must have heard of his failed courting of Dmitrieva and its burlesque-like aftermath. It could easily have been her anger over this that fueled the next poem, the first of Akhmatova' poems about Nikolai Gumilev to be included here.

> And when we were cursing one another
> In our passion as it glowed white hot,
> Both of us still could not understand how
> For two people earth could be so small,
> And that raging memory can torment,
> A fiery ailment—torture of the strong!—
> And in abyssmal nights the heart will teach us
> To ask: "Where is my friend who now has gone?"
> But when piercing through a wave of incense,
> Menacing, exulting rings the choir,
> Into my soul, stubbornly, severely,
> Inescapably look those same eyes.
>
> Anna Akhmatova
1909[17]

Swan Songs
Akhmatova and Gumilev

Angry accusations fly, fired by passion, jealousy and unforgettable memories. The stern, fixed, penetrating gaze of the lover, who knows her as no other does, signals Gumilev's presence in this poem.

It was in Kiev in November, 1909, at an event called "The Island of Art," that Kolya, accompanied by friends and his cousin, Mariya Kuzmina-Karavayeva, and Anna met again. As the two talked over coffee at the Hotel Europa, it is likely that he told her every detail of the story of the duel with Voloshin. Anna would not have been very amused, indeed may have been quite frightened at Gumilev's latest flirtation with death. Perhaps it was that duel, clumsy and ridiculous in its execution, yet terrifying in its possible outcome, that finally forced Anna Gorenko to give in to the insistent and undeterable Kolya. That evening when Kolya again asked her to marry him, convinced that it was inevitable, Anna agreed to become his wife. She wrote in January, 1910:

1

They came and they told me: "Your brother is dead."
I don't understand their meaning...
Today how long the scarlet sunset
Weeps over the sea in the evening.

I can bring back my brother from wandering paths,
I'll find my beloved brother.

> In my house I'll cherish and care for the past,
> On the past I'm a secret sorcerer.
>
> 2
>
> "Brother! I've waited for this shining day.
> In which countries did you wander?"
> "Sister! Turn round and do not look at me,
> This breast is bloody and wounded."
>
> Anna Akhmatova
January 25, 1910, Kiev[18]

At the death of the poet's "brother" (and Akhmatova's first poems about Gumilev addressed him as "brother"), the sky bends weeping over the sea as the world of nature joins in mourning him. But the poet refuses to accept the reports of her "brother's" death, confident that she can find him alive and bring him back from his "wandering paths," which presumably not only stretch over the African plains, but into the beds of other women. Then she will not only preserve the story of their past love, but will transform it into art with her magical powers. On his return, perhaps as a spirit, she welcomes him without a murmur of reproach. But he warns her to look away, so that he can hide from her sight the bloody wound on his breast.

This poem reveals how deeply shaken Anna was by Kolya's brush with a senseless and wasteful death. It was just such a duel, caused by a dispute over a woman, that had tragically cut short the life of

Alexander Pushkin. From her youth until the end of her life, Akhmatova would be nourished by the poetry and life of Pushkin, whose ubiquitous presence, as seen in her poem, she sensed in Tsarskoe Selo. The duel between Gumilev and Voloshin, so hilarious to the gossiping writers of Petersburg, clearly had a much graver impact upon Anna Gorenko.

Kolya's rather puzzling response to his hard-won success in love was to set off for Africa again. He wrote to Bryusov that he planned to shoot two or three panthers, loll about under the palm trees and come back just in time to hear his lecture at the "Academy of Verse." At the end of December, 1909, he wrote from Ethiopia: "As you see, I am writing you fom Djibouti. Tomorrow I will travel into the depths of the country in the direction of Addis Ababa...Along the way I will hunt. Here they eat everything, including lions and elephants. The sun burns unmercifully, the negroes are naked. Real Africa. I write poems, but few. The more I turn brown, the stupider I get and I am getting browner by the hour. But there are masses of impressions. Enough to write two books of poems."[19] He planned to return at the end of January.

No notes or diaries of this journey, if there were any, have survived. But in a letter to Mikhail Kuzmin from Harare he describes his adventures with his usual bravado:

Yesterday I did 11 hours (70 kilometers) on a mule, today I had to go another 8 hours (50 kilometers) to find leopards...Here there is only one hotel and the prices, of course, are terrible. But tonight I plan to sleep in the open air, if sleep is possible, because the leopards usually appear at night. There are lions and elephants here but they

Frances Laird

are as rare as elk are for us…I am a terrible sight—my clothes are torn with the thorns of mimosa, my skin is burned to a brassy-red color, my left eye is inflamed from the sun, my legs hurt because my mule fell on a mountain pass and crushed me with its body. But I wave it all off. It seems to me that I am dreaming two dreams at once—one difficult and unpleasant for the body, the other delightful for the eyes. I am trying to think of the last and forget about the first.[20]

Gumilev returned to Russia early in 1910. An intimate moment when the two young lovers are at last together is captured in the next poem. Palpable is the poet's tender anticipation and joy in the presence of his beloved, when the slightest touch of her hand is charged with emotional electricity. The love of Anna and Kolya hangs in a delicate balance, freed for a moment from the warring passions that led up to it and that would inevitably follow.

> There is none more anxious, more capricious,
> But long ago I gave myself to you.
> You know how in only one existence
> Many lives could willfully be fused.
>
> And today…the sky above was gray as
> Day passed in a dull and feverish fog.
> Out the window on the square's wet grasses,
> Children were not playing at leap-frog.
>
> You were looking at the old engravings,

Swan Songs
Akhmatova and Gumilev

Propping up your head upon your hand,
The figures there, amusing and outrageous,
Passed before us in a boring train.

"Look, my sweet, a bird there—do you see it?
And a horseman rides, his steed's so fast.
But how strangely frowning and bad-tempered
Is that burgermeister of high class."

You began to read about a prince then.
He was gentle, pious, pure and chaste.
And with the tip of your little finger,
You touched my sleeve when you turned the page.

As the moon, though, rose above the city
And the sounds of day began to fade,
Suddenly you wrung your hands, uneasy,
And then you so poignantly turned pale.

There before you, I, confused and timid,
Then fell silent, dreaming of one thing,
That to you about a golden heaven
A caressing violin would sing.

Nikolai Gumilev
1910[21]

Frances Laird

This poem rings with a striking authenticity often absent in Gumilev's more aesthetically contrived poetry. The details of time and place—young lovers spending a wet, foggy afternoon leafing through a book of old engravings and speculating on the oddities of the people pictured in its pages—are vividly conveyed. The heroine reads to the poet about a prince who possesses all the qualities that the poet knows he lacks—piety, gentleness, purity. Outside the window, the gray twilight thickens slowly into night and the moon rises. The atmosphere of the room is languorous, muted, even stifling, yet it is charged with emotional, even sexual, energy. In this intimate space the words and gestures of the heroine are magnified and invested with enormous meaning. Still the two seem held apart, whether by timidity, convention, or unease until the touch of her fingertip on the poet's sleeve suddenly connects them with a powerful current of feeling.

What is conveyed clearly in the poem is what Gumilev found so fascinating in the young Anna—her whimsical imagination, her sensitivity to the world around her and her mysteriously unpredictable, changeable moods. Anna seemed especially affected by the appearance of the moon, as here when she turns pale and anxious as it rises in the night sky. The poem ends with the poet standing shy, silent, and confused before her. The conquistador has been conquered and rendered powerless, no doubt an uncomfortable position for Gumilev. Whether he has come dangerously close to revealing his deepest feelings and baring his vulnerable emotional flanks or whether he cannot find concluding lines that will lift the poem into a larger realm of meaning, the poet again slips into that safe Symbolist harbor, the golden paradise.

Before their wedding, Anna came to visit Nikolai in St. Petersburg, where she read for the first time *The Cypress Chest*, Innokenty Annensky's last collection of lyric verse. When Gumilev showed her the galley proofs of the book in the Bryullov room of the Russian Museum, she was overwhelmed by the poems and read them "as if the world had ceased to exist." "…Immediately I stopped seeing or hearing, I couldn't tear myself away, I repeated those poems day and night…they opened up a new harmony for me."[22] And a new understanding of poetry that led her to declare: "I find my own 'origin' in Annensky's poems."[23] A door had opened for her out of the misty, stifling, mannered world of Symbolism into one with fresh, real poetic vistas. Akhmatova considered Annensky's poetry, so original and rich in possibilities, as the source of not only her own and Gumilev's poetry, but that of Khlebnikov's sonorous verse play, Pasternakian cloudbursts, and Mayakovsky's free-ranging accents and absent rhymes. It was not that these poets imitated Annensky, but that they already were "contained" in Annensky's poetry.[24]

Gumilev had dropped out of St. Petersburg University for a time, but upon his return from Africa, he began to attend classes again. On April 5, he applied for official permission from the rector of the university to "enter into the lawful state of marriage with the daughter of a Councillor of State, Anna Andreevna Gorenko." Soon after Gumilev received permission on the 14th of April and a leave of absence until August 20, he left St. Petersburg for Kiev.

He wrote to Valery Bryusov of his approaching marriage to "A.A.Gorenko to whom 'Romantic Flowers' was dedicated. The wedding will probably be on Sunday and then we will leave for Paris." These bare facts are all he reveals about the triumphant conclusion to this passionate and difficult courtship. His own literary activities receive most of his attention. "*Zhemchuga (Pearls)* [his third collection of poems] has come out. Vyacheslav Ivanovich in his review of it in *Apollon*, calling me your sword-bearer, says that with this book I earned from you the ritual blow of the sword on the shoulder initiating me into knighthood," a metaphor that must have pleased Gumilev. He sees *Pearls* as a completion of a cycle of experience and now is prepared to go in a new direction. "What this new thing will be is still not clear to me but it seems that it is not the path on which Vyacheslav Ivanovich sends me."[25]

On April 25, 1910, Anna Gorenko and Nikolai Gumilev were married in the seventeenth-century Church of St. Nicholas in Nikolska Slobodka, the village where Anna's mother was then living, on the banks of the Dnieper River near Kiev. Her mother and father were so doubtful about the marriage that they refused to attend the wedding ceremony, which hurt Anna deeply. Standing before the gilded iconostasis glittering softly with the light of candles, the two young people submitted themselves to the ancient rituals. In the dark, smoky, incense-sweet church, they held up white candles as the priest suspended the marriage crowns of martyrdom above their heads and intoned the ageless words of the Russian Orthodox marriage service as a small choir sang the responses. Gumilev presented to Anna on their wedding day a copy of *Pearls* inscribed: "To A.A. Gorenko. To Caesar what is Caesar's," acknowledging her inspiration, and the following poem:

Ballad

You lovers, whose sadness is like clouds,
And gentle ladies given to reflection,
Your yearning leads you on along what roads,
On to what triumph that is yet unheard of
Above the chalice destiny extends you?
Where for your endless sadness and your tears
Is there prescribed a balsam that will heal?
Where does the heart take fire but not be burned?
In what deserted place will it appear,
A rosy paradise's glowing gleam?

Frances Laird

> But look—I found now easy comes my song,
> Like a memory of some long past delirium.
> Upon me fell a great and powerful hand.
> As armored in chain mail of burning copper
> To drowsy Andromeda flew Perseus.
> Let the false temple flame up far away
> Where to shadows and to words I prayed.
> Oh, sacred homeland, it is you I greet!
> You lovers, try fate and then for you
> A rosy paradise's glow will gleam.
>
> A peaceful river flows within my land.
> And much sweet food is in its fields and copses.
> A stork there catches snakes among the reeds.
> Inebriate at noontime with gum's odor,
> The reddish-brown bears somersaults are turning,
> And like young Adam in a youthful world,
> I smile at all the varied fruits and birds
> And I know that when evening comes on, playing,
> The Christ Child will pass by along the stream,
> A rosy paradise's glow will gleam.

Swan Songs
Akhmatova and Gumilev

Premise

To you, dear friend, I will give back my song,
Believing in your metres all along,
When, coddling and chastising, you would lead,
For you knew all, you knew that for us, too,
A rosy paradise's glow would gleam.

Nikolai Gumilev
1910[26]

In a poem written as a paean to his new bride, one would expect that she would be featured as its central figure. Yet Anna is absent in the main body of the poem. In a rhetorical gesture, Gumilev directs his attention to his readers, those "lovers" and "ladies," and only in the concluding "Premise" does he addresses the "friend" whom he has just married. In fact, this wedding poem to Anna Gorenko seems to be about Gumilev himself.

With opening lines steeped in *toska*, a peculiarly Russian mixture of vague sorrow, yearning and ennui, Gumilev asks his lovelorn readers questions that have sprung from his experiences along the painful path to this fateful day, when destiny has handed him the "chalice" he has so desperately sought. His winning of the woman around whom his highly romanticized poetic world has centered provides the healing balm for the pain he has suffered. Now he can approach that long-sought "rosy paradise" existing beyond this world, that mystical realm free of sorrow, contradiction and conflict. This poem, he claims, came with amazing ease, arising out the vague memories of dreams, the feverish, uncontrolled images of delirium.

The vision of Perseus coming to the rescue of Andromeda had gripped his imagination like a powerful fist. In this Greek legend, owing to a quarrel between Queen Cassiopeia and the Ocean nymphs, Poseidon sends a sea monster to devour all living things in the kingdom. Only the sacrifice of Andromeda, King Cephus' only daughter, would save it from the creature's ravaging. When Perseus discovers the beautiful Andromeda chained to a rock and awaiting death, he kills the monster and frees her from her chains. Does Gumilev suggest with this mythic imagery that he is the heroic rescuer who will liberate Anna Gorenko, the pale virgin bound to the rock of a spirit-stifling bourgeois life beside the Black Sea? By marrying her will he break the chains of sadness and ennui that entangle her and carry her off into a wider world of life experience? Certainly repeating their wedding vows in the face of their families' opposition had been for both Kolya and Anna an act of defiance that freed them to choose from a wider range of possibilities in the life they would lead together. The young lovers have taken up the challenge Fate had thrown down and accepted its role in their lives. The attainment of that "rosy paradise" of self-realization would now perhaps become real for them.

In the third stanza, Gumilev creates an idyllic vision of his spiritual homeland—a fertile, bountiful, Eden-like garden filled with animals and plants over which he presides as a "young Adam." In this garden, the snakes hidden in the reeds may hint at the evil that lurks near-by. But they are kept firmly under control by storks that stride along the riverbank and snatch them up in their beaks. The brown bears, intoxicated with the smell of sap, roll and frolic like overgrown puppies in the warm sun. Even the Christ Child makes a playful appearance in Gumilev's "rosy paradise." But where in this Garden of Eden is Eve? Strange that in a hymn to marriage the presence of the other half of the primal pair is lacking.

It is only in the closing "Premise" that Gumilev brings Anna into the poem, though this short stanza seems tacked on almost as an afterthought. Recognized as the recipient of his song, she is the one to whom it has been returned or given back, indicated by the use of the Russian verb "*otdam*.". For as she has encouraged him, "coddling and chastising him" in his work and his life, Gumilev, he assures her, believes in her poetry. He acknowledges Anna's conviction that destiny had marked them out for marriage and led them at last into their own "rosy paradise" of marital bliss.

But the marriage rites carried out in blue clouds of incense and the trembling light of candles, blessed by the priest and witnessed by the stern ranks of saints staring down from the iconostasis, was only their outward union in the eyes of society and the Russian Orthodox Church. The real "marriage" of Nikolai Gumilev and Anna Gorenko was of a rarer kind, a close, profound and intimate connection of poet with poet, mind with mind, spirit with spirit that outstripped and outlasted the bonds of this legal marriage. It would endure beyond this brief moment in a "rosy paradise," beyond the flights of passion and clashes of wills that would follow. It was the deep and abiding respect in which they held one another's poetry, the trust in one another's taste and critical perception, the keen mutual appreciation of the workings of the mind, the spirit, the heart and the imagination. This "marriage" outlasted betrayal, divorce, other relationships and even the death of Gumilev. In fact, Akhmatova, looking back, believed that the rituals of the Russian Orthodox church that had joined them together on that bright April day in 1910 marked, not the beginning of marriage in its conventional sense, but the beginning of the end.

Chapter V
At the Fireside

In the spring of 1910, Anna and Nikolai set out for Paris for a month-long honeymoon. There "they gave themselves up with their whole souls to the museums of the leading light of a city and to French literature."[1] Much of what we know of the young couple's sojourn in Paris comes from Akhmatova's essay on the artist Amadeo Modigliani, written in 1964. This brief prose piece combines her memories of her wedding trip with another visit to Paris a year later. The Paris that Anna and Nikolai experienced in 1910 was the *vieux Paris* captured in the dream-like streetscapes of Atget's photographs. It was a city of green squares and narrow, cobbled streets, although the broad boulevards of Haussmann's grand designs were even then being laid "onto the living body of Paris..."[2] If a lone motorcar lumbered noisily into view, it had to honk its way through a tide of horse cabs and carriages, wagons, hand-barrows, and horse-drawn omnibuses that thronged the streets and avenues. Along the Seine, the booksellers laid out their old volumes in the bookstalls beneath the linden trees. The streets were lined with wine shops, bakeries, tabacs and coal-merchants, and gleaming piles of lettuces, new peas and bunches of rosy radishes were heaped on the stands of the neighborhood markets. Although a daring few among the women of Paris had attempted wearing *jupes-culottes*, a loose-fitting trouser, most kept to the prevailing fashion—ground-sweeping skirts and close-fitting jackets or blouses with muttonleg sleeves. The fashionably dressed Parisiennes who strolled the avenues with their ruffled parasols and wide-brimmed hats, fancifully decorated with feathers, fruits and flowers, were then, as now, the unquestioned arbiters of style and taste.

The newlyweds strolled the narrow streets of the Latin Quarter, watched the passing crowds from sidewalk cafés, leafed through the yellowed pages and spidery engravings in bookstalls along the quais. The sight of the Eiffel Tower made a lasting impression on Anna: "At that time the early light airplanes…which, as everyone knows resembled book-cases on legs, circled round my rusting and twisted contemporary, the Eiffel Tower. To me it resembled an enormous candlestick holder, forgotten by a giant in the capital of the dwarves…"[3] As Russians they weren't alone in Paris, for Diaghilev's Ballet Russe, featuring Stravinsky's *The Firebird,* with the famous dancers, Vaslav Nijinsky and Anna Pavlova, and the stage designer, Leon Bakst, was then taking the city by storm.

Anna's imagination may have been overly colored by the haunting and mysterious images of French Symbolist poets, for she was disappointed in Paris. "Poetry was in a state of total neglect, and people bought it only for designs by the more or less famous artists. Even then I understood that in Paris painting had swallowed up French poetry."[4] Cubism, with its revolutionary ways of envisioning the world, splintering and dissolving its subjects into hovering, monochromatic constructions of lines and planes, was just starting its massive sweep through the world of art. Everyone was talking of Picasso and Braque and their amazing experiments.

The only painter Anna seems to have become acquainted with was the young Amadeo Modigliani, one artist who remained largely unaffected by the Cubist fever. "All that was divine in Modigliani only sparkled through a sort of gloom. He was not at all like anyone in the world. Somehow I have always remembered his voice. I knew him when he was poor, and I did not understand how he survived—he didn't possess even a shadow of recognition as an artist."[5] To Anna he seemed poor and alone, isolated from the rest of the Parisian artistic community. She saw him only rarely on this first visit to Paris, but after corresponding with Modigliani throughout the winter, she would come to know him much better on her next trip to Paris.

Strangely, in her reminiscences of Paris Akhmatova barely mentions her new husband. Perhaps the early intimations of disillusionment had already surfaced. Or perhaps her memories of what should have been a happy period in her life were colored by the subsequent painful events in her life with Gumilev. Gumilev left no record in letters or diaries of their honeymoon trip.

In June, 1910, the young couple returned to Russia, accompanied by Sergei Makovsky, whom they had run into in Paris. Makovsky wrote: "In a railroad carriage, with the soothing rumble of the wheels, it was easy to talk to one another "heart to heart." Anna Andreevna, I remember well, interested me immediately, and not only in the capacity as the lawful wife of Gumilev, an absolute rake, with whom in my eyes so many romances were tangled up and untangled 'without consequences,' —but the whole appearance of Akhmatova then, tall, slender, quiet, very pale, with a sad set to her mouth, provoked either a kind of affecting curiosity or else pity. As Gumilev talked with her, I got the feeling that he loved her seriously and was proud of her. Up to then he had never once spoken to me of his marriage. Subsequently, he spoke of this as his only real love..."[6]

Back in Tsarskoe Selo, they moved into the Gumilev family house on Bulvarnaya Street. For Anna, her hometown had changed since her childhood. The summer village of the tsars had lost its special magical atmosphere. "Tsarskoe Selo seemed dead to me after Paris. There's nothing surprising about that. But where did my Tsarskoe Selo life vanish to in five years? I did not find even one of my fellow students from school and did not cross the threshold of one Tsarskoe Selo home. The new life in Petersburg had begun."[7]

She and Kolya spent the summer at the Gumilev's summer home, Slepnevo, described by Makovsky as: "...not distinguished by any kind of country beauty. A modest estate, a wooden house of an ordinary kind in the taste of the styleless construction of the last century. The terrace of the garden facade looked out on a round field in the middle of which grew a tall oak tree..." "The only oak in this part," Akhmatova wrote. "The old park was surrounded by an earthen bank. Along one side of it ran the road...Beyond the road, separated from the park were gardens for vegetables and fruits."[8]

Valeriya was amazed to hear that her two childhood friends had married. From Anna's letters she had heard only of her repeated rejections of the importunate Kolya. When they saw each other again in Tsarskoe Selo, Valeriya was struck by how little Anna spoke of her marriage, unlike the typical new bride who will chatter at length about the idiosyncrasies of her husband and the domestic details of her new household. "…I thought she had not changed at all…It was as if this event had absolutely no significance for her or me…"[9]

Anna continued to appear as the subject of Gumilev's poems after their marriage, but his depictions of her gradually began to move away from those romantic fairy-tale images of the rusalka and the sad princess. His poems lose that breathless enthrallment and anticipation of the lover, turning darker, more equivocal. Akhmatova wrote how one of her own dreams was the inspiration for Gumilev's poem "Margarita," written after their return from Paris: "When I was young I had a strange dream in which somebody said to me…: 'Faust never existed—Margarita made it all up…There was only Mephistopheles…' I do not know why we dream such terrifying dreams, but I told my dream to N.S. He made a poem out of it. He needed the theme of a death caused by a woman—in this case, the sister."[10]

<u>Margarita</u>

In a tavern Valentin speaks of his sister,

Frances Laird

    And he praises her mind and her face,
    And upon Margarita's left hand finger
    A precious ring has been placed.

    And at Margarita's is hidden a chest,
    Beneath the window in gold ivy vines.
    The malicious mocker in his scarlet cape
    Brings her so many earrings and rings.

    Margarita's room has a window set high,
    But the mocker has a ladder to climb.
    Let the students' songs ring out in the streets,
    Singing praise to Margarita's name.

    Too languid is April, the rubies too bright
    To know nothing at all, to forget…
    Lovingly Martha strokes a full sack,
    Only…a sulphurous smell comes from it.

    Valentin, Valentin, forget your disgrace.
    Ah, what will not happen on some summer night!
    Was not sly Riggoletto hump-backed and lame,
    His own daughter laughed at him, mocking the sight.

    All in vain with your threats do you call Faust to battle!

> *Swan Songs*
> *Akhmatova and Gumilev*
>
> He's not here..he was dreamed up by maidenly shame.
> Just the mocker in his cape, scarlet and tattered,
> Will you find…and you will be slain.
>
> Nikolai Gumilev
> July, 1910[11]

According to the well-known tale, the world-weary Faust, preparing to die by drinking poison, has cursed God, whereupon Mephistopheles, an agent of the devil, appears, promising to grant him his wish to become young and handsome, so that he can taste again the joys of love. At the sight of Margarita, a beautiful village girl, Faust willingly signs his fateful pact with Mephistopheles. Valentin, Margarita's soldier brother, believes that Margarita has been insulted and attempts to defend her honor, but he is thwarted by Mephistopheles' magical powers. When he goes off to war, leaving her alone and unprotected, Margarita is wooed by Faust, with the enticement of a casket of jewels provided by Mephistopheles. Martha, her neighbor, is impressed by this expensive gift. Inevitably Maragarita is seduced by Faust and, when Valentin returns and discovers this, the two fight a duel and Valentin is killed. Margarita, abandoned by Faust, ends her life in prison, having murdered her illegitimate child.

In Gumilev's poem, Valentin sings of his sister's virtues among his fellow soldiers at the village tavern. But the ring from Mephistopheles' casket that she wears on her left hand makes her deception obvious. The easy accessibility of Margarita's room and her name on the lips of the students suggest her sexual promiscuity that disgraces her brother. As in Akhmatova's dream, Faust is not present to dignify Mephistopheles' sordid machinations. Margarita has given herself up to pure, unmitigated evil and consorts shamelessly with the devil himself. There is no one Valentin can challenge to a duel that would restore honor to the family's name. The themes of betrayal and death in a poem written by Gumilev in the first months of their marriage strike a decidedly minor note, hinting at an incipient disillusionment that gradually will creep into the poetry as into the marriage reflected in it.

Tsarskoe Selo was the setting for a poem permeated with a dreamy, rather wistful nostalgia that Akhmatova refers to in her memoirs of Gumilev: "I agree that it is difficult in the 'Giants' Palace' to make out the Tsarkoe Selo tower [the ruined tower by the Orlov gates in the imperial gardens] from which we (Kolya and I) watched the cuirassier's chestnut steed kick, and how the horseman skillfully calmed him…"[12]

>Remember the palace of giants
>In the pool of silvery fish,
>The *allées* of lofty plane trees
>And the towers of blocky schist?
>
>How the goldenish steed at the towers

Swan Songs
Akhmatova and Gumilev

Reared up, playing, on his hind legs
And the white saddle cloth decorated
With patterns of delicate threads?

Remember in cloudy hollows
The cornice that you and I found,
Where stars like grapes by the handful
Came swiftly hurtling down?

Oh, say, without turning paler,
Now you and I are not of these
Who may be stronger and braver,
But are only strangers to dreams.

Our hands are so finely-modeled
And beautiful are our names.
But to deadly, tedious boredom
The soul if forever condemned.

And we have not yet forgotten,
Though it's destined to slip from our minds,
That time when we loved one another,
That time when we learned to fly.

       Nikolai Gumilev
       1910[13]

Gumilev looks back on the time when he and Anna as young lovers had wandered past the ruined tower and down the gravel paths of the imperial gardens, when together they had watched a golden-brown horse rear up and had counted the stars that fell down the sky like grapes. Although still at home in the world of dreams, Gumilev sensed a "deadly, tedious boredom" had crept into their lives. He looks back longingly at that tender and innocent stage of their love, when they had been "learning to fly," discovering one another and living out new emotions and experiences, a time when they had loved one another simply. But in those few short months of marriage, familiarity seemed to have poisoned for Gumilev the union that he had so long and ardently sought.

To judge from the poetry written in 1910, Nikolai Gumilev had scarcely become a husband before he felt the confines of marriage. He took his usual escape route when, on September 25, wed for barely six months, Gumilev boarded the *Oleg* in Odessa and sailed for Africa again. After stopping in Djibouti on the Gulf of Aden, he ventured again into Ethiopia to Harare and Addis Ababa. In this poem, composed enroute, Gumilev's enthrallment with Africa and his role as the great, white master goes unappreciated by the woman who has tried to imprison and domesticate him.

<u>At the Fireside</u>

Swan Songs
Akhmatova and Gumilev

Shadows floated up and the fire died out.
He stood all alone, arms across his chest.

Into distance reached his unmoving stare,
Bitterly he spoke of his sorrow there.

"I made my way deep into foreign lands,
Eighty days or more rode my caravan.

There were forests and mighty mountain chains
And strange cities of people far away.

Many times from them, in the quiet night,
Out to our camp flew strange, unearthly cries.

We dug ditches and we cut down the trees,
Lions in the dust would walk up to me.

But among us there were no timid souls,
We shot at them, aimed right between their eyes.

From the sand I dug out an ancient shrine
And the river's name was made the same as mine.

Five great tribes of men in the lands of lakes,

They obeyed my words and honored laws I made.

In the grip of sleep, I have now grown weak
And my soul is sick, most painfully sick.

Now I know, I know just what terror is,
Buried as I am inside these four walls.

Even flashing guns, even splashing waves
Cannot break the hold of this binding chain…"

Malice melted in her triumphant look,
In a corner there, the woman heard him speak.

Nikolai Gumilev
September, 1910[14]

There is a tense interplay of emotions between a man and woman in a quiet sitting-room, much as in that pre-nuptual poem of loving indulgence, "There is none more anxious, more capricious…" written less than a year before this. In this domestic scene a man stands beside the fireplace, the very heart of the home, his arms folded across his chest, while a woman is seated in an armchair in a far corner. They are isolated in space, distanced from one another by the shadowy reaches of the room. He proudly recounts to the silent woman his past adventures, with himself in the starring role as hero.

There is no real communication between the two—he speaks into the darkness and she listens without responding. In alien and forbidding lands of mountain precipices, savage lions, and unpredictable tribesmen, he was the wielder of power over the native tribes he found. But no matter how extreme the dangers, nothing had charged his heart with such terror as did his "imprisonment" in the "binding chain" of marriage within the four walls of that house. The woman, apparently unmoved by his words, betrays her feelings only in her eyes where a look of malice turns to triumph.

The apotheosis of Gumilev's love for Anna Gorenko has tarnished, the light of the long-awaited "rosy paradise" has dimmed. Like the flames that flicker weakly on the hearth, the fire of passion is dying out. While this was not the whole truth of their relationship, it seems in this poem that Gumilev intended to convey his view of the married state to his bride.

To Andrei Bely, this poem demonstrated the aesthetic strides Gumilev was making as a poet. "Gumilev...is making rapid and successful achievments in lyric poetry. His poems are becoming much more interesting both in form and content." In particular, Bely was impressed by the newness of Gumilev's rhythms in this poem, constructed of what he saw as "coiling pentameters."[15]

Anna left no thoughts on Gumilev's sudden departure with their honeymoon hardly over. In his absence, she began to study in the Rayev Higher Historical-Literary Course and, more importantly, to discover her unique style with the inspiration of Annensky's poems and to write with new assurance and determination. Before he had left, Gumilev had taken her to Vyacheslav Ivanov's "Tower," where Akhmatova encountered the literati of Petersburg among whom she would soon find her place. When on her first visit Ivanov had asked her if she wrote poetry, she recited two of her poems for him. He "very indifferently and ironically pronounced: 'What lush Romanticism!'"[16] She may not have understood the disparaging nature of this comment, but no doubt Gumilev had.

After Nikolai had sailed for Africa, Anna encountered Ivanov by chance when he lectured at her Rayev course and he invited her to his Monday evenings. She began attending regularly, read her poetry several times and had her first taste of recognition. "All around everybody praised me—Kuzmin, Sologub and at Vyacheslav's. (They didn't like Kolya at Vyacheslav's and they tried to tear me away from him; they used to say: 'There you are, there you are, he doesn't understand your poetry.')" [17] Attempting to persuade her to leave Nikolai, Ivanov assured her, "You'll make a man out of him by doing that."[18]

Although Ivanov was extremely perceptive as a critic, Akhmatova found him hypocritical, difficult, and completely self-absorbed. He would "weep over poems tête-a-tête and then lead the way to the 'salon,' where he would quite caustically tear them to pieces..."[19] Ivanov needed his own circle of devotees. "You would go to see him, he would lead you into his study: 'Recite!' Well, what could I recite then? Twenty-one years old, plaits down to my heels and fantasies of unhappy love...I would recite something like 'The slender shepherd boy.' Vyacheslav was ecstatic: 'Since the time of Catullus and so on.' Then he would take you into his sitting room: 'Recite!' You would recite exactly the same thing. And Vyacheslav would demolish you."[20] But Ivanov recognized talent and was convinced that Anna Akhmatova would bring Annensky's poetic innovations to fruition. Seating her on his right in the late poet's place of honor, he is said to have declared: "Here is a new poet, to reveal to us what still lay deep within the soul of Innokenty Annensky."[21]

Alone in her room in the Gumilev house on Bulvarnaya street, Anna wrote and read a great deal. The poems seemed to flow from her pen as never before; she sensed that she was beginning to find her way. In Petersburg she often visited Valeriya or travelled to Kiev to visit her mother. Without her well-known husband, she moved about with growing confidence in the artistic world of Petersburg, attending poetry readings and art exhibitions. Encouraged by her friends, Akhmatova began to publish her poems in small magazines. "And then they began to praise me," she wrote. "And you know what praise was like on the Parnassus of the Silver Age! To this exorbitant and shameless praise I replied rather coquettishly: 'But my husband doesn't like them.'"[22] This rather insincere attempt at modesty was the basis for all the rumors that arose afterwards that Gumilev did not approve of her poetry.

The writer Georgy Chulkov noticed her, surrounded by Gumilev's colleagues from *Apollon,* at the opening of a World of Art exhibition.

He met her again at the home of Feodor Sologub and when the evening drew to a close, he accompanied her to the train station. "In the evening Petersburg fog she resembled a large bird which was used to flying high in the air, but was now dragging her wounded wing along the ground. 'You know I write poetry,' she said as we waited for the train...She began to recite some of the poems which became *Evening*. It was a new, unique melody."[23]

Sergei Makovsky, now married himself, would visit Akhmatova on occasion, finding her "...always somehow enigmatically sad and evoking a tender compassion toward herself. Sometimes when Gumilev was on a trip, she stopped in to see my wife and read her poems. She still hadn't published in magazines; Gumilev 'didn't allow it.' Having listened to a few of her poems, I immediately suggested printing them in *Apollon*. She wavered: what would Nikolai Stepanovich say when he returned? He was decisively against her publication. But I insisted: 'Good, I'll take the responsibility on myself. Allow me to say that I simply stole these verses from your album and printed them on my own authority.' And so it was arranged...The poems of Akhmatova, as they appeared in *Apollon*, brought so much praise that Gumilev, having returned from "faraway lands," had to accept this *fait accompli*."[24]

On March 25, 1911, Gumilev returned from Africa. Akhmatova maintained later that she had hardly gone out of the house in the five months of her husband's absence. But on the evening of his unexpected arrival back in Tsarskoe Selo she had slept at a girlfriend's house. "She came back in the morning, saw him, and, caught unawares, said that that was just the sort of thing that would have to happen—the first time in months she had spent the night away from home, and it had to be that day."[25] One of the first things Kolya did upon his return was to ask to see the poems that Anna had written in his absence.

In Amanda Haight's biography of Akhmatova, the poet's description of this moment was quite dramatic: "When Akhmatova met him at the railway station, he looked at her sternly and asked, 'Have you been writing?' When she said she had, he demanded to see the work then and there on the platform. He cast his eye over it, nodded, and said, 'Good.'"[26] Akhmatova told Lydia Chukovskaya that when she read the poems that would make up *Evening*: "He gasped. From that time onwards, he always loved my poetry very much."[27]

Although Anna had already written at least two hundred poems, Kolya could not abide her early ones. "He'd agree to listen and pay close attention because it was me but he was very critical; he suggested I occupy myself with something else. He was right: I really did write appalling poems then…like those published in little magazines as fillers…"[28] Now Akhmatova had received the blessing of her ultimate critic and without hesitation could call herself a poet. Soon after this, her poems appeared in *Apollon* (1911, No. 4).

Gumilev, a keenly perceptive critic of poetry, must have been enormously relieved that his wife would not embarrass him with sentimental rubbish, turning him into an object of derision for his *Apollon*-ian friends and fellow poets. Yet he may have wondered how his wife's literary vocation would affect his cherished, self-created identity as the poet/conquistador, which might well be compromised if she were to be recognized as a poet in her own right.

Despite the troubling undercurrents in their marriage, there were also times of pure happiness in that first year, when they could enjoy the close comradeship of their shared calling. "One Evening," which Gumilev sent to Valery Bryusov in May, 1911, captures such an intimate, harmonious moment.

<u>One Evening</u>

In tall vases was languidness of dying lilies.
Copper-red was the west and palest blue the night.
Of Leconte de Lisle you and I were conversing,
It was for the cold poet that you and I pined.

More than once we had opened the silky-smooth volumes
And we calmly had read and had whispered "Not there."
But then flashed to us all of the words, all the languors,
Like the stars for a nomad that rise once a year.

In our souls rose a world unexpectedly vast and
The strange, singing rhymes of an ages-old sun.

> Through the twilight of evening, thrown back in an armchair
> The sharp profile of the Creole with the soul of a swan.
>
> Nikolai Gumilev
Spring, 1911²⁹

As evening falls, Anna and Kolya sit with a volume of the French Parnassian poet, Leconte de Lisle, conversing about his poetry and searching for a particular passage. In his words, new and unsuspected meaning suddenly reveals a mysterious world, vast, ancient, with a sun that sings in strange harmonies. The two feel the presence of the poet himself, as if he sat beside them in the gathering dusk. Endowing the French poet with "soul of a swan," Gumilev acknowledges Leconte de Lisle as worthy to join the sacred circle of Tsarskoe Selo poets.

According to legend, the city of Kiev, where Anna had lived for two years, was founded by three brothers. One of these, Kii, had succeeded in killing a huge snake that had menaced the townspeople, so that his name was given to the village on the banks of the Dnieper river. This is the background for Gumilev's depiction of Akhmatova in a poem which, while humorous, has an underlying seriousness. In it, Gumilev gently mocks Anna's unearthly powers with his reference to "Bald Mountain," a high hill in the vicinity of Kiev where witches were said to gather.

Out of a Serpent's Lair

Frances Laird

From out of a serpent's lair,
From out of Kiev's fine squares,
I took not a wife, but a sorceress.
I thought—an amusing thing,
I guessed—a self-ruling thing,
A cheerful and merry bird-songstress.

She'll frown when you whistle,
Embrace her—she'll bristle,
But let the moon shine—she will languish.
She watches and moans as
If she'd buried someone
And to drown herself is all she wishes.

I say: "For a christened man,
With you it's so singular
That I can no longer be bothered.
So take all your languor to
The broad river Dnieper's pools,
To the sinful slopes of Bald Mountain."

She's silent, she hesitates
And doesn't feel well today.
The guilty one, I can but pity her,

> A bird that no longer flies,
>
> A birch tree that's undermined
>
> Above a fate to which God curses it.
>
> Nikolai Gumilev
June, 1911[30]

The image of the serpent, with its negative associations—temptation, disobedience, cleverness, duplicity, poisonous venom—is a questionable image for describing one's wife. But this is also Gumilev's tongue-in-cheek reference to Akhmatova's snake-like litheness and flexibility of body. Vera Nevedomskaya, a Slepnevo neighbor of the Gumilevs, remembered how Nikolai had staged an amateur circus one summer with Anna featured as the "Snake Lady." "She had an amazing flexibility—she easily put a leg behind her neck or touched the back of her head with her toes, maintaining all the while the severe face of a novice nun."[31] Akhmatova was proud of these acrobatic abilities. "I could bend backwards and touch the floor with the back of my head. I could lie on my belly and touch my feet with my head. Without the least bit of training, I was able to do things which are ususally only achieved by constant, daily practice."[32] (This ability is illustrated in a Modigliani drawing of a limber Akhmatova bending back her head to touch it with one foot that curves up from behind her.[33])

Gumilev charts the extremes of his wife's personality, on one hand—an amusing, capricious, merry song bird—on the other—a witch. No decorative plaything to amuse and entertain him, she is a mysterious, unknowable woman, the possessor of magical powers. With her own complex and rich inner life, she exists independent of and quite distinct from him. She is closely attuned to the world of nature, with a refined and acute sensibility keyed to the changing phases of the moon that cause her to be moody, difficult, and often sunk in depression and ennui.

What fascinated Gumilev before their marriage, Anna's inscrutable air of mystery, unpredictability and dreamy languor, seems now a source of irritation, even exasperation. In the third stanza, he tells her in effect to go off and drown herself in the Dnieper if that is what she wants. She responds with silence and withdrawal which arouses his reluctant compassion. He regards her with pity, seeing her as somehow broken, needy, limited— "a bird that no longer flies."

The final lines ring with the dark prevision that repeatedly echoes out of these poems. The image of Anna as the birch tree hanging out over an abyss, the earth falling away from its roots, is powerful and full of meaning as we look ahead at Akhmatova's life after Gumilev. Through the Stalinist terror and the long decades of overt and covert political oppression, she clung to life tenaciously, rooted like the birch tree clinging to the cliff and teetering over the brink of destruction.

In 1911, Gumilev attempted a poetic acrostic formed with the name of Anna Akhmatova and inspired by his African adventures.

Addis Ababa, city of roses,
Nestled on banks of glassy streams,
Nurtured by a heavenly wonder,
A diamond set in dark ravines.

Armida's garden—there a pilgrim
Kept his promise of vague love.
May we all bow low before him,
As red and stifling blooms the rose.

There filled with deceits and poisons
One's gaze into his soul looked deep.
Vast sycamores stood in the gardens
And *allées* of twilit plane trees.

Nikolai Gumilev
Tsarskoe Selo, 1911[34]

The city of Addis Ababa is transformed in Gumilev's imagination into a "city of roses" created miraculously, a flowery oasis surrounded by wilderness and desert and set like a precious gem glittering out of the earth. There a pilgrim (Gumilev) has kept his vow "of vague love" in "Armida's garden." Armida, in a poem by Tasso, "The Deliverance of Jerusalem," spirits away her lover, Rinaldo, to a far-off island where, in her enchanted gardens, he loses all memory of his past. By implication, Anna, the enchantress, has cut the poet off from his former life. While in "To Beatrice" Gumilev used the white rose as a veiled reference to the pure and innocent Anna Gorenko, here the roses are red with the fire of passion. Gumilev's poem implies that, even seas and continents away from her, he has kept his vow of fidelity in love. Yet he cannot escape the malicious and deceitful gaze—presumably Anna's—that plunges deep into his soul. Gumilev seems to cast Anna out of the role of the adored ideal of womanhood into the exact opposite, the perfidious and false wife. For in so doing Gumilev could more easily justify his own betrayals of his marriage vows. The last lines carry us back beneath the plane trees of that *sanctum sanctorum* of memory—the imperial gardens of Tsarskoe Selo.

It is difficult now to understand the evident cooling of Nikolai Gumilev's passion for Anna, as evidenced in his poetry, within a few short months of their marriage. Perhaps it stemmed from an irreconcilable clash between the Anna his imagination had created and the earthly Anna. In the seven years he was obsessed with the fantasy images of the rusalka, the tsaritsa, the whimsical child of nature, he seldom depicted Anna Gorenko as a flesh and blood human being with her own thoughts and passions. For him she was the vessel for his romantic, mystical idea of womanhood. He had pursued this creature of his imagination relentlessly and, despite amorous distractions, with a single-minded zeal. Now that he possessed the real woman, the rusalka had slipped from his grasp and vanished.

Or perhaps Gumilev's emotional withdrawal from the marriage grew from the conflict between his role as husband and as the Nietzschean poet/holy warrior who prized above all his courageous and willful independence of action. Solitary and autonomous, he must venture to prove his worth, a never-ending test of the self, perhaps driven by Gumilev's need to reassure himself of his strength, identity and self-worth as a man. Apparently he had never asked himself before he married how a wife and children would fit into the scenario of this freely lived and self-focused life. Marriage assumes not only the compassionate understanding of the desires and needs of the other, but demands trust and an intimacy in which the heroic cannot long be sustained. Gumilev was unable or unwilling to make that transition from the superficial, exciting stage of adolescent falling-in-love to a mature and lasting love relationship. It was impossible for him to release the world of dreams so as to fully embrace this world and enter into a deep, long-lasting and mature partnership with a woman. Always driven to find yet another seemingly unattainable woman to take the place of the one he had conquered, he must feel the thrill of a fresh love and begin the pursuit all over again. By means of this "Don Juanism," which would follow the pattern set in his premarital behavior, he was continuously proving himself through sexual conquest, an activity Gumilev thought crucial for the poet/conquistador.

A special terror for Gumilev was that he would be sucked in and destroyed by the petty bourgeois provincialism and the tedious monotony of daily life. This may have contributed to the soul sickness recognized by Akhmatova: "…Everything (the good and the bad) arose from this feeling—both his travel and his Don Juanism."[35] For Gumilev, new sights, new experiences, new love affairs kept adventure alive in his life, fed fresh imagery into his poetry and nourished his self-image and self-esteem.

But this behavior could only corrode the foundations of a marriage. Makovsky was only one witness to the gradual disintegration of the Gumilev marriage. "No kind of mirages can substitute for everyday reality, when 'at home' a young wife is miserable in solitude, especially such an 'unusual' one as Akhmatova…Its not easy for a poet to reconcile a poetic 'self-will,' and thirst for more and more novel impressions, with a settled family life and with love, which also was as necessary to him as air…Gumilev never managed to solve this problem. He overrated his own strengths and underrated those of a woman who was able to forgive, but was no less proud and self-willed than he was."[36]

No young bride, once so adored and so avidly pursued, could have easily suffered in silence such behavior in a husband, especially one as proud, determined and independent as Anna. To judge from a poem which Gumilev wrote in 1910, a fierce battle of wills was carried on, whether it was engaged openly or simmered beneath the surface of daily life. Gone in the next poem is any trace of Symbolist fantasy. Jarringly frank and brutally direct, it carries us down into the deep and dirty pits of human experience where the theme of dominance and submission becomes frighteningly real.

> More than once it has happened, and will more than once,
> In our battle, surpressed and persistent,
> You've rejected me now, but as always, I know
> That tomorrow you'll come back submissive.
>
> But don't wonder about it, my quarreling friend,
> My enemy seized by dark love,
> If the moaning of love turns to moans of torment
> And our kisses are stained with blood.
>
> Nikolai Gumilev
1910[37]

Perhaps the outward semblance of a marriage could have been maintained if Gumilev had chosen a wife who could more easily fit into the traditional role. But Anna, who had little knowledge of or interest in the practical matters of running a household, was not merely dabbling prettily in the arts when writing poetry. The high calling of the poet would soon govern her life with the power that it exerted over that of Nikolai Gumilev.

Chapter VI
Poisoned

Two months after Nikolai Gumilev's return from Africa, in May of 1911, he and Anna set off again for Paris. There Anna renewed her friendship with Amadeo Modigliani, with whom she had been corresponding throughout the winter months. Akhmatova later recalled a line from one of the artist's long, beautifully-written letters: *'Je tiens votre tête entre mes mains and je vous couvre d'amour'* ('I hold your head in my hands and cover you with love'). Of course, he had to draw the address on the envelope with great care because he did not know the Russian alphabet."[1] In writing of her friendship with Modigliani, Akhmatova gave a somewhat reserved account. Only with the recent discovery of previously unknown drawings of Akhmatova by Modigliani from the collection of Paul Alexandre, works first exhibited in Venice in 1993, has real evidence cast more light on their brief, but intimate relationship.

It must have been disturbing to Anna to realize that, for Kolya, the marriage vows did not exclude the possibility of other lovers. Evidently he had soon made it clear that he could only live the life of a poet completely if he had absolute freedom of action, which included making love when, where and to whom he wished. It is conceivable that Anna, feeling emotionally abandoned by Gumilev, may have welcomed the warmth of Modigliani's admiration. She may have come to feel that, if this was Kolya wanted, she would show him that she, too, could live by his rules.

But the mutual attraction that Kolya could see growing between Anna and Modigliani was too much for him. When Modigliani objected to Gumilev's rudeness in speaking Russian in front of him and his French friends, the two clashed in an angry argument. Gumilev, no doubt seething with jealousy, abruptly left Paris and returned to St. Petersburg. He never mentioned Modigliani's name again, except for one occasion. Significantly, this was in 1918, when their marriage was ending and they made a last visit together to see their son in Slepnevo. Then Gumilev made a reference to Modigliani as a "drunken monster."[2] Perhaps he was attempting to blame Anna and her relationship with Modigliani for the failure of their marriage.

Anna had noticed little change in the handsome, dark-eyed young artist since she had last seen him the year before, only that: "He had become somber and a little thinner," for he had been ill that winter.[3] She could not understand how the poverty-stricken Modigliani could survive in Paris. She often visited his ramshackle studio at 14 Cité Falguiere, where the walls were hung with enormous portraits that extended from the floor to the ceiling. In the little courtyard behind it, Modi, as she called him, was at work on a sculpture which he referred to as *la chose* (the thing) and the rap of his mallet echoed through the deserted alleyway. Akhmatova remembered: "It was exhibited at the Salon des Independants in 1911. He asked me to go and have a look at it, but he didn't come up to me at the exhibition because I wasn't alone, but with friends."[4] Modigliani gave her a photograph of this piece.

To Akhmatova it seemed that Modigliani had no friends. "He seemed to be surrounded by a dense ring of solitude. I don't recall that he exchanged greetings with anyone in the Luxembourg Gardens or the Latin Quarter, where everyone more or less knew one another."[5] And she saw no evidence of other women in his life. Modi may have encouraged her illusions of his solitary life to keep this lovely Russian poetess to himself, for actually he had a wide circle of friends in Montmartre. Soon after arriving in Paris in 1907, Modigliani had found a patron in Paul Alexandre, a young doctor fascinated with contemporary art.[6] Struck by his talent, Alexandre had given the penniless painter a room in a house he rented on Rue du Delta as a refuge for his needy artist friends. On Saturday evenings in the Delta house, riotous theatricals, film scenarios, music, poetry readings and chess matches would go on among the artists, their wives and girlfriends as well as an unending parade of pretty models and seamstresses. Modigliani, with his simple, generous nature and aristocratic bearing, soon became the dominant personality there.

The sculptor Constantin Brancusi, a close friend of Modigliani's, frequented the Delta house, joining enthusiastically in the pagan dances, wrapped in a bed sheet. Brancusi had helped Modigliani find his Montmartre studio on the Cité Falguiere and when Modigliani took up sculpture, it was Brancusi who advised him on how to choose his materials and cut the stone. Contrary to Akhmatova's impression, difficult though his life may have been, Modi was not without good friends.

Born into a cultured Italian-Jewish family in Livorno, Amadeo Modigliani had a love of poetry, something Akhmatova found to be rare among artists. Akhmatova remembered how they would sit on a bench in the Luxembourg Gardens under Modigliani's huge, black umbrella as the Paris drizzle sifted down and recite lines of French poetry together. "…A warm summer rain would be falling, and nearby slumbered *le vieux palais à l'italienne.* Together we would recite Verlaine, whom we knew well by heart, and we were happy that we could remember the same things."[7]

Modigliani loved to wander about the city at night and Akhmatova would often recognize his footsteps in the quiet street. "I would go to the window and, through the Venetian blinds, watch his shadow lingering below…"[8] They explored in the moonlight what remained of *le vieux Paris* in the blocks behind the Pantheon. Once Anna arrived at the Cité Falguiere studio and, through some misunderstanding, Modigliani was not at home. "I was clutching an armful of red roses. A window above the locked gates of the studio was open. Having nothing better to do, I began to toss the flowers in through the window. Then, without waiting any longer, I left." When they next met, Modigliani could not believe that she had not been in the room for the roses had fallen onto the floor and "…were lying there so beautifully."[9]

Modigliani regretted that, not knowing Russian, he could never really understand Akhmatova's poems. "...He suspected that there was something miraculous lurking in them; but they were only my first uncertain attempts."[10] Modigliani, who was fascinated by spiritual knowledge and the occult, was impressed most of all, Akhmatova recalled, "by my ability to guess people's thoughts, to see their dreams, and other trifles to which those who know me have long been accustomed. He would say repeatedly: '*On communique.*'"[11]

Then in his *periode negre*, Modigliani was fascinated by Egyptian art and visited the Louvre almost daily, often taking Anna along. In the weeks they spent together, Modigliani made many drawings of Anna. Akhmatova wrote in her memoirs: "I didn't pose for his drawings of me; he did them at home and gave them to me later. There were sixteen in all, and he asked me to mount and hang them in my room in Tsarskoe Selo. They vanished in that house during the first years of the Revolution. The one that survived bears the least resemblance to his future nudes..."[12] Until now, the only drawing of Akhmatova known to have survived is the often reproduced reclining figure of Akhmatova with its arcing lines and delicate profile.

It appears, however, that Modigliani made many drawings of Anna Gorenko Gumileva. In fact, the poetess he called affectionately his "Egyptyanka," or "little Egyptian girl" may well have been the artist's most fertile inspiration during this period of his career.[13] In the pages of *The Unknown Modigliani; Drawings from the Collection of Paul Alexandre,* Anna's image appears repeatedly. A female nude, seen from the rear, the face in profile, with a drooping chignon of dark hair, bears the unmistakable Akhmatovian nose.[14] The head of woman, simplified to the purest, most essential forms, shows the fringe of hair and the necklace of beads that the young Anna wore then.[15] "He used to say: *'les bijoux doivent être sauvages';* (apropos my African beads), and he drew me wearing them."[16] Three studies of a seated female nude, in a pose that could have been taken from an Egyptian frieze, with arms akimbo and face turned back in profile, again with the mane of dark hair and the Dantean nose, are unquestionably of Anna.[17] Anna as the limber acrobat appears in a drawing entitled "Female Trapeze Artist," where she has drawn her legs up behind her, nearly touching her head with one foot.[18] Many of the caryatid figures strongly resemble Akhmatova's body form and the fringe of hair over the forehead, with one dated 2 July 1911 by the artist, precisely the time of their close friendship.[19] The female nude lying on her stomach on a bed with a darkened window in the background is surely Anna.[20] Akhmatova's description of one drawing: "He made a drawing of my head in the attire of Egyptian queens and dancers..."[21] may refer to Modigliani's studies of a female head with decorative headpieces, dated August 20 and August 22.[22] Clearly, in Modigliani's Egyptian period, the face and form of this young Russian poetess was an important stimulation to his creativity.

Despite her assertion to the contrary, Akhmatova must have posed for these drawings, many of which depict her nude, for it is difficult to believe that Modigliani could have executed these drawings otherwise. And in conversation, she admitted that she did so. When she showed her precious remaining Modigliani drawing to Lydia Chukovskaya, she said: "You understand, he was not interested in the likeness. The pose fascinated him. He drew me about 20 times."[23] Since Akhmatova was not a paid model, the assumption can also be made that the friendship of Akhmatova and Modigliani was rather more than a platonic one. Excepting portraits where the she is clothed and identified, the unpaid female model was usually the artist's wife or mistress.

Looking back later in her life upon that summer in Paris, how did Akhmatova remember the love affair? "It is likely that neither of us understood one essential thing: that everything that was happening was the pre-history of both our lives: his—very short, mine—very long. The breath of art should have been the light, bright hour that precedes the dawn. But the future, which as we know casts its shadow long before it appears, knocked at the window, hid behind lampposts, cut through our dreams, and threatened with the terrible Baudelairian Paris concealed somewhere nearby. And all that was divine in Modigliani only sparkled through a sort of gloom."[24] In the sixties, when she asked Joseph Brodsky for his opinion of the storied affair, he replied: "Well, Anna Andreevna. It's *Romeo and Juliet* in a production by the members of the royal house."[25] This delighted her tremendously.

The intriguing question remains—what happened to the other drawings that Modigliani gave to Anna Gumileva? It was Modigliani's practice to quickly draw several versions of each pose, starting with a fresh sheet of paper each time instead of correcting any mistake in the drawing. So it is likely that the drawings Akhmatova claimed were lost were in fact versions of those same poses found in Paul Alexandre's collection. The question of the fate of her drawings was a touchy one for Akhmatova. When asked about them, Akhmatova was unusually evasive in her answers, even appearing offended that anyone, knowing the terrible conditions of her life, would even inquire. She told Joseph Brodsky that soldiers of the Red Guard, billeted in her home in Tsarskoe Selo, had used the drawings to roll their cigarettes.[26] The soldiers' choice of heavy drawing paper covered with drawings of female nudes for their cigarettes seems unlikely when there presumably would have been heaps of manuscripts and writing paper at hand. Still that scenario is not impossible.

However, it could be that Akhmatova, even if she were well aware of the value of the drawings, had destroyed them herself. In 1921, in a foreign magazine she came upon Modigliani's obituary. "Once during a meeting [of the Writers' Union], someone handed me a copy of a French art magazine. I opened it, and there was a photograph of Modigliani...and a little cross...The long article was an obituary. From it I learned that he was a great artist of the Twentieth century..."[27] In the thirties, trying to survive through Stalin's reign of terror, she became obsessed with thoughts of her own destruction. At that time she burned many poems written during and shortly after her 1911 trip to Paris, poems that may have grown out of her love affair with Modigliani.* Possibly fearing that these drawings might be used as a weapon to compromise or slander her, she might well have destroyed them herself.

Akhmatova's striking appearance did not go unnoticed even in Paris, a city filled with enchanting women. The wife of Georgy Chulkov wrote: "She was very beautiful and everyone on the street would turn around to look at her...She was tall, elegant, and wore a white dress and a wide-brimmed straw hat with a large ostrich feather which her husband, the poet Gumilev, had brought her. He had recently returned from Abyssinia..."[28] The French aviator, Blériot, who had flown his little wooden plane across the English Channel from Calais to Dover in 1909, was also attracted to Anna Akhmatova. She told of how: "'The six of us Russians went off to Montmartre to some house. It was not an entirely respectable place, rather dark...I sat down straightaway at a table with a long cloth, right down to the floor, and took off my shoes—they were hurting my feet like mad—and looked round at everyone imperiously. On my left sat Blériot, the aviator, who was then a real celebrity...When we got up to go I found Blériot's visiting card in my shoe.'"[29]

---

* Only one poem from *Evening*, "*Mne s toboyu pyanym veselo—*" (You and I are merry when we're drunk—"), dated Paris, 1911, Seems to refer to Modigliani.

Swan Songs
Akhmatova and Gumilev

Back in Russia, Gumilev wrote "Poisoned," a poem that tells of a woman whose hand trembles as she pours out a goblet of poisoned wine for her lover, thus betraying her guilty secrets.

Poisoned

"You are strangely and terribly pallid,
You are quite, you are quite white as snow!
As you serve golden wine to me, dearest,
Why is it that you're trembling so?"

Then she turned away, sad and lissome…
What I know, I knew long ago,
But I'll drink up, smiling I'll drink up
All the wine that is poured by her.

But when all of the candles are snuffed out
And the nightmares arrive at my bed,
Those nightmares that slowly can stifle,
Deathly drunkenness fills up my head…

And I'll come to her, I will say: "Dearest,
I have seen an astonishing dream.
Ah, I dreamed of a plain without limits
And a sky with a golden-bright gleam.

You must know, I'll be cruel no longer.
Be happy with him if you may,
I'll not give in to spite or to sorrow,
I will leave and go far, far away.

From the heavens, from the cool heavens
White reflections of day can be seen…
And it's sweet to me—don't cry, my dearest—
To know that you've poisoned me."

Nikolai Gumilev
1911[30]

Knowingly drinking the golden wine that brings on suffocating nightmares and intoxication, the poet see in his dreams, not the blissful golden paradise envisioned in his wedding hymn, but an endless plain stretching beneath a golden sky. His nocturnal vision offers a life without boundaries or limits, one of absolute freedom. The poet regrets his cruelty and will leave the woman to be happy "with him," the other, if that is what she wishes. In the final stanza, his destination presumably is heaven, but not one inhabited by blissful lovers. He will look down on the vague, white reflections of light cast up from the earthly world and be comforted that the woman he once loved weeps over him, even though his death came by her hand.

Gumilev has transformed his jealousy into generosity, imagining himself freed from her even if the price of his freedom is death.

Anna returned from Paris to spend what remained of the summer at Slepnevo, with its "squares of ploughed field in hilly country, mills, bogs, dried swamp, gates, wheat and more wheat..."[31] Back in the Russian countryside, did her thoughts turn to Paris and Modigliani? Akhmatova only records: "In 1911, I arrived in Slepnevo straight from Paris and the hunchbacked servant in the ladies' room at the station in Bezhetsk, who had known everybody in Slepnevo for years, refused to recognize that I was a lady and she said to someone: 'A French girl has come to visit the Slepnevo masters.'"[32]

If Anna found disconcerting her abrupt arrival back in the Russian provinces, the locals found her just as strange. Her exotic air and her slender figure, unusual among the robust, well-upholstered country women, made her known in the surrounding countryside as the famous London mummy who brought everyone bad luck. Gumilev no doubt had dropped casual remarks about the "Egyptyanka." At dinner one night, a neighbor seated beside Akhmatova, embarrassed at finding nothing to talk about, remarked: "You probably find it very cold here after Egypt."[33]

Kolya was soon bored with tennis games and horseback riding and would disappear on mysterious sorties, no doubt pursuing the village girls. Akhmatova kept to herself or "just gathered mushrooms in both of the Slepnevo gardens, while Paris still glowed behind me in a sort of final sunset..."³⁴ Vera Nevedomskaya tells of her meeting that summer Gumilev and Akhmatova:

> Gumilev entered from the garden onto the veranda where we were drinking tea. On his head was a lemon-colored fez, on his feet purple socks and sandals and with this a Russian blouse. I later understood that in general Gumilev loved the grotesque in life and in his costumes. He had a very unusual face—not really Bi-Ba-Bo, not really Pierrot, not really a mongol, but with light eyes and hair. His intelligent, intent eyes were slightly squinting. With his markedly ceremonious manners and slightly smiling mouth and eyes, you felt as if he wished to play mischievous tricks and make fun of his good aunties, their drinking of tea with jam, the conversations about the weather, the wheat harvest and so forth.³⁵

Nevedomskaya's recollections of Akhmatova are not so affable:

> Akhmatova had the severe face of a novice nun from an Old Believer's monastery. All her features were too sharp to call her face beautiful. Unsmiling grey eyes. She must have been 21 or 22 years old. At the table she was silent and one immediately felt that she was alien in her husband's family. In that patriarchal family, Nikolai Stepanovich and his wife were like white crows. His mother was annoyed that her son didn't want to serve in the guards or in the diplomatic service but became a poet, went off to Africa and brought home a wife who was rather queer. She also writes poems, is always silent, dresses either in a dark cotton dress like a sarafan or in extravagant Parisian clothes (then she was wearing a narrow skirt with a slit).³⁶

Nikolai provided entertainment during the endless, hot Chekovian afternoons by organizing amateur circuses in which they all performed. When the rain drove them inside, he wrote and directed a fanciful verse drama in the pseudo-classical style. Anna remained silent and withdrawn, coming to life only when there was conversation about poetry or when she and Gumilev read their poems. But she was not so lost in her own thoughts as to be unaware of the flirtation that had sprung up between her husband and Nevedomskaya. Gumilev was no doubt taking his revenge for Modigliani. Akhmatova wrote: "I remember that I found her letter to Kolya which did not leave much to the imagination..."[37]

Dmitri Bushen, an artist who visited them there, observed what he felt to be Akhmatova's love for Gumilev, although he also noticed tension between them.[38] Gumilev was soon deep in another infatuation, this time with his cousin Masha Kuzmina-Karavayeva, who was then visiting her aunt at Slepnevo.

The sisters Mariya and Olga Kuzmina-Karavayeva, both charming blondes, were cousins of Nikolai and they had known one another since childhood. Olga, with her entrancing voice, was the more lively of the two. Masha was quieter, with a lovely complexion that turned rosy at night, the unmistakable sign of tuberculosis. Anna Gumileva, Kolya's sister-in-law, wrote: "I remember Masha was always dressed with great taste in a pale lilac dress...She had weak lungs and when we went for a drive with the neighbors, the poet always requested that their carriage go ahead 'so that Mashenka wouldn't breathe in the dust.' More than once I saw Kolya sitting at Masha's bedroom when she was resting during the day. He waited for her to come out with a book in his hands open to a page and his gaze fastened on the door. Once Masha said to him openly that it wasn't right to love someone and become attached to them, when she had been sick for a long time and felt that she wouldn't live much longer."[39]

It was from Slepnevo that Gumilev wrote to Valery Bryusov with his first, rather tentative reference to his wife's poetry. "What did you think about the poems of Anna Akhmatova (my wife)? If you aren't too lazy, write briefly but frankly. Positive and negative your opinion will make her ponder, and its always useful."[40] Later that summer, Anna and Nikolai travelled to Moscow and Kiev before returning to 63 Malaya Street in Tsarkoe Selo, the two-storyed green house purchased by Nikolai's mother. Makovsky described how the young people lived in four rooms on the ground floor: "…Gumilev's library was full of books, standing on shelves and littered everywhere. Here was a wide divan on which he slept. Opposite in a dark blue room stood the couch of Akhmatova. In the third, with windows looking out on the courtyard, hung canvases of Alexander Ekster, her gifts to Gumilev. In that room stood modern-style furniture…The fourth room…served for Gumilev as a working office…[with] a roomy writing desk and walls hung all over with African maps, among which were hung bracelets of ivory."[41]

That Gumilev's frequent desertions hurt Akhmatova deeply comes through in a poem she wrote that autumn.

> He left me at the new moon's coming,
> My dearest friend. What can I say?
> He joked, "My little tightrope walker!

Swan Songs
Akhmatova and Gumilev

How will you live on until May?"

I answered as if to a brother,
Not grumbling, without jealousy.
But even four new capes could never
Make up for the loss to me.

Let my way be dangerous, fearful,
More fearful still is yearning's path...
My Chinese parasol, how crimson,
My slippers, how well rubbed with chalk!

The orchestra plays something jaunty
And lips are smiling all around.
But my heart knows, it know that empty
Remains the seat in the fifth loge.

Anna Akhmatova
November, 1911[42]

Akhmatova chose the highly artificial, flashily theatrical, but dangerous world of the high-wire circus performer as a setting for this poem about the withdrawal of love and the fear of abandonment. The persona of the tightrope walker provided the poet with a disguise behind which to conceal herself as well as a highly expressive, metaphorical identity. Akhmatova shrank from the risks of self-revelation, still unready to "throw herself wide open," as she advised the poet to do much later in her "Secrets of the Craft."

The theme of abandonment is clearly conveyed in the opening lines of the poem. The tight-rope walker's "dearest friend" has left her at the waxing of the new moon, the starting point in a cycle of nature that might be compared to the first months of a marriage. The intimate relationship of the two had been abruptly broken off by the "friend's" departure. But the absent lover hasn't comprehended the impact of this on the tight-rope walker, even jokingly asking "How will you ever live without me?"

The tightrope walker, keeping her emotions tightly under control, responds to him as if he were her brother (as Akhmatova had previously addressed Gumilev). She forces herself to view their relationship as familial, not one charged with the passion of sexual love. But she cannot contain the enormity of her loss which bursts out in the next lines. Not even four new capes—things unimaginably costly and unattainable—could make up for his absence. In this anguished exclamation rings Akhmatova's confession of the emotional toll, so carefully hidden up to this point, that Kolya's betrayals had taken upon her. Yet even this has its ironic twist, for if four new capes could not make up for the loss of her lover, maybe five capes could? The reader is left to question the absolute value she places on his love.

Fighting back her emotions, the rope-walker must retrieve a sense of calm and self-control as she considers the path before her. She can launch herself out from the platform along a rope high over the abyss, a terrifying, life-risking act. Or she can remain safely on the ground, a prospect even more frightening than death itself. As the orchestra strikes up its music and the audience waits in breathless expectancy, she takes up her gaudy Chinese parasol to begin her perilous, teetering walk. The audience will applaud her skill when she leaps from the rope onto the platform at the other side. But the one person whom she wishes would witness her triumph will not be in the crowd to see it.

Akhmatova's use of the persona of a tight-rope walker is especially illuminating. First, the performer is an ordinary woman who has developed highly specialized skills for her glittering role in a circus act. She has put on her exotic, theatrical identity for the entertainment of her audience, concealing her prosaic self beneath the glamorous artifice of make-up and costume. In the circus ring, this not only offers her a new persona, but protection as well. For stepping into the arena, she is suddenly transfixed by the dazzling, unforgiving illumination of the spotlight, becoming the object of the crowd's intense scrutiny. With her naked exposure to the eyes of the audience, each mistake she makes, each slip of her foot or awkward movement will be seen. And not every observer will feel a benevolent wish for her safety. For the secret desire lies in every human heart to witness failure, even if it is as deadly as a fall from the tight-rope. Akhmatova, through this image of the circus performer, expresses her own uncertainty and fear upon entering the public world

Frances Laird

as a literary personage. Perfecting her skills as a poet, she, too, will attract the clamorous attention of the crowds. With her azure shawl draped gracefully over her shoulder, holding herself with the bearing of a princess, she, too, will assume the persona of a celebrated and elegant poetess of St. Petersburg's bohemian world.

Akhmatova's poetic voice rings out fresh and original in this poem with a style inimitable from the first published poems—the colloquial language, the laconic reticence, the sudden bursts of intense emotion and the vivid and colorful details of her imagery. This terrifying walk along the tight-rope with the eyes of the world upon her suggested Akhmatova's own progress toward self-realization as a poet, step by step, poem by poem, over the abyss of insignificance and failure. Yet what she expresses most keenly in this poem is the absence, whether physical or emotional, of the most important witness to her transformation into a poet, her dearest friend, her most valued critic, and her husband, Nikolai Gumilev.

Gumilev wrote "The Animal Tamer," as his poetic response to Akhmatova, choosing for himself the persona of another circus performer, the indomitable, whip-cracking lion trainer.

<u>The Animal Tamer</u>

    My Chinese parasol, how scarlet,
    My slippers, how well rubbed with chalk!
                    —Anna Akhmatova

Swan Songs
Akhmatova and Gumilev

Again with a step that is brave, calculated,
I am approaching the most sacred doors.
Long have the beasts been awaiting me there,
Beasts of all colors beyond the strong grating.

They will be snarling, afraid of my whip,
Either today they will be more submissive
Or be more treacherous…what does it matter,
If I am young and my blood is on fire?

Only…I seem to see more and more often
(See and yet know that I may be just mad)
A terrible beast, which I know is not there,
Silent it is, six-winged and golden.

It watches me long with a vigilant eye,
Following each of the movements I'm making.
It never joins with the other beasts playing,
And never approaches at feeding time.

If I am sentenced to death at ring center,
The death of the animal tamer, I'm sure
Unseen by the public this beast will be first
To bite through my legs at the knees in an instant.

Frances Laird

> Fanny, the flower that you gave me I wore.
> You, as always, are gay on the tight-rope.
> My beast is slumbering there at your bedside
> And looks in your eyes like a long faithful hound.
>
> Nikolai Gumilev
March, 1912[43]

Again appear the familiar themes of control and submission. The animal-tamer, armed only with a whip, enters a cage filled with snarling, unpredictable, and dangerous wild animals. With the force of his personality, courage and will, he must master and subdue the beasts that surround him. This act of domination demands patience, skill, bravery, intuition and strength of purpose. But in Gumilev's poem the taming of lions takes on an added spiritual dimension. For the poet refers to the doors through which he must enter the cage as "the most sacred doors," suggesting the Holy Doors of the icon screen that open onto the high altar of a Russian Orthodox church where the Mass is celebrated. The lion tamer's encounter with the beasts is a spiritual trial by which his body, Christ-like, is offered for sacrifice and his faith is tested. But it is not a faith in a higher Presence that will protect him; it is an absolute faith in himself. The lion-tamer is supremely confident in his youthful strength and ardent spirit. He knows that, with the power of his will alone, he can overcome these savage beasts.

But a mysterious animal has slipped into the cage among the others, a creature of his own fevered delusions. This beast is radiantly golden and six-winged like the cherabim. Remote, passive, watchful, it lacks the overt aggressivity of the other animals. Yet he knows that when his back is turned it will be the first to leap upon him, to bite through his knees, crippling him and rendering him helpless. This beast, tamed by Fanny the tight-rope walker, sleeps beside her bed as would a faithful and protective dog.

Assuming Akhmatova's circus metaphor, Gumilev has projected into an imagined external world the struggle that is going on within himself. The wild beasts over which he has established his control are the struggling aspects of his own self. But one dimension of the self remains malevolent, ungovernable, and potentially dangerous. This "beast" cannot be subdued by the poet himself, but only by the hand of a woman. Perhaps this creature represents the self-destructive element that drove Gumilev to his repeated suicide attempts and into dangerous behavior—the reckless horseback riding, the journeys into the depths of Africa, and, later, his military exploits in the First World War. It is the beast of self-destruction that Akhmatova's love has pacified and tamed. This reading of the poem would suggest that at least one aspect of the Kolya's complicated, multi-faceted self remained faithful to Fanny/Akhmatova.

As Symbolism was approaching the inevitable limits of its viability, Gumilev began to distance himself from Bryusov and Ivanov. Akhmatova wrote: "…as a boy he believed in Symbolism like people believe in God. It was an inviolable, sacred object, but as he drew nearer to the Symbolists, in part to the Tower (V. Ivanov), his faith wavered and he began to sense that something had been profaned."[44] The moment had come when the expressive potential of one literary style had been nearly exhausted and must give way to the next.

In the autumn of 1911, Nikolai Gumilev and Sergei Gorodetsky had started a group called the Guild of Poets. Assembled at their first meeting, in addition to the founding members, were Anna Akhmatova, Mikhail Kuzmin, Osip Mandelstam, Alexander Blok, and Vladimir Narbut, among others. At first, it was not the intention of the Guild of Poets to break with the Symbolists in any overt or dramatic way. But Gumilev had been outspoken in his criticism of Ivanov's latest book of poetry, *Cor ardens,* in *Apollon:* "An immeasurable gulf separates him [Ivanov] from the poets of line and color, Pushkin or Bryusov, Lermontov or Blok. Their poetry is a lake which reflects the sky, the poetry of Vyacheslav Ivanov is the sky reflected in a lake."[45] Ivanov, accustomed to greater respect, was outraged. At a meeting of the Academy of Verse which he was leading, Gumilev read his "Prodigal Son." Ivanov ripped it to shreds. Akhmatova recalls: "Vyacheslav attacked him in a tirade which was practically obscene. I remember that when we were making our way back to Tsarskoe Selo we were absolutely crushed by what had happened..."[46]

Swan Songs
Akhmatova and Gumilev

The Guild of Poets met two or three times a month at the homes of its members. Akhmatova, acting as secretary, sent out the invitations decorated with the drawing of Apollo's lyre. At their meetings, the poets would read their latest work, then discuss the poems. But all was not utterly serious; there were some amusing moments. When Akhmatova recited poems by other poets, they somehow took on the intonation of her own poetry. Everyone laughed at her recitations of Nekrasov.[47] During dinner, the poets would compose in an inflated, artificially formal style contributions to the "Anthology of Ancient Stupidity," a collection of parodies and silly verses about one another. This poem was written after the birth of Lev (Lyova), the son of Akhmatova and Gumilev:

>Nikolai Gumilev has
>His leg raised high,
>As he tosses out pearls
>For romantic sowing.
>Who cares if Lyova is bawling in Tsarskoe,
>Nikolai Gumilev has
>His leg raised high.

And about Akhmatova:

>Akhmatova peers at everyone
>With a sad and beckoning gaze.

> Her sweetsmelling fur
> Was real muskrat.
> She looks into the eyes of the silent guests.[48]

For Akhmatova the readings and endless discussions could sometimes be tedious, but when Osip Mandelstam read his poetry, she came to life. "You sat for several hours and read poetry, some good, some ordinary. Then suddenly your attention would be distracted. You listened because you had to—and suddenly, as if some swan flew in above you...Osip reads."[49]

Akhmatova had first met Osip Mandelstam at Ivanov's "Tower" in the spring of 1911. She recalled: "He was a wiry boy then, with a lily of the valley in his lapel, his head thrown way back, with fiery eyes and lashes that reached almost halfway down his cheeks."[50] They ran into one another often in Petersburg, at the homes of friends, at the offices of *Apollon* or *The Hyperborean* (the journal of the Guild of Poets), at art galleries and at the Stray Dog, a basement cabaret frequented by artists and writers. Akhmatova loved her conversations with Mandelstam, for "he didn't just listen to himself and answer himself, which is what almost everyone does nowadays. In conversation he was polite, quick to react, and always original."[51] He would tell her silly stories to amuse her. "We used to make each other laugh so hard that we would fall off the couch with the singing springs at Tuchkov Lane...and we giggled until we almost fainted, like the confectionary girls in Joyce's *Ulysses*."[52] Osip would confide in her details of his love life and ask her opinion on the women with whom he had fallen in love. Gumilev, who had met Mandelstam as a student in Paris, shared Akhmatova's affection and respect for him and for his poetry.

At a meeting of the Guild of Poets held at the Gumilev house, an exciting, new direction in Russian poetry called Acmeism, initiated by six members of the Guild, took shape. In his article for *Apollon*, titled "Acmeism and the Legacy of Symbolism," Gumilev acknowledged the debt that he and other poets owed to their ancestors, the French Symbolists—the attention to purely literary problems, the use of free verse, the more individualistic style, the importance of metaphor and the "theory of correspondences." But, he wrote, the expressive power of Symbolism was growing weaker, creating a stylistic vacuum. "Acmeism," also called "Adamism," would reinvigorate the poet's way of looking at the world in the early twentieth century.[53]

According to Gumilev, the name "Acmeism" came from the Greek *akme*, meaning the "the highest degree of something, a blossom, a time of blossoming." "Adamism," another name for this movement, conveyed the elemental, masculine nature of its firm, clear view of life. While Russian Symbolism was "born in the misty gloom of German forests," Acmeists associated themselves with the bright, Romantic world of the French language. Like the French Symbolists, they would "break the fetters of metre" and look to native speech patterns and expressions for the directness and clarity they desired. Every phenomenon would have value in its own right, its own "specific gravity," and would not be plugged into the hierarchy of an all-encompassing philosophical system.

The Acmeist poets, determined "always to keep in mind the unknowable but not to insult one's idea about it with more or less verifiable guesses…" rejected Symbolist forays into mystical realms. The literary qualities of Acmeism are so broad and general, that is was difficult, aside from their common rejection of Symbolism, to define how the poems of Acmeist poets resembled one another. But putting theory aside, Akhmatova believed that Gumilev's conception of Acmeism grew directly out of her poetry and that of Mandelstam.[54] While sharing a love for the beauty and the mystery of the things of this world, the Acmeists also saw themselves as deeply rooted in the traditions of Western European art and literature. All had travelled and lived in France and Italy, knew the languages and had read the classic works of literature.

The Acmeist poet liked to view himself as a simple craftsman, a turner and shaper of the solid material of the word. Osip Mandelstam, who likened the poet to an architect, titled his first book of poems *Stone (Kamen)*. "It was as if the stone thirsted after another existence. It revealed its own dynamic potential hidden within itself, as if it were begging admittance into the 'groined arch' in order to participate in the joyous cooperative action of its fellows."

The poet must embrace this world, this "God-given palace," with his whole heart, not whine and pine for another one more beautiful, more perfect, perhaps, but purely hypothetical. For Mandelstam, that was as if, while being entertained at a sumptuous banquet, one secretly detested and plotted against one's host. "We do not want to distract ourselves with a stroll through the 'forest of symbols,' because we have a denser, more virgin forest-divine physiology, the infinite complexity of our own dark organism."[55]

The battles that arose in the pages of little journals. between the advocates of the two styles of poetry, one waxing, one waning, turned fierce and uncompromising. These literary arguments would occasionally break out into noisy brawls in the Stray Dog where the poets socialized or at public readings. Akhmatova writes: "In the winter of Acmeism's *Sturm und Drang* we sometimes gave recitals as a group. Gumilev and Gorodetsky read lectures. I remember how the elderly Radetsky, with his great beard, shook his fist and shouted: 'Look at these Adams and this skinny Eve,' referring to me."[56]

Chapter VII
Evening

In the spring of 1912, Anna Akhmatova's first book of poetry, *Vecher (Evening)*, was published by the Guild of Poets, with the familiar drawing of Apollo's lyre on its cover. *Evening* contained forty-six poems, with an introduction by Mikhail Kuzmin. The three hundred copies of its first printing were sold out almost immediately. The small volume of poetry received praise from the critics with even Valery Bryusov writing favorably of it in his review.

The publication of *Evening* brought the Acemist vision of poetry into sharper focus and proved to be a defining moment in that style. The Akhmatova poem is grounded in a world that the reader recognizes, is rooted in the earth the reader walks and vaulted with the same ever-changing skies. The poet's view of this palpable, terrestrial world is clear-eyed and vivid. The details of sight, sound, and smell she includes, though spare and chosen with great care, are those that the reader can envision. We need only look back at Akhmatova's tight-rope walker, with her bright red parasol, her slippers whitened with chalk and her passion for new capes. It is a concrete, accessible and inclusive world as opposed to that of the Symbolist poet, who favored a dream-like, distant and indefinable poetic landscape, a realm meant for the spirit, not for flesh and blood. Akhmatova revels in the earth-bound and the tangible, for it is through this world that the spirit speaks.

Comparing Akhmatova's poem of the tight-rope walker with Gumilev's "The Animal Tamer," we can see how Akhmatova's poetry embodied the Acmeist ideals, even more than did Gumilev's. The golden, six-winged beast of his poem, silent, wary, crouched and ready to attack the animal tamer, exists as a creature of the poet's imagination. Whether as a symbol of an uncontrollable facet of the self, of a fierce angelic guardian, of an urge towards self-destruction, Gumilev's image has been chosen for its symbolic power, evidence that he has not yet made a complete break from his Symbolist past.

When religious imagery appears in Akhmatova's poems, it is never pious, effete or cerebral. The shadow of the elaborate philosophical scaffolding beloved of the Symbolists cannot be discerned looming behind the scenery of her poems. For Akhmatova the religious dimension is revealed in the actions of a human being. The drama of her poems is intensely interior, unfolding in the heart and mind of the heroine. One tiny gesture, one glance, one exclamation will reveal the depths of spirit and the extremities of emotion. Articulated in her poems are the passions and pains of a life lived through a woman's body and mind—love, jealousy, boredom, lassitude, anxiety, despair. It is a world that invites the reader in, for at its center is the human heart. Osip Mandelstam saw Akhmatova's poetry as introducing "all the enormous complexity and wealth of the nineteenth century novel into the Russian lyric."[1] The sprawling dramatic events of Dostoevsky, Tolstoy and Turgenev are concentrated by Akhmatova in the dazzling, pin-point focus of a circus spotlight. We look at the tiny, brightly colored tragedy of the tight-rope walker as if gazing through a telescope the wrong way.

For all its originality, Akhmatova's poetry was firmly based in the established patterns of Russian versification. There were few purely formal innovations in *Evening*. Feeling in no way compelled to "break the fetters of metre," she carried forward the traditional forms of classical Russian prosody. Her rhymes form so naturally and her rhythms flow of effortlessly that they seem almost a feature of her native tongue. It was Mandelstam's opinion that Akhmatova's lyrics were shaped by the asymmetrical parallelism of the simple Russian folk-song.

Poems included here that first appeared in the original edition of *Evening* are "In Tsarskoe Selo," "The Song of a Last Meeting," and "The Grey-eyed King." Two others, "When we were cursing one another..." and "He left me at the new moon's coming...," were added to the collection in subsequent printings. Critics and biographers have been reluctant to correlate the themes of *Evening* with the facts of the poet's life. But reading the poems of *Evening*, one is struck by the overwhelming sense of loss, disappointment and disillusionment found there. Again and again the poet speaks of the hopes of a radiant and fulfilling love crushed, the promising bud of a happy life plucked off before it could blossom. Love has gone strangely and unexpectedly wrong, leaving the poet puzzled and disoriented as she casts her mind this way and that to find answers to the questions that haunt her. Will I weep about you, strange one, and will your face smile at me? Do you love a blonde or a red-head? Who will I dream of today? Who did you kiss? Were you close to me or did you just love me? At times the poet loses her sense of self and, struggling to claim some kind of identity, she turns herself into an object—an amusing toy like a pink cockatoo, a cold, marble statue, the painted cuckoo in a clock. In one poem, she feels her soul has been sucked up through a straw and all that is left of her is an empty husk.

And how is marriage depicted in these poems? Invariably as a terrible mistake. In a poem about the coming of autumn, she declares almost as an aside that she should never have become a wife. In the poem about the three things her husband loved best—evensong, old maps and white peacocks, his wife was not among them. The poet's wedding ring, like the shiny, swollen welt of a wasp's sting on her finger, has brought her nothing but a sharp and lingering pain. She feels betrayed and abandoned by her lover/husband and asks—why did you leave me? In one poem, she seems to encourage him to go, if that is what he really wants; they are not chained together. Poem after poem speaks of the lover's desertion.

Death often hovers in the background of the poems of *Evening*. The poet asks herself, has she poisoned her lover with her own sorrow? She imagines that passers-by think she has been newly widowed. "The Grey-Eyed King," in Russia one of Akhmatova's most popular poems, takes on new meaning when it is read with these

Frances Laird

ideas in mind. It was written December 11, 1910, soon after Gumilev's departure for Africa.

The Grey-Eyed King

Glory to you, irremediable pain!
Yesterday perished the grey-eyed king.

The autumnal evening was stifling and red.
Having come home, calmly my husband said:

"They carried him back from hunting, you know.
They found his body beside the old oak.

Pity the queen. So young! And they say
That overnight her hair has turned grey."

Near to the fireplace he found his pipe
And he went out to work for the night.

My little daughter I now will awake.
Into her grey-shining eyes I will gaze.

Outside the poplars are rustling in wind,
Sighing: "No longer on earth is your king…"

Swan Songs
Akhmatova and Gumilev

Anna Akhmatova

December 11, 1910, Tsarskoe Selo[2]

This poem depicts the humble drama, powerful in its simplicity, of a fairy-tale or folk song. A husband returns home to tell his young wife that the king has been tragically killed while out hunting. So grief-stricken and distraught is the queen upon hearing of his death that her hair has suddenly turned grey. When her husband leaves for work, the wife wakes her baby daughter so that she can gaze into her eyes, grey as those of the king. What the queen can express openly, the tumultuous feelings of grief and loss, the wife must conceal at all costs. They burst out only in the rustling leaves of the poplar trees beyond her window that utter the truth which she cannot acknowledge—the dead king was her secret lover.

It has been speculated that Akhmatova's model for the unfeeling husband was Nikolai Gumilev. But if the king is also seen as Nikolai, if the husband and the king were two aspects of one person, the poem takes on a fuller meaning. "The Grey-Eyed King" expresses the poet's realization that the royal suitor, the tsarevich created in her adolescent imagination whom she hoped would rescue her from the stifling boredom of her provincial world, was now dead. The ardent young Kolya, the prince of her girlish romantic dreams, who had once loved her so fervently, had died. She was left with a self-interested and distant husband who seemed only too eager to escape from her presence. Akhmatova would elaborate the identical theme—death of the prince/lover—in a long poem, *By the Sea Shore*, that she finished in 1914.

In the poems of *Evening,* Akhmatova often used features of the natural world, as the poplar trees in this poem, to reveal the emotions that roiled beneath the seemingly calm, controlled surface of the poem. In "I came here, an idler…," written in February, 1911, Akhmatova wrote about the pond, grown shallow and covered with slime, where the rusalka lived. But what did it matter—the rusalka was dead.[3] When we recall Gumilev's first poem about Anna, this image of the dead rusalka takes on a striking significance.

The risk that the reader would peg a poem too neatly into the facts of the poet's biography, distorting or trivializing a reading, making of it a rummage through the private corners of the poet's personal life, was always present. Akhmatova, fearful of this kind of invasion, protected herself with the masks of various poetic personae, the shepherdess, the tightrope walker, the peasant girl. In the spring of 1912, when the poems of *Evening* were revealed to the eyes of the world, Akhmatova felt, not pride, but deep embarrassment. Kolya, she later recalled, laughed at her diffidence and encouraged her to savor her literary triumph. He recited this verse:

> Retrograde or another George Sand,
> What does it matter, now you can gloat!
> You have a dowry, governess,
> Spit on them all and enjoy your triumph![4]

But Akhmatova remembered stuffing the journal containing her poems out of sight beneath the sofa cushions, claiming: "I never liked seeing my poems in print. If there was a copy of *Russkaya mysl* or *Apollon* containing my poems on the table, I would grab it and hide it. I considered it indecent, as if I had left a stocking or a brassiére on the table."[5] Her anxiety over her newly published book forced her, in the spring of 1912, to find refuge with Kolya in Italy and Switzerland. Sitting on a tram and looking about her at the other passengers, she remembered thinking to herself: "How happy they are—they haven't had a book published."[6] Safely anonymous in Italy, Akhmatova needn't bear the curious gazes and the unspoken questions her poems aroused in her readers. But she was left face to face with the intractable problem of her unhappy marriage. Moreover, she now knew that she was pregnant with Kolya's child.

Visiting the great cities of Italy, Akhmatova soaked up the eternal, ineffable beauty of the churches and palazzos, sculpture and paintings, storing in her imagination for a lifetime these cherished sights. But by the end of the trip, their relationship was apparently so strained that the two were living in separate cities, Gumilev in Florence and Akhmatova in Rome. When Kolya returned to Russia to spend the summer in Slepnevo, Anna went to stay with her mother at her cousin's estate near the Austrian frontier. Fifty-two years would pass before she would be free to return to Italy.

Although for both the marriage was tinged with bitterness and disappointment, Kolya's feelings of affection for Anna remain warm and genuine as he conveys the family news in a letter he wrote from Slepnevo that summer:

Dear Anichka,
    How are you, you don't write. How are you feeling, you know this is not just an empty phrase. Mama has been sewing a lot of tiny shirts, swaddling bands, etc. She asks me to send you a big kiss.
    I wrote one poem despite your warning not to write about dreams, about my Italian dream in Florence, remember? I'm sending it to you, it seems rather ungainly. Write please what you think about it. I'm living here quietly, modestly, almost without books, continuously with a grammar, sometimes English, sometimes Italian. I am already reading Dante, although of course I only grasp the general sense and some expressions. With Byron (in English) it goes worse, but I do not despair.
    I've also taken to riding, particularly equestrian vaulting or something like it. Already I can jump into the saddle at a trot and jump out of it without using the stirrups. I'm trying to do it at a gallop but am unsuccessful as yet. Olya and I are going to arrange for tennis and are going to order racquets and balls tomorrow. That way at least I'll lose some weight.
    Our Moka has been about to have her pups for the last few days and she has a basket with straw in my room. She is so sweet everyone falls in love with her. Even Aleksandra Alekseevna [wife of Gumilev's cousin] said that she is the most lovable of our animals.
    Every evening I go for a walk alone along the Akinikhsky road to experience what you call God's melancholy. All the malicious gossip about Acmeism disappears before it. Then it seems to me that in the whole universe there is not a single atom that is not full of deep eternal sorrow.

Swan Songs
Akhmatova and Gumilev

I have come full circle and am back to the period of *Romantic Flowers*...but it is interesting that when I think of my latest work it seems to me from inertia to be in the enlightened tones of *Foreign Sky* [Gumilev's fourth book of poems, published in 1912]. It seems our earthly roles are changing, you will be the Acmeist, I the gloomy Symbolist. All the same, I hope to get by without an abcess.

Anichka my dear, I love you very very much always. Give my regards to everyone.

Love,
Kolya[7]

Kolya, as we see in this letter, could be charming and attentive. His warm, still lovable personality radiates through this letter in his anxiety about her condition and his surpressed, childlike excitement over the coming baby, his eagerness for Anna's opinion of a new poem, his clumsy but enthusiastic deciphering of Dante with Italian dictionary in hand, his love of trick-riding and tennis games, his solitary walks in a world permeated with sorrow, where poetic theory bumps up against toothache. It may have been then that, far from Kolya and with a certain perspective on their difficult relationship, Akhmatova wrote this tenderly nostalgic and rueful poem:

> Pencil case and books in straps of leather,
> I would come back home from school each day.
> The lime trees certainly can still remember
> Our meetings there, my gay and cheerful boy.

> Only then he changed, the pale grey cygnet,
> Having turned into a haughty swan.
> Sorrow lay then, as a ray undying,
> Upon my life, my voice has lost its song.
>
> Anna Akhmatova
1912[8]

Akhmatova recalls their school days in Tsarskoe Selo, when the whispering lime trees were the only witnesses to those tentative, tender hours of their budding love. The image of the pale grey cygnet that grows into a swan is particularly apt and evocative. The awkward and unattractive young Kolya had matured into a proud and self-confident man, a cause of satisfaction, if not joy. The change from cygnet to swan also describes Gumilev's transformation into an acknowledged poet. Yet it is the loss that has come with this change that Akhmatova dwells upon. Into the swan/Kolya has come an arrogance and self-will that has brought only sorrow into Anna's life. With that sadness, Akhmatova has lost her own song.

With a problematic marriage and the fears and uncertainties of approaching motherhood, Anna must have found writing poetry difficult enough. She would have been anxious about her future, knowing that she could expect little support from Kolya after the child was born. The prospect of caring for a baby in an increasingly unworkable marriage, without the time, space or energy to devote to her own poetry, must have been very real. Akhmatova may have feared the loss of her poetic voice in the life she saw ahead.

Although he had no doubt attempted to persuade her that his love affairs did not imply his rejection of her, she would naturally assume that she had been found wanting by her husband. Kolya, as we have seen, could be endearing, but his adultery, self-justified though it may have been on the aesthetic grounds of his philosophy of life, she could not accept. Sergei Makovsky wrote: "Loving both him and his poetry, she wasn't able to come to terms with his masculine self-assertion. Gumilev continued to behave like a bachelor, unencumbered by the presence of a wife."[9] Valeriya saw the relationship between Akhmatova and Gumilev as "a secret dueling—from her side, for her own affirmation of her status as a free woman; from his, because of a desire not to submit to any bewitchment and himself to remain independent and powerful…"[10]

We see Akhmatova through Gumilev's eyes in "She," a poem begun the year before.

She

I know well a woman: silence,
A bitter weariness of talk
Exists in the mysterious shining
Within her pupils, wide and dark.

Frances Laird

>With greed her spirit opens only
>To brassy music of a poem.
>Before life, earthly and consoling,
>She can be haughty and remote.
>
>Inaudible and never hurried,
>So strangely fluid is her step.
>You could not say she is a beauty
>But she holds all my happiness.
>
>When willfulness is what I yearn for
>Then, brave and proud, I go to her
>The aching, wise and sweet, to learn in
>Her ravings and her lassitude.
>
>She shines out in the hours of languor
>And holds the lightening in her hand.
>The dreams she has are sharp, like shadows
>Upon the burning, heavenly sands.
>
> Nikolai Gumilev
1911-12[11]

In "She" Gumilev may have given us the most real and affirming poetic portrait of Akhmatova from the early years of their marriage. Recognizable are her silences, her mysterious gaze, her hunger for poetry, her seeming remoteness from earthly affairs, her graceful and elegant carriage, her unusual beauty. Gumilev acknowledges his dependence upon her for access to a woman's experience of life, one far removed from his determinedly masculine existence. He even sees in Akhmatova a goddess-like power as she "holds the lightening in her hand." Her more contained, quiescent nature, imbued with the mystery of the feminine, while exerting its own kind of energy and power, lay directly opposite to the engaged, willful action which Gumilev glorified in his life and poetry.

During their separation that summer, Gumilev finished three other poems about Akhmatova that often ring in a minor key, yet demonstrate his attempt to come to grips with the complex nature of their relationship. But it is difficult to recognize her in "To a Cruel Woman," so drastically has Gumilev's point of view changed. He is the first of many writers and critics who would compare Akhmatova to Sappho, the legendary Greek poet who lived on the island of Lesbos in the seventh century B.C. Sappho served as a priestess in a religious cult of young girls who worshipped Aphrodite and the Muses. In the Russian version of the poem, the word "friend" is masculine and indicates an intimate male friend or lover.

To a Cruel Woman

"To you, enchanting, evil woman, really
Amusing is the sacred word of 'friend'...?

Frances Laird

> You would prefer upon your moon-like body
> To trace the touch of only female hands,
>
> The touch of lips, both bashful and impassioned,
> And gazes—yes?—of undemanding eyes?
> Perhaps till now in vague day-dreaming never
> Have you been tortured by a childish smile?
>
> A man's love is the flame brought by Prometheus
> And makes demands and in demanding gives.
> Before it stands the soul, anxious and weakened,
> And like the burning bush it burns and speaks.
>
> I love you. Just forget your dreams." In silence
> She, almost shuddering, lifted up her eyes,
> And then I heard the clang of lyres ringing
> And the loud thunder of the eagle's cries.
>
> Sappho's eagle soared above the white cliffs,
> In triumph flying and the beauty stark
> Of the green, shadeless vineyards there on Lesbos
> Closed these blaspheming lips beneath its lock.
>
> Nikolai Gumilev
1911-12[12]

Here, as in "At the Fireside," a powerful, even overbearing male figure confronts an "evil" and "enchanting" woman whose mysterious strength he struggles to fathom. The passion that had bound them has cooled, for she laughs ironically when he calls himself her "friend." Her rejection offends the poet, for he sees the role of the lover as exalted, even sacred. Unwilling to admit the real reasons her love has cooled, Gumilev implies that, like Sappho, she may prefer instead of his the more tentative, less assertive, and thus inferior love of a woman.

The poet lectures her on the superiority of a man's love. With some arrogance he compares it to the gift of fire that Prometheus stole from the gods on Mount Olympus and brought to earth for the use of mankind, thus implying that creative power, in an artistic as well as a biological sense, is channeled through the love bestowed upon a woman by a man. Unlike a woman's love, which is generous and nurturing, a man's love is urgent and demanding. But if it asks much of the woman who accepts it, its gifts to her are many. A woman's soul will flutter and faint before the awesome fire of this love, until it bursts into flame and, out of the heat of passion, begins to speak. In another grandiloquent simile, Gumilev compares the ignited soul to the burning bush from which the voice of God spoke to Moses, a Biblical reference that gives the masculine profession of love its authoritative, even divine heft. Gumilev seems to suggest that a woman's ability to express herself, her eloquence, is generated in the fire of a man's passion. This being so, she has no need of daydreams, for his declaration of love should be sufficient in itself to satisfy her.

The woman's response, her body "almost shuddering," is highly dramatic. Without speaking a word, she lifts her eyes to him and he is suddenly struck with a flash of recognition. He hears the loud ringing of the lyre and the shriek of Sappho's eagle sounding in his ears, sees a vision of the sun-drenched island of Lesbos and is struck dumb by its beauty. With his vision comes the realization that this "cruel woman" whom he loves is a poet who one day will equal Sappho in her greatness. It is Gumilev who has been guilty of uttering the blasphemous words that questioned her sacred vocation as poet, one even loftier than that of lover. In "To a Cruel Woman" Gumilev validated Anna Akhmatova, the poet, and honored her high calling. Despite his insatiable need for stimulation and adventure that put their marriage at risk, Gumilev conveyed powerfully and unequivocally the significance that Anna Akhmatova held for him both as woman and poet.

Inevitably raised with Gumilev's association of Akhmatova and Sappho was the issue of lesbian love. His insinuation that Akhmatova was sexually attracted to women may have been a way of rationalizing her coolness towards him, while allowing him to overlook the fact that it was his own behavior that was the cause. However, the initial, exasperated questions of Gumilev, the man, in the first two stanzas are then answered by Gumilev, the poet, with his full recognition of Akhmatova's gift. It was in the art of poetry, not in the gender of their lovers, that Akhmatova and Sappho were kinswomen.

In "That Other One," Gumilev's discontent with Akhmatova, and women in general, resurfaces. Bored by their frivolous conversations and emotional manipulations, no longer hoping for a deep relationship with a woman, he must wait for the spiritual comrade fated to be his companion for eternity.

<u>That Other One</u>

Filled with reproaches, I am waiting
Not for a gay and cheerful wife
And heart to heart conversations
About what was in former times.

Nor for a lover: I find boring
The broken whisper, languid glance,
For, trained to rapture and to torment,
A hundred times more proud I am.

I'm waiting for the comrade given
To me by God for centuries,
Because I felt a keen homesickness
For silence and for lofty peaks.

Frances Laird

> How criminal is he, the stern one,
> To trade forever for an hour.
> He impudently took for fetters
> The daydreams that are joining us.
>
> Nikolai Gumilev
1912[13]

Gumilev, the roving womanizer, declares his refusal to love an ordinary woman, be she lover or wife, in the ordinary way. He rejects the intimacy and shared history of marriage as haughtily as he scorns the amorous tricks of the mistress. Only love experienced at its absolute extremes, whether of ecstasy or torment, will satisfy him. The comrade for whom he waits, the eternal soulmate provided by God, would rescue him from those female entanglements, as well as the flurry of words that assail him, and would restore him to the elevated realm of the spirit.

But the last stanza is puzzling, for it is unclear to whom the "stern one" refers? Akhmatova's memory of this poem merged with the one that follows, "The Eternal One," as in a quote cited earlier: "…I am not touching upon that special, exceptional relationship…where I am called 'That Other One' ('And he is like a criminal, stern') who 'puts down the staff, smiles and simply says, "We've arrived."'"[14]

Akhmatova assumes that the "stern one" refers to herself, the comrade whose identity is disguised by the masculine gender. Presumably her "criminality" consisted in exchanging for his hour of amorous dallying the eternal bond that connected them. Yet the chains that joined them together were no more substantial than dreams.

The last of the 1912 poems expressing Gumilev's changing view of Akhmatova and their marriage is entitled "The Eternal One." He again changes Akhmatova's gender, perhaps to obscure the reference to her. Or perhaps in eliminating sexual love in this union of two souls, Gumilev intended to underline the lofty, asexual, highly spiritual dimension of their relationship.

<u>The Eternal One</u>

In the corridor of days close-crowded,
Where even the sky is a heavy yoke,
I gaze on ages, live in moments,
For the Day of Days I wait and hope:

The end to worries and successes,
To the blind wanderings of the soul…
Oh, day when I will gain my sight and
Be strangely knowing, hurry on!

Another soul I will discover,
Grasping what had teased me once,
And I will bless the golden pathway,

Frances Laird

>The one that leads from worm to sun.
>
>And he who walked beside me, going
>In thunder and in gentle quiet,
>One who was cruel towards my pleasures
>And clearly gracious towards my faults,
>
>Taught me silence, taught me struggle
>With all earth's knowing, ancient, wise,—
>He'll lay his staff down and then, turning,
>Will simply say: "We have arrived."
>
>   Nikolai Gumilev
>   1912[15]

Gumilev finds himself back in the Symbolist territory of apocalyptical judgement and golden worlds beyond this one, where he can come to know the unknowable and penetrate the mysteries of life. His companion on the journey "from earth to sun," one who knows him well, condemns his self-indulgence, yet looks upon his faults with understanding and forgiveness, is unmistakably Akhmatova. She has taught him how to be silent, how to struggle for his art, how to learn from the ancient wisdom of the earth. Their life's journey will end when the two poets finally set foot in that long-sought, yet elusive "golden paradise." In this poem Gumilev acknowledges the love that exists beyond the problematic earthly one and a vision of their lasting union in an eternal, otherworldly place.

At summer's end, Anna returned to Tsarskoe Selo from her cousin's estate. Gumilev, having enrolled in courses in philology at St. Petersburg University, had rented a room on Tuchkov Street where Anna would frequently stay. Such close quarters could hardly have been comfortable for Akhmatova, as she was nearing the end of her pregnancy and may even have discovered by then that Gumilev had begun another love affair, this with the actress, Olga Vyotskaya.

On a morning in early October, 1912, at the Gumilev home on Malaya Street, Anna went into labor. Nikolai took her by train to the highly respected maternity clinic of Professor Otto in St. Petersburg, where he dropped her off and promptly disappeared. After spending the night drinking in taverns with Dmitri Kuzmin-Karavayeva, a cousin and priest, he returned to discover that his son, Lev, had been born. Entertaining stories about the event went the rounds of St. Petersburg. Makovsky wrote: "It was as if Gumilev, insisting on his scorn for the 'marital knot,' went carousing till morning with his cousin, reeling along the various merry establishments, never once inquiring about his wife by telephone…In the words of Father Dmitri, all of this was intended to have the appearance of a proud, foolish pose, the desire not to be "like everyone else…"[16] When Gumilev had taken his wife and baby home, Valeriya and her husband came for lunch and they all toasted the happy event with champagne.

Frances Laird

While Kolya was preoccupied by educational and amatory pursuits in Petersburg, Anna stayed at home in Tsarskoe Selo. In his early months she nursed her son herself, but gradually was able to pass the care for the child into the hands of a nanny and his doting grandmother, who was only too eager to take charge of the baby boy. Despite her confinement and the constant attention needed by an infant, Akhmatova managed to write a few poems. In a letter to Valery Bryusov dated October 22, 1912, she wrote: "I am sending you a few of the poems I wrote just the other day. I couldn't do so earlier because I had a baby and I haven't written anything all fall.' But it was not long before she took up her life again in the literary world of St. Petersburg.[17]

Chapter VIII
At the Stray Dog

In the spring of 1913, Nikolai Gumilev was preparing for yet another journey to Abyssinia (Ethiopia) and Somaliland, this time as the official head of an anthropological expedition under the auspices of the Academy of Sciences. This was one of the first government-sponsored ethnographic expeditions from Europe sent out to explore this part of Africa and the objects Gumilev collected on it would form the core of the African collection in the St. Petersburg Ethnographic Museum. For company he would take along his young nephew, Nikolai Sverchkov.

The preparations for the journey were arduous and time-consuming. The War Department had given the expedition five rifles and a thousand cartridges, but Gumilev still had to find tents, saddles, packs, cameras, letters of recommendation and the many necessary certificates. On the eve of their departure, when the baggage had already been sent ahead, Kolya suddenly fell ill with a high temperature and severe headache. The doctor's diagnosis was typhus. When Georgy Ivanov stopped by to say good-bye, he found Gumilev delirious with fever and raving about talking rabbits. But in a moment of clarity, he was able to say his farewells, insisting that he would leave the following day. When Ivanov came by the next day, he was met by a weeping Akhmatova who told him that Kolya had just left. Hours before the ship was set to sail, he had asked for his clothes and water for shaving, then rested a moment, drank a glass of tea with cognac and was gone.

Soon after the trip was underway, he wrote to Akhmatova from Odessa:

Dear Anichka, I'm already in Odessa and in a café almost abroad. I'll write to you and then try to write some poetry. I'm completely better, even my throat, but still a bit tired no doubt from the journey. But then I've stopped having nightmares as before; once I dreamt of Vyacheslav Ivanov wanting to do some horrible thing to me, but in the dream it all came out all right. In a bookshop I had a look at *The Harvest* [probably referring to *Zhatva* (Moscow), IV, 1913]. Your poems look very well and it's funny how Boris Sadovskoy had toned down his comments.

Here I saw a poster that Vera Inber is to give a lecture on Friday about the new women's dress or something like that; as well that [Leon] Bakst and [Isadora] Duncan and all the heavy artillery are here.

All day I've been remembering your lines about the 'girl by the sea' ["By the Sea Shore"]. It's not just that I like them, they intoxicate me. So much is said so simply. And I am completely convinced that out of all post-Symbolist poetry, you and of course Narbut (in his own way) will prove to be the most significant poets.

Dear Anya, I know that you do not like it and do not want to understand it, but it is not only pleasant for me but absolutely necessary that, as you deepen for me as a woman, I strengthen and foster the man in myself; I never would have been able to guess that hearts can decay hopelessly from joy and fame [quotes from an Akhmatova poem], but then you would never have been able to concern yourself with research into the country of Gaul or understand seeing the moon that it is the diamond shield of the goddess of the warriors of Pallas.

Curious, that I am now again the same as I was when I wrote *Pearls* and it is closer to me than *Foriegn Sky*.

Young Kolya has been a fine companion up to now and will, I believe, continue to be.

Kiss Lyova for me (strange, I'm writing his name for the first time) and teach him to say Papa. Write to me till 1 June to Diredawa, Abyssinia, Africa, then till 15 June to Dijbouti and 15 July to Port Said, then to Odessa.[1]

Kolya's boyish charm, what had attracted Anna to him and held her in the marriage while making his extramarital activities so difficult to accept, permeates the few letters to her that have survived. This letter in particular offers a rare insight into Kolya's thinking about their marriage. Clearly he values Anna and the relationship which allows him entry into a woman's experience and the depths of her inner life. But at the same time, he insists that it is vital for him to "strengthen and foster the man in myself," begging for her understanding of his need to test his physical courage and exercise his masculine power to widen his experience of the world, including its women. He and Anna are very different creatures, he insists, she with her subtle and profound insights into the realm of emotions, he with his intellectual command of ancient history and Greek myth. As readily as she can accept this, she must accept their disparate views of marriage.

Striking, too, is Gumilev's high estimation of Anna's poetic gift, seeing it as exceeding his own in some ways. And his enthusiasm was not idle flattery, for Gumilev was a perceptive and exacting critic and never made claims for a poet's work that he didn't fully believe. His one mistake was in thinking that Narbut—not Mandelstam—would be the other important post-Symbolist poet. Although Kolya knew that Anna was aware of his "Don Juan" activities, in his letter, warm, confiding, affectionate, chatty, there is no hint of the defensiveness, awkwardness or emotional distance one might expect.

On a postcard bearing a photograph of the Suez Canal, Gumilev wrote on April 13, 1913:

> Dear Anika, just imagine, not one poem since Odessa. I translate Goethe listlessly, write the journal better. A terrible winter is reported, I am resting like a beast. No conversations about literature, about friends, the sea is good, as before. I am waiting impatiently for Africa. Teach Lev to talk and don't get bored. Write me so I find many letters in Diredawa. And mark them with numbers.
> I kiss you and Lev warmly; stroke Molly.
>
> Always your
Kolya[2]

And a third letter, written in June of 1913:

> My dear Anika, I am already in Djibouti, arrived and disembarked very well. The magical open page already saved me fifty rubles and in general rendered a whole lot of good services. My poor health has completely passed and my strength grows with every day. Yesterday I wrote a poem, I'll send it to you. Write to Diredawa what you think of it. On the ship I tried once to write in the style of the Hylaea [the Futurists], but I couldn't. That raised my respect for them. My journal is going successfully and I am writing it as if it were going to be printed directly. In Jedda from the ship we saw a shark; it was really a sight. It took up two pages of the journal.
> What are you doing? Really, go in June to Inna Erazmovna [Anna's mother]. If there is not enough money, borrow some, on my return to Petersburg I will have some. Send your new poems to me here without fail. I want to know

how you have done. Tell Lev that he will have his golliwog. Let him be happy. The Turkish consul assigned to Harare is travelling with us. I am very friendly with him. He is going to collect Abyssinian songs for me and I will stay with him in Harare. I finally made up with the present vice-consul Galef, with whom, you remember, I had quarreled and he has done a lot of important things for me.

I kiss you and Lev.
Your Kolya[3]

But letters from Anna filled with news from home did not pile up in Diredawa. For when Kolya's mother asked her to clean his desk, she had discovered love letters from Olga Vyotskaya. Jealous, hurt, tortured by the intimate details of his betrayal, perhaps even the news of her pregnancy by Kolya, Anna refused to write to him.

Nikolai Gumilev, as he wrote above, kept a diary of this journey, chronicling its progress and recording matters of ethnographic interest.[4] Unfortunately, only the pages covering the first stages of the expedition have survived. Gumilev, travelling under the auspices of the government, sailed on a ship from the Russian fleet, the *Tambov*. He and young Kolya made a stop in Constantinople, where they toured the Hagia Sophia, once a magnificent Christian cathedral, now a Moslem mosque with the ghostly outline of Byzantine angels circling around inside the whitewashed dome. Prevented from disembarking at Port Said—it was feared that they carried cholera—they sailed on through the Suez Canal into the Red Sea to Djibouti.

After days of waiting, they boarded a train to Diredawa. But when heavy rains washed out the railroad bed, the hardy travellers rode the tracks through the bush on open handcars. The way was slow, dusty and hot under the blistering African sun, but they were rewarded with the sight of jackals, gazelles and a maribou. Reaching Diredawa, Gumilev put together a caravan of mules and hired a translator and drivers. He planned to push south into the region lying between the Somalian Peninsula and Lake Rudolph, there to record local songs and legends, collect ethnographic materials and take photographs.

Sadly, it is at this point that the journal, discovered by his mother at Slepnevo after his death, abruptly ends. The remaining chapters were lost when the family moved to Bezhetsk. But hair-raising tales of his uncle's exploits were told by "Little Kolya," and recorded by his mother, Gumilev's step-sister, A. S. Sverchkova. At some point on their trek through the bush, they reached a river where, instead of a bridge, there was a basket large enough to hold three people suspended on ropes attached to a tree on either bank. When seated in the basket, a man could draw it hand over hand to the opposite shore. "Noticing that the trees were rotting or the roots were loose, Uncle Kolya began to rock the basket, risking an imminent fall into a river swarming with crocodiles. Scarcely had they crawled out of the basket when one tree fell over and the rope broke."[5]

Another adventure involved Hussein, king of one of the fiercest Somalian tribes in East Africa, who lived in a village 300 kilometers to the southwest of Djibouti. The natives of his caravan told Gumilev how Hussein had transformed an enemy army into stones and how a mountain had moved behind him from one place to another. Intrigued by the tales of his extraordinary powers, Gumilev wanted to meet this king and prophet. When they arrived in the village, Hussein, placated with presents, allowed the two white men to look around, but had them closely watched. Sverchkova continued: "The tribal justice system was at rather a primitive level. There were two large rocks between which was a narrow opening. To test the innocence or guilt of a person in a crime, he had to strip naked and crawl between the rocks. If the person became stuck, he died in terrible torment, for no one was allowed to extend a hand to him nor give him a piece of bread or a cup of water. Skulls and bones were scattered over the ground. No matter how hard Little Kolya tried to dissuade his uncle, Gumilev insisted on trying the experiment himself—to crawl between the rocks." As Little Kolya watched terrified for his uncle, Gumilev passed the test. Sverchkova's view of the stunt: "It was not bravery but a kind of madness!" She must have harbored some regrets at having entrusted her precious son to Uncle Kolya's care.

In Slepnevo, where Anna had taken the baby Lev for the summer, her imagination, fed by jealousy and hurt, dwelled upon her husband's latest betrayal.

> Obedient is imagination,
> Your grey eyes' image came to me.
> In solitude in the Tver region,
> You I remember bitterly.

> In lovely arms, a happy captive
> Upon the Neva's left bank slopes.
> So, my well-known contemporary,
> It turned out just as you had hoped.
>
> You ordered me, "I've had enough, so
> Just go away, destroy your love."
> And here I am, weak-willed and wasting,
> But strongly listless is my blood.
>
> But if I am to die, then who will
> Write down the poems I meant for you,
> Then who will help to make them ring out,
> All those as yet unspoken words?
>
> Anna Akhmatova
July, 1913[6]

Bitter, isolated, deceived, humiliated, Akhmatova lived out the hot summer months in the bosom of her husband's family with no one to confide in, with no relief but poetry from the painful and turbulent emotions that ruled her heart. If her husband would not obey her will, at least her imagination would. She pictures Kolya in the arms of Olga Vysotskaya, perhaps in the very bed on Tuchkov Lane where she had often slept beside him. Gumilev must have been pleased, living the life he had always wished for, freely exploring the varied possibilities of love, never allowing his marriage vows to deter him. If Anna demanded exclusivity, then she must destroy her love for him, for he would not be made a prisoner to one woman's love. Akhmatova, immobilized by a loss of willpower, feels her life force seeping away in the halting flow of blood through her veins that is ever "more keenly tedious," the exact translation. Her lethargic pulse slows inexorably and soon nothing will be left for her but death.

But when she comes to face death, the poet realizes that it will be their shared love of poetry that joined their spirits. If she were to die, the poems meant for Gumilev's eyes would be left unwritten. Here Akhmatova acknowledges Gumilev as her primary reader, the one for whom she writes and whose response she most treasures. Her recognition of the rare value of what remained to join them may have helped to ease the pain of his betrayal and to release her from yearning for a kind of marriage Gumilev could never accept.

Nikolai returned from Africa in September, 1913, loaded down with exotic animal trophies and a parrot with a bright yellow head and pink breast. But his enthusiam for travel had been tempered by disappointment. For if the trip had been successful in a scientific sense, Gumilev had not found that "golden door" for which he had searched so assiduously in his travels. There was no escape through some mystical portal opening onto a higher plane of experience, no exit through the walls that enclosed and isolated the self. Gumilev would never return to Africa, for war and revolution would intervene and irrevocably change his life and his world.

At the Stray Dog, a tiny cabaret where artists, musicians, and poets met, mingled, dazzled and outraged one another, two of the regular patrons were Anna Akhmatova and Nikolai Gumilev, reigning stars in Petersburg's bohemian world. The Dog was run by Boris Pronin, who, influenced by the innovative director Vsevolod Meyerhold, oversaw the productions on its tiny stage as well as the spontaneous performances that arose off-stage. Nightly he stood guard at the door to admit the genuine denizens of the art world and a small selection of "pharmacists," as he termed those bourgeois citizens curious to watch the strange antics of Petersburg's artists and writers. Each customer played his or her role in the unpredictable, fascinating, often uproarious theatrics running nightly.

To reach the Stray Dog, which occupied a couple of low, dank cellar rooms of a large house on Mikhailovsky Square, one passed through an iron gate and descended a narrow, precipitous stone stairway where the stench of neighboring garbage pits and outhouses hung heavy in the air. The doorway was so low that a man had to doff his top hat before entering. But: "...in nineteen thirteen, it was the only little island in nighttime Petersburg where the literary and artistic young people...not having a penny to their names, felt themselves at home."[7]

The two rooms were crowded with little tables and a buffet that extended along one wall. The stage, though small, had sufficient space for plays, poetry readings, and concerts. Sergei Sudeikin, a stage designer, had painted the stone walls and ceiling with brightly-colored images of birds and flowers. In the hours before midnight, after the theatres had closed, the cabaret opened. Then:

...as into an incubator the unhatched enthusiasms of the theatrical hall were quickly transported, so that in an atmosphere warmed by wine fumes they broke out in unrestrained applause, the signal for which was given by the cry *Hommage! Hommage!*
Here like a hot dish in a thermos flask, prepared at the other end of the city, by horsecab, taxi, tram they brought the freshly cooked triumph which they liked to prolong, to savour again and again until it acquired the rancid flavour of yesterday's success.[8]

Akhmatova and Gumilev played their appointed roles in the nightly spectacle at the Stray Dog. Benedict Livshits witnessed their grand entrance: "Sheathed in black silk, a large oval cameo at her waist, Akhmatova sailed in. At the insistence of Pronin, who flung himself over to meet her, she lingered at the entrance in order to write in the 'pigskin' her latest poems, about which the simpleminded 'pharmacists' would construct their conjectures. In a long, black frock coat, leaving no beautiful woman without his attention, Gumilev retreated, moving backwards between the tables, whether in this way he could observe royal etiquette or was apprehensive about a 'rapier' glance in the back."[9]

Poets of every persuasion, Symbolists, Acmeists and Futurists, collected in the Stray Dog, recited poems, argued noisily or proudly cut their enemies dead. Of Futurists there were Hyleans, Ego-

Frances Laird

Futurists, Budyetlans, Cubo-Futurists, motley and vociferous cliques unified only in sharing in some way the ideas of the Italian poet, Marinetti, and a desire to cut poetry off from the "wasteland" of its past in order to bring it into the age of speed and the machine. With their gaudy costumes, painted faces, scandalous outbursts, and shrill, dogmatic manifestos, they galvanized the attention of the public.

The Russian Futurists' experiments with words led them to claim that a word possessed a singular power in and of itself, without reference to its conventional meaning. Thus arose *zaum,* or *zaumnnyi yazyk*, a "beyond the mind" language, the brilliant invention of two Cubo-Futurists, Velimir Khlebnikov and Alexei Kruchenikh. Pure sounds, rhythms, dissonances and aural analogies were intended to convey meaning in an intuitive, irrational process. If there were disorder in language, it only mirrored the outward disorder of that chaotic age.

Gumilev was often offended by the pranks and excesses of the Futurists, especially their manifesto, "Go to the Devil!" published in January, 1914, and signed by Mayakovsky, Khlebnikov, and Livshits, among others. Proclaiming that "The appearance of new poetry has had the effect on the crawling dodderers of Russian literature of a white-marbled Pushkin dancing the tango," they poked fun at the Symbolists and the Acmeists, including Gumilev, calling them "a pack of 'Adams with parted hair.'" The manifesto taunted them, proclaiming that: "They endeavored to stick the labels of acmeism and apollonianism on dull songs about Thule samovars and toy lions and then joined the motley procession around the established position of the Futurists..."[10] The poetic wars reached a crescendo in the fall of 1913.

Gumilev, stung by their insults, refused to speak to any Futurists at the Stray Dog, which proved rather difficult as they were jammed together around crowded little tables nearly every night of the week. Velimir Khlebnikov would brood alone, absorbed in his philosophical cogitations. Georgy Adamovich remembered how: "...Osip Mandelstam, who was by nature cheerful and sociable, was talking animatedly about something. He talked and talked, then suddenly looked around, as if looking for someone, and stopped short: 'No, I can't go on talking when Khlebnikov is silent.'"[11]

Mandelstam, an even-tempered and easy-going presence in the Dog, paid no attention to the Futurist cant and even initiated Livshits into "the mysteries of Petersburg *savoir faire*, beginning with the secret of getting credit at the Stray Dog buffet and ending with the Polish laundry, where for three times the usual price you could receive in one hour an excellently washed and stiffly starched collar—an invaluable convenience indeed with the skimpiness of our wardrobe."[12]

Mandelstam was even on good terms with Vladimir Mayakovsky, the most notorious and most talented of the Futurists, who had trumpeted "I am neither cubo- nor ego-...I am a prophet of the mankind of the future!" Mayakovsky, in his bright yellow tunic, would sprawl like a wounded gladiator, watching the entrance so that he could honor each Futurist poet who wandered in by thumping his drum. Anna remembered how: "Once at the Dog, when everyone was eating loudly and the dishes were clanking, Mayakovsky took it into his head to recite poetry. Osip went over to him and said: 'Mayakovsky, stop reciting poems. You're not a Romanian orchestra.'"[13]

Even Nikolai Gumilev's icy hauteur toward the Futurists could soften. When Khlebnikov was desperately in need of money to impress a young woman and her actress friend with supper and wine at the Dog, he told Livshits his idea:

—Why don't we get the money from Gumilev?
—From Gumilev? But why from him?
—Because he isn't hard up and because he is our rival.
—It's awkward to turn to a person who, after our manifesto, scarcely puts out his hand to us.
—Rubbish! First I'll tell him everything that I think about his poetry, and then I'll ask for money. He'll give it to me. I'll go to Tsarskoe now and today you invite Lelia and Lilia to the Dog.

He disappeared, having put on for the great, solemn occasion my ill-fated top hat. Toward evening he returned, visibly satisfied with the outcome of his trip. Whether he fulfilled exactly his intention or not, only Akhmatova, who was present at his conversation with Gumilev, would have been able to say, but he brought the money.[14]

The productions staged at the Stray Dog might include a lecture on poetry, a Symbolist play, or the ballerina Tamara Karsavina dancing to the music of Couperin. Olga Glebova-Sudeikina, a frequent performer, played the role of the Virgin in *The Flight of the Virgin and Child to Egypt*, with script by Kuzmin, music by Sac and staging by Sergei Sudeikin and danced in the title role of *The Goat-Legged Nymph*. Arthur Lourie, a young composer, might play a new composition or Mikhail Kuzmin recite his poems, accompanying himself with starkly monotonous chords on the piano. It was at the Stray Dog that Russian audiences were introduced to the avant-garde music of the early twentieth century, to Ravel, Schoenberg and Debussy.

The Stray Dog was always full for poetry readings, especially those of Akhmatova. Standing tall on the tiny stage, her elegant head with its distinctive profile held high, the folds of an azure shawl falling artfully over her shoulders, Akhmatova displayed a rare dignity that ennobled everything around her and created a lasting impression on those who saw her. Mandelstam compared her to Phaedra, seeing even then a tragic shadow beneath her vivacious personality. Adamovich remembers her as lively and amusing until she began to read, when her whole demeanor would suddenly change and her face go pale. "I was stunned by Anna Andreevna's appearance. When people recall her today they sometimes say she was beautiful. She was not, but she was more than beautiful, better than beautiful. I have never seen a woman whose face and entire appearance, whose expressiveness, genuine unworldliness and inexplicable, immediate appeal set her apart anywhere and among beautiful women everywhere."[15]

The artist Yury Anennkov was also struck by her strange loveliness, describing her as "…beautiful in an unusual way with her 'uncurled fringe' covering her forehead and a rare grace of movement and gesture. I do not recall anyone else among the other poets who could read their poems so musically. Her manner of recital, the way she read her poems, was in itself already poetry."[16]

At the Stray Dog, Akhmatova was often surrounded by a cluster of admirers, men who rushed up to her with fervid declarations of love. Akhmatova remarked of one: "'Strange, he didn't mention the pyramids. Usually in these circumstances they would say: 'We met before in the time of Ramses II, don't you remember?'"[17] Mayakovsky, while loudly condemning her poetry, was attracted in spite of himself. "One day he held her delicate, thin hands in his huge paw and with derisive admiration exclaimed for all to hear: '"My God! What little fingers!' Akhmatova frowned and turned away."[18] Even Nikolai Gumilev was impressed by the number of attentive young men and jokingly protested: "Anya, more than five is indecent."[19]

But the poetry readings could turn raucous. Mayakovsky was on stage when the 'pharmacists' took offence at his insults. "Men rose from their seats with shouts of indignation, ladies with tears. The artists turned to Pronin, the owner of the Stray Dog: 'After this hideous incident we would consider coming here below our dignity.' Pronin replied, 'Good riddance.'"[20]

Akhmatova enjoyed being in the company of her artist and writer friends. She recalled: "In my youth I was very sociable, I loved having guests, I loved being a guest myself. Kolya Gumilev explained my sociability this way: 'When left alone, Anya writes poetry non-stop. She needs people in order to rest from her poems, otherwise she would write without even taking a break or resting.'"[21] Nadezhda Mandelstam also noticed Akhmatova's love of company: "She adored sitting around a table drinking tea with friends of all ages; she loved the noise and lively table conversation …People would fall off their chairs laughing when she gave in to her mischievous nature. She could not keep up the role of a lady for long…"[22] The friendships that Akhmatova made at the Stray Dog were of lasting importance to her. Decades later, after war, revolution, emigrations, terror, and more war, the ghosts of these and the other habitués of the Stray Dog gathered to surface again in Akhmatova's *Poem Without a Hero.*

One tragic incident then that involved Olga Glebova-Sudeikina left a deep impression upon Akhmatova and would provide an important theme in *Poem Without a Hero*. Olga, an enchanting young actress and dancer, was married to Sergei Sudeikin. Although her roots were in the peasantry of the Pskov region, she had grown up in St. Petersburg. With her blonde beauty and ample talents, Olga had quickly made a name for herself in the role of Columbine in Meyerhold's experimental production of *Columbine's Scarf* and in leading roles in *Confusion* and *Psyche,* plays by Yury Belyaev.

Arthur Lourie affectionately described Olga: "Long golden braids, like Melisinde's, or Debussy's *la fille aux cheveux de laine;* large grey-green eyes that sparkle like opals; porcelain shoulders, the 'bosom of Diana' virtually exposed by the sharp decolleté of her bodice; a captivating smile; fleeting, soft laugh, fleeting, soft movements—who is she? a butterfly? a Columbine? Perhaps a fairy in a shimmering doll kingdom, where everything is happiness and joy, where every day is a holiday?"[23]

Olga had created the perfect setting for displaying herself: "Her exquisite little house contained Elizabethan furniture made of Karelian birch, harpsichords, Venetian mirrors, Russian glass, portraits by Borovikovsky, and paintings of beautiful women by Venetsianov. Olga Afanasyevna reigned among these treasures like a queen."[24] It was a shrine created for her worshippers, an exquisite stage, "gaudier than a circus wagon," where her elusive mystery and unusual beauty could be best appreciated. In *Poem Without a Hero,* Akhmatova wrote of Glebova-Sudeikina, decked out in flowers like Botticelli's *Spring*, receiving her visitors while reclining on her bed "adorned like a bower." The cupids suspended on the azure walls (painted by her husband) kept "watch over the altar of Venus" and golden candlesticks flickered with an ethereal glow.

But for another writer, Olga was "the living embodiment of her desperate and piquant epoch."[25] She possessed an almost magical power over men. A young poet and officer in the dragoons, Vsevolod Knyazev, fell desparately in love with her. In Riga where he was stationed, the handsome, blonde Knyazev, who had once been Mikhail Kuzmin's lover, carried on a torrid affair with Olga that inspired a bundle of passionate, but mediocre poems. So tangled were the sexual attachments among these artists that Kuzmin, who had moved in with the Sudeikins, began an affair with Olga's husband, Sergei, until she discovered it and tossed Kuzmin out. Sergei, amazingly forgiving of his wife's infidelities, then consoled himself with the pretty actresses who flocked about him. But Olga soon grew tired of Knyazev. One evening in April, 1913, he watched as she returned home with another man, rumored to have been Alexander Blok. While standing on her doorstep, Knyazev shot himself in the head. His death, as dramatic and pointless as it was, was only one in a plague of suicides reported daily in the Petersburg newspapers.

The philosopher Nikolai Berdyaev condemned the frenetic, intensely creative yet claustrophobic atmosphere of pre-war St. Petersburg: "All this took place within a very small, elite circle totally cut off from the masses. There was a feeling of breathing the putrefied air of a hothouse rather than fresh air. There was *Angst*, tension, but no joy. Serious creativity was combined with cheap imitation and a following of fashion. There were too many aesthetes, mystics, disciples of the occult, with a dominance of the erotic and aesthetic over the ethical...There was something poisonous in the air of Petersburg at this time."[26]

Adamovich sensed that the frenzied pleasure-seeking in the Stray Dog was underlain with a palpable anxiety: "It was very crowded, very stuffy, and not exactly merry. I would have great difficulty in coming up with the precise word to describe the atmosphere in the Stray Dog. But no one who once frequented the place has forgotten it to this day."[27] For many of its patrons, the smoky cellar was the center of their life. The Acmeist poet Vladimir Pyast wrote: "We (Mandelstam and I and many others) began to imagine that the whole world was in fact concentrated at the Stray Dog, that there was no other life, no other interests than the Doggy ones."[28]

Akhmatova captured that air of a reckless, superficial gaiety undercut by spiritual alienation that reigned on New Year's Day in the Stray Dog.

> We're harlots here and carousers,
> How unhappy are we all!
> On the walls the birds and flowers
> Are homesick for the clouds.
>
> The black pipe you are holding—
> So strange the puffs of smoke.
> To appear even more slender
> I put on my narrow skirt.
>
> Blocked forever are the windows.
> Is there frost or a storm outside?
> But the eyes of a wary house cat

Are not unlike your eyes.

Oh, how my heart is aching!
Do I wait for the hour of death?
But the woman who now dances
Will surely be in hell.

                        Anna Akhmatova
                        January 1, 1913[29]

Caught in the noisy holiday celebration by an instant of penetrating moral insight, the poet suddenly sees the party-goers—and herself—as degraded and frivolous. They are trapped inside these stuffy, crowded rooms where even the inanimate birds and flowers painted on the walls yearn for the open sky. The puffs of smoke from Kolya's pipe, defamiliarized in this intense moment of profound vision, take on odd, unsettling shapes. Perhaps unnerved, Akhmatova quickly returns to the superficial, her own fashionable appearance in her close-fitting Parisian skirt with the slit. The windows onto the outside world are opaque, obscured by frost or rain, so those inside can remain happily oblivious to what is happening there. Only the eyes of Gumilev, as intuitively knowing as a cat, seem strangely wary. Could the doomed dancer in the last lines be Olga Glebova-Sudeikina? Thoughts of suffering and death intrude upon the raucous jollity.

Despite their frequent appearances together in the Stray Dog and around Petersburg, the marriage of Akhmatova and Gumilev continued to unravel. In 1913, Orest, Gumilev's son by Olga Vysotskaya, was born. Twenty-six years later, in the depths of the Yezhov Terror, Akhmatova would spot Olga in the prison lines and whisper to Lydia Chukovskaya: "'Her son is Lyova's brother…He is only a year younger than Lyova. He has Kolya's hands exactly.'"[30]

Gumilev went on to the next affair with Tanya, the sister of Georgy Adamovich. When she insisted on marrying Gumilev, Anna readily agreed to a divorce. But Gumilev's mother was horrified, for one of the conditions Akhmatova set was that she would keep Lev. Gumilev's mother spoke forcefully to her son: "I must tell you the truth. I love Lev more than Anna does and more than you."[31] They agreed to remain married, whatever that might mean. Akhmatova tried to reconcile herself, at least outwardly, to Kolya's wandering ways and treated Tanya in a friendly manner. But one wonders what she felt when Gumilev dedicated *Kolchan (The Quiver),* his next book of poems, to Tanya Adamovich.

In the fall of 1913, Akhmatova gave her first poetry reading in a large theatre at the Bestuzhev Institute for Women. The patroness of the reception was Ariadna V. Tyrkova-Vergezhskaya, a writer in the forefront of the fight for equal rights for women. With the remark, "Anichka has won equality for herself," she set her stamp of approval on both Akhmatova and her poetry.[32]

Reading at a large, public gathering was a new and intimidating experience for Akhmatova. She wrote: "If the theatrical stage is capable of hiding a person, then reading alone on stage can mercilessly expose him. The stage is similar to an executioner's block...Perhaps, I experienced that for the first time then. The audience begins to look like a many-headed hydra to the performer. It's very difficult to command the hall..."[33]

It was here that Akhmatova had an encounter with Alexander Blok, a reigning cultural icon of his day. Not only was Blok immensely gifted and prolific, his romantic appearance and reputation as a lover fulfilled the idealized image of the poet. Blok's popularity can only be compared to that of a movie star or rock musician today. His refined and sensitive features, his crown of golden curls, full, sensuous lips, dreamy blue-grey eyes appeared on picture postcards sold to his admirers. When a student informed the two poets that Akhmatova follow Blok on the program, she protested. "'Alexander Alexandrovich, I cannot read after you.' He—with a reproach in his voice—replied: 'Anna Andreevna, we are not tenors.'" Akhmatova continued: "...Nobody knew me and when I came out there was a cry of 'Who's that?' Blok had advised me to read 'We're all harlots here...'I started to resist: 'They laugh when I read 'I put on my narrow skirt. He replied: 'They laugh at me when I read 'And the drunkards with their rabbit eyes.'"[34]

Petersburg audiences were enthralled by Akhmatova's readings, especially young people, who crowded about her at intermissions.

While most poets recited in a highly dramatic manner, Akhmatova read with understated emotion and restraint. She prepared with great deliberation, making a careful selection of the poems she would read and the sequence in which she would read them. Then, standing before a mirror, she would decide how to present herself and what she would wear. She would practice for hours, repeating the poems and weighing each word for its proper intonation and expressive force.

Although Akhmatova's acquaintanceship with Blok never progressed beyond brief and superficial meetings at readings and other literary events, the myth took root in the public mind that there was a secret love affair going on between them. Perhaps Petersburgers believed that a romance between Blok, who was involved in an endless series of affairs, and Akhmatova was destined to happen. Gossip circulated that the hero of "The Grey-eyed King" was Blok and that Lev Gumilev was really Blok's son, which incensed Akhmatova, for "The Grey-eyed King" was written four months before she had even met Alexander Blok. Yet even Lydia Chukovskaya admitted to thinking that the words "my well-known contemporary" in Akhmatova's poem "Obedient is imagaination..." referred to Blok.[35]

Just who was Alexander Blok's latest lover was a frequent subject of speculation. He had married Lyuba Dmitrievna Mendeleyeva, the fiercely beautiful daughter of the great chemist, Gregory Mendeleyev. She was Blok's ideal incarnation of the Divine Feminine and, inspired by her, Blok had written over eight hundred poems collected in

Verses to a Beautiful Lady. Although they remained emotionally dependent upon one another, the two lived largely separate lives, Blok in the literary world and Lyuba as an actress.

But Akhmatova believed Blok's behavior with women was strange. She told Lydia Chukovskaya: "...I know a bit about his affairs...Two women at different times told me about their relationships with him—essentially it was the same story...Both were young and beautiful...One visited him late, in his empty flat...the other at The Stray Dog...Both were the *femme fatale* type...But he pushed them away at the last moment: 'My God...It's dawn already...farewell...farewell...'"[36] At this time, Blok was involved with Mlle. Delmas, a tall, red-haired actress, who was playing the role of Carmen at the Mariinsky Theatre.

In December, 1913, Akhmatova visited Alexander Blok at his tall, grey house near the Neva river so that he could inscribe copies of his books for her. Akhmatova recalls: "In each one he simply wrote: 'To Akhmatova from Blok,'...but in the third volume he wrote out his madrigal dedicated to me: 'Beauty is frightening, they'll tell you.' I have never had the Spanish shawl in which Blok portrays me, but at the time Blok was mad about Carmen and made a Spaniard out of me, too."[37] No one who read Blok's poem to Akhmatova could understand what precisely it meant and neither could she. "One thing is clear, that it was written like that (with her palms she made a warding-off gesture): 'Do not touch me.'"[38] Akhmatova wrote about this meeting in the poem, "I visited the poet..."[39]

Frances Laird

There were strains upon the Gumilev marriage other than Kolya's love affairs. Akhmatova's poetry was receiving praise from critics and growing ever more popular with readers. Alhough as a critic Gumilev was highly respected within the rather narrow world of Russian poets, his poems did not have a large audience outside it. Some thought that he had failed to meet the criteria he laid out so clearly for others. Adamovich wrote about a meeting of the Guild of Poets: "[Gumilev's] criticism was detailed and, as a rule, unerringly correct. He had an exceptional ear for poetry, an exceptional feel for words. But I confess that even then I felt that he was incomparably more perceptive to the poems of others than to his own. He seemed not to notice or sense some vapidness and decorativeness in his own work."[40]

The poems that Akhmatova wrote in 1913 show that, behind the facade of dignified calm, she was still struggling to understand Gumilev's attitude towards her. In the following poem, she tries to come to terms with his egregious behavior.

> My smile is a certain smile—so,
> Just a barely seen movement of lips.
> I will look after it just for you,
> For love gave it to me as a gift.

Swan Songs
Akhmatova and Gumilev

> Who cares you give others your love,
> Who cares that you're wicked and bold.
> Beside me my gray-eyed groom
> And before me a lectern of gold.
>
> Anna Akhmatova
> 1913[41]

Akhmatova acknowledges the gifts that Gumilev's love have bestowed upon her and has persuaded herself of her indifference to his "Don Juanism." What did it matter if he were cruel and unfaithful to her, when she can still envision him at her side before the golden *analoi* upon which holy texts and icons are placed, presumably at their marriage ceremony just three years earlier in the church of St. Nicholas on the Dnieper. She implies that she sees them joined together in the eyes of God, in an unbroken spiritual bond untarnished by the outside amatory interests of Nikolai Gumilev.

Still other poems of this period reveal that, beneath Akhmatova's stoicism, lies suffering.

> Hello there: hear the slightest rustle
> Right beside your desk?
> Those lines you won't finish writing—
> I have come to you.
> Really—will you try to hurt me
> Like you did the other time?

> You can't see my hands, you're saying,
> Neither hands nor eyes.
> Here with you it's bright and simple.
> Do not drive me to that place
> Beneath the bridge's stifling vault where
> Dirty water turns to ice.
>
> Anna Akhmatova
October, 1913[42]

As he sits in his study absorbed in his work, Anna, betrayed only by the slight rustling of her dress, enters. Intending to distract him from the poem over which he pores, she reminds him of another time when he had caused her pain. Now he can no longer see her hands or her eyes, features he once celebrated for revealing the mysterious depth and subtle power of her character. As she gazes about this room, where everything seems light, clear and uncomplicated, she sees that his life, revolving around the axis of his own ego, is a simple existence fully satisfying his needs and desires. The impact of his actions upon her is irrelevant and meaningless in the world that he has constructed.

But shifting ominously from light into darkness, the poet pleads that he not force her down beneath the arches of the bridge, that "stifling vault," like the stone roof of a tomb, "where dirty water turns to ice." For a woman betrayed, suicide by drowning was the method of choice in St. Petersburg, a city laced through with rivers and canals. Not that Akhmatova was seriously considering suicide; there was in her poetry a self-dramatizing inflation of images and emotions to create a poetic impact. But here sounds an ironic echo with "Rusalka," where Gumilev envisaged her once as a maiden betrayed in love who, in her despair, drowned herself.

Anna's thoughts of suicide could be more easily dismissed if this image had not been repeated in a poem written in the autumn of 1913, where Akhmatova clearly sees herself as the abandoned woman gazing down at ice-crusted water.

> For the loved one—so many requests!
> It's not so for the one loved no longer.
> I am glad that the water that rests
> Under colorless ice is not flowing.
>
> And yet I—may Christ help me!—will stand
> On this shroud that is bright and brittle.
> But if one day we will be judged by
> Our descendants, you must save my letters.
>
> So that you, brave and wise, can be seen
> By them more distinctly and plainer.
> For how can blank spaces remain
> In your famous biography's pages?

Frances Laird

>Earthly drink is too cloying and sweet,
>Too close-knotted a love net's meshes.
>Someday let the schoolchildren read
>My name as they do their lessons.
>
>And then, learning this sorrowful tale,
>Let them smile at it playfully, slyly...
>Love and peace were not granted to me,
>So bestow on me bitter glory.
>
>>Anna Akhmatova
>>1913[43]

No longer beseiged by the untiring attentions of the lover, Akhmatova considers the icy river as a way out of the pain and humiliation she suffers in being overlooked, cast aside. Yet she turns away from that ultimate act of self-destruction. Appealing for God's help, she will stand on the ice's brittle shroud, or *pokrov* (referring to the burial wrapping for the dead), that coats the still, dead waters beneath. Had she chosen to jump, the ice would have become her burial shroud.

Halfway through the second stanza, Akhmatova's micro-view of their two lives suddenly expands into a global perspective. Gazing into the future, she suddenly comes face to face with us—her readers of today! Her calm, yet implacable assurance was that we—her descendants—would look back upon her life, examining its extraordinary details and wondering at its fateful unfolding. It is astonishing that Akhmatova possessed this uncanny understanding of the lasting significance of her life and work at a time when her career as a poet had barely begun. Akhmatova knew then that we would draw our own conclusions about her, about Kolya Gumilev and the poetry that grew out of their painful and complicated relationship. All she asks is that he preserve the letters (poems) that would illuminate her story, allowing readers to see clearly the "brave and wise" Gumilev, (just the slightest hint of mockery here) as well as to appreciate the role she had played in his "famous biography."

In the fourth stanza, Akhmatova's poetic view-finder draws back even further so that she looks down upon life as if from the perspective of eternity, taking in the vagaries and delights of earthly life, while questioning their ultimate value in the context of the infinite. With prophetic assurance, Akhmatova predicts that her story will take its place in the cultural history of Russia and that one day children will read of it in their school textbooks. Yet they must not take it too seriously, for hers, after all, is just one more story. In the portentous closing lines she already forsees what lies ahead for her—no lasting love and precious little peace. As for "a bitter glory," though slow in coming, her reputation has grown as new readers have discovered her inimitable verse and learned of the hard-won triumphs of her life.

Another whose life would follow a tragic trajectory was her good friend, Osip Mandelstam. Akhmatova wrote: "I see him now through the sparse smoke and fog of Vasilyevsky Island, and where the Kinshi Restaurant used to be on the corner of the second line and Bolshoi Prospect…where once, according to legend, Lomonosov drank away his governmental watch, and where we (Gumilev and I) used to go for breakfast when we lived on Tuchkov Lane."[44] Mandelstam would confide in Akhmatova on the progress of his love affairs with the poet Marina Tsvetaeva and Salomea Andronikova. But when he turned his amorous attentions to Anna, she resisted: "Osip tried to fall in love with me twice, but both times it seemed to me to be such an insult to our friendship that I immediately put a stop to it."[45] Seeing her read at the Stray Dog, Mandelstam compared her to the great French actress, Rachel, who starred in Racine's play, *Phedre*.

> Oh, sadness, she, turned halfway round,
> Gazed out on the indifferent faces.
> The pseudo-classical shawl falling
> Down from her shoulders turned to stone.
>
> The ominous voice—the bitter fumes—
> Unchains a yawning depth of spirit,
> So once as an indignant Phaedra
> Rachel had stood in former times.
>
> Osip Mandelstam
1914[46]

Another friend was Mikhail Lozinsky, a gifted translator, whom she described as a "unique and wonderful individual, who combined fantastic powers of endurance, a most refined wit, nobility and loyal friendship."[47] They were introduced at the second meeting of the Guild of Poets, Akhmatova recalled. She dedicated two poems to him in 1913. Others friends were Arthur Lourie, a composer, and Vladimir Shileiko, a student of the ancient culture and language of Assyria and a poet, who was intoxicated by Akhmatova's poetry. He appeared at the Stray Dog as "...a tall, emaciated figure in a student uniform with large volumes of Persian poetry under his arm, which he brought for Akhmatova." With his erudition and his dark, almost demonic good looks, he called to mind Dr. Faustus.[48]

Within the Guild of Poets, the strains produced by powerful but conflicting personalities moving in various poetic directions began to undermine the group's happy cohesion. Gumilev and Gorodetsky were constantly quarreling. Akhmatova wrote that she and Mandelstam "...began to think of the Guild as a burden and even submitted a petition to Gumilev and Gorodetsky to have it shut down. Osip and I wrote it. Gorodetsky passed a resolution: 'Hang everyone and imprison Akhmatova. Malaya Street, No. 64.'"[49] The Guild of Poets would ultimately disband in 1914.

Despite Akhmatova's outwardly stoic acceptance of Gumilev's philandering, a poem dated 1914 expresses her bitter mockery of his love affair with Tanya Adamovich.

Frances Laird

> I am not begging for your love.
> The place it now rests can be trusted.
> And I will write, please do believe me,
> No jealous letters to your bride.
> But I will give you this wise counsel!
> That you give her my poems to read,
> And let her, too, preserve my portraits—
> Two such solicitous lovebirds!
> More needed by these little fools
> Is consciousness of total triumph,
> Than friendship's bright, warm conversations
> And memories of first tender days…
> When with your dear friend you run through
> The kopecks of this happy present,
> And to your satiated soul
> All suddenly grows so repellent,
> Into my solemn festal night
> Do not come. I do not know you.
> How ever could I be of help?
> Of happiness I am no healer.
>
> Anna Akhmatova
> 1914[50]

In a tone drenched with bitter irony, the poet gives her directions to Kolya as he embarks upon his next affair, while reassuring him that she will not behave badly towards his new "bride." All she asks is that this latest mistress understand exactly whom she replaces, for Akhmatova will not allow herself to be conveniently erased from the picture. With the exclamation, "Two such solicitous lovebirds!" we finally see Akhmatova the woman, spurned and cheated, striking back. Let the new "bride" savor her "victory," for, she predicts, when the happy couple have squandered the small change of their hapless love, Kolya's passion inevitably will turn to disgust. Then the poet warns him against turning to her for sympathy, intruding upon her "solemn, festal night." Indeed, with the finality of "I don't know you," she declares both her frustration in trying to comprehend him and her refusal to acknowledge him as the person she had once loved. Anyway, she would be powerless to cure him of the "disease" of happiness afflicting him, referring to Gumilev's idea of the full, manly life that had to include the dauntless and exhilerating search for new women to conquer.

Frances Laird

Chapter IX
The Real Twentieth Century Begins

Anna Akhmatova's second collection of poems, *Chetki (Rosary),* was published on March 15, 1914. The first edition was printed in 1,100 copies and sold out within the year. Akhmatova saw its success as the triumph of the Acemist movement over the ferocious attempts of the Symbolists, Futurists, and Ivanov to strangle it. This book marked a significant point in the history of Russian poetry; it was to be the tombstone on the grave of Russian Symbolism.[1]

The title, *Chetki,* can also be translated as "Beads," mitigating somewhat its religious overtones. Akhmatova may have had in mind a favorite necklace of heavy, agate beads that she compared to a rosary in a poem entitled "In a Mirror." Like the beads of a necklace, poems are strung together, reflecting and refracting different aspects of her world. Although religious imagery does appear, the poems of *Rosary* are largely secular in tone and content. When images taken from Russian Orthodox Christianity do appear, they often serve primarily as vivid details of the cultural milieu in which Akhmatova lived.

The epigraph for the book is taken from a poem by the nineteenth century poet, Evgeny Baratynsky: "Then good-bye forever! But know/that the names of two guilty ones/not one, will be found/in my poems, in my love/legends." As the epigraph suggests, the dominant theme of *Rosary* is that of the ending of a love that once bound together two people, both of whom are guilty in the death of a relationship, with corallary motifs of captivity, falseness, betrayal, separation, rejection, and abandonment.

If the poems of *Evening* were set for the most part in Tsarskoe Selo, those of *Rosary* stem from Akhmatova's life in Slepnevo and St. Petersburg, a city whose sights, smells and sounds she vividly recalled: "Smoke over the rooftops. The Petersburg Dutch ovens...The Petersburg fires during bitter frosts. The peal of bells that would deafen the city with their sound. The drum roll that always made one think of an execution. The sleds that collided with all their might against the curbstones of the humpbacked bridges..." Then there were the sounds of the courtyards, of the thunder of loads of firewood being thrown down into cellars and the itinerant tradesmen who wandered the streets: "Organ-grinders ('Sing, my little sparrow, sing, soothe my heart...), knife-sharpeners ('I grind knives, scissors...'), secondhand-clothes dealers ('Dressing gowns, dressing gowns...'), who were always Tatars. Tinsmiths. 'I've got Vyborg pretzels.'" From the backstairs of the Petersburg apartments wafted the evocative aromas of "bliny at Shrovetide, mushrooms and fast-day oil during Lent, and smelt from the Neva in May. When cooking something pungent, the cooks would open the door onto the back staircase 'to let out the fumes' (that's how they termed it), but nevertheless, the back staircase, alas, more often that not smelled of cats."[2]

Frances Laird

As Akhmatova was preparing the manuscript of *Rosary* for printing, Gumilev had said thoughtfully: "...maybe it will have to be sold in every small shop," so convinced was he of the book's likely success.³ But Akhmatova was unhappy at the book's publication: "I bored my husband with complaints. Once, angered at my whining, he said, 'Well, if you want the book to be good—include Pushkin's *Anchar.*'" ⁴ Justifying Gumilev's high opinion, *Rosary* was even more popular than *Evening*. It even became a game among her admirers to "say the *Rosary,*" with one person reciting the opening lines of a poem, then another finishing it.

Most reviews of *Rosary* were enthusiastic. Nikolai Gumilev, maintaining a herculean control over his subjectivity, reviewed the book in *Apollon* in his column "Letters about Russian Poetry." The article, included here, would be of interest, if only for Gumilev's acute perception of Akhmatova's poetic gift.⁵ But it is even more fascinating to read between the lines, bearing in mind that Gumilev himself and the anguish caused by her love for him, had been the source of many of the poems.

In Rosary *by Anna Akhmatova, the eidological aspect [i.e. the figurative-sense aspect of poetry] is thought out least of all. The poetess does not "make up herself," does not, in order to unify her experiences, place at their center some sort of external fact. She doesn't address herself to something known or understood only by herself. And in this she differs from the Symbolists. But, on the other*

Swan Songs
Akhmatova and Gumilev

hand, her themes are often not reduced to the limits of a given poem. Much in them seems unsubstantiated, because not proven.

As with the majority of young poets, in Anna Akhmatova's work often such words as pain, ennui, death are encountered. This youthful pessimism, quite natural, and therefore beautiful, until now was the property of the "test of the pen" and, it seems, in the poems of Akhmatova for the first time it has taken its place in poetry. I think that everyone is surprised how great in youth is the ability and the inclination to suffer.

The laws and the objects of the real world suddenly take the place of earlier ones permeated by the dream in the fulfillment of which [the poet] believed. He cannot but see that they are self-sufficiently beautiful and he is unable to conceive of himself among them, to make the rhythm of his own spirit agree with their rhythm. But the force of life and love in him is so strong, that he begins to love his very own orphanhood, he comprehends the beauty of pain and death. Later on, when an "unexpected joy" begins to reveal itself to his spirit, tired of being always in the same condition, he will feel that man can joyfully apprehend all aspects of the world and from the ugly duckling which he was until them in his own eyes, he will become a swan as in the fairy tale of Andersen.

To people who are not fated to attain such a transformation or to people who are possessed with a cat-like memory, attached to all the past stages of the soul, the book of Akhmatova appears thrilling and precious. In it is found the voice of a host of existences mute until

Frances Laird

now—women in love, sly, dreamy, rapturous, finally speak their own genuine and, at the same time, artistically convincing language. That connection with the world of which I spoke above and which is the destiny of every genuine poet, is nearly achieved by Akhmatova because she knows the joy of the contemplation of the outer and knows how to convey this joy to us.

> *The dry lips are closed up tightly,*
> *Hot are three thousand candle flames.*
> *In this way lay the Princess Eudoxia*
> *On perfumed, sapphire-blue brocade.*
>
> *And bent over, tearless, a mother*
> *For her son gone blind prayed to her*
> *And a voiceless, hysterical woman*
> *Tried to catch with her lips at the air.*
>
> *And an old man who'd come from the country*
> *In the south, with humped back and black eyes,*
> *To the darkened stairstep drew nearer*
> *As to the doors of heaven's paradise.*

Here I turn to what is most significant in the poetry of Akhmatova, to her stylistics. She almost never explains, she demonstrates. This is achieved by her extremely inventive and original choice of images, but the main thing is their detailed elaboration. *Epithets designating the evaluation of a subject (such as beautiful, horrible, happy, unfortunate and so forth) are rarely met. This evaluation emerges with the description of the image and mutual relationships of images. In Akhmatova there are many devices for this. I will show a few: the confrontation of the adjective defining color with the adjective defining form:*

>...And thickly dark-green ivy
>Twined around the high window.

or:

>...There is the raspberry-red sun
>Above the shaggy, blue smoke.

The repetition in two adjacent lines doubles our attention to the image:

>...Tell me how they kiss you,
>Tell me how you kiss them.

or

>...In your snowy branches black jackdaws,
>Black jackdaws you must shelter.

The conversion of an adjective into a noun:

Frances Laird

> ...*The orchestra plays a merry [thing}...*
> *and so forth.*

There are very many color attributes in the poems of Akhmatova and most often yellow and grey, until now the most rare in poetry. And, perhaps, as a confirmation of the non-accidental quality of her taste, the majority of epithets emphasize precisely the poorness and subdued quality of the objects: a threadbare rug, worn-down heels, a faded flag and so forth. For Akhmatova to love the world, she must see it as nice and simple.

The rhythmics of Akhmatova contribute a great deal to her stylistics. Paeons [four-syllable metrical foot '∾∾∾] and pauses help her single out the most necessary word in the line. And I did not find in the whole book one example of a stress falling on an unstressable word, or, conversely, a word stressed by the meaning without a stress. If anyone takes upon himself the effort to look through a collection of any contemporary poet from this point of view, then he will see for himself that things are usually quite different. A weakness and halting quality of the breath is characteristic for the rhythmics of Akhmatova.

The four-line stanza, and almost the whole book is written in this, is too long for her. Her units of expression are enclosed most often into two lines, sometimes three, sometimes even one. The causal connection by which she tries to replace the rhythmical unity of the stanza for the most part does not achieve its goal. The poetess must *elaborate the stanza if she wishes to master composition. One spontaneous outburst cannot serve as the basis for a composition. This is why Akhmatova knows for the present only a sequence of logically developed ideas or a sequence in which subjects fall into the circle of her vision. This does not constitute a deficiency in the poems, but it closes before her the way to the attainment of much that is valuable.*

In comparison with Evening, *published two years ago,* Rosary *presents a great step forward. The poems have become more solid, the contents of each line fuller, the choice of words chastely-spare and, what is best of all, the disconnectedness of thought, characteristic of* Evening *and constituting more of curiosity of psychology that a feature of the poetry, has disappeared.*

Gumilev demonstrates his ability to grasp the essential nature of Akhmatova's poetry and to convey his understanding of it to the reader. First, Gumilev distinguishes her work from that of the Symbolists, who wrote out of their own mystical, religious and philosophical understanding of a world that existed in some rare, ethereal sphere. Akhmatova, Gumilev emphasizes, does not write about a reality beyond her own sensory experience of the world, nor create an artificial persona through which to see and speak of the world as the Symbolist poet did. Her themes extend beyond the limits of a single poem and a single life. Her poetic ideas are not developed in clearly articulated steps then brought to a conclusion, but, as in life, are left hanging.

Frances Laird

For Gumilev this poet strikes no poses. The ideas and emotions she expresses are genuine and grounded in her own life experience, her "youthful pessimism" "beautiful" and "natural." Knowing the circumstances from which the poems sprang, Gumilev's attempt to aestheticize, discount or, at the least. diminish the truth of the emotions she expresses is not surprising. Striking the pose of a seasoned poet, he seems to be saying, "It's amazing how these young people choose to suffer!" Yet he is the very source of the pain and confusion which Akhmatova gives voice to!

Gumilev locates Akhmatova's poetry solidly within the Acmeist movement, where the laws and objects of the earthly world, with their inherent beauty and meaning, take precedence over those of a world of pure imagination and dreams. It is the poet's work to open our eyes to the wonder of the actual. In his loving apprehension of the real, the poet will come to see himself as part of its beauty, transforming himself from the ugly duckling into a swan, a now familiar metaphor.

Gumilev properly acknowledges the voices of "women in love, sly, dreamy, rapturous," that had been mute until then. In Akhmatova's poems, the reader hears women speaking in an artistically convincing language of their own. Yet, strangely, the poem Gumilev quotes to illustrate this, "The dry lips were closed up tightly…" concerns peasants praying over the holy relics of Princess Eudoxia, saint and wife of Dmitri Donskoi, one of the few poems in

Rosary not written about love or the disillusionment of love, a subject which Gumilev seems to have carefully chosen to avoid.

In his treatment of the stylistic aspects of Akhmatova's verse, Gumilev is on less perilous ground. He calls attention to the poet's vivid imagery, the way her viewpoint emerges indirectly from the description of an image and its relationship with other images, the use of repetitions and the rhythms of the lines. Only at the end does Gumilev venture to be mildly negative, when he criticizes Akhmatova for the limited scope of her poems. One passionate outburst of emotion, he believes, cannot take the place of a more rational and logically developed progression of ideas and images. It is a fascinating dance that Gumilev executes in this review, attempting to maintain his critical distance, touching down on one subject, carefully avoiding another. Those readers of *Apollon* who knew both reviewer and reviewee doubtless followed his every step with fascination as he tiptoed through the quicksands of this potentially dangerous literary territory.

Akhmatova saw the year 1914 as the beginning of the "true twentieth century," one that would come to be known for its destruction of peoples, lands, and cultures on an unprecedented scale. She wrote: "In early May the Petersburg season was beginning to die down; little by little *everybody* was going away. This time the parting with Petersburg turned out to be forever. We returned not to Petersburg, but to Petrograd; from the nineteenth century we suddenly found ourselves transported to the twentieth, everything had changed, beginning with the city's appearance..."[6]

In May, Anna travelled to Derazhnya, near Kiev, to visit her mother, while Kolya, after seeing Tanya Adamovich in Vilnius, went on to Finland. He wrote to Anna:

> Dear Anichka, I thought I'd receive your letter at the Tsarskoe Selo station, but didn't. Did you forget me or have you already left Derazhnya? Libava bored me terribly and here I am in the Teriokas. Near here are Chukovsky, Evreinov, Kulbin, Lozinsky, but at the latter's either today or tomorrow a baby will be born...
>
> I spent the whole day at [Kornei] Chukovsky's. He read me a piece of his future article about Acmeism, very kind and benevolent. But it's only a piece and, of course, that's not where the dog is buried! Yesterday I talked with Makovsky, long and stormily. We could hardly kiss one another and hardly not fight with one another. It seems, however, that he will try to create a department of *belle-lettres* [in *Apollon*] and still other improvements...I am writing a new letter about Russian poetry—Kuzmin, Balmont, Borodaevsky, perhaps someone else. Then an article about African art...I expect that I will write down the poems.
>
> My melancholy, it seems, is passing. Write to me, dear Anichka, at the address of Terioka (Finland), the Ideal coffee-house. In this coffee-house I took a room for a ruble a day, really not bad.
>
> You know I am waiting for a letter, but till then I kiss you warmly.
>
>   Your Kolya
>   Kiss the hand of Inna Erazmovna.[7]

Anna travelled back to Slepnevo by way of Moscow, where she caught an early morning mail train and had a startling encounter with

Alexander Blok. "I was smoking on the open platform [of the train.] Somewhere near an empty platform the engine slowed down and they threw on a bag of mail. Suddenly Blok appeared before my amazed eyes. I shout, 'Alexander Alexandrovich!' He looks around and, since he was not only a great poet but also a master of the tactful question, he asks: 'Who are you traveling with?' I manage to answer: 'I'm alone.' And the train pulls out."[8]

From Slepnevo, Anna answered Kolya's letter on July 13, 1914:

> Dear Kolya, I arrived in Slepnevo on the 10th. I found Lyovushka healthy, happy and very affectionate. Your mother will probably write to you about the weather and business. Yasinsky speaks very favorably of me in the June issue of *New World*. I try to avoid the neighbors, they're very insipid. I've written several poems which not one person has heard yet, but that, thank God, does not bother me much. Now you are *au courant* with all the Petersburg and literary news. Write me, is there any news?...
>
> Will you return to Slepnevo? Or will you be in Petersburg from early August? Write me about all this as soon as possible I'm sending you the drafts of my new poems and am very much waiting for news. I kiss you.
>
> Yours,
> Anya[9]

Four days later, she wrote:

> It's getting boring, the weather has turned bad and I forsee an early autumn. For days at a time I lie on the couch in my room, I read a bit, but write poems more often. I'm sending you one of them which seems to have a right to exist. I think money will be very tight for us this autumn. I don't have any and probably you don't either. You'll get a pittance from

Apollon. And in August we'll need several hundred rubles. It would be good if we got something for *Rosary*. All this worries me a great deal. Please, don't forget that the things are pawned. If possible, redeem them and give them to somebody to hide…

Kolya, write and send poems. Good luck, my dear.
I kiss you.

Yours,
Anya[10]

Whatever the *modus vivendi* the two had worked out in a marriage that was pulling apart like two separating strands of a cord, Anna was still concerned about how they could put order into their future. As yet there has been no final and irrevocable split. Anna vividly remembered that summer at Slepnevo:

"I wore a green malachite necklace and a cap made of fine lace in those days. In my room (which faced north) hung a large icon—Christ imprisoned. The narrow bed was so hard that I'd wake up in the night and sit for a long time to rest…A small portrait of Nicholas I hung over my bed, not like the Peterburg snobs did to achieve an almost exotic touch, but simply and genuinely as Onegin had done …I've forgotten whether there was a mirror in the room. The remnants of an old library…stood on the shelves."[11]

To Georgy Chulkov Akhmatova described the uneasy atmosphere of Slepnevo as the rumors of war rumbled in the distance: "It's quiet, boring, and a bit terrifying here. News from the outside world sounds absolutely improbable. I don't see anyone, and, in general, I am leading a quiet life. Recently I finally began to write a big piece ["At the Edge of the Sea"], but the quiet seems to be hindering me. And everything around me is faded, worn, and mainly, connected with a number of sad events."[12] It was the lull before the storm of the Great War to come.

One of the poems Akhmatova wrote, reclining on the couch in her bedroom, was the following:

<u>July 1914</u>

1

There's a charred smell. Four weeks has been burning
The dry peat in the depths of the marsh.
Now even the birds have stopped singing
And the aspen is trembling no more.

The sun lacks God's grace. Since Pascha
Not a shower has sprinkled the fields.
A one-legged wanderer passed by
And alone in the yard he said:

"Dreadful times are approaching. Soon crowded
With fresh graves will be the land here.
Expect earthquakes and plagues and hunger
And eclipses of heavenly spheres.

And our enemy for his amusement

Will not split up only our earth.

The Mother of God will spread over

Our great sorrows a snow-white cloth."

2

The sweet odor of juniper rises

And floats out of the burning woods.

The boys' wives moan over their soldiers,

A widow's cry rings through the streets.

The prayer services weren't sung for nothing.

The earth was longing for rain!

With red moisture warmly were sprinkled

The trampled-all-over fields.

Low, low is an empty sky hanging,

And now quiet the praying voice:

"They are wounding your most holy body,

For your mantle they're casting dice."

Anna Akhmatova
July, 1914[13]

The sense of dark foreboding is tangible in the prophetic ring of Akhmatova's voice. Before the war has even begun, she envisions the terrible destruction, the murder of the earth which she likens to Christ's body.

On August 1 (July 19 by the old Julian calendar), the Germans declared war on Russia. The following day, there was a massive demonstration near the Winter Palace with vast crowds of people carrying icons, flags and portraits of Tsar Nicholas II. Inside the Palace a religious service was held at which Nicholas invoked the blessing of a miraculous icon, the Vladimir Mother of God. When the Tsar and Tsarina made their appearance in the balcony overlooking the immense square, the enormous crowd that filled it knelt and sang the imperial anthem. Waves of patriotic demonstrations swept the country and young men signed up for the army by the hundreds of thousands. The streets of St. Petersburg, renamed Petrograd by Tsar Nicholas II, thundered with the booted feet of soldiers marching down Nevsky Prospect toward the Warsaw Station where crowds packed the platforms to wave them off.

Nikolai Gumilev could not resist this chance to put his valour to the test on the field of battle. He immediately joined the cavalry, enlisting in Empress Alexandra's Guards Regiment of Uhlans. Dressed in his new uniform, he set off for the front from the Tsarskoe Selo railroad station on August 4. There he and Akhmatova had run into Alexander Blok, who was also fulfilling his patriotic duty. The three dined together at the railway station and Akhmatova remembered: "Blok then was making the rounds of the recruits' families in order to offer them assistance. When the two of us were left alone, Kolya said, 'Can it really be that he will be sent to the front? That's the same thing as roasting nightingales.'"[14] Although he took no part in the fighting, Blok would serve near the front in Pinsk until March of 1917.

Anna visited Kolya while he was in training in the village of Navoloki, near Novgorod. Of his cavalry exercises she wrote: "…he told me that he was learning to ride all over again. I was surprised—he had been an excellent horseman, used to ride beautifully and could ride for a long time, for many miles. It turned out not to be the kind of riding required in the field. The arm absolutely had to be held like so, the leg like so, otherwise either you or your horse would get tired, etc. And whipping was an essential part of the exercise. The riding instructors would even whip a grand duke about the legs."[15] Gumilev would spend most of the war on horseback and, dreaming of nights alerts, would suddenly shout in his sleep: "Mount your horses!"[16]

As soldiers everywhere quickly realize, military life consists of endless days of excrutiating boredom interspersed with hours of intense activity, if not mortal terror. Writing from his camp near Novgorod, Kolya spoke of the difficulty of filling the long, empty hours when he wasn't training and waiting for the relief, like some "heavenly kingdom," that a call to action would bring.

> Dear Anichka, (Forgive my crooked handwriting, I have just been working with a bayonet on horseback—it's tiring.) Congratulations on your success. As far as I can calculate, it has an enormous significance and, perhaps, we will greet the New Year as before at the Dog. I have a very efficient orderly

and it seems he will manage to secure himself the tall, black horse called Chernozem. We are both healthy but terribly bored. Training happens twice a day for about one and a half to two hours. The rest of the time is completely free. But it is impossible to occupy oneself with anything such as writing—from visitors (volunteers and hunters) there is no retreat. The samovar doesn't leave the table, our chess sets are busy twenty-four hours a day and, in most cases, people are pleasant. But all the same it's depressing.

Only today we decided to shut ourselves away. I don't know whether it will help. However, everyone shares our boredom and dreams of the march as of the heavenly kingdom. I already feel much and very much want to work. I don't know whether I'll be able to.

I firmly kiss you, mama, Lev and everyone.

Yours, Kolya[17]

Soon after this, Gumilev was posted to the Polish front and wrote to Anna on her return to Tsarkoe Selo in the late summer of 1914:

My dear Anichka, I am already in the real army, but we are not fighting yet and it's not known when we will begin. Still we have to wait, but now with rifle in hand and sabre drawn. And I am beginning to feel that I am a suitable husband for a woman who "gathered French bullets, like we gathered mushrooms and bilberries" [lines from Akhmatova's "At the Edge of the Sea"]. This quote compels me to remind you of your promise to quickly write down your poem and send it to me. It's true, I am homesick for it. I wrote a verse, I'm sending it to you. Sell it or read it to somebody, as you wish. I have lost my critical abilities here and don't know whether it's good or bad...

I am hale and healthy: all the time in the fresh air (and the weather is beautiful, it's warm), I ride horseback and at night sleep like the dead.

They are carrying out not a few wounded men and the wounds are so strange: they are wounded not in the chest, not in the head, as described in novels, but in the face, the arms, the legs. A bullet went through the saddle under one of our uhlans, just at the moment when he had risen up in a trot. One second before or after and he would have been wounded.

Now by chance we are standing in such a place from which it is easy to write. But soon we'll have to begin to cross over and then it will be more difficult to write. But you absolutely don't need to worry if there is no information about me. Three volunteers know your address and if anything happens to me, they will write to you immediately. So that the lack of letters will only mean that I am on the march, healthy, but there is no way to write. Of course, when it is possible, I will write.

I kiss you, my dear Anichka and also mama, Lev and everybody...

Your Kolya[18]

To Mikhail Lozinsky, he was more explicit about the joys and excitements of war. In the following letter, written November 1, 1914, he tells of taking part in a major attack on a Lithuanian town. It is obvious how stimulated, even inebriated Gumilev could become by the sights and sounds of the battlefield.

Dear Mikhail Leonidovich, I am writing to you already as a veteran, one who has been many times on reconaissance, many times under fire and now is resting in a stinking tearoom. All that you read about the battles around Vladislovo [now Kudirkos-Naumiestis, east of Kaliningrad] and the latest encounters I have seen with my own eyes and took part in all of them with all my strength. I served in the firing upon Vladislovo, went on the attack (alas, repulsed by weapons fire), froze standing watch at night, drank myself sick with plum brandy, stuffed myself with chicken, goose and pig meat while patrolling the movement of a detachment of Germans.

Generally speaking, I can say that this is the best time of my life. It reminds me a bit of my Abyssinian escapades but is less lyrical and excites me much more. To be under fire almost every day, to hear the screech of shrapnel, the clicking of rifles aimed at you—I think such is the enjoyment an inveterate drunkard experiences before a bottle of very old, strong cognac. However, a reaction sets in, a minute of silence—at the same time a moment of exhaustion and boredom.

I now know that success depends not on the soldiers—soldiers are the same everywhere. But only in the strategic calculations. So I would suggest a general and energetic attack, which alone would lift the spirit of the army. With an attack, all are heroes, with a retreat, all are corpses—that applies to us and to the Germans...But as it applies to pillaging, rout...really a soldier is not a member of the Army of Salvation and if you re-read Schiller's "Camp Wallenstein" you will understand this psychology."19

Gumilev sent his regards to "Master Shileiko," adding: "Anya told me that Shileiko has poems about me. Could you send them." Gumilev, one of their own in the midst of military action, seems to have become a popular subject for his fellow Petersburg poets.

Unlike Kolya, Anna was not carried away by the fever of patriotism that swept Russia with its entry into the war. Her trepidation over what awaited the Russian people cast a gloomy shadow over the future. The last thing she expected was triumph, glory and peace. Her anxiety about Gumilev's safety, knowing the risks to which he would expose himself, occupied her thoughts. The absence of letters or news of the army's movements was cause for constant worry. In September, 1914, she wrote this poem, which quickly became popular and was widely published in collections of patriotic poetry.

Frances Laird

Consolation

> There Michael the Archangel
> Enlisted him in his hosts.
> —N. Gumilev

You will not receive news from him anymore,

You will not hear about him again.

In grieving Poland, embraced in fire,

You will not find his grave.

So let your soul become quiet, at peace.

He'll be one of the lost no more.

He is now a new warrior in God's fighting force,

For him you must not mourn.

It is sinful to weep and sinful to pine

In your dear, native home.

Just think, you can raise your prayers up high

To an intercessor of your own.

Anna Akhmatova
September, 1914, Tsarskoe Selo[20]

Already Anna was trying on a widow's weeds, tentatively accustoming herself to the disappearance of Kolya from her life with his death in battle, his burial in an unmarked grave. With the ironic play of fate, he survived the Great War untouched, but Kolya's end finally did come with bullets and an unmarked grave.

Frances Laird

Chapter X
Love and War

Nikolai Gumilev was not swallowed up in the fiery jaws of war as Akhmatova had feared. In fact, with the Polish front so near, he often returned to Petrograd to attend to his literary projects, to visit his wife, his son and his friends and to cultivate his current *amoureuse*. In December, 1914, when Anna again saw him off to the front in Vilnius, a religious festival was being celebrated in the town. As an act of penitence, it was the custom for the townspeople to crawl to the icon of the saint they were venerating and the street outside her hotel window was filled with people inching along the cobbled street on their knees.[1] It was a strange and moving spectacle. She went on alone to Kiev to visit her mother, before returning to Tsarskoe Selo.

The artistic and cultural life of Petrograd continued despite the war. Now poetry readings were held to raise funds for the wounded. In January, 1915, Nikolai Gumilev was awarded the Russian military's highest honor, the St. George Cross for bravery. Because he had to remain at the front, Akhmatova read Gumilev's poems at a special ceremony held by the Duma in the Parliament building. When Kolya returned on leave to Petrograd, a celebration was held for him at the Stray Dog. In the crowded cellar with its gaudily painted walls and air blue with cigarette smoke, glasses and crockery clinked festively while outside a snowstorm howled. Gumilev read his poems to a warm and sympathetic audience of fellow poets and friends. It was a very special evening, the last one he and Akhmatova would spend together at the Dog, for after Kolya had returned to the Polish front, the Stray Dog was closed down by the government, supposedly in the interests of military censorship.

By that time, as evident in a letter to Lozinsky written January 2, 1915, Gumilev's elation with the war was subsiding. War for him now is "the sewage disposal of Europe." And he was annoyed that poets like Shileiko, safely distant from the battlefield, were using his experiences to write their own poems.

> Dear Mikhail Leonidovich…You…await from me the words of a wise soldier. I will speak frankly: in my life there are three things of merit—my poems, my journeys and this war. Of them everyone exaggerates with annoying persistence the last, which I value the least of all…I am not speaking about the poems, they are not very good and I am praised for them more than I deserve. I am annoyed about Africa. When half a year ago I returned from [Abyssinia], nobody had the patience to listen to my impressions and adventures. So really it's true, all that I thought out alone and for myself alone, the neighing of the zebras at night, crossing rivers filled with crocodiles, the fights and reconciliations, the bearish leaders in the middle of the desert, the majestic holy man who had never seen white men in his African Vatican, all this is much more significant than those works on the sewage disposal of Europe in which now millions of the ordinary men in the street are involved, and I among them. And Master Shileiko has also forgotten about my "sweet-smelling legend." What labors do I manage, what chains do I bear? True, he wrote those poems for himself and saves them till the time when the last manifesto will be published calling forth him alone.
>
> Forgive me my grumbling. We are now having our weekly rest period and, as there is no prospect of "epic tomorrows," I really have the blues. The only hope that supports me is that a better day of my life is approaching, a day when the guard cavalry along with the

troops of England and France will enter Berlin. Probably they will give out parade uniforms to everyone and the whole enormous city will be like a living album of lithography. Imagine the whole expanse of Fredrickstrasse lined with hussars, cuirassiers, sepoys, Senegalese, Canadians, Kazaks, their varicolored full dress uniforms with decorations of the whole world, their happy faces, white, black, yellow, brown...Into the head of no Hoffman could come what was playing out then in taverns, coffeehouses and the back streets of his good city of Berlin.

In my regiment, my own George [St George medal] sent to me is waiting. It is number 134060...[2]

On his return to the front, Gumilev plunged back into the war. Despite his disillusionment with the ineptitude of Russia's military leaders, the stupidity and vast waste of human life and material, the terrible conditions in muddy, wet, stinking, lice-ridden trenches, Gumilev kept his doubts hidden and continued to play the warrior-hero. As one friend wrote:

...He accepted the war with complete simplicity, with a straightforward zeal...His patriotism was as unlimited as his religious creed was unclouded. I didn't see another man to whom the nature of doubt would have been more foreign...His mind, dogmatic and obstinate, knew no duality...As earlier in the African bush, finally Gumilev with his rifle moved into the wide spaces to meet the unknown, to meet danger. His experience of the war was easy, enthusiastic. A heroic act was joyful.[3]

But Gumilev sometimes went beyond the extremes of personal courage on the battlefield. At times his attitude to death was one of outright defiance. To stand teetering upon the thin line separating life and death while cheekily challenging fate seemed to nourish and enliven his creative powers. Before the horrified eyes of his men, he could flaunt his life boldly, even recklessly on the battlefield. As one friend observed:

> In the World War he was such a fiery and intrepid paladin, meeting danger face to face. His comrades in the cavalry talked a great deal about him. In the most terrible moments, when all around him was lost, he was restrained and calm, as if taking the measure of death with his prominent grey eyes.
>
> It so happened that his squadron was spread out in trenches. And the horsemen served behind the infantry. The enemy trenches came close together with ours. Gumilev would stand up on the banks of the breastwork from which the Germans and Russians were throwing grenades back and forth and, without considering that he was a living target, he would look out into the greening distance with eager eyes. There in a veil of smoke stood trees made leafless from the shooting, barely visible roofs torn apart by the shells, a wounded belltower, a river, barely glimmering, floating by. Gumilev is from the waist up under the steely-blue gunbarrels. They shoot at him. The steel bees whistle around his very head...His comrades said: "He is testing fate." Others thought: "He is testing his nerves for some secret reason." And he doesn't retreat from his dangerous post until the soldiers grab him and drag him down below.
>
> In cavalry attacks he was always in the front ranks...He wrote from the front: "I know death is not here—not on the field of battle. Like a thief, it lies in wait for me, unexpectedly, suddenly. I see it far off in the miserly, dreary dawn, not with the red point of an unending line—not with the inspiring chord of the heroic deed." This half-prose, half-poetry, too, was prophetic...[4]

Gumilev walked away from these hair-raising stunts without a scratch. The poet/wanderer in the realms of fantasy and dream, effete inhabitant of the world of art, whose militancy had only been aroused before in the defence of poetry, plunged into the chaos, muck and terror of warfare. Was he trying to plumb the depths of himself and come to some understanding of his own nature, under enemy fire pushing the boundaries of his nerve to the ultimate point? Was he hardening and honing the blade edge of his courage for some future challenge? Or was he flaunting his disdain for death in a self-dramatizing display to impress his fellow officers and men? One friend had another answer: "Heroism seemed to him the height of spirituality. He played with death as he played with love. He had tried to drown himself—he didn't drown. He had opened up his veins, so that the blood would flow—and remained alive...He looked at death face to face and survived."[5]

But, always the writer, Gumilev used the raw material of his battlefield experiences in columns for a Petrograd newspaper, *The Birzhev Gazette*.[6] As reports from a special correspondent, his "Notes of a Cavalryman" appeared from February, 1915, to January, 1916. During that time, Gumilev's cavalry division ranged over an area extending from Radom, south of Warsaw, north into Lithuania, then down into Belorussia to Luninets, south of Minsk.

To his friends and fellow soldiers, Gumilev may have seemed exceptionally courageous. But seldom could he have been reckless and foolhardy and come out of the war whole. For he was ordered to go out on patrol under fire, to reconnoitre villages with German snipers hidden in huts and haystacks, to pass through dark forests where the enemy might lurk behind any tree, to ride for miles through the night to the next battle front, coated with ice and exhausted to the point of falling asleep in the saddle. Hunger and fatigue were constant and a warm place with a steaming samovar where he could spend the night was a rare luxury only too likely to be interrupted by the sudden command to take the saddle again on an important mission. Gumilev described his entry into Eastern Prussia:

> Like a huge sledge-hammer the German cannons fired away with the Russian salvos answering them. Somewhere, with convincing rapidity in its childish and strange language, a machine gun babbled incomprehensibly. An enemy airplane, like a hawk above quail hiding in the grass, hung over our patrol and then began slowly to sink into the south. I saw through my binoculars its black cross.
> This day will always remain sacred in my memory. I was on patrol and for the first time in the war I felt how the will exerts itself to the point of becoming, in a physical sense, turned into stone. This happens when it is necessary for one to go into the forest where the enemy line may lie, to gallop along the ploughed ground which prevents the possibility of a quick escape, toward a moving column in order to find out whether it is firing on you. And on the evening of that day, a clear, gentle evening, for the first time I heard beyond the scanty coppice the growing roar "Hurrah" with which V. was taken. The fiery bird of victory on that day lightly touched me with its enormous wing."[7]

In the encounter that won him his second St. George Cross for bravery, Gumilev was ordered to reconnoitre a near-by village where German scouts had been spotted. As clouds obscured the moon, Gumilev and another soldier sneaked into the village to try to capture the German scouts alive. They crept stealthily along a canal to the village fence, then darted from the corner of one house to the next. It reminded Gumilev of playing hide and seek in summer with the village girls, the same bated breath, the same happy awareness of danger, the same instictive knowledge of how to sneak along and hide oneself. The moon came out and at the far edge of the village, he spotted the enemy trenches and the outline of an enemy soldier who, gazing at him, whistled quietly.

It was the moment of truth. "There was just one thought, alive and powerful, like passion, like fury, like ecstasy. It will be him or me! He indecisively raised his rifle. I knew that he must not shoot at me, so many of the enemy were close by. I flung myself forward with drawn bayonet. An instant passed and before me there was no one. Perhaps the enemy soldier had sat down on the ground or crawled away. I stopped and began to look around. Something grew blacker. I drew closer and touched it with the bayonet. No—it was a log." Suddenly there was a shot and a bullet whistled by, uncomfortably close to his face. Then firing broke out from the enemy trenches. Gumilev and his comrade managed to make it safely back to their detachment. In a peasant's hut they compared notes and ate bread with salt while the officer wrote up the dispatch. Outside the wind had blown the clouds away and the round, red moon made everything bright, ending their heroic forays for that night.[8]

With his columns Gumilev wanted to convey to the reader at home in Petrograd some sense of the cavalryman's life, from the torture of waiting for an impending attack to the joy of a glass of hot tea. His most practical bit of advice for keeping warm: never lie down to sleep wearing your overcoat, but lay it over you like a blanket. Occasionally in the tumult of war he paused to drink in the beauty of the skies and countryside around him.

In stanzas nine, ten and eleven of "Iambic Pentameters," Gumilev expresses the glorification of war as a stage for heroic acts:

> And in the roaring of the human throng,
> In the rumble of the heavy cannons passing,
> In battle trumpets call, shrill and incessant,
> All at once I heard destiny's song.
> And where the others ran, I set out running,
> Saying humbly to myself: "Wake up, wake up!"
>
> Loudly soldiers sang and their songs' words
> Were inarticulate but my heart seized them.
> "The grave is just a grave—men, forward, faster!
> For us the sweet, fresh grass will be our couch,
> Green leaves will be the curtains hanging round,
> Our ally—the archangelic powers."
>
> This song flowed on, enticing and so sweet
> That I set out and they accepted me
> And gave to me a rifle and a steed,
> And fields filled with the foe, strong and mighty,
> Bombs that droned their threat and bullets sighing
> And skies with glowing clouds, shot through with lightening.[9]

Frances Laird

Summoned forth by destiny, Gumilev found the attraction of war irresistable. He seemed not unduly shocked or disillusioned by what he found there, the chaotic jumble of mud and broken bodies, the lack of rifles, the brutal discipline, the squandered waste of human lives in the trenches. In his reference to "the archangelic powers," he points to the lofty spiritual signficance of war, a joint effort of God and man. It is clear in the next stanza of "Iambic Pentameters" that Gumilev believed God to be situated firmly in his own camp.

> And with such happiness my soul took fire
> From then on, filled with gaiety and cheer,
> With wisdom and with clarity it chatted,
> Conversing about God with the stars.
> It heard God's voice in the alarms of battle
> And it called God's its own roads and its pathways.

Under the constant threat of sudden death, Gumilev felt thrust closer to God, detecting His voice in the call to battle and feeling His directing hand upon his soul. That he never believed man could take the place of God, making God irrelevant, contradicts the view that Gumilev pictured himself as a Nietzschean Superman. Gumilev's religious beliefs lay well within the traditions of Russian Orthodoxy.

Back in Petrograd, in April of 1915, a benefit poetry reading was held at which Akhmatova appeared along with Mandelstam, Blok and

Swan Songs
Akhmatova and Gumilev

Kuzmin. But lung problems began to plague both Akhmatova and Gumilev. Kolya was sent back from the front and confined to a clinic in Moscow for three months for the treatment of severe bronchitis. Anna, too, suffered from bronchitis exacerbated by the effects of tuberculosis, the illness that had ravaged her family.

As for their marriage, stanzas five, six and seven from "Iambic Pentameters" illuminate the point to which it had come by the summer of 1915.

> You for whom I seached through the Levant for
> A royal mantle's undecaying purple,
> I lost you in the game, as Damayatin
> At one time lost in play the crazy Nal.
> The dice flew out with ringing sound like steel,
> Down dropped the dice and then—a sadness fell.
>
> You said to me pensively, severely:
> "Once I believed and I loved much too dearly.
> Not loving nor believing, I will go
> To stand before the face of God All-seeing.
> In this I may destroy myself somehow
> But I renounce you now forevermore."
>
> I wasn't brave enough to kiss your hair or
> To even press your cold and slender hands.

> Tormenting, terrible was every sound
> And I repelled my own self, like a spider.
> You left dressed in a dark and simple gown,
> A figure from an ancient Crucifixion.

Gumilev recognized that their marriage may have reached a point of no return. His "game of love" had undermined their irreplaceable relationship. Like Damayatin, a character from an Indian folktale, he had gambled away Anna in a game of chance. The end comes without emotional fireworks and high drama, only her stern declaration that she had loved him too much and trusted him too absolutely. Now disillusioned, she will let the God before whom she spoke her marriage vows be the final judge of her actions. Gumilev, overcome with pain and self-loathing, idealizes Akhmatova as Mary standing beneath the Cross, an image taken from an icon of the Crucifixion. By placing Anna on this high spiritual plane, he is again aestheticizing her rejection of him and distancing himself from pain and his responsibility for this rupture. (Years later, in Poem X of *Requiem,* Akhmatova, lamenting her imprisoned son, chose for herself the image of the suffering Mother of God standing beneath the Cross.)

Many artists were eager to capture Akhmatova's striking appearance in stone or on canvas. That winter she had posed for Natan Altman in his studio in rooms opposite the Winter Palace. When she grew bored by the interminable hours of sitting, they would crawl out the window to get a breath of fresh air, look out over the snowy Neva, then creep along the ledge to visit friends in a neighboring flat. Sometimes Osip Mandelstam would drop in for a visit. In later years the two would giggle about the Italian artist, Grandi, who had lived next door and, viewing the nearly-finished portrait, had "…uttered an immortal phrase that Mandelstam like to repeat: 'there will be a big loaf.' (he evidently meant to say *laugh).*"[10]

In Altman's painting, Akhmatova, in an ink-blue silk dress with a deep, ivory neckline, a saffron-yellow shawl falling from her shoulders, sits serenely in an armchair. Her body, set diagonally with her knees sharply angled up, conveys a sense of awkward grace. Her dark hair is drawn back severely and her bangs fall over her forehead above the broken line of her nose. Behind her a window opens out upon a landscape of cube-like shapes. Natan Altman's painting was first shown in 1915 at an exhibition organized by the World of Art. Because of Altman's innovative modern style, it was a groundbreaking artistic as well as literary event in St. Petersburg. This portrait of Akhmatova became the manifesto of a new mini-movement, called the "Punin group," after the art critic, Nikolai Punin (who would become Akhmatova's third husband). "This portrait rejected the traditions of Impressionism and introduced the problem of Constructivist forms," Punin wrote.[11] Although Altman refused to be labeled a "Cubist," his work showed an interest in inherent structural and formal qualities.

Kornei Chukovsky, who first met Akhmatova in 1915, was impressed by her air of dignity, which he attributed to her upbringing in Tsarskoe Selo.

At times, especially among guests, among strangers, she behaved with an intentionally regal air, like an elegant woman of the world. That's when you sensed within her that polish by which we native Petersburgians unmistakably recognize people raised in Tsarskoe Selo. I always felt that imprint in her voice, manner and gestures...The signs of this rare type of person are a strong sensitivity to music, poetry, and art, refined taste, an irreproachable correctness of carefully polished speech, extreme (slightly cold) politeness regarding strangers, and a total absence of passionate, strong, unrestrained gestures typical of a vulgar lack of control. Akhmatova had absorbed all these Tsarskoe Selo qualities.[12]

With the failure of her marriage, Anna turned to deepening other friendships. In 1914, Akhmatova had met a young officer, Boris Anrep, at Nikolai Nedobrovo's apartment in Tsarskoe Selo. Anrep recalled: "Nedobrovo had already written me about her; on our first meeting I was captivated by her charm. She was an intriguing woman capable of subtle and astute observations. More that that, she wrote beautiful, poignant poetry. Nedobrovo thought her to be the best poet of the time."[13] When on leave, Anrep would often visit Nedobrovo and Akhmatova. His interest in her soon turned to adoration.

The parks of Tsarskoe Selo and the streets of Petrograd provided the background for their developing relationship traced in the poems she wrote that spring and summer of 1915. They would meet in restaurants or go sleighing, but always Anrep begged her to recite her poems. "She would smile and chant the words softly. Often we sat silent, listening to the sounds around us. During one of our meetings that year, I spoke of my lack of faith and of the futility of religious hope. Anna strongly reproached me, saying that the key to happiness lay in faith: 'One cannot live without faith.'"[14]

This poem, written that spring of 1915, is one of several that spoke of this new love.

> Broad and yellow is evening light,
> Tender is the April coolness.
> Though by many years you're late,
> I'm glad that you've come despite this.
>
> Sit down closer here by me
> And gaze at me with eyes that are cheerful.
> The dark blue notebook I have here
> Is filled with all my poems of childhood.
>
> Forgive me that I've lived to grieve
> And was not filled with joy by sunshine.
> Forgive me for the fact that I
> Mistook for you so many others.
>
> Anna Akhmatova
Spring 1915, Tsarskoe Selo[15]

Frances Laird

    The poet welcomes the one for whom she had long been waiting, to whom she will allow an intimate look into her past in the poems she had written as a child. Clearly Akhmatova was opening herself up to this new relationship and expected much from it. Anrep left with her a copy of his long poem, *Fiza*, which she sewed into a silk purse like a sacred relic.

    Nikolai Nedobrovo, another hopeful admirer, feared that Akhmatova loved Anrep in a way that she could never love him. Akhmatova, who held a deep affection for Nedobrovo, dedicated to him a moving poem about the subtle and ungovernable nature of human emotions.

> There is in people's closeness hid a sacred line.
> Infatuated love and passion cannot cross it—
> Although in awful quietness lips may be joined
> And hearts break into pieces out of loving.
>
> And friendship will be powerless, and years
> Of happiness, fiery and exalted,
> When still the soul is free, a stranger yet
> To sensual delight's slow, sweet exhaustion.
>
> But crazy are the ones who strive to reach this line
> And those attaining it are then struck down by
> A yearning anguish…Now you can see why

Swan Songs
Akhmatova and Gumilev

> Beneath your hand my heart's not throbbing.
>
> Anna Akhmatova
>
> May, 1915, St. Petersburg[16]

Kolya, released from the clinic, returned to Tsarskoe Selo, where he continued his various literary activities. When Makovsky asked him to write a play for marionettes, Gumilev leaped into the project with his usual enthusiasm and produced "The Child of Allah." Because of the war, it was never produced, though it was later published in *Apollon*. In July, Gumilev left again for the Polish front.

Anna had been ill with tuberculosis and her health did not improve at Slepnevo, where she went in June. In the countryside, cut off from Anrep, Nedobrovo and her other friends, she wrote five poems, four of which were addressed to Boris Anrep. In one, Akhmatova imagines for herself a very different life as a simple, village girl.

> Somewhere there is a simple life and world,
> Transparent, filled with kindness, cheerful...
> Across a fence there, talking with a girl,
> At dusk a neighbor leans and only bees are hearing
> Those tenderest of any words.
>
> But we live solemnly, with difficulty
> And carry out our bitter meetings' rites,

> When reckless wind sweeps down all of a sudden
> To tear away our speech just as it starts—
>
> Yet for nothing would we change this splendid granite
> City of misfortune and renown,
> The shining ice of its broad river's run,
> Its gardens, gloomy and bereft of sun,
> And the Muse's voice heard only barely.
>
> Anna Akhmatova
June 23, 1915, Slepnevo[17]

Akhmatova was fated to live in the fierce and pitiless "granite city," her meetings with her lover a sacred ritual carried out against its backdrop. Here the forces of nature and history conspired to thwart communication, whether between lovers or on a higher artistic level. Yet she would choose to live nowhere else but in this ominous and magnificent city of Peter where her Muse's voice comes as a barely audible whisper.

The condition of her lungs continued to deteriorate and Anna returned to Tsarskoe Selo in mid-July with her doctor's insistence that she spend hours everyday in bed. But despite her fragile health, Anna was swept up in family troubles when her father fell gravely ill. She helped his mistress care for him until his death on August 25. Anna's lingering illness and the death of her father took its toll, for she wrote only two more poems that year. Not surprisingly, the theme of death was central. In October, she spent three weeks in Huvinkka, a sanitorium in Finland, where she wrote a poem about visiting white death along the road to darkness. Weak and unable to write, she feared that in the face of death her Muse had abandoned her, fleeing down an "autumnal, steep, narrow road." Akhmatova was confined to bed throughout that winter.

Kolya had visited her at the sanitarium, but when Anna returned to the Gumilev house in Tsarskoe Selo, he remained in Petrograd. He was waiting for permission to transfer to Her Majesty's Alexandriisky Hussars, which eventually came through in March, 1916. He was delighted with the dazzling new uniform with its gold buttons and braids that reminded him of Pushkin's.

Perhaps as a result of his war experiences, Gumilev became increasingly drawn to religion, visiting churches, attending services and reading theological works. Akhmatova may have had something to do with encouraging this, as she recalled: "In 1916, when I was regretting that everything had turned out so strangely, he said, 'No, you taught me to believe in God and to love Russia.'"[18] But this new preoccupation with Russian Orthodoxy put no crimp in his love chases. At a clinic in Tsarskoe Selo, he met Anna Englehardt, a nurse, who would one day become his second wife.

Finally breaking away from his Symbolist past, Gumilev wrote with new immediacy, simplicity of expression and authenticity of emotion about himself.

Frances Laird

Childhood

As a child, I loved the meadows
That lay honey-scented and vast,
The dry grasses and the copses
And the bulls horns in the grass.

Every dusty bush by the roadside
Cried to me: "Let's have some fun.
If you walk around me carefully
You will know just who I am."

But the untamed wind of autumn
As it roared by stopped our play.
Still more blissful did my heart beat.
I believed that I would die

Not alone—with my companions,
With the burdock and colt's-foot,
And away beyond far heavens
I'd wonder about all of it.

I love the ventures of thundery
Military fun for this—
That people's blood is not holier

>   Than the emerald juice of grass.
>
>   Nikolai Gumilev
>   March, 1916[19]

The conquistador/poet has vanished without a trace, to be replaced by the boy he once was, a true native of the natural world who lived with the plants and trees as his playmates. It is not alone, but among these friendly roadside weeds that he envisions his death will come. Again sounds Gumilev's strangely prophetic foreseeing of his end.

The final stanza of "Childhood" offers another insight into Gumilev's passion for "military fun," when he claims that human blood and the juice of grass are equally sacred in his eyes. He sees all earthly life bound up in one mystical, dynamic system of birth and death, blooming and withering, thriving and perishing. Man is one with nature and cannot be arbitrarily separated from it. Perhaps it was on the battlefield, where living and dying went on at a heightened, accelerated rate, that Gumilev felt transported into the unceasing flow of life into death.

Slowly recovering from tuberculosis at home, Anna lacked the strength to do more than receive a few visitors. A notable one that Christmas was the "peasant poet," Sergei Esenin, who wore his blonde hair in long curls and affected his own exotic version of peasant dress, a full-sleeved, silk blouse and high, shiny leather boots. Esenin had received little education and, taking his themes from rural and village life, aimed his appeal to the mass of ordinary Russians.

The brilliant young Moscow poet, Marina Tsvetaeva, read her poetry in one of the private literary salons. Tsvetaeva, who had written a cycle of poems entitled "To Akhmatova," the first opening with: "Oh, muse of weeping, most beautiful of muses!" had longed to meet Akhmatova and was bitterly disappointed at her absence.

That winter Nikolai Gumilev was often away at the front, but he did make an appearance at the Comedian's Halt, the cabaret that had replaced the Stray Dog. Nikolai Otsup recalled his reading:

He reads the poems with difficulty, as if he doesn't have enough air. A few of the vowels he pronounces quite inarticulately, a little through his nose, and his whole voice sounds sure and loud.
  They applaud Gumilev. He walks down from the stage into the public and stands before the table of a lady who is calling to him. The lady says something in a quiet voice, indicating with her eyes A. Tolmachev, one of the poets associated with Igor Severyanin. She evidently is asking Gumilev, the master of ceremonies that evening, to invite Tolmachev to read his poems. Gumalev answers with a voice purposely loud so that it is heard by Tolmachev: 'I cannot allow, when I am master of ceremonies, the appearance of a Futurist.'"[20]

As Anna lived quietly, her growing love for Boris Anrep had taken hold upon her imagination and is reflected in the lyrical poems she wrote that spring. Anrep had given her a carved wooden cross he had found in a ruined church in Galicia, and with it a poem he had written:

> I lost my words, I didn't say my pledge
> I stretched my hands to a defenseless girl

> To save her from a crucifix,
> A token of soul I'd given her.[21]

When Akhmatova later copied Anrep's poem into an album of poems dedicated to her, her version show some interesting changes:

> I quite forgot the words and didn't make a promise;
> Along the sickly girl, I, stupid, lay my hands
> To save her from the cross's sorcery and torment
> Which I, as token of our meeting, gave to her.
>
> Boris Anrep
> February 13, 1916[22]

In Anrep's version, the poet found himself expected to make some kind of vow to the girl, but he had failed to do so. In her version, Akhmatova has the poet describe himself as "stupid" for this omission. He spreads his hands over the girl's body in the attempt to protect her from the power of the crucifix, that is, the fascination with suffering and self-sacrifice. Anrep sees the wooden crucifix as respresenting his soul, while Akhmatova calls it a token of their meeting. Long after the love affair was over, Akhmatova could put her final stamp upon it. Although Anrep didn't date the poem, Akhmatova did—February 13, 1916.

This date marks both an emotionally charged event and a sudden change in their relationship. Anrep was being sent to London for six weeks on official military business. Before leaving on February 13, he was invited by Nikolai Nedobrovo to his elegant apartment to hear a reading of *Judith,* a play Nedobrovo had just finished writing. Nedobrovo greeted Anrep with his usual warmth, yet Anrep sensed a tension between them. Akhmatova was seated on a small sofa, watching them with a smile. As Anrep sat down beside her, he felt the indescribable pain and agitation he always experienced in her presence. Akhmatova had been bequeathed by her grandmother a mourning band coated with black enamel and set with a small diamond. Anna always wore the ring, "...bestowed upon her by the moon," believing it held a special power.[23] As Nedobrovo, seated at an antique Italian Renaissance desk, began to read his tragic drama, Anrep recalled:

...Sometimes I looked at the profile of Anna Andreevna and saw her gazing somewhere into the distance. I tried to concentrate. The measured verse filled my ears like the sound of train wheels. I closed my eyes and placed my hand on the seat of the sofa. Suddenly I felt something in my hand: the black ring. 'Take it,' Anna whispered. I wanted to say something. My heart began to pound and I looked questioningly at her face. Silently, she gazed again into the distance. I squeezed my hand into a fist as Nedobrovo continued to read.[24]

This incident was the subject of two poems by Akhmatova, "Like an angel stirring up the water..." written shortly after, and "The Tale of the Black Ring," which was not completed until 1936. The day before Anrep left for London, Anna sent him a copy of *Evening,* with the inscription: "To Boris Anrep—One hope fewer now beguiles me,/But one more song I have for singing. Anna Akhmatova, Tsarskoe Selo, 13 February 1916."[25] (A variant of this line appears in "I have stopped smiling..." written in April, 1915.) She may have sensed already that their love affair would be over with his departure.

But her poems of that spring of 1916 still centered on her love for Anrep. In March, she wrote "Little Song," a short acrostic poem of ten lines, each beginning with a letter of Anrep's name. As the months passed and spring grew into summer with no letter or sign of Anrep's return, Akhmatova's poems begin to change. In Slepnevo, she wrote "Like a white stone in the depths of a well..." about the memory of happiness and suffering that lay within her. As the gods had transformed people into objects, her beloved had been changed into a stone/memory that was visible by gazing deep into the well of her eyes.

Waiting expectantly to hear from Anrep, Anna must have been brooding upon her role in the failure of the marriage. In a poem written then, she imagines the scene of a husband's sudden entrance into the house where his conscience-stricken wife meets him.

> Ah! it is you again. Not as the boy in love, but
> The husband, stern, inflexible and overbearing.
> You come into this house and fix me with your stare,
> In pre-storm quiet is my spirit struck with fear.
> What have I done to you, once more you ask me,
> The one bestowed on me by love and fate forever.

Frances Laird

> I have betrayed you. And all that you must repeat—
> Oh, if only sometime you would tire of it!
> So speaks a dead man who disturbs his killer's slumber,
> So does Death's Angel wait close by the fateful bedside.
> Forgive me now. The Lord has taught us to forgive.
> My flesh is languishing, with sorrow it is sick.
> And yet now my freed spirit peacefully is resting.
> I remember just a garden, bare, autumnal, tender,
> And crying calls of flying cranes and black-soiled fields,
> Oh, how with you the earth was sweet delight to me!
>
> Anna Akhmatova
July, 1916, Slepnevo[26]

The psychological acuteness and complexity of the nineteenth century Russian novel that Osip Mandestam saw in Akhmatova's poetry is evident in this brief, concentrated drama. The husband returns from his wanderings, powerful, severe, accusatory. But it is not *his* infidelity that is central, but that of the woman who has betrayed him, chosen for her by love and by fate. His accusations are inescapable judgements, like the ghost that haunts the dreams of the murderer or the Angel of Death that hangs over the bed of a dying person. She begs him to forgive her. In the closing lines, the poet looks back to a time when they stood together looking out over the bare, black fields of Slepnevo as a wedge of cranes swept over the autumnal sky. In an anguished exclamation, she realizes that her joy in the earth was bound up with him.

In August, 1916, Gumilev returned to Petrograd where, hoping to be made an officer, he prepared to sit for an examination on military fortifications. Doubtless he visited Anna and his family in Tsarskoe Selo. But Gumilev failed the examination and, in October, he returned to his military duties. Anna went by train to visit her mother and brother at Pesochnaya Bay, near Sebastapol. Having rented a room for herself, she stayed on that fall and winter to escape the damp, piercing cold of Petrograd and speed her recovery from tuberculosis. The poems Akhmatova wrote then speak of loss and betrayal, of disappointment and the pangs of conscience, of sacrifice and repentence, of the stony silence of her Muse, all themes that sprang from her disappointed love for Boris Anrep. In one that begins "When in the dreariest of capitals…," she speaks of the cross he had given her:

> I only took the cross with me,
> Your gift that day of your betrayal,—
> So wormwood on the steppes would bloom,
> And blowing winds would sing like sirens.
>
> And there upon the empty wall
> It saves me from my bitter ravings.
> And nothing that I can recall

> Is awful—even that last evening.
>
> Anna Akhmatova
>
> August 1916, Pesochnaya Bay[27]

Nikolai Nedobrovo, also seriously ill with tuberculosis, was living in Bakhchisary, a town northeast of Sebastapol. In love with Akhmatova himself and having watched the blossoming of her relationship with Anrep, he could now offer her welcome consolation. The two friends had long, nostalgic conversations about Tsarskoe Selo and its parks. Akhmatova dedicated two poems about the imperial gardens to Nedobrovo. In "A Tsarskoe Selo Statue," she wrote of the bronze figure of a slender, graceful young girl seated on a rock, with her broken water jar. Akhmatova envies her for the delight she gives Nedobrovo. "And how could I forgive her that—/The pleasure of your loving praises…/Just look, she's happy being sad/This one who is so smartly naked."[28] The autumnal images in both poems reflect not only the time of year, but the approach of parting and death. These hours with Nedobrovo, exchanging memories in the paradisical setting of Bakhchisaray, would mark the end of this long, close relationship of mutual admiration.

> Once more drowsiness has given me
> Our last starry paradise,
> City of pure running fountains—
> Golden-toned Bakhchisaray.

Swan Songs
Akhmatova and Gumilev

There beyond the motley fences,
By waters lying deep in thought,
With joy and comfort we remembered
The gardens of Tsarskoe Selo.

All at once we recognized it,
Catherine's eagle—there it was!
It flew down into the valley
From the magnificent bronze gates.

So that the song of painful parting
Long in our memory would live,
Dusky autumn in her skirt hem
Brought a heap of scarlet leaves

And scattered them upon the stair steps
Where you and I said our farewells,
And into the realm of shadows
From there you, my comfort, went.

                          Anna Akhmatova
                          Autumn 1916, Sebastapol[29]

Meanwhile, Gumilev, enjoying the unfettered life of the "Don Juan," had ended his relationship with Tanya Adamovich with the publication of *Quiver,* his fifth book of poetry, which he had dedicated to her. That fall, he had an brief affair with Margarita Tumpovskaya, an anthroposophist immersed in study of the occult. Longer lasting was his subsequent attachment with Larisa Reisner, a writer, then just twenty years old, that yet unformed and adoring stage that Gumilev preferred. Born into a family drawn to revolutionary causes, she had begun a journal of political satire, *Rudin*. In the gushing letters they exchanged when Gumilev had returned to the front, the two called one other by the pet names "Lefi" and "Gafiz." Although Larisa claimed she had declined his marriage proposal because of her deep respect for Akhmatova, her scruples did not prevent her from carrying on a love affair with Akhmatova's husband.

Off in Crimea, Akhmatova remained ignorant of Gumilev's latest dalliance. She told of an encounter that probably took place early in 1917.

> Once I was at the Comedian's Halt—the only time—and was just leaving. I was walking towards the door through the empty room—there sat Larisa. I said 'goodbye' to her and shook her hand…I was putting my coat on, suddenly Larisa appears, two tears in place on her cheeks: Thank you! You are so magnanimous! I'll never forget that you held your hand out to me first!" —What was that about? A young, beautiful girl, why this self-deprecation! How could I know then that she had had an affair with Nikolai Stepanovich? And had I known—Why shouldn't I have held my hand out to her?[30]

But Anna could not have felt entirely innocent of deception herself when that December she was introduced by Nedobrovo to Boris Anrep's wife, Yuniya, and was her guest at Belbek, near

Sebastapol. Yuniya Anrep, now separated from her husband, was a nurse on leave from the war. Akhmatova's hidden feelings did not prevent their friendship, for she dedicated a poem to her. Soon after, Anna was found to be healthy enough to return to Petrograd, then to Slepnevo for Christmas with her husband and son. She remembered that after "gloomy, wartime Sebastapol, where I was short of breath because of my asthma and would freeze in a cold, rented room, it seemed that I had found myself in some Promised Land."[31] Those wintry days in the countryside encapsulated for a moment a world that would soon disappear irrevocably. "It was magnificent. Everything was somehow transposed into the nineteenth century, almost back to Pushkin's time. The sleds, felt boots, bearskin rugs, enormous fur coats, the ringing quiet, the snowdrifts, the diamond-like snow."[32]

Chapter XI
Revolutions

During the last Christmas and New Year holidays that they would spend together at Slepnevo, Anna and Nikolai may have finally confronted the fact that a genuine marriage between them no longer existed. Whatever happened there, quiet but intense discussions, stormy arguments, or even Kolya's usual complacent acceptance of the staus quo, the moment of decision for Anna had arrived. Now she would take her life into her own hands. When she left Slepnevo, she did not return to the Gumilev house on Malaya Street in Tsarskoe Selo, but moved in with her friend, Valeriya Sreznevskaya, at 9 Botinskaya Street in Petrograd.

Valeriya was delighted for: "Anna had a pleasant disposition and this made it easy for others to live around her. In my home, she stayed in a small but comfortable room with a window overlooking our clinic's shady, quiet garden. Her door was almost always opened, so we would talk without leaving our rooms. I had a very keen sense of hearing and sometimes would call out to her: 'Why aren't you sleeping? 'How did you know I wasn't?' 'From the sound of your breathing.' Then she would come and sit on my bed and tell me that she was having trouble falling asleep. She would often whisper her poems at night, listening to how they sounded."[1]

The break with Gumilev would bring serious consequences for Anna. At a time when divorce was still considered scandalous, even disreputable, the social and economic costs for a woman were enormous. With her father dead and her mother living on a modest pension in Crimea, Akhmatova had no family to fall back upon for help. She had little or no money of her own and could never hope to support herself writing. The political climate was ominous with the recent murder of Rasputin just another blow at a weak and wavering monarchy. War had ravaged the Russian economy and prospects for future prosperity were exceedingly dim. Although she did not know it then, Akhmatova had taken the first step down in a precipitous spiral into a life of poverty. But she was freeing herself from a marriage in which she must have felt continually betrayed and humiliated in the eyes of the world.

Akhmatova was not sorry to leave her blue room in the Gumilev house, where she had never felt at home in all the years she'd lived there. For her a strange and depressing atmosphere hung over the place, a dark cloud that proved to be a portent of the tragedy to come. She wrote at Slepnevo that January:

> My shadow stayed behind, and it is pining,
> In that same dark blue room it's living still,
> It waits past midnight for the city guests
> And presses to its lips the enameled icon.
> In that house things never were quite right[2].

Boris Anrep had returned from London and, on the evening of February 24, 1917, the day that the February Revolution broke out, he accompanied Anna to the Imperial Alexandrinsky Theater for a dress rehearsal of Meyerhold's sumptuous production of Lermontov's play, *Masquerade*. They took a horse cab through the streets, now dark and eerily empty. Rifle shots echoed out occasionally in the distance. It had been a tumultuous day, the streets mobbed with curious crowds and plastered with manifestoes. They had watched while the demonstrators, with banners flying in the wind, marched through the streets, evading the batons of the tsarist police. Trolleys and buses had stopped running, bringing the Petrograd transportation system to a standstill. But rows of shiny, black automobiles were lined up in front of the Alexandrinsky Theatre. Inside, on a last festive evening of the old, tsarist world, the stalls were packed with glittering crowds of the wealthy, cultured and aristocratic elite of Petersburg society.

Masquerade, depicting as it did the society of imperial St. Petersburg sunk in frenzied self-indulgence and rushing toward its doom, presented a chillingly symbolic reflection of the lives of those who watched from the audience. The lavish sets and opulent costumes astonished even such a sophisticated audience as this. The play ended ominously with a Russian Orthodox church choir intoning the memorial service for the old regime.

After the performance, Akhmatova and Anrep had great difficulty in making their way from the theatre to the Vyborg side of the Neva where she was living. The cabmen, terrified by the erratic shooting in the streets, had all disappeared. It was at that moment, she remembered "...when I was standing with my companion on Nevsky Prospekt...and a Cossack cavalry charged down the road," that she heard inside her head the first words of the *Poem Without a Hero*.[3]

As the pitch of revolutionary activity heightened and life in Petrograd became more problematic, Boris Anrep departed again from Russia, this time for good. England, where he had lived for a time, attracted him with its civilized calm and order. He had already found his way into the literary world where he had met Lytton Strachey and others of the Bloomsbury group. Deeply hurt by his decision to leave Russia, Akhmatova viewed his emigration as a betrayal of his native land as well as of her. Anrep wrote this rather sentimental account of their parting:

I walked across the frozen Neva River in order to avoid the barricades around the bridges...I reached the Sreznevsky house and rang the bell. Anna Andreevna opened the door.
"Is it really you? On a day like this? They are seizing officers on the streets, you know."
"I took off my epaulets."
She was obviously moved that I had come to see her. We went into her room and she reclined on her sofa. For a while we spoke of the significance of the revolution. She was worried, saying that enormous changes were in store.
"It will be the same as it was in France during the Great Revolution, perhaps ever worse."
"Let's not talk about it any more," I said, and we were silent. She looked at the floor.
"We will never see each other again. You are going away."
"I will come back. Look, I have your ring." I opened my jacket and showed her the black ring I wore on a chain around my neck.

Anna touched the ring. "Good, it will preserve you." I pressed her hand to my chest.

"Wear it always," she said.

"Always," I whispered and then added "It is sacred."

Her eyes clouded with emotion, and she stretched out her hands to me. I burned with spiritual ecstasy, kissed her hands, and stood up to leave.

Anna smiled gently: "It's better this way."[4]

Boris Anrep was only the first of Akhmatova's friends to escape the worsening situation in Russia by leaving for the West. She knew that one day she, too, must decide whether to emigrate or, whatever the consequences for her, to remain in her native land. As her conversation with Anrep reveals, Akhmatova understood that with the coming revolution there would be enormous changes in Russian life. Perhaps even then she suspected that there would be no place for her poetry in the tough, visionary utopia promised by the Bolsheviks.

That winter Akhmatova and Osip Mandelstam were together frequently and often talked over this troubling question. Earlier, Mandelstam, one of the first poets of the Silver Age to write on civic themes and about the "people," had been completely caught up in the idea of revolution, anticipating the creative energy and renewal change could bring to a moribund society. But he, as many others, was soon disillusioned. Akhmatova recalled:

Mandelstam would often come to take me out for rides in a horse-drawn cab past the incredible potholes of the revolutionary winter, amidst the celebrated bonfires that burned almost until May, and we would listen to the gunfire wafting from who knew where. That is how we would drive to readings at the Academy of Arts, where they held benefits for the wounded and where we both read several times.[5]

Akhmatova delighted in her conversations with Mandelstam, but when she sensed that Mandelstam's feelings for her were becoming those of a lover rather than a friend she grew uneasy. When she suggested that they not meet so often, Mandelstam apparently felt deeply hurt and, in March, 1917, he abruptly vanished from Petrograd. Nadezhda Mandelstam, who later became his wife and Akhmatova's close friend, assumed that Akhmatova told Osip how she felt in her "usual clumsy manner." "At any rate, Osip was terribly offended. He was not in love with her, at least this is what he told me. He differentiated between the nuances of a relationship, and he was constitutionally incapable of lying or concealing anything. Besides, he felt that Anna was his equal or even above him; a woman, in other words, made for comradeship, not for love, which for him was either a lengthy affair or a momentary spark, a game, a madness—but always with someone weaker."[6] Akhmatova was not surprised by Mandelstam's disappearance as the maelstrom of revolution into which they had been plunged made everyone's lives then unpredictable.

The civil unrest and the anxiety it caused Akhmatova clearly affected her work, for she wrote only a handful of poems that winter and spring. It was only when she had retreated to the uneasy peace of Slepnevo again that she could find the quiet she needed. But the violence she had witnessed in the streets of Petrograd haunted her.

Frances Laird

No longer was death a poetic abstraction—it had become as real and as immediate as the black, gelid puddles of blood and the shapeless bodies she had seen sprawled over the snowy cobblestones of Petrograd.

Nikolai Gumilev had missed the revolutionary events of February, for the war, however ineptly and disastrously it was being waged, bore relentlessly on. When he did return to the capital from Okulovka, where he was stationed, he showed little interest in the evolving political situation. Disillusioned with the Russian command and the war on the western front, he had hoped to be transferred to the southern front. But suffering again from bronchitis, Nikolai was forced to return from his posting and enter a clinic in Petrograd for treatment. Soon after his release, Gumilev said his tender good-byes to Larisa Reisner and set out for London and Paris, where he intended to act as a foreign correspondent for a Russian newspaper.

Nikolai Gumilev left Russia at just about the time that Lenin made his triumphant return at the Finland Station. In an acrostic poem, Gumilev makes it clear that he could see no place for Akhmatova in the dark, satanic world of post-revolutionary Russia.

Acrostic

At the sky's edge was an angel lying,
Netherwards she leaned, stunned at the chasm,
New worlds down below were dark and starless,

Swan Songs
Akhmatova and Gumilev

And no groan was heard. For Hell was silent.

As bright crimson blood's beat, shy and modest,
Keen fear and the fragile hands that trembled,
Most holy angel's image in reflection
Again fell to the whole world's possession.

The world is crowded! Let her live on, dreaming
Of love, of sorrow and of shadows, making
Visible in the predestined twilight
Alphabets of her own revelations.

Nikolai Gumilev
1911—March, 1917[7]

In London, Gumilev spoke in an interview of his desire to see mystical and spiritual elements return to poetry, qualities which are evident in the dreamy, elusive imagery of this poem in which Anna is a shy and tremulous angel, leaning from heaven over a hell-ish world in which she can have no part. What is clear from this poem and the one that follows is that, though the marriage had broken down and his intimate relationship with Anna had been fractured beyond repair, her presence loomed large, enduring and irreplaceable in his psychic life.

Sometime in 1917, Gumilev wrote a poem beginning with the lines, "You pitied me and you forgave me..." which can also be read

Frances Laird

as addressed to Akhmatova. The final stanzas are again stunningly prophetic.

> You pitied me and you forgave me,
> And even gave to me your hand,
> When in my soul where death was pacing
> There was no stone left upon stone.
>
> So does the noble-hearted victor
> Without a trace of doubt bestow
> Upon the one now liberated
> His life and his possessions, too.
>
> All that with sleepless nights I summoned
> From my soul's darkness into light,
> All that which by the gods was given
> To me, the warrior and the poet,
>
> All, down before your power bowing,
> All will I give and nothing hide
> For the blinding happiness you'd bring me
> If I could be with you sometime.
>
> Just don't request of me sweet songs, as
> Those songs at one time I composed.

Swan Songs
Akhmatova and Gumilev

You know I have no strength to sing them
With the castrato's squeaky voice.

Don't punish me for words I've written,
Don't plunge into the chasm once more,
For sometime when the moonlight glitters,
A weary slave, I'll disappear.

Across the fences and the ditches
In the deserted field I'll run,
Forgetting self and all conditions,
All contracts and the fear of pain.

You never will discover where,
Your gaze displaying worry's torment,
In what cursed, God-forsaken swamp
The road I took has finally ended.

Nikolai Gumilev
1917[8]

In the moment of reconciliation depicted here, whether real or imagined, the poet recognizes that it is the woman, not he, who has been victorious in their terrible struggle of wills. He promises that, if she will allow him back into her life, he will give her everything he possesses. But she must not ask him for the "sweet songs" he once composed for her, because he can no longer sing them with the "castrato's squeaky voice." Perhaps Gumilev sees himself as emasculated if denied the role inextricably tied to his sense of his manhood—the love chase and seduction of other women. He ends with the uncannily accurate prevision of his final, tragic disappearance four years later. Even more haunting still is the way he foresees the torment of Akhmatova's agonized, untiring, secret search for his unmarked burial place. If Mandelstam saw Akhmatova as the Cassandra of her age, Gumilev was surely the Tiresias, another Greek seer punished by the gods.

Surprisingly, when Nikolai Gumilev reached London, Boris Anrep was the first person he got in touch with. Anrep helped him to get settled and introduced him to other writers, including G.K.Chesterton and the art critic, Roger Fry, whose articles Gumilev had published in *Apollon*. In his memoirs Aldous Huxley wrote of a conversation he had with Gumilev at one of Lady Ottoline Morrell's literary salons for the Bloomsbury set. In June, Gumilev moved on to Paris and, when the job as a foreign correspondent didn't materialize, he worked for the new Provisional Government of Russia in its office of military affairs. He quickly made the acquaintance of Nataliya Goncharova and Mikhail Larionov, Russian artists living there. When Nikolai Minsky ran into Gumilev in Paris, he was struck by the change in him. "His earlier talkative nature had changed to a silent pensiveness and in his wise, naive eyes were set in an expression of hidden resolution. He took little part in the general conversation and only came to life when the conversation turned to his Persian miniatures."⁹ The sorrows of unrequited passion may have accounted for his moodiness, for Gumilev had fallen in love with a young Russo-French woman, Elena Dubouchet. She, unfortunately, was already engaged and was cold to his advances. But this unreciprocated love was not wasted; it provided material for a collection of poems entitled *The Blue Star*.

As was usual for her, Anna left for Slepnevo to spend the summer with Lev. It would be the last summer visit that she would make to the Gumilev estate, for the social and political disintegration was spreading out from Petrograd into the provinces. Akhmatova wrote to Mikhail Lozinsky of her anxiety for their safety in the Tversk countryside: "The peasants swear that our house is standing on their bones...Deserters keep coming, saying that the war is going splendidly, and the peasants believe them."¹⁰ She wanted to return to Petrograd but was afraid that the peasants would burn the Gumilev house on August 6 in celebration of a local holiday. From Valeriya she learned that in Petrograd things were getting even worse. Akhmatova debated whether to take refuge in Paris or stay in Slepnevo for the winter.

Despite the tension and worry, Akhmatova was very productive that summer, writing a dozen poems at Slepnevo. Still preoccupied with her disappointment at Boris Anrep's emigration and his silence, she dedicated four poems to him, although she dropped the dedications when they were published. She wrote: "My poems came

Frances Laird

with an easy, free gait. I waited for a letter that did not come—and never came. I often saw that letter in my dreams; I would unseal the envelope, but either it was written in some incomprehensible language or I was going blind…"[11] The fact that Kolya, too, had gone abroad could only have increased her sense of isolation and abandonment. In one poem, she wonders how her lover would react to the news of her death. In another she concluded that he had never really loved her and asks herself why she is always drawn to a man who belongs to someone else. She feels nostalgia for the past underlain by a gnawing fear of what the future will bring.

That summer Akhmatova continued to struggle with the question of whether to emigrate or to stay in Russia. In one poem she imagined how it would be if she could follow Anrep to England.[12] In another, addressed to Anrep, Akhmatova speaks with a barely suppressed anger about his emigration, a spiritual betrayal of his country.

> You're an apostate: for a green island
> You have given up your native land,
> Given up our songs and our icons
> And the pine tree on the quiet pond.
>
> And for what, valiant Yarolavets,
> If you haven't lost your mind at last,
> Were you overcome by red-haired beauties

And by houses, elegant and grand?

Go ahead then—blaspheme and swagger,
Desolate your Orthodox soul.
Stay there in that kingly city
And grow to love your freedom for a while.

Why do you come moaning and groaning
Beneath that high window of mine?
You know that in the sea you won't be drowning
And from battle will escape unharmed.

Neither battle nor the sea is awful
To one who has lost a paradise.
It's because of this that you have begged us
To remember you in prayers we raise.

      Anna Akhmatova
      Summer 1917, Slepnevo[13]

For Akhmatova, Russian-ness was closely tied to Russian Orthodox Christian spirituality. Anrep is the "apostate," who has rejected his ancestral faith and abandoned its icons for the attractions of English women and a comfortable life. The fears and misgivings he voices are all for show, for he has safely lived the most blessed of lives, untouched even by war. But, though he doesn't realize it yet, as an exile he will suffer for his forsaking of the "paradise" of his native land.

At summer's end, Anna reluctantly returned to Petrograd where: "...since there is a new custom of flooding the sidewalks with the citizens' blood every month, it has lost its charm in my eyes."[14] She, too, was being picked up and swept along on the tide of revolutionary events. Almost unnoticed in the anarchy engulfing Petrograd was the publication in September of *Belaya Staya (White Flock)*, Akhmatova's third collection of poems. The title is taken from a poem of 1915 in which she wrote of the "white flocks of my poems." "White flocks" can suggest the sheaf of white pages on which her poems were written as well as the familiar imagery of the white dove and the swan. With life in Petrograd turned upside down and with "hunger and ruin...mounting with each day," there were tremendous difficulties in producing and distributing a book. Akhmatova wrote: "Transportation was coming to a standstill—it was impossible to ship the book even to Moscow, it was sold entirely in Petrograd. The paper was coarse—practically cardboard. The journals were closing down, as well as the newspapers. Therefore, unlike *Rosary, White Flock* did not have a sensational press."[15]

With the October Revolution of 1917, Petersburg was in a state of near anarchy. The Sreznevsky's house where Anna was living and Dr. Sreznevsky's psychiatric clinic were located in the Vyborg district, the first in Petrograd to join the revolt. Although the house and clinic were surrounded by a high stone wall that separated them from the revolutionary activity in the streets, the crack of rifle fire and rattle of machine guns could often be heard in the distance. One afternoon, as Valeriya and Anna sat sipping tea in the dining room, there came a loud ring at the door and the strident babble of men's voices. A detachment of Red army soldiers and sailors was clamoring to see Valeriya's husband, who was acting as director of the mental clinic of the Naval Academy. Into Valya's hand they thrust a paper with the names of five patients at the clinic who had been condemned to death. The horrified Valya discovered that the names of her husband and herself were included on the list. Dr. Sreznevsky immediately telephoned the Cheka, where an official promised to investigate. But the raucous band of soldiers refused to be held off by the young doctor on duty. An official from the State Health Organization finally intervened and was able at least to postpone the executions. Later it was discovered that the accusations had been made by a mentally-ill commissar confined in the ward next door under orders of Dr.Sreznevsky who was taking his revenge. Such was the tenuous and fragile safety of innocent people during these chaotic times.

Having witnessed the ruthless and barbaric way Lenin and the Bolsheviks had seized power, Akhmatova, like many others, was filled with anxiety about the intentions of the new Soviet government. At the same time, Russian troops were falling back as the Germans forced their way inexorably ever closer to Petrograd. It was then that Akhmatova made final a choice crucial in determining the direction of

Frances Laird

her life and her art. The temptation to abandon a doomed and foundering Russia for Italy or France, whose culture she knew and loved almost as dearly as her own, must have been almost achingly irresistable. With her intuitive understanding, she knew what kind of future lay ahead for her and for the Russian people under a Communist government. But as this poem, written that autumn, witnesses, she had made her decision not flee to safety in the West, but stay in her motherland to suffer at the side of her people whatever the future might bring.

> When in a suicidal anguish
> The people awaited their German guests
> And when Byzantium's stern spirit
> Took flight out of the Russian Church,
> And when the city by the Neva
> Forgot the greatness of her past
> And, like a drunken, whoring woman,
> Did not know who would take her next,
> I heard a voice. It called in comfort.
> It said to me: "Come over here.
> Just leave your lost and sinful country,
> Leave Russian lands forevermore.
> I'll wash the blood from off your hands and
> From out of your heart I'll pluck black shame.
> The pain of your defeats and injuries

I'll cover over with some new name."
But calmly, with complete indifference,
With both hands I closed up my ears,
So that this talk, debased and worthless,
Would not defile a soul in grief.

Anna Akhmatova
Autumn, 1917[16]

With this poem comes a dramatic change of tone and imagery in Akhmatova's poetry and a new, authoritative resonance to her voice. With unwavering gaze she looks upon the plight of the unfortunate inhabitants of Petrograd, caught between the killing inflicted upon them by their own people and that of the invading German troops. Whatever its shortcomings over the centuries, the Russian Orthodox Church was the bedrock of Russia's cultural and moral as well as its spiritual life. Emptied of "Byzantium's stern spirit," not only would the faithful lose direction, but the ethical equilibrium of Russia would be destroyed. But Akhmatova saved her strongest, most shocking imagery to describe what had become of Petersburg, comparing the city whose gardens and palaces, skies and waters she had celebrated in so many poems to a drunken whore offering her body to any taker. Akhmatova's words ring out, powerful and uncompromising, like the words of the Prophet Isaish: "How the faithful city has played the whore,/ once the home of justice/ where righteousness dwells—/but now murderers!" (Isaiah 1:21).

Frances Laird

But a quiet voice, insinuating itself into her consciousness, calls enticingly to the poet, promising her consolation and the chance to leave behind the failure, disorder and death now gripping her as well as her country, mired in evil and destined for destruction. If she leaves, she would be cleansed and redeemed, not only from the moral pollution that clung to Russia's tragic history, but the guilt and shame she has brought upon herself there. She can be reborn, be "given a new name" in a place where no one will know the failures of the life she had lived, the disillusionment and humiliation of her marriage to Gumilev, the disappointment of her unrequited love for Anrep, her inadequacies as a mother. But the poet covers her ears and will not listen to such filthy and loathsome talk. Although she is sick with sorrow at the wretched plight of Russia, it would be sinful for her even to entertain the thought of leaving her people in exchange for her own comfort and security.

The prediction of Nedobrovo that Akhmatova's poetry would expand out of the realm of the intimate love lyric into larger, more widely significant public themes has been fulfilled. It is as if with this poem the poet had stepped out of the safe confines of her blue room, that private poetic universe with its exultations and disappointments, and stood exposed on an open stage before the world. Akhmatova has assumed the mantle, honorable but weighty, of the Russian poet, one which she would wear for the rest of her life. Now she speaks not only for herself, but for all the Russian people with the oracular voice of the prophet.

This poem would be published in April, 1918, in *Volya Naroda (The Will of the People)*, but not as Akhmatova wrote it. The first eight lines were excised by the Communist censors; in this and all future printings the poem would be known to Russians as "I heard a voice." Already the Bolsheviks had begun to impose their political line upon what appeared in print. Neither the German threat nor the Orthodox faith were to be openly acknowledged. Nor would Petrograd, the heartland of the revolution, be demeaned by comparison to a drunken prostitute. In this truncated form, the poem would prove useful in promoting the idea of unswerving faithfulness to the motherland. But even without its opening eight lines, the poem made a powerful impression on readers. In the coming years, many Russians would recite this poem from memory. It was only in 1967 that the complete poem was finally published in the Soviet Union. The silencing of the poet, though state censorship here was only partial, reminds us of Gumilev's previsionary "Rusalka," who, removed from her elemental world, lost her voice.

As the Bolshevik regime insinuated itself into every corner of Russian cultural life in order to establish absolute control, poets and poetry soon became the subjects of its scrutiny. An article written by the critic, Vygodsky, and published in *New Life* in December, 1917, initiated the process of separating the "new" poets from the "old." He wrote: "In present-day poetry one can observe two streams, two directions. In one we find the attempt to resurrect classical accuracy of expression and artistic perfection of form, which has found its best expression in the poetry of Akhmatova and Mandelstam. The other, at whose base lie Futuristic theories, is at the moment represented by Mayakovsky. And almost all young poets, expressing their own individuality to a greater or lesser degree, move consciously or unconsciously in one or the other of these directions."[17]

With Communism's proclaimed goal of establishing a utopian paradise for the proletariat, stripped clean of every trace of the tsarist past, it was not difficult to predict which poets would be chosen to herald this new, futuristic age and which would be considered the dusty relics of the pre-revolutionary past. From this point on, Akhmatova would experience the relentless, ever increasing pressure of official displeasure towards her work. She would be forced from her place in the literary spotlight, back into shadowy edges, then completely out of Petrograd's cultural life. Ultimately, her very survival would depend on this imposed invisibility. Akhmatova attempted bravely to face and accept the possible end of her life as a poet in this, perhaps her "last song."

> Nobody now will listen to my singing,
> The days long prophesied have come about.
> Last song, this world is wonderful no longer,
> Don't tear apart my heart, do not ring out.
>
> Not long ago like a free-soaring swallow,
> You carried out your early morning flight.

> But now that you'll become a hungry beggar,
> You won't go knocking at a stranger's gate.
>
> Anna Akhmatova
1917[18]

Implicit in the closing lines is Akhmatova's determination that, whatever she may be forced to endure in the years ahead, rejection, poverty or hunger, she will never allow her poetic gift to be degraded to serve values alien and antagonistic to her own.

Another poem that came to public attention at this time, one Akhmatova had written in 1915, was entitled "A Prayer" and appeared in *Pravo naroda (The Right of the People)*, the newspaper of a Petrograd labor union, on November 26, 1917.

A Prayer

> You can give me bitter years of illness,
> Choking, sleepless nights and feverish heat,
> Take away my dear friend and my baby,
> Take my mysterious singing gift.
> At your liturgy I will pray this
> After so many tortured days,
> That the black clouds over darkened Russia
> Turn to clouds in a glory of rays.
>
> Anna Akhmatova

Frances Laird

May, 1915, Feast of the
Holy Spirit, Petersburg[19]

In the first year of the war, Akhmatova offered to God the sacrifice of her well-being, her "dear friend," presumably Nikolai Gumilev, her son, even her poetic voice, if the Great War could end and Russians could live in peace. But two years later, in the revolutionary clamor, the poem took on new meaning. When set on the newspaper page, not yet fully under Communist control, surrounded with articles condemning the actions of the Bolsheviks, its political message was clear. Akhmatova read "A Prayer" at a public reading on the day that elections for the Constituent Assembly were held. Its closing lines expressed the flicker of cautious but hopeful optimism that Russia might emerge intact from the turmoil of revolution.

Osip Mandelstam wrote of Akhmatova's prophetic gift in "To Cassandra" where he envisioned her as the daughter of Priam, the king of defeated Troy, brought back by Agamemnon to Greece as part of his booty of war. Apollo had given her the gift of prophecy, but also ensured that no one would ever believe her.

To Cassandra

I did not search in the blooming moments
For your, Cassandra, lips, for your, Cassandra, eyes,
But recollections of the solemn vigil

Swan Songs
Akhmatova and Gumilev

In December torment us.

And in December, the year nineteen-seventeen,
Loving, we lost everything.
One robbed by the will of the people,
Another robbed by his own self.

Someday in the capital gone crazy,
On a Scythian holiday upon the Neva's banks,
With sounds of their disgusting dances,
They'll tear the shawl from off your lovely head.

But if this life is the necessity of raving
And forests made of ships and buildings rising high,
I have loved you, armless victory,
And wintertime diseased with plague.

On the square with armoured carriers,
I can see a person—he
Frightens off the wolves with logs of burning embers:
Freedom, law, equality.

Sickly, silent, calm Cassandra,
I can do no more—but why
Shone the sun of Alexander

Frances Laird

> A hundred years ago for all?
>
> Osip Mandelstam
> 1917[20]

Where Akhmatova saw Petersburg as the degraded prostitute, Mandelstam saw a city that had lost its sanity and been turned upside down. In the Scythians, the pagan tribes and ancient precursors of the Russian people, Mandelstam finds the crude barbarism of the Bolsheviks. Elated with their triumph, they are out to destroy the culture and traditions of old Russia, replacing them with their own. Even then Mandelstam understood that he and Akhmatova would become anachronisms. With the line "They'll tear the shawl from off your lovely head," he predicted that Akhmatova would be brought down. The lone defender of the old values might ward off the attack of the "wolves" with the brightly glowing sticks of "freedom, law, equality." But these sparks of fire would die out, leaving the darkness and the predatory ravages of the "wolves." What would be the place of the poet in this new world? Mandelstam looked back to "the sun" of Russian poetry, Alexander Pushkin, asking why he had shone for *all* the Russian people. Following on his initial rush of hope and expectation about the good that could come with revolution, came Mandelstam's realization of the immensity of the threat to all that he held precious.

Meanwhile, in Paris, Nikolai Gumilev had lost his post when the Bolsheviks took power and restructured the Russian Military

Commission. The military aims of the new government had shifted and Russia withdrew from the southern front in Salonika where Gumilev had once hoped to serve. He put in a request for a commission in London to take effect in January, 1918. A poem that he wrote at this time suggested that that he regretted his lost relationship with Anna, but did not view their separation as final.

Angel of Pain

Righteous are your pathways, my tsaritsa,
Those along which you are leading me.
Only, like a bird, my heart is beating
Terribly from out of dark blue flame.

Since that time when I was but a child still
And trembled sweetly, standing in the church
Before your delicate and girlish profile,
Singing from the psalms, I prayed and dreamed.

And until that time when, in the temple
Of my ever powerful memory,
Lit up with the consecrated candles
Were so many luring lips and eyes,

I did not know of a yoke so heavy,
Neither did I know of fire so sweet,
As if you had knowledge then of something
That would always be concealed from me.

In the brilliance of defenseless beauty,
Like pain's angel, close to me you drew,
You gave slavery sweeter far than freedom,
Languishing in mortal sadness…you

Would confide in me about your sorrow,
You would give me boughs of lilac white,
Coming in return my poems resounded
And they sang about you day and night.

Like a bird, let my heart keep on beating,
Let death keep descending to me…Ach,
Keep me and preserve me, my tsaritsa,
In such dazzling chains, such blinding bonds.

Nikolai Gumilev
1917-18[21]

Gumilev is in a very different space, poetically speaking, than the poets caught in the swirling vortex of revolution. As in "Acrostic" and "Forgiveness," also written in 1917, he appears to be reverting to the poetic language of the Symbolists, addressing Anna again as "tsaritsa." In returning to the style of his early poems to Akhmatova, perhaps he is attempting to recapture a time when their love for one another had a purity, intensity and innocence now lost. Admitting that Akhmatova's decision to separate was the right one, whatever anguish and regret it has caused him, Gumilev recalls standing beside her in church on their wedding day and the dreams that came to him then. However, with the irresistable attraction of "so many luring lips and eyes," the "yoke" of fidelity with which she had harnessed him was too heavy. With her mysterious depths and her vulnerable beauty, his "angel of pain" had made him her slave, a condition he realizes was far sweeter than the freedom he demanded. Gumilev recognizes her power to inspire him, how his poems "sang about [her] day and night." And again comes a prevision of his death. With the exclamatory "Ach" (or "Akh"), the first syllable of Akhmatova's name, Gumilev longs to be bound by her in chains of a spiritual slavery even as in life the legal bonds of their marriage were dissolving. Although these poems of 1917 may recall Gumilev's Symbolist poems, a stronger sense of immediacy and necessity governs his imagery. In "Angel of Pain" the bird, yoke, fire, and chains are not arbitrarily chosen for their aesthetic appropriateness, but are weighted with meaning. Gumilev doesn't merely speak through the hollow mouthpiece of a heroic persona, but expresses emotional truths.

Frances Laird

Gumilev's military commission in London lasted only until April, 1918. He presumably renewed his contacts with English writers and saw Boris Anrep, who had begun working in the medium of mosaic. Anrep had never written to Anna, having been warned that after the October Revolution it might be dangerous for her to receive letters from a Russian emigré. He had continued to wear the black ring Anna had given him on a chain around his neck, until it broke and he placed the ring in a small box of treasured momentoes.

Anrep tried to dissuade Nikolai from returning to Russia, but homesick for his native land, he was determined to go back despite the hardships he would meet there. Anrep recorded the following interchange in his memoirs. He had asked Gumilev to take as a gift to Akhmatova a length of silk for a dress and a large, well-preserved ancient coin stamped with the profile of Alexander the Great. Anrep wrote: "He unwillingly took the objects, saying: 'What is this, Boris Vasilyevich? She is my wife, after all.' I gasped at him in surprise. 'Don't be a fool, Nikolai Stepanovich,' I said coldly."[22] Gumilev obviously believed he was being asked to be a courier for his wife's lover. Anrep's shocked and haughty response may, in such delicate circumstances, have been feigned, but does leave in question the exact degree of intimacy that existed between Anrep and Akhmatova. After a brief stop in Paris, Gumilev arrived back in Petrograd. Boris Anrep never did discover if Akhmatova had received his gifts.

Chapter XII
Dying Petersburg

In the closing months of 1917, Vladimir Kasimirovich Shileiko, a friend from her Stray Dog days, was taking an increasingly important role in Akhmatova's life. Shileiko, with his dark hair, heavy brows and penetrating black eyes behind glittering, oval eyeglasses, was, according to Valeriya,"…exceptionally, inexpressibly handsome…tall, slender."[1] Shileiko was a poet as well as a brilliant specialist in the language and history of ancient Assyria. As a precocious boy of fourteen he had deciphered the hieroglyphics of an ancient Egyptian text. After attending St. Petersburg University, he had worked as a tutor to the wealthy Sheremetev family and in the research department of the Hermitage Museum. In January, 1917, Shileiko had been drafted into the army where he had been issued the thick, woolen military overcoat that he then wore constantly, indoors and out.

In a poem which he wrote some years earlier, Shileko had expressed his long preoccupation with Akhmatova.

> My life is hard and agonizing,
> And I grow tired and I drink wine:
> Met with a fate that's marvellous,
> I've loved sternly, for a long time.

Frances Laird

> It seems, obsessed with one idea,
> Into the waiting shade I'll take
> A July day and the memory
> Of a woman, wild, insane.
>
> Vladimir Shileiko
1914-16[2]

Here Shileiko admits to two defining traits in his personality—an earnest, even obsessive approach to love and work and a stern, demanding temperament. Akhmatova found fascinating his scholarly work, the ancient stories and poems from Babylonian and Egyptian texts that he recited in the strange, impenetrable music of unknown tongues. She was drawn by his seriousness of purpose, his almost monkish dedication to his laborious and demanding vocation. She also may have been attracted by a stability and constancy that she craved after her years with Gumilev. For Shileiko was not a womanizer. Left alone amidst the chaos and increasing hardships brought by the Revolution, Anna may have hungered for the emotional and physical security he could provide. Despite his difficult personality, she could expect that the self-discipline, even self-denial Shileiko displayed in his work would carry over into his life.

And although Shileiko wrote poetry, his talents, unlike Gumilev's, lay in a field safely removed from Akhmatova's. The unexpressed but real rivalry between the two leading poets in Petersburg clearly could have exacerbated the discord in their marriage. For although Gumilev was older, had been a poet longer, was respected and influential as an editor and critic and had published more books, he lacked Akhmatova's dramatic presence and charisma. His poetry was appreciated by a rather narrow circle of readers mostly made up of other poets, while hers had achieved a wider popular success. Though he may have taken great satisfaction in guiding Akhmatova into the world of poetry, he may have felt some resentment at seeing her books outsell his own.

A poem addressed to Shileiko written in December, 1917, indicates that Akhmatova knew precisely what she was getting into in a relationship with him. It also goes far in explaining why only four poems date from the year 1918.

> You are always new and enigmatic.
> And I am more obedient each day.
> But your love, oh my stern friend and lover,
> Is a trial by fire and iron for me.

> You forbid all singing and all smiling,
> And forbade all praying long ago.
> Just so that from you I'll not be parted,
> Leave all as it is right now!

Frances Laird

> So, a stranger to the earth and heavens,
> I live on and I no longer sing,
> As if you had taken my free spirit
> From both hell and paradise.
>
> Anna Akhmatova
December 1917[3]

With this new love, Akhmatova has abandoned the struggle to assert her independence and autonomy in exchange for a lasting relationship with a man. She refuses to fight the endless, enervating battle of wills that had characterized her years with Kolya, when their emotional duelling had found its way into poems such as "And when we were cursing on another…" and "More than once it has happened…"

Akhmatova's friends were horrified at her new regimen of self-abnegation. Valeriya described a visit to Shileiko's flat in the servant's wing of the Sheremetev Palace when he was ill and Anna was caring for him. Her enthusiastic first impression of the handsome Shileiko had been tempered by what she found there:

> The labyrinth of the Sheremetev Palace—the inner courtyard, passageways, staircases leading through corridors—cold, dark, hunting trophies on the walls, finally a door. I entered, an oblong room, bed, couch, a large round table, everything strange and gloomy. A lamp on the table burning oil, leaving the corners of the large room in shadow. By the table sat a man in a soldier's coat, his face very thin, an unwholesome look on his face, a wry grin, caustic

conversation, erudite, interesting. He spoke quietly, with his head bent slightly to one side. He talked about Egypt, Babylonia, Assyria, he recited tablets from Assyrian by heart. I listened, excited, but noticed his great egotism. I went home with Anya. I saw she was tired, pale. "You know, he didn't sleep all night. He was analyzing his tablets and drinking tea." "And you got up and warmed it and poured it for him." "Well, of course, he is very nervous, very suspicious, and demands undivided attention. All my other relationships and feelings must be excluded."[4]

To judge by her poem, Akhmatova seemed almost proud of her self-abnegation, as if she had taken up some rigorous training program for the spirit ("I'm more obedient to you each day.") It was not easy for her to become the person he wanted her to be, but "a trial by fire and iron." She feels that, though she is still alive, her lover has separated her from her connection to the earth and her access to the heavens. Yet she would gladly sacrifice everything if they could remain together.

"Oh, Russia," a fund-raising evening to benefit the Red Cross, was held in Petrograd on January 5. Olga Glebova-Sudeikina danced, Arthur Lourie performed his music on the piano and Anna Akhmatova, Zinaida Gippius and others read their poetry. But because of what had happened that day, the event took on the atmosphere of a political protest. It was the opening day of the long-awaited Constituent Assembly, the lawfully elected legislative body of the new government. When it became clear that the Bolsheviks were vastly outnumbered by more moderate parties, bands of Red soldiers were sent to pack the hall. They prevented the elected delegates from taking their seats and shouted down anyone who attempted to speak. Eventually the Constituent Assembly had to be dissolved. If there was little reaction from the general public to this, at least the Petersburg intelligentsia could express its outrage.

The long, frigid winter shrank by two weeks as the days from February 1 through February 13 vanished from Russian calendars. Lenin had decided to bring Russia into the modern world by changing from the old style of dating based on the Julian calendar to that used in the West based on the Gregorian calendar. Another of Lenin's decrees had a more profound and lasting impact on the city of Petrograd—his decision to move the official capital of Russia from Petrograd to Moscow.

Although this was officially cast as an attempt to move the capital city out of the range of German guns, actually it was Lenin's way of taking revenge upon the intellectuals of Petrograd for their staunch opposition to his rule. So began the decline of the once-glorious capital founded by Peter the Great. The population of the city immediately began to shrink. With severe shortages of coal and firewood, people burned their books and furniture to keep warm in the exceptionally harsh winter. Water pipes froze. Long lines of hungry shoppers queued up to buy the few rotting vegetables and loaves of moldy bread left in the markets. Yet the impoverished city displayed a rare and pristine loveliness. With the factories closed by strikes and no longer spewing black smoke into the air, the sky cleared to an intense, bright blue. As the surging, ubiquitous crowds thinned, the classically harmonious vistas of broad avenues and squares revealed their breathtaking beauty.

As Vladimir Shileiko was Nikolai Gumilev's friend as well as Anna's, in April, 1918, when Kolya arrived back in Petrograd and heard that Anna was at Shileiko's, he dropped in to see her there. The three sat around drinking tea and chatting amicably. It wasn't until he visited her the next day at the Sreznevsky's that Anna told Gumilev she was in love with someone else and wanted a divorce. Valeriya wrote: "Sitting on my large sofa, Anna told Nikolai she wanted to leave him forever. Nikolai turned deathly pale and, after a prolonged silence, finally spoke: 'I have always said you were perfectly free to do whatever you wanted!' He stood up and left." When he heard it was Shileiko that she wanted to marry, Gumilev was incredulous, but forced himself to behave with restraint.[5]

Akhmatova described how the marriage had ended: "He did not object at all, but I could see that he was deeply hurt...At the time he had just returned from Paris, after his unrequited love for the 'Blue Star.' He was full of her—yet my wish for a separation stung him all the same..." Soon after this, the two travelled to Slepnevo to visit Lev. As she recalled: "We were sitting on the divan and Lyovushka was playing between us. Kolya said:' And what did you start this for?' That was all...I believe we were engaged for too long. I was in Sebastopol, he was in Paris. When we got married in 1910, he had already lost his passion..."[6]

If Akhmatova's desire to end their marriage had injured his pride or caused him inordinate distress, Gumilev revealed it to no one. He moved into the vacant flat of Sergei Makovsky, who was then living in Crimea. Petrograd was a changed city. As if playing over the face of a fading beauty, the pale winter sun picked out the classical facades tinged with grime and streets grew dusty and filled with trash. Although its pulse still beat strong, literary life had changed irrevocably. In the new Soviet establishment, Gumilev would encounter challenges that, as the plains of Africa and the trenches of Poland, would provide yet another arena for the testing of his courage and steadfastness.

On May 13, 1918, Gumilev took part in a significant literary event—the first public reading of Alexander Blok's highly controversial poem "The Twelve." It was held in the hall of the Tenishevsky school, where both Osip Mandelstam and Vladimir Nabokov had once been schoolboys, at the unlikely hour of two o'clock in the morning. Fearful of the scandal it would arouse, several poets, Akhmatova among them, had declined to take part in the reading.

"The Twelve," the most extraordinary and powerful poem written about the Russian Revolution, came to Alexander Blok in a frenzy of inspiration that lasted barely two days. With pounding pace and strident voices, a band of twelve Red Guard soldiers are marching through Petrograd's dark streets, whipped by the snowy blast of a blizzard. Voices, some unknowable and mysterious, others identifiable, echo out over the howling winds in scraps of conversation, political slogans, lines from Russian Orthodox liturgy, crude epithets and insults. Katya, a prostitute, has been murdered, either slashed by Vanka or shot through the head by Petka, both Red soldiers. Through the raging blizzard, the band of soldiers pushes relentlessly on beneath a red banner, firing their rifles down the dark streets. They are trailed by a limping, mangy dog that symbolizes the old world. Out ahead leading them on, almost hidden in the swirling snow and wreathed in white roses, strides Jesus Christ. It was a striking and enigmatic work, the dramatic impact of which was heightened in the reading given by Blok's wife, Lyuba Dmitrievna Mendeleeva. Heated discussions erupted as people argued about what it meant.

One member of the audience remembered the tumultuous event:

> The first part ended with the first public reading of Blok's "The Twelve," effectively declaimed by his wife, who appeared under her stage name: Basargina. By the end of this reading, bedlam had erupted in the hall. Part of the public applauded, the other whistled and stamped their feet. I went over to the tiny green room which was absolutely stuffed wih poets. According to the program, after the intermission Blok was to appear, then another poet. But Blok kept repeating with trembling lips: "I won't go on, I won't go on." And then a middle-aged blonde woman walked up to Blok and said, "So, Alexander Alexandrovich, you wrote that, but to tell the truth, it would have been better if you hadn't." After that, he [the other poet] turned and walked to the door leading to the stage. It was Nikolai Gumilev.
> Returning to the hall, which continued to be in an uproar, I saw Gumilev calmly standing, leaning with his elbows on the lectern and viewing the audience with his grey-blue eyes. It was probably the way

he looked at the wild animals in the thick forests of Africa, holding his trusty rifle ready. But now his weapon was poetry. And when the hall quieted a little, he began to read his "gazelles" ["Persian Gazelles"] and at last from his poems and he himself flowed such a magical power that his reading was accompanied by stormy applause. After that, when Blok appeared, there no longer were any demonstrations."[7]

Dmitri Gumilev, Kolya's brother, and his wife were also in the audience. Anna Gumileva, the poet's sister-in-law, wrote proudly of "our Kolya" and his mastery of the nearly-rioting crowd. She added: "Only the next day did Kolya tell us that Blok refused after the poem "The Twelve" to go out on the stage. Then Kolya decided to rescue him and went out earlier than his time on the program," in this way calming the unruly audience for Blok.[8]

Nikolai Gumilev soon adapted to the difficult life that all residents of Petrograd were forced to endure and made friends among the younger generation of poets. Vladislav Khodasevich visited him in Makovsky's apartment on Ivanovskaya Street:

He invited me to his place and greeted me as if ours were a meeting of two monarchs. In his ceremonious politeness there was something so inauthentic that at first I wondered—is he joking? ...In a Petersburg deserted, starving, reeking of cockroaches, both of us hungry, emaciated, in frayed jackets and holey boots, we sat and chatted with exorbitant importance in the unheated and uncleaned study. Remembering that I was from Moscow, Gumilev thought it necessary to offer me tea. But he did so with such an uncertain voice (probably there was no sugar) that I refused and, it seems, got him out of his difficulty.[9]

Swan Songs
Akhmatova and Gumilev

As he was leaving, Khodasevich encountered little Lev, playing soldier with a toy sword and his father's uhlan helmet.

But in Petrograd there existed one haven for cold, hungry artists and writers in the House of the Arts (Dom Iskusstv). Opened in late 1918 under the direction of Maxim Gorky, now the most powerful man of letters in the Soviet government, the House of the Arts occupied a spacious apartment on three floors of a palace overlooking the Moika River. It had been requisitioned by the government from a wealthy Moscow merchant, Yeliseyev. In its mirrored hall were held concerts, lectures and classes in prose writing, poetry and translation. In the pale blue salon decorated with sculptures by Rodin, Gumilev led poetry workshops for young proletarian poets. But most importantly, the members could buy an inexpensive hot meal, a bowl of kasha or cabbage soup and bread, and relax for a time with their writer friends in the oak-paneled dining room. In the House of the Arts there was warmth and food for body and spirit, precious in those years of hunger, cold and isolation.

Both Akhmatova and Gumilev sat on the board of the House of the Arts, so they encountered one another there frequently. Akhmatova, always sensitive to Kolya's feelings, avoided the parties and other social events he was sure to attend. But they still shared the care of their son and, despite his bitterness over the divorce, he often brought Lev (who was being cared for by Gumilev's mother) to visit her. Their careful but amicable relationship continued as Gumilev and

Shileiko worked together on a translation of the Sumerian epic, *Gilgamesh*.

Nikolai Gumilev married again, to a woman he expected to be simpler, more "manageable" than Akhmatova. Anna Nikolaevna Englehardt, a nurse in the clinic where he had been treated for bronchitis, had been in love with Gumilev since before he had left for Paris and London. With her rosy cheeks, fluffy, blonde curls and wide blue eyes, Asya, as she was known, was of a feminine type exactly opposite Akhmatova's. Gumilev, with his usual dexterity, had carried on a love affair with Englehardt simultaneously with his romance with Larisa Reisner. Asya had written to him at the front and abroad affectionate, if banal and rather whiney letters. This is an excerpt from one she wrote to him in Paris, dated more than a year earlier, December 4, 1917.

Kolya dear...It's sad to write knowing that it will take at least a half year for this letter to arrive. I am really driven to despair from such a delay. Dearest, already we have been parted for 1/2 year. Sometimes it seems to me that it has been forever! I can't nor do I wish to call you back here, Kolya, to insist that you come. It would be too egotistical. You know here in Petersburg now it is vile and boring, everyone is taking off somewhere...But there in Paris life is probably different—you have interesting business, dear friends, your collection of paintings, not the coarseness and devastation that reigns now. I endlessly want to see you, as ever I love only you, but it's better for you to be there, where it's pleasant and where you are getting along well. Perhaps the war will finally end soon and then you will come or, perhaps, before long you will be able to come here. I am afraid, and it will be painful to me to see your regret, if you come back now thanks to me, because here, really, it is difficult to live! You summon me, you dear! But I am afraid to travel alone on such a long trip at the present time, perhaps earlier I would have come, but now it is so difficult to travel at all and the more so as it's so far. Because suddenly you may be sent somewhere else, and I would be left alone, no, I have a thousand reasons. Ah, Kolya, Kolya, I love you, I often think of you, and I can't but believe that sometime we'll be together again...[10]

Gumilev's marriage to the second Anna was even less successful than that to the first. She may have been remembered as "very pretty, with a meek, gentle little face and a pink ribbon around her forehead."[11] But Akhmatova revealed what lay behind this winsome and charming facade: "It was a hasty marriage. Kolya was deeply hurt when I left him and he married somewhat hastily, on purpose, out of spite. He thought that he was marrying a simple girl made of wax, that he would be able to shape a person out of her. But she was made of reinforced concrete. Not only was it impossible to shape her, you couldn't even make a mark, a scratch on her.'"[12] Taken in by Anna Englhardt's pink ribbons and gushing prattle, Gumilev was soon exasperated with her willfulness and bad temper and packed her off to Slepnevo. His sister-in-law, giving this a more positive twist, maintained that it was because more food could be found in the countryside. But Asya refused to stay there and pestered Gumilev with her insistent requests to return to the city.

Little concerned with the political upheavals going on around him, Gumilev viewed the Bolsheviks with barely concealed disdain. But they had transformed the world within which he worked. All private publishing had been abolished and in December, 1917, Gosizdat, the

State Publishing House, was formed to oversee the publishing of books and other printed materials. This was the first step in establishing a system of strict governmental control and censorship.

In its early years, Gosizdat provided welcome opportunities for Russian writers. World Literature (Vsemernaya Literatura), a publishing house devoted to making the classic works of world literature available to the masses, was inaugurated under the direction of Maxim Gorky. In those lean days Petersburg's best scholars and writers could earn a small wage and receive ration cards by editing and translating texts from all over the world. At least for a time they may have been distracted from the realization that their freedom to publish what and as they chose had vanished.

The section of World Literature devoted to poetry, housed in offices on Liteiny Avenue, was headed by Nikolai Gumilev and Mikhail Lozinsky. In this new Soviet order, Gumilev would find new roles to play as poet, teacher, critic and translator. His only real rival in the literary world of Petrograd was Alexander Blok, also a member of the board of World Literature, whom he often encountered at meetings or other literary functions. Their relationship was strained and prickly as they jockeyed for position, not so much for political power within the literary bureaucracy as for influence over younger poets. Their views on most subjects were sharply antithetical and the two kept up a continuously running, elaborately polite but deadly serious argument over the nature of poetry. But in the end, the destinies of these two were closely tangled in their tragic deaths, which brought down the curtain upon the once insouciant, avant-garde literary stage of St. Petersburg.

As Vsevelod Rozhdestvensky, a Tsarskoe Selo poet and friend of Gumilev, observed the two:

> They obviously disliked one another but in no way expressed their hostility. What is more, the talk of each of them was presented as an elegant duel of mutual politeness and courtesies. Gumilev extended himself in refined and ironic compliments. Blok listened sternly and, with an especially cold clarity and a bit more often than was necessary, added to every sentence: "esteemed Nikolai Stepanovich," distinctly pronouncing every letter of his first and second name.[13]

Blok was unenthusiastic about Gumilev's poems, which he felt lacked depth, having "only two dimensions." Yet he respected his erudition and his critical acuity. Gumilev had the highest esteem for Blok and had written a rapturous article about his poetry for *Apollon*. After one long and fruitless argument between the two, Rozhdestvensky wrote, an obviously irritated Blok walked away, leaving Gumilev:

> "Just look at that," he said to me. "That man is unusually obstinate. He doesn't wish to understand the most obvious truths. In that conversation, he nearly upset my equilibrium..."
> "Yes, but you were chatting with him exceptionally politely and you weren't able to object about anything to him."
> Gumilev quickly and surprisingly stared at me:
> "And what could I do? Imagine that you were talking with the living Lermontov. What could you say to him, what could you argue with him about?"[14]

Gumilev's admiration for Blok as a person and a poet was clear when he told a friend: "He's not only the best Russian poet, but the best of any I have met in my life. A gentleman from head to foot. A pure, noble spirit. But—he doesn't understand anything in poetry, believe me."[15]

Outwardly, the differences between them were as striking. Blok had been blessed with a refined, classical beauty as a young man and, despite his dissipated life-style, he retained the ravaged good looks and personal magnetism of the young, romantic poet. Whereas Gumilev, with his coarser features, his lisp, his prominent eyes, could not match Blok in looks. Blok seldom frequented Petersburg's literary events and prided himself on never having descended into the crowded, noisy cellars of the Stray Dog. But his premiere place in the world of Russian poetry remained unquestioned. Though he was only six years older than Gumilev, Alexander Blok, having published his first book in 1903, belonged to an earlier generation of poets. He had written more poems than Gumilev and was beloved throughout Russia, while Gumilev was still relatively unknown to the average Russian reader.

But there were many similarities between them, a fact which will do much to intensify such a rivalry. For no matter how Gumilev advocated his Acmeist poetics, when it came to practice, many of his poems were rooted in the Symbolist idiom. Khodasevich, a friend of both poets, wrote: "Blok, at times storming against Symbolism, was one of the purest Symbolists. Gumilev, to the end of life never emerging from the influence of Bryusov, imagined himself a deep, constant foe of Symbolism."[16]

Others in Petrograd's literary world thought the two poets had much in common. Vladimir Shklovsky wrote: "The last time I saw them both was at World Literature. Tall, erect...both read aloud their poems with the special sing-song, recitative tone characteristic of Petersburg poets when they declaim for one another...With both poets there are repeating moments in their work. For one 'the beautiful lady,' for the other...is repeated the image of the seraphim..."[17]

And they were alike in other ways. Both poets came from prosperous families securely positioned in the intelligentsia, were educated at St. Petersburg University and had lived most of their lives in or near that city. Both created for themselves a quasi-mythic, self-conscious persona of "the Poet," a role which shaped and amplified their personal lives and, though it took them in different directions, determined their poetic development.

Although Gumilev could be obsessively concerned about his place in the hierarchy of Russian poets, it was not merely questions of ego or their relative importance in the world of poetry that underlay the rivalry of Gumilev and Blok. Khodasevich saw important and basic differences:

Their understandings of the world were conflicting, sharply opposed literary problems. The main thing in Blok's poetry, its "secret motive" and its emotional-spiritual sense, must have been alien to Gumilev. For Gumilev, the hostile and not easily understood sides of Symbolism must have appeared to him with special clarity in

Blok. It's not for nothing that the manifestoes of the Acmeists were directed first of all against Blok and Bely. In Gumilev, the "emptiness," the "un-necessity," the "exterior-ness" would have offended Blok.[18]

Blok particularly disliked Gumilev's analytical approach to poetry, his way of weighing and "dismembering" a poem. Blok once spoke with Rozhdestvensky of how he wrote a poem:

"...First of all, I hear some kind of sounding. The intonation of an earlier idea. Someone speaks to me—passionately, with conviction, as in a dream. And then the words come. And it's necessary only to follow after them, so that they lie exactly in that intonation, in no way contradicting it. That then is truth. Every poem at the beginning is a ringing dot spreading out in concentric circles. No, it's not even a dot but more an astronomical fogginess. And out of it worlds are born."[19]

And Gumilev's approach:

"Gumilev looks at it differently," I noted. "He maintains that he sees a poem as a whole, in all its colors and forms. And it remains for him only to write it down so that not one detail is left out. What is more, he has the firm conviction that it is possible to set out the theme of a future poem beforehand, like a chess problem, and solve it in all its possible variations."
Blok laughed bitterly. "Happy man! But I don't envy him."[20]

If their differing views on the nature of poetry were all that separated them, the gulf between the two poets might have been bridged. But there were two complicating factors that fed Blok's hostility—Gumilev's past relationship with Bryusov and his present one with his "Gumilyats," the young post-revolutionary poets who clustered about him. Blok considered his influence upon them "spiritually and poetically pernicious."[21]

On the translation of literature, an art form highly prized in Russia, Blok and Gumilev again held very different opinions. For Blok, though he was a meticulous editor and translator, it was the "spirit" or mood of the work, rather than its formal elements, that he believed necessary to convey. Gumilev, on the other hand, insisted that the translator must duplicate in the second language the exact form as well as the substance of the original poem. The formal characteristics of metre, rhyme, line length, whether chosen by the poet or emerging naturally in the process of writing, were not accidental, but an intrinsic part of the poem that contributed to the poem's total meaning.[22]

Yet one more difference between the two leading poets of Petrograd was their starkly opposing views on the cataclysm of revolutionary change. Gumilev was arrogantly dismissive of the bold machinations and political maneuvering of the Bolsheviks. He had to accept the changes imposed upon his life because he had no choice and outwardly attempted to make a place for himself in the "utopia" of Communism. If he could not enthusiastically support the new order, neither would he actively oppose it. Gumilev did not feel that, by teaching the proleteriat to write poetry or providing workers with classic texts from other traditions, he was compromising himself. But he made no secret of his scorn for the crude, unlettered bumpkins who had seized power, a view no doubt shared by others of Petersburg's intelligentsia.

Blok, however, had long been intrigued with the idea of revolution. His poems are pervaded with images of storms, whirlwinds, blizzards, like the wild, uncontrollable forces that would scour Russia clean of the accretions of centuries of social, political and moral rot. Blok's article entitled "The Intelligentsia and the Revolution." published on January 9, 1918, in *The Banner of Labor*, was addressed to Gumilev and all those other artists and writers who scoffed and jeered at the Revolution.[23]

Blok compares Russia to Gogol's run-away troika, rushing forward into the future. In the aftermath of war, the culmination of centuries of baseness and horror, the revolutionary fervor roared like the new music of a world orchestra. Revolution, like a force of nature, would bring destruction and unexpected consequences. The artist must not retreat into his private world, but must listen to its music. Blok excuses the wholesale destruction wreaked upon Russia, of the social order, of the Orthodox Church, of Russian culture. He condemns the intelligentsia for their weeping and handwringing, for keeping silent on important political questions, for pronouncing the beautiful word, "comrade," ironically, as if in quotation marks. He insists that the writer of the future must not look down on the unenlightened masses, but speak new words to new readers. If out of pride and malice the intelligentsia hardens its resistance to the Revolution, the struggle for renewal would only be more bloody.

Blok ends by calling writers to "Listen with your whole body, whole heart, whole consciousness—listen to the Revolution!"

By January, 1919, the whirlwind of revolutionary fever was beginning to subside. The Bolsheviks had taken the country firmly in their grip and had begun their massive undertaking to "re-make" Russia. But clearly it would not be according to the dreams of poets, but those of commissars. The "world music" that Blok was straining to hear was sounding flat and far-away.

Blok had been well-treated by the Soviet authorities. In response to a poll carried out by the *Petrograd Echo*, with the question— "Can the intelligentsia collaborate with the Bolsheviks?" —Blok had responded: "...It can and it should...Quite apart from personal reasons, the same music is sounding for the intelligentsia as for the Bolsheviks. The intelligentsia has always been revolutionary...The intelligentsia's anger against the Bolsheviks is superficial, and it seems to be passing. A man thinks differently from the way he speaks publicly. Reconciliation, a musical reconciliation, is on the way..."[24]

But on February 21, 1919, Blok was arrested by the Cheka and locked up in the Petrocheka's center, a building on Gorokhovaya street which had earlier housed the Petrograd city offices. The accusation against him was that he was involved in a "conspiracy of the Left Social Revolutionaries" against the Soviet government. After two days of questioning and the special intervention of Anatoly Lunacharsky, the People's Commissar of Education, Blok was released. Although he continued to work on the committee of the Bolshoi Dramatic Theatre and the editorial board of World Literature, this terrifying experience of suddenly finding himself viewed as the "enemy" must have deeply shaken Blok's faith in the Bolsheviks and the rightness of their cause. In the arena of political opinion, Blok and Gumilev would not remain irrevocably opposed, as over the next two years until his death, Blok's disillusionment with the new government deepened. His pessimism about Russia's future under the Bolsheviks would come to surpass even that of Nikolai Gumilev.

Chapter XIII
The Lost Streetcar

If Vladimir Shileiko had been attracted to Akhmatova for her beauty and mysterious depths, it was an obliging and dutiful wife that Shileiko really needed—someone to help him with the arduous task of organizing his papers and taking down dictations as he translated Assyrian texts, to provide food, tea and cigarettes, to care for him when he was sick, to keep the apartment clean, orderly and heated. This was not a role that Akhmatova could easily fill. Although she did learn to light the big iron stove, she was as hapless and impractical in managing the exigencies of ordinary life as her mother before her had been. In normal times it would have been difficult enough. But with the drastic shortages of food and fuel in Petrograd, life was made nearly impossible even for the most practically-minded.

In a time of revolution and civil war, one could understand Akhmatova's sincere, but misguided attempt at spiritual redemption through self-denial. Relinquishing her personal freedom, even her poetic voice, and submitting herself to Shileko's demands may have been her way of chastising her spirit, of scouring it clean of pride and willfulness. That year, if she had not abandoned completely the writing of poetry as Shileiko had asked her, she may have destroyed many poems too steeped in the misery she was suffering.

Frances Laird

Anna's reckless, unsparing giving of herself, her total submission to a trial of the spirit, took its toll upon her, as this poem of July, 1918, suggests:

> From your love, strange and mysterious,
> I cry out as if in pain.
> I've become epileptic and yellow, I
> Can scarce drag my feet along.
>
> Don't go whistling any new songs to me,
> For long you can deceive with a song.
> But with claws, claws rage against
> My consumptive breast.
>
> So that blood from my throat will come flowing out
> Faster onto the bed.
> So that from my heart intoxication will
> Be extracted forever by death.
>
> Anna Akhmatova
July, 1918[1]

Her lover as a predatory bird, clawing the poet's breast, already weakened by illness, and spilling a gush of blood over the bed is a graphic, powerful, even horrifying image. But the poet feels that it is only a cruel and bloody death that can release her from the hypnotic spell woven around her by love.

The ominous news of the Tsar's death and the disappearance of the imperial family cast a pall over Petrograd as well as Akhmatova's beloved parks and palaces of Tsarskoe Selo, now renamed Detskoe Selo (Children's Village). It was in the forlorn ex-capital, soon after her divorce from Nikolai Gumilev was finalized in August, 1918, that Akhmatova and Shileiko were married and she moved into his apartment in Fontanny Dom, the eighteenth-century palace on the Fontanka Canal that in pre-Revolutionary days had belonged to the Sheremetev family. As Shileiko was a member of the Russian Academy and, before the Revolution, had tutored the Sheremetev children, he was allowed to live in a room in the servant's wing. It would be beneath the family coat-of-arms and the motto, *Deus conservat omnia,* that she would live most of the rest of her life.

Akhmatova described the hardships then: "Three years of hunger. I left the Gumilevs' without taking anything with me. Vladimir Kazimirovich was ill. He could do without anything but tea and tobacco. We rarely cooked—there was nothing to cook or to cook in. We had to ask the neighbours for every little saucepan: I didn't have a fork, a spoon or a saucepan...The most humiliating thing was matches. There weren't any and in the morning I had to run into the street to get a light off somebody."[2]

Frances Laird

In the fall of 1918, Shileiko was given work in Moscow and they moved to a flat on Zachatevsky street. Akhmatova recalled the months she lived there in a poem she wrote in 1940.

<u>Three Zachatevsky Street</u>

Little back alley, little back…
It tightened a loop around my neck.

From the Moscow River it draws cool air,
In the windows little lights glare.

A vacant lot on the left-hand side,
And a monastery on the right.

A tall maple tree across the street
Listens to a long groan in the night.

A rotting streetlamp leaned to one side,
From the bell tower the bell-ringer strides…

If only I could find that little icon,
For I feel my time will be here soon,

If only again I had my black shawl

Swan Songs
Akhmatova and Gumilev

And Neva water to fill my mouth full.

Anna Akhmatova

1940[3]

The noose that she feels tightening around her neck and choking her "song" cuts off her words mid-sentence. The world around her is spare, bleak and lonely, with only a maple tree as witness to her suffering. She feels that her life will soon end and longs only for her familiar shawl, for comfort and as a reminder of her fleeting moments of recognition on the Stray Dog's stage, and a swallow of water from Petersburg's great river. The fear-frozen air of the Stalinist terror emanates from this poem, written at the same time as *Requiem*, with the same bright emptiness, haunting silence and desolation that permeates Poem VII, "The Sentence." At least Akhmatova's loneliness in the Moscow flat was occasionally mitigated by visits from Osip Mandelstam.

Shileiko and Akhmatova returned from Moscow early in 1919 and moved into an apartment in the Marble Palace, another of Petersburg's exquisite eighteenth-century buildings, once the residence of a Romanov prince. Their room looked out over the statue of General Suvorov and the Field of Mars, a military parade ground dotted with the graves of those killed during the October Revolution. The large living space was divided into two rooms by a plywood screen. The living-room held a large, round dining table, a rickety, overstuffed sofa with protruding springs, a china cupboard and a bookcase stuffed with rare books. There was also a bedroom and a small kitchen. The apartment was usually littered with the books and rare manuscripts Shileiko was working on. Adding to the clutter was a St. Bernard dog, Tapa, that had followed Shileiko home, one of thousands let loose by owners who could no longer feed them. To acquire the food ration cards that were issued to Shileiko and that kept them both alive, Akhmatova, as everyone else, was forced to stand in the long queues. But with the shortage of fuel, it was impossible for them to take the chill from their spacious, frigid rooms and they moved back into the one room flat in Fontanny Dom sometime in 1919.

Akhmatova's unending struggle was to find enough food for herself and Shileiko, to find oil for the kerosene lamp and wood for the stove so that ice crystals would not fur the blankets at night. In the bleak darkness of a dying Petrograd, she faced a future filled with questions, as friends and acquaintances fled to what they imagined would be an easier life in the West. But it was out of the depths of such suffering, when strength and vitality were being sucked from her, that she wrote one of her most moving poems:

> What makes this age much worse than those before it? Really,
> As if while dazed with anxiousness and grief,
> It fingered lightly its own blackened sore place,
> But healing was beyond its reach.
> While in the west the earthly sun still keeps on shining

And cities' rooftops there are gleaming in its light.
But here the white one marks the houses now with crosses
And calls the ravens, and the ravens all take flight.

Anna Akhmatova
Winter, 1919[4]

Akhmatova is not just speaking for one unhappy woman, but for all the people of a suffering Russia, as she would in the coming years. The era of civil war and revolution, with its violence, terror and wholesale destruction like none before in Russia's tragic history, is the subject of the first stanza. Stunned and paralyzed by loss, this age can only dumbly finger its wound, like a stupified child picking at a scab on his knee. Once time would have worked to heal the wounds of the body and spirit. But the poet can see nothing around her, neither from nature nor man, which would mend this profound rupture that has been made with the past. The poet gazes westward toward the civilized world of Europe and her beloved Paris, where the sun comes up each day and people live out their lives beneath secure and familiar roofs. Despite the ravages of war, there is a predictable continuity to life there. But in Petrograd there are no certainties. Death marks out the houses where it will strike, choosing at random who will live and who will die, then summons the black ravens to pick the bones of the corpses clean. In Akhmatova's Cassandra-like vision, there is a chilling premonition which echoes in the calm, elevated, almost transcendent voice of the poet.

Frances Laird

While Akhmatova shrank back from the Soviet world into isolation, gazing down upon it as if from a high tower, Gumilev dove into the fray. He had heeded Blok's advice—at least in part—and stepped courageously out into the new cultural landscape. For in a time of chaos he saw poetry as a haven of spiritual freedom and consolation. In his efforts to keep Russian poetry—and himself—alive, he taught and lectured anywhere in Petrograd where he was granted a room, a stage, an interested audience. He became a familiar, if odd, sight on the streets of Petrograd. As Nikolai Otsup wrote:

What Petersburger doesn't recall Gumilev's strange fur coat with the smooth fur on the outside and the white patterns on the bottom (such a fur coat as a prosperous Laplander wears). In this fur coat, in a hat with ear flaps, in great, blunt-nosed boots which he got from KYBA (the Commission on the Improvement of the Life of Scholars), the grand and affable Gumilev, usually surrounded by his disciples, went from one lecture to the next in the Institute of the Living Word, the House of the Arts, Proletkult [Proletarian Culture—an organization to promote culture among the masses], Baltflot and such establishments. He read his lectures without taking off his fur coat, as we all did, so cold was it in the unheated auditoriums. The steam poured from his mouth, his hands turned blue, but Gumilev lectured about the new poetry, about the French Symbolists, taught how to translate and even to write poems. He did this not only in order to feed his family and himself, but because he loved poetry with his whole being and believed that it was necessary to help every person relieve his perplexity when he asks himself: why am I living? For Gumilev, poems were a form of religious service.[5]

Like a missionary Gumilev worked to spread his gospel of poetry, giving readings in Petrograd and in Moscow, teaching eager but unlettered proletarian youth the stringent rules of metre and rhyme, replacing with his living words the magazines and journals banished by the Bolsheviks, and warming his shivering listeners with his passion and enthusiasm. He took upon himself the mantle of guardian of the poetic culture in Petrograd.

Although Gumilev believed the role of poet to be exalted, almost god-like, he was equally convinced that poetry was an art available to everyone. Once asked if there weren't already too many poets, Gumilev responded: "Every person is a poet. The Castalian spring of his soul is stopped up with rubbish. It must be cleansed."[6] In Greek myth, Castalia was a young girl of Delphi who threw herself into a spring on Mount Parnassus to escape the lecherous pursuit of Apollo. This spring became sacred to the Muses and its waters granted poetic inspiration to those who drank of it. Gumilev often spoke of the elusive images that drew him into his poems:

In the old times of knights, the paladins were troubadours, like the German guild artisans were meistersingers...I sometimes dream that I, in one of my previous lives, was master of the sword and song. Talent is not always a gift, often it's a memory. Unclear, vague, unreadable. You go after it, groping, into the dusk and fog towards the wonderful ghosts melting away there once in your past life...[7]

Gumilev was especially attentive to his students, his little band of "Gumilyats." In the turmoil of a newly-forming culture with alien values, they shared his love and respect for the written word.

Gumilev knew that it was through them that the rich tradition of Russian poetry would be kept alive and passed on to a new generation. He was especially sensitive in his response to their work, prizing their originality, however awkwardly it might be expressed, and was always prepared to find "the pearl in the piles of manure," as he put it. Yet he was demanding and exact, for the young poet must be stubbornly persistent in perfecting his difficult craft.

Gumilev enjoyed the company of young people in a social way, for he himself often seemed to be sixteen years old. Khodasevich wrote:

> He was surprisingly young of spirit. He always seemed like a child to me. There was something childish in his head, his hair closely cut with electric clippers, in his bearing which was sooner a schoolboy's than a military man's. Also, his childishness showed through in his great attraction to Africa, to war, finally—in his feigned grand manner which so surprised me with our first meeting and which suddenly slipped away, evaporated somewhere until he suddenly remembered and drew it back to himself again. Like all children, he liked to represent himself as a grown-up. He loved to play the "master," the literary "boss" of his "Gumilyats," the little poets and poetesses who surrounded him. He loved the poetic kiddies. Sometimes, after lectures about poetics, he played blind-man's-bluff with them—in the literal sense of the word...Then Gumilev was like the praised high school student who plays around with the elementary students.[8]

Nikolai Gumilev was not a man of caution and calculation. Although he never spoke of his political opinions in public, in his conversations with friends and students he was irrepressibly frank. He refused to tone down his outspoken opinions and eccentric ways, to make compromises in the face of Soviet power. Although he must have been aware that he was flirting with danger, that was something he had never hesitated to do. He would not be frightened into mute submission by his new political masters. Maxim Gorky, the highest-ranking Soviet man of letters and a poet, attended a lecture at which Gumilev was giving instruction in versification. When Gorky asked if it was really necessary that a poet know all those rules, Gumilev assured him that it was. Gorky posed a trickier question:

"Nikolai Stepanovich, what can you say to me about my poems?"
"I don't know them well. I confess, I don't remember that I read them."
Gorky didn't take offense, but replied:
"By the way, one of my poems had great success, especially among young people, students and workers. They declaim it now. It's called 'The Stormy Petrel.'"
"Yes, yes, I remember, trochaic tetrameter with nothing but feminine endings. The metre is an imitation of 'Gainavat.' Excuse me, Alexei Maximovich, it is effete. One of your lines somehow came to my attention: '*Vysoko v gori vpolz uzh i leg tam.*' If you had known Russian prosody, you wouldn't have made a trochaic out of one syllable words. You can't do that, it isn't grammatically correct. "*Vpolz uzh i leg tam.*" Perhaps your ear of a talented writer doesn't hear that absolutely impossible collision of words—and not only in poetry?"[9]

When Kolya told Akhmatova of this, she first burst out laughing, then worried that if Gorky had become angry, he could take away Kolya's work or his ration card. Nikolai Otsup didn't believe that Gumilev intended to provoke those in power, nor did he deliberately seek out an audience where his views would be acceptable. However, if an audience were hostile, he would fall silent, wishing neither to provoke a scandal nor "cast his pearls before swine." Gumilev knew that he often aroused anger, even malice, in his listeners. He spoke out not merely to promote his own poetic ideals, but because he preferred to remain oblivious to ideas hostile to his own. If he could, he would ignore the Revolution. Once when speaking about the lofty civic vocation of the poet-druids and poet-priests, he suddenly overheard a rude reply from the audience to a question he had rhetorically posed. If he couldn't bear to listen to it, yet in those circumstances he could not confront and attempt to reason with the person who said it. So Gumilev chose to keep on speaking. To go against the prevailing opinions of everyone was what he loved to do.[10]

Gumilev's lectures in a small way were a challenge to Bolshevik power, so Otsup believed. Before an audience of Proletkult, he jokingly but provocatively proclaimed "I am a monarchist!"[11] In a lecture in the literary studio of Baltflot, before a hundred sailors and a commissar, Gumilev was asked: "What then, citizen lecturer, helps one to write good poems?" "In my opinion, wine and women," calmly answered the citizen lecturer. To those who knew Gumilev, the purpose of such an answer was the teasing of the "bosses." With respect to poetry, the bosses were already spreading everywhere a system of education in the spirit of Marxism. Not surprisingly, at the conclusion of the lecture, the commissar demanded that Gumilev end his classes at Baltflot.[12]

Swan Songs
Akhmatova and Gumilev

At the Institute of Art History in June, 1919, Nikolai Gumilev lectured on the work of Alexander Blok, who sat impassively before him in the audience, where he criticized the end of the "The Twelve." Gumilev felt that the sudden appearance of Christ was artificially tacked on for purely literary effect. At the end of the lecture, Blok said thoughtfully: "I don't like the end of 'The Twelve' either. I wanted it to turn out differently. When I got to the ending, I was surprised myself: why Christ? But the closer I looked, the more clearly I saw Christ. And so I made a mental note: "Yes, unfortunately, Christ."[13] Gumilev looked at Blok with his usual arrogance, unable to imagine how one could not have absolute control over what one wrote. According to Chukovsky: "He [Gumilev] was a master, not a *commander* of his inspirations, and he didn't like it when poets acted like passive victims of their own poetry." But Blok was always eager to hear what others thought of "The Twelve," as if someone else might be able to reveal to him the meaning of what he had written.[14]

In the spring of 1919, Kolya and Asya moved out of the family house into their own flat at 5 Preobrazhenskaya Street. Soon after, Asya gave birth to a daughter, Yelena. Supposedly Kolya, who had dreamed of having a daughter, was delighted when the doctor handed the newborn to him, saying "There's your dream." But he could be no more faithful to this wife that he had been to Anna Akhmatova. With an actress from the Alexandrinsky Theatre, Olga Arbenina, he had carried on a two-year love affair. And other temptations were

Frances Laird

always near in the covey of adoring neophyte poetesses who flocked about him.

As living conditions in Petrograd grew worse, as the Soviets pressed the Marxist ideology upon them and more freedoms were taken away, writers were severed from their readership. The question of emigration was warmly but circumspectly argued wherever two or three gathered. Akhmatova had already made her decision to stay, even as she was more fully realizing the implications of it and the consequences for her. Along with Boris Anrep, Salomea Andronikova was now in England. The ballerina Tamara Karsavina had emigrated as had the Nabokov family, whose son, Vladimir, had yet to begin his career as a novelist. In December, 1919, Zinaida Gippius and Dmitri Merezhkovsky, mainstays of the Symbolist movement, left Russia.

Akhmatova knew even then that those who chose to stay behind in Russia would be abandoned by those who had found freedom in the West. As the walls of tyranny closed in upon her, she imagined the glorious city of St. Petersburg as the funeral monument for those who would preserve Russian culture.

<u>Petrograd, 1919</u>

>Imprisoned in a wild capital,
>Forevermore we have forgotten
>The steppes, the cities, the clear lakes

Swan Songs
Akhmatova and Gumilev

And dawns of the great land of our fathers.

By day and night in the bloody round

A cruel and brutal langour grows.

Nobody wants to help us now

Because we chose to stay at home,

Because, loving our city best,

And not drawn off by winged freedom,

We have preserved, saved for ourselves

Its palaces, its fire and water.

Another time is drawing near.

Death's wind cools my heart already.

But our unwitting monument

Will be Peter's holy city.

Anna Akhmatova[15]

That "holy city" was sliding into an abyss of decay and desolation. As the winter of 1919-20 tightened its icy grip on the once grand capital of Russia, Osip Mandelstam came to Petrograd. His name on the advertising posters slapped up over flaking walls appeared beside those of Alexander Blok and Nikolai Gumilev. Akhmatova remembered:

The old Petersburg signboards were still all in place, but behind them there was nothing but dust, darkness, and yawning emptiness. Typhus, hunger, execution by firing squad, dark apartments, damp wood, and people swollen beyond recognition. You could pick a large bouquet of wildflowers in Gostiny Dvor [the department store on Nevsky Prospekt near where Anna and Kolya had first met]. The famous Petersburg wooden pavement was rotting. The smell of chocolate still wafted from the basement windows of Kraft. All the cemeteries had been pillaged. The city had not just changed, it had turned into its exact opposite. But people still loved poetry (mainly the young people)...[16]

Conditions were even worse in Tsarskoe, now Detskoe, Selo. Nikolai Otsup recalled Gumilev's ironic and humorous verse:

> Not Tsarskoe Selo—unfortunately,
> But Detskoe Selo—hey, hey.
> What's better: being under the tsar's fist
> Or being amusement for malicious kids?[17]

For Akhmatova, the destruction of this beloved place of her childhood was but another crushing blow.

All the fences had been burned. Rusty beds from World War I field hospitals stood over the open drains of water pipes, the streets were overgrown with grass, roosters of all colors wandered around crowing...The gates of Count Stenbock-Fermor's house, which not long before had been noted for its magnificence, sported an enormous sign: Mating Center. But in autumn the oaks on Broad Street, witnesses to my childhood, still smelled as tart as ever, and the crows on the cathedral's crosses cawed the same way they had when I listened to them on my way to school through Cathedral Square, and the statues in the parks looked exactly as they had in the teens. I would sometimes recognize residents of Tsarskoe Selo in tattered and frightening figures. The arcade was closed.[18]

Swan Songs
Akhmatova and Gumilev

It would take the bombs of a future war to finally obliterate the gardens, bridges, pavillions, and statues of the imperial gardens and the little wooden houses of Tsarskoe Selo. Although she was only thirty years old, Akhmatova sees herself in the next poem as an old woman whose youth has suddenly receded into a far distant past and who turns to an outlawed God for help.

> I am old and I am bitter. The wrinkles
> Cover over with their web my yellow face.
> My back is bent and my hands are trembling.
> But my executioner gazes with cheerful look
> And he boasts of his skilled and artful work,
> Examining on my pale and withered skin
> The traces of his blows. Lord, have mercy!
>
> Anna Akhmatova
> 1919, Sheremetev House[19]

That gay, amorous and carefree young poetess, with her unusual beauty and languorous grace, whose fresh and unmistakable voice had enchanted St. Petersburg, had disappeared. In a regime determined to wipe out any traces of her and the era of which she was part, she had been replaced by a yellowed, wrinkled crone.

As Akhmatova turned back to the intensely personal lyric to express what was happening to and around her, Nikolai Gumilev discovered fresh and startling imagery that enabled him to break through to a new level of visionary expression. In December, 1919, he wrote one of his most powerful and frighteningly prophetic poems, "The Lost Streetcar." Otsup recalled:

> ...In Russia in the epoch of war communism, among his terrorized, starving colleagues, Gumilev was steadfast and calm, but more than ever he had to escape into a region of visions and dreams.
>
> It might be interesting to the future biographer of the poet to know how and when "The Lost Streetcar"...was written. At that time, Gumilev and I were close friends; day and night we would sit around my place on Serpukhovskaya street. We spent the night of the 29th to the 30th of December, 1919, at the place of my friend, an 'improvised' patron of the arts, the engineer Alexander Vasilevich K...
>
> K. apparently didn't intend to republish Gumilev but, knowing that the poet needed money, he signed a paper by which the author of *The Quiver* received thirty thousand rubles. We were happy and we were drinking. It was impossible to go out at night, so we left as morning broke.
>
> When we set out toward the bridge, despite the very early hour, a streetcar came thundering down unexpectedly behind us...Gumilev set out running.
>
> The following day Gumilev read me "The Lost Streetcar.[20]

The Lost Streetcar

The street I walked along was unfamiliar

And all at once I heard a crow's caw

And a ringing lute and far-away thunder,

There in front of me a streetcar flew.

How I leaped up onto its stairsteps

Swan Songs
Akhmatova and Gumilev

Still remains a mystery to me.
A fiery streak trailed in the air, left
Behind it even in the light of day.

Rushing along, storm-like, dark, wings flying,
In the abyss of time it lost its way...
Bring this streetcar to a stop, tram driver,
Stop the streetcar at once, I say!

Too late. We were skirting the wall already,
We went racing through a grove of palms,
Across the Nile, the Seine, the Neva,
Over the three bridges we thundered on.

Then past a window frame we were flashing
As after us an old beggar threw
A curious look—he was exactly
The one who'd died a year ago in Beirut.

Where am I? So languid and so anxious
My heart is beating in response. Do you
See the station where you can purchase
A ticket to the India of the Soul?

A shop signboard...the blood-soaked letters

Frances Laird

    Read out— "Greengrocer." Here I know well
    Instead of cabbages and rutabagas,
    They have the heads of dead people to sell.

    In a red shirt, his face like an udder,
    The axe-man cuts off a head—it's mine.
    It lay together with the others
    There at the bottom of the slippery bin.

    And a plank fence standing in a side street,
    A house, three-windowed, a lawn all grey.
    Bring this streetcar to a stop, tram driver,
    Stop the streetcar at once, I say!

    You lived here, you sang and wove me
    A rug, Mashenka, for the one you'd wed.
    But now where is your voice, your body,
    Could it be, perhaps, that you are dead?

    How you were moaning in your bedroom,
    While I, done up in a powdered braid,
    Went to present myself to the Empress
    And we didn't see each other again.

    Now I understood this…That our freedom

Swan Songs
Akhmatova and Gumilev

Is just light beating through from somewhere far.
Shades and people are standing at the entrance
To the planets' zoological park.

And all at once the wind is sweet, familiar.
From past the bridge comes flying at me
A horseman's palm in a glove of iron
And the two hooves of his rearing steed.

As Orthodoxy's stronghold, true and faithful,
Cut into the sky is St. Isaac's dome.
There prayers for Mashenka's salvation
And my panakhida I'll have intoned.

Still the heart's gloom is never ending.
It hurts to live and it's hard to breathe.
I never would have thought, Mashenka,
It possible to love so and so grieve.

Nikolai Gumilev
1919[21]

With a heart-stopping sense of his time, Gumilev speaks for himself, while speaking for everyone, as Akhmatova did in "Petrograd, 1919." In the "The Lost Streetcar," with its mix of images—dreamlike, philosophical and brutally real—Gumilev displays a new mastery of his craft. At last he has fused fantasy, reality and profound, moving passion into a powerful, authentically expressive whole. The streetcar has jumped its tracks and is hurtling at terrifying speed through time and space, carrying the helpless poet along with it. This central image gains resonance when we remember the end of part one of Gogol's *Dead Souls,* when the driver whips up the horses of the troika and Chichikov sits back to enjoy the sensation of speeding through the Russian countryside.

And what Russian does not love fast driving? And how should his soul not love it?...And is not a galloping *troika* like a mysterious force that has swept you away on its wings, so that you find yourself flying along, and everything else flying with you? The milestones fly past to meet you, the merchants in their carts are flying by, on each side of you forests of dark fir and pine trees are flying past to the thump of axes and the croaking of crows, the whole of the highway is flying on, no one knows where, into the receding distance; and there is a lurking terror in that glimmer of objects that keep flashing by rapidly and are gone before they can be identified...Russia, are you not speeding along like a fiery and matchless *troika*? Beneath you the road is smoke, the bridges thunder, and everything is left far behind. At your passage the onlooker stops amazed as by a divine miracle. 'Was that not a flash of lightening?' he asks. What is this surge so full of terror? And what is this force unknown impelling these horses never seen before?...Russia, where are you flying? Answer me! There is no answer...[22]

Alexander Blok saw Gogol's troika as Russia in revolution, but in Gumilev's poem, it has been transformed into its modern, mechanical equivalent, the streetcar. We see many parallels with the passage by Gogol—the terrifying sense of a speeding vehicle propelled by a mysterious force and out of control, the passenger's terror as objects rush past, the sensation of flight, wings, croaking of crows, axes, bridges, thunder, storms, fire.

In "The Lost Streetcar," the poet finds himself walking down an unfamiliar street in a vivid dream world. He hears the cawing of a crow, an ordinary sound from the unchanging world of forests and villages, followed by the ringing tones of a lute, an instrument associated with song (i.e.poetry). Then comes the ominous thunder of an approaching streetcar bearing down upon him. He clambers aboard and the streetcar, now transformed into a demonic, winged creature that swoops down into the "abyss of time," carries him back into his past. Scenes from his earlier life flash past. He sees palm trees and a bridge spanning the Nile River in Africa. The streetcar rumbles over another bridge crossing the Seine, returning him to his student days and his honeymoon with Akhmatova in Paris. Flying over a bridge that spans the Neva River, he is back in St. Petersburg again. From there he is propelled through countries strange and mysterious to him, past a dying beggar, who gazes at him with a curious look. But the poet feels nothing, for his heart is numb with anxiety and lassitude. Perhaps in India he might find in ancient religions the answers to his soul-questions, if he only knew how to get there. The cruel, brilliant clarity of a nightmare grips him as the streetcar swoops past a greengrocer's shop, where the scarlet letters of its sign are dripping with blood and, instead of cabbages and turnips, on display is a heap of decapitated human heads. An ugly, axe-wielding executioner stands ready to provide fresh ones. To his horror, the poet recognizes his own head among those at the bottom of the blood-smeared bin.

The streetcar sweeps inexorably onward, past the house and wooden fence where Gumilev and Akhmatova had lived, where now he sees himself enjoying a simpler life with a simpler woman—Mashenka, an idealized incarnation of his dead cousin, Mariya Kuzmina-Karavayeva, who sings to him as she weaves him a rug. But she is dying even as the poet, his hair powdered, steps into the world of Alexander Pushkin, where he, like Pushkin, must make his forced obeisance to the state.

The vision of freedom beating down like sunlight, bountiful, radiant, life-giving, eternal, is immediately countered by a scene of human beings, past and present, standing in line to be allowed entry to "the planets' zoological park," the Earth. This is Gumilev's terrifying image of the regimentation imposed upon human kind, upon history and upon the natural world at the hand of a thorough and unrelenting totalitarian state.

Suddenly the poet sniffs the familiar scent of his native city as the streetcar crashes past the the massive bronze figure by Falconet of Peter the Great on his rearing horse. If this sculpture embodies the historical and cultural traditions of the city, the near-by Cathedral of St. Isaac embodies those of Orthodox Christianity. It is there that the poet wants prayers sung for his Mashenka and the rites of his own death carried out. To dead Mashenka, Gumilev expresses his suffering and love in that stifling, sorrow-soaked year.

Life for Akhmatova and Shileiko, as for so many others, grew more difficult with each passing day. Shileiko was frequently ill with lung problems and Akhmatova was painfully thin. Although their marriage was not a success, they still cared for one another. Kornei Chukovsky wrote in his diary for January 19, 1920:

> Yesterday I saw Anna Akhmatova. She and Shileiko are together in one room, with a bed behind a screen. The room is dark and cold. Books are on the floor. Akhmatova has a strident voice. It's as if she's talking to me over the phone. Sometimes her eyes seem to be blind. She is tender with Shileiko, sometimes brushing away the hair from his forehead. He calls her Anichka; she calls him Volodya. She told me what a wonderful translator of poetry he was and that he dictated a whole ballad to her in its exact form. Then he succumbs to lunacy.[23]

Shileiko had completed the translation of *Gilgamesh* for World Literature, on which he had worked with Gumilev, and no longer received the stipend that kept the two of them alive. Without official support for his research, without permission to publish her poetry, he and Anna had become merely two more souls overlooked, devalued, and stranded without the resources to support themselves. Shileiko and Akhmatova were in desperate straits, now completely dependent for their survival on handouts from friends.

Surprisingly, one of these turned out to be Larisa Reisner, who sent a large sack of rice to the starving couple which, with her customary generosity, Akhmatova immediately shared out with her neighbors. Larisa had fallen on her feet with the coming of the Communists. Born into a family of revolutionaries, her political credentials were impeccable and she had worked diligently to recreate herself as the embodiment of the new "Russian revolutionary woman." Since her affair with Gumilev, she had married Fyodor Raskolnikov, an official in the Russian navy. In that time of widespread starvation and want, they kept a town house staffed with servants where they served magnificent meals. As Nadezhda Mandelstam wrote: "…Larisa and her husband justified themselves by saying that, as people engaged in building a new order, it would have been sheer hypocrisy for them to deny themselves their due as incumbents of power."[24]

Yet Reisner maintained a great respect for Akhmatova, although she was one of the out-dated intelligentsia that the Communists were eagerly erasing from the face of the earth. Akhmatova wrote: "At that time, I was poverty-stricken, hungry, sleeping on bare boards—a real Job…Then I once went to see her on business. She lived in the Admiralty: three windows looked out on the Bronze Horseman, three onto the Neva. She took me home in her carriage. On the way she said: 'I would give everything, everything to be Anna Akhmatova.' Stupid words, aren't they? What is everything? Three windows onto the Neva?"[25]

Even in such dire conditions, Akhmatova was careful of her appearance. Kornei Chukovsky witnessed this feminine side of her and an encounter with Blok, recorded in his diary entry for March 20, 1920:

> A few days ago Grzhebin phoned Blok: 'I bought Akhmatova,' meaning that he had managed to get hold of her poetry. What had happened was that Akhmatova had been brought a dress that she instantly liked, a dress she had always dreamed about, and she had gone immediately to Grzhebin and sold him her books for seventy-five thousand rubles.
> Blok, Zamyatin, and I ran into her as we were leaving World Literature Publishers. It was the first time I had seen Blok and Akhmatova together. It was very interesting: Blok's face was impenetrable, except that something almost imperceptible and 'responding' was in constant motion around his mouth. The same with Akhmatova. Nothing about their eyes or their smiles expressed anything, but much was said nonetheless.[26]

Akhmatova had realized that she had paid too high a price—the silencing of her poetic voice—for what little emotional and physical security she had received from Shileiko. She had to break out of a marriage that had become imprisoning and take her life back. With the help of friends, she found work in the library of the Agronomy Institute that, as well as a small salary, would provide her with a room, a ration card and a supply of firewood to see her through the coming winter. Taking advantage of Shileiko's convalescence in hospital, she moved into a government flat on Sergievsky Street. There in a space of her own, she could begin writing again. On his first visit, Osip Mandelstam brought news of the death from tuberculosis of Nikolai Nedobrovo in Yalta. A grief-stricken Akhmatova tried to find out more about the circumstances of his death. She wrote in her memoirs: "*Nobody* has *ever* been able to tell me any more details. That was what it was like then!"[27]

Gumilev, the "iron man," as his friends jokingly called him, continued his valiant attempt to live and work as if the Bolsheviks were not there. Andrei Levinson, a co-editor at World Literature, wrote about the enormous translation project that was keeping them all alive:

> For two or more years we were consolidated in the common work, the hopeless and paradoxical work of planting the spiritual culture of the West on the ruins of Russian life. Anyone who experienced the "cultural" work in Sovdepia knows the bitter taste of useless efforts, the feeling of doom in the struggle with the bestial animosity of the masters of life. But we lived this whole magnanimous illusion in those years, setting out the hopes that Byron and Flaubert, penetrating the masses as though to the glory of Bolshevik "bluff," would fruitfully astound more than one soul.[28]

At meetings of the editorial board of World Literature, Levinson learned to appreciate Gumilev's grasp of European poetry, the excellence of his poetry and his exceptional gift for teaching. Khodasevich remembers the grand importance with which Gumilev "met" at those conferences of editors and how his manner reminded him of the poet, Bryusov, once Gumilev's mentor.[29] Gumilev was known for his staunch defense of his fellow artists at those meetings, where "with extraordinary sharpness and fearlessness [he] stood up for the worth of the writer."[30]

The Studio of World Literature, a poetry workshop supported by the publishing house, was then Gumilev's primary pulpit, where he "clarified the rules of his poetics in the form of 'commandments' as if he were certain of the unarguableness of their foundations."[31] He was drawn to the rules of poetry as an Orthodox Christian is drawn to the precepts and rituals of his religion. "He was genuinely attracted to laws, to the symmetry of numbers, to measure. He was always setting out to put together tables of images, an encyclopedia of metaphors, where the myths of all peoples would be side by side with historical legend."[32] Gumilev wanted to make of poetry an exact science, freed of the mystical unrealities of Symbolism and the verbal non-sense of the Futurists. His poetry workshop was a special place, as one friend attested: "In the cruel, bestial situation of Soviet life, it was a bright oasis where young people, not yet dirtied by idleness and speculation, found a response to aesthetic inquiries…He knew how to engender in young people a love for poetry, to develop in them taste and an understanding of artistic beauty. And young people respected him, valued his advice and more than one of the young poets developed thanks to his instruction."[33]

Gumilev couldn't bear critics of the "seminarian" or "people's" type, who were becoming all powerful in the Soviet era. "'You know,' he said, 'Not long ago there were two kinds of critics. One type drank vodka, sang *"Gaudeamus igitur,"* and despised the French language. The others read Mallarmé, Maiterlinck, Verlaine and hated the first for their dirty underwear and rudeness. So there you are—honest *narodniks* are simply dung not needed by anyone and out of supposedly "rotting decadents" came the whole of today's literature.'"[34]

Rare then was a person like Gumilev who, in his dealings with poets and writers, could hold tenaciously to what was for the good of Russian literature while avoiding entanglement in the political manipulations and plots that tempted others. Nikolai Otsup wrote: "...I always had confidence in him. He was immeasurably higher than the petty intrigues with which the little people, who can be divided by vanity, always and everywhere poison the literary atmosphere, hindering the genuine poets in their lofty, disinterested service."[35] Otsup admired Gumilev for his firmness: "In Russia in the epoch of War Communism, among his starving, terrorized colleagues, Gumilev was strong and calm, but more than any other time, he needed to preserve himself in the realm of dreams and visions."[36]

The legends and myths of other cultures lifted his imagination out of the claustrophobic confines of an increasingly authoritarian society. A Celtic tale of a magic violin or lute provided the inspiration for "The Enchanted Violin," the first poem of Gumilev's book, *Pearls*, and his verse play, *Gondla*. He studied the Cabala, read the prophecies of astrologers and believed in the protective powers of amulets.[37] He even tried drugs to artificially induce the visions he sought. Erik Gollerbakh wrote: "Once he asked me for a pipe for the smoking of opium...He poisoned himself with the smoke of this blissful potion. Many people laughed at these 'experiments' of his."[38] But it was difficult to condemn him for trying to find some escape from the hostile world closing in around him, a world he viewed with indignation and disgust.

But the Bolsheviks reasoned that the most rebellious, free-thinking element of Russian society, its poets, must be made to serve the ends of the state. They gradually imposed control over poets through official organizations to which all must belong to find work and receive ration coupons for food. Organized into an official union, the All-Russian Union of Poets would serve the Communist party, contributing what it could to the formation of a new society. Membership in the Union of Poets was the price Gumilev paid to lecture and teach at Baltflot, Proletkult, the Studio of World Literature and the other official "cultural" organizations, the price he paid to continue his life as a poet.

Levinson admired the way that "into a stormy auditorium Gumilev carried his poetic teaching unchanged. He spoke out with absolute frankness his condemnation of a pseudo-proleterian culture, and right beside it revealed forthrightly his patriotic creed. Perhaps, Gumilev was able to go everywhere because nowhere would he lose himself."[39] But this freedom of expression, ever more narrowly circumscribed, would not be tolerated any longer than it would take for the Communists to establish absolute authority over all facets of the cultural life.

As cold, disease, starvation ravaged the people of Petrograd, Nikolai and his friends would gather in the evening to read their latest poems to one another, talk endlessly, and drink black tea, for vodka and wine were nowhere to be found. It was then that the Cheka made its silent nightly runs, inexorably weeding out the "enemies of the people." Death was becoming a ubiquitous presence in that city when, as Otsup wrote: "...after nine o'clock in the evening it was impossible to go out on the street, when the backfire of an engine at night made you strain your ears in horror: whom had they come for? When they didn't have to pick up the carrion—it was torn apart right on the street by emaciated dogs or hauled away piece by piece by even more emaciated people."[40]

Times of terror and desperation could bring out the best in people as well as the worst. Otsup from time to time would disappear from the capital, to return from some far-off place with treasures: dried fish, cranberries, baranka [ring-shaped rolls], dried peas, vegetables and even—wonder or wonders—lumps of sugar. He would deliver these, beautifully wrapped in packages tied with ribbons, to his starving poet friends. In payment they would give him their most precious possessions—a sonnet, a ballad, an elegy.[41]

Chapter XIV
The Silver Age Tarnishes

In the fall of 1920, Eric Gollerbakh encountered Nikolai Gumilev at the House of Rest, a government-sponsored resort on the banks of the Neva, where the poet had come to lecture on poetry. By this time, Gumilev's idealism and enthusiasm for teaching workers the rules of versification were wearing thin. He had deliberately regressed and now found his escape in play:

>...I was surprised at the change in his tone and appearance. He didn't talk at all with the workers, he didn't notice them (although he was appearing before them on the stage of the House of Rest with poems that didn't have great success). With his literary colleagues, he carried himself coldly, almost arrogantly. He talked to them with an icy tone and sometimes he "forgot" to greet them.
> He occupied himself happily with the young ladies, not in the figurative but the literal sense of the word. He made them squeal and giggle, read them poems endlessly, ran through the park with them. In other words, he was "sixteen years old."[1]

As a gift, Gollerbakh gave Gumilev a portrait in poetry which he had composed, inspired by lines and images from Gumilev's poems about Africa.

> I don't know who you are—a pious aesthete
> Or a savage disguised in a jacket?
> To the sound of an organ or castanets

Do you compose canzones and sonnets?
What if suddenly in a felucca you slip away,
Having taken the Neva for the Ganges,
Or you throw out a whistling boomerang
At a plane soaring over the city?
Are you related to the refined giraffe?
Like the hippopotamus, slow and important,
And the boa constrictor melting into the grass,
And the rhinoceros, fierce and courageous?
They found their place and their refuge
In your patterned and measured poems.
And the mandragoras sigh and bloom
In harmonies strange and stupefying.
But in the drunken, ominous voice,
In the Buddha-like face's features,
A yearning for the unearthly hides,
Gazing at us confusedly, wildly,
Like a deathless call in a world of decay,
Like a burst towards some other being,
Shining in an exotic paradise
Are Fra Angelico's sinless visions.
And bending low before them on stoney ground
The poet makes his prostrations,
Combining the cold light of his grey eyes
With the brownish twilight of the icon.

Swan Songs
Akhmatova and Gumilev
Erik Gollerbakh
1920[2]

Gollerbakh has captured essential and often noted qualities of Gumilev—his love of beauty and the exotic, his refined nature combined with a brazen courage, the probing gaze of his grey eyes set in a calm, Buddha-like face, his yearning for other worlds. Nikolai Gumilev's reaction was enthusiastic. "'A portrait, a portrait, a portrait very like me,' exclaimed N[ikolai] S[tepanovich], reading through this poem. 'You must have noticed in me the combination of the exotic and the orthodox.'"[3] Unfortunately, their friendship soured when Gollerbakh wrote an ironic and less than flattering review of Gumilev's recent poems published in the anthology, *Drakon (The Dragon)*.

Late in 1920, Gumilev attempted to resurrect the Guild of Poets with roughly the same format as that of 1911. Perhaps he felt that the close community of Petersburg poets was unraveling under the dissension within and assaults from without. Or he may have been attempting to retrieve a happier time of his life as a poet. But the philosophical foundations set forth by the new Guild of Poets, based on strict discipline and work, could only have been shaped by the rigorous atmosphere of the times. The founding members were Gumilev, Georgy Adamovich, Georgy Ivanov, Mikhail Lozinsky and Nikolai Otsup. This new incarnation of the Guild of Poets did not go unnoticed by Alexander Blok, who wrote in his diary: "Gumilev rules the roost—quite interesting and clever. The Acmeists, one feels, are in a kind of conspiracy, have a special manner towards one another. All under Gumilev."[4] Blok must have sensed the power shift in the influencing of young poets from himself to Gumilev.

The hostility between Blok and Gumilev erupted into the open in a dispute over the leadership of the Petrograd Union of Poets, a branch of the All-Russian Union of Poets. Gumilev's role in this affair was the closest he ever came to involving himself in political maneuvering. Alexander Blok had initially been chosen to preside as chairman. But one night, Osip Mandelstam appeared at the door of Khodasevich's room in the House of the Arts and announced that the "Blok-ian" directors of the Union had just been rejected and replaced by members of the Guild of Poets, including Khodasevich, with Gumilev as chairman. Khodasevich was puzzled:

> The coup was carried out somehow so strangely. The information was sent out barely an hour before the meeting and not everyone living far away even received it. I didn't like all this and I said that, not having asked me, they had elected me in vain. Mandelstam began to persuade me not to make an issue of it, so as not to offend Gumilev. From his words I understood that the "re-elections" were arranged by several members of the Guild who had to get the stamp of the Union so that they could arrange matters of a commercial nature. For this they hid behind the name and position of Gumilev. Gumilev, like a child, was dazzled with the title of chairman.[5]

Blok, as apolitical as Gumilev, had found his duties as Chairman of the Petrograd Union of Poets—making sure that poets received ration cards and firewood, writing annotations of poems of new members, and settling conflicts between poets and publishers—onerous and time-consuming. But Gumilev's manner of seizing that position clearly offended him. For when Gumilev and his friends carried out their "struggle for power," the poets associated with Blok had been blackballed and replaced by "Gumilyats."

But Blok would take his revenge upon Gumilev in "Without Divinity, Without Inspiration," an article aimed squarely at the Acmeist poets.[6] In it Blok vented literary opinions infused with bitterness and irony that he had kept bottled up inside himself for years. It is as if, shaking off the inner restraints that had kept him from speaking out, in one of his last articles Blok had decided to leave a final message to those who still valued the Russian culture to which he had devoted his life.

The title of Blok's essay is taken from lines of one of Pushkin's most famous love poems, "K***". In the boredom and isolation of exile, Pushkin had forgotten the vision of his beloved's face: "Far off, in deep gloom of confinement,/My days had quietly dragged out,/Without divinity or inspiration,/And without tears or life or love." Blok maintained that divinity and inspiration, the essence of the poet's nature, were absent in the work of the Acmeist poets, more precisely, in that of Gumilev.

Blok's fear was that the great river of Russian poetry and prose was being broken up into separate streams of specialist literary movements, dissipating and weakenings its flow. Attacking Gumilev's Acmeist manifesto, "Acmeism and the Legacy of Russian

Symbolism," Blok rejected Gumilev's claim that the purely literary qualities of French Symbolists had influenced Russian Symbolism. As for Acmeism, Gumilev's assertion that it was "the flowering of physical and spiritual powers" was, if not presumptuous, no more than what Blok claimed for his own poetry. For Blok there was something cold and foreign in Gumilev's poetry and in Akhmatova, whom Blok questions even being an Acmeist, "it would be impossible to find the 'flowering of physical and spiritual powers' in her exhausted, diseased, female and self-absorbed manner." However abhorrent were the Futurists, at least they provided a prevision of the caricatures and absurdities of war and revolution. But most repugnant to Blok was Gumilev's quasi-legalistic conception of a poetry based on laws governing a complex of words and his purely analytical approach to the poetic process. With supreme arrogance the Acmeists assumed that only they could fulfill all the criteria of the true poet. They must not be entrusted, Blok warned, with the precious burden of Russian culture.

Blok's hostility may have been fed by the assumption that, since Gumilev was involved in literary activities under Soviet control, he must be acquiesing to it. Yet Blok, too, served on official committees and participated in governmental organizations, it being the only way of acquiring a salary, firewood and food ration cards for himself, his wife and his mother. Perhaps Blok feared that the spiritual values of his poetry and his creative life as a whole were now being judged as irrelevant in the world taking shape around him. The prophetic voice of the poet, now being choked out in the insidious spread of governmental control and the bureaucratization of the poetry, would be considered irrelevant, worthless. It would have been easy to cast Gumilev, the leader of the Acmeists who had mounted the first real opposition to Symbolism, as the enemy. But the real enemy to Blok's conception of poetry was a world that was being transformed so drastically as to bring all long-held values of tradition, morality and spirituality, not just literary ones, into question. This essay was Blok's anguished and futile attempt to influence the future direction of Russian poetry, the precious inheritance handed down through generations of poets who had lived, suffered and ultimately triumphed with the gift of words.

As the desolate year of 1920 drew to an end, the writers of Petrograd made a brave attempt to at least go through the motions of their former lives. With the approaching holidays, a ball was held in the Institute of the History of the Arts. Khodasevich was a guest in the vast, freezing halls of a former residence on Issakievsky Square filled with fumes from the smoldering fires of damp wood and remembered the feeble lighting and the clouds of steam which rose from the mouths of the guests as they spoke:

> Music rang out. People moved about in the half-darkness, crowding close to the fireplaces. My God, how that crowd was dressed! Felt boots, sweaters, mangy furs which one couldn't part with even in the dancing hall. And there, fittingly late, appeared Gumilev and on his arm a lady in a low-cut black dress who was shivering from the cold. Erect and haughty in his evening dress, Gumilev proceeded through the spacious rooms. He was trembling

from the cold, but grandly and politely bowed to the left and the right. He chatted with acquaintances in a worldly tone. He was playing that it was a ball. His whole appearance said; "Nothing has happened. A revolution? I didn't hear anything about it."[7]

The lady on Gumilev's arm was Irina Odoevtseva, one of his poetic "disciples" and his current love interest. Nikolai greeted the New Year at Slepnevo, where he joined his mother, his brother, Dmitri, and sister-in-law, Anna, Asya and the two children. Anna Gumileva remembered the holiday as warm and lively. She would go into Kolya's study, where he was always seated in a deep armchair with a pen in his hand, and they would carefully discuss the next day's menu. She saw him "cheerful, full of the life force, at the zenith of his fame and personal happiness with his second lovely wife, devoting himself completely to his work."[8]

As 1921 began, Gumilev left his family in Slepnevo and returned to Petrograd. As Peter Ryss recalled, the city was heaped with the hulls of sunflower seeds chewed by the starving population to ease the excrutiating pains of hunger. "The automobiles of comrade commissars drove insolently through the city. All those who were wearing handcuffs were rotting in prison. It was starving, grey, foul. And you just wanted to run from this despair, wherever your eyes gazed. But the heavier became the Bolshevik grave, the more difficult it was to leave."[9]

Although he revealed his thoughts to few, Gumilev began seriously to consider emigrating. He and Vasily Nemirovich-Danchenko discussed the various possibilities of "an escape from the

Soviet paradise." But Nemirovich-Danchenko had twice been refused a passport and could see no way out for himself. Gumilev yearned for the sun-drenched south, captivating Nemirovich-Danchenko with stories of his adventures in Abyssinia. "If one could believe in the transmigration of spirits, one could recognize in him a brave seeker of new islands and continents in the unknown spaces of the oceans of time. Amerigo Vespucci, Vasco da Gama, conquerors like Cortez and Pissaro."[10]

But they couldn't agree on the best route out of the country. Nemirovich-Danchenko thought it would be less risky to leave through Finland, while Gumilev was convinced that a way through Latvia would be more certain. They finally compromised on Estonia where Gumilev knew there were fishermen in the seaside villages who could be paid to ferry them across the Baltic Sea. Unfortunately, neither possessed the millions of rubles that it would cost. The two poets would stroll the decaying streets of Petrograd where they could talk without fear of being overheard about their anxieties for Russia's future under Soviet power. His friend remembered Gumilev saying:

"There is no hope of turning back in Russia. All the efforts of those who love Russia and feel pain for her will be broken apart against a solid wall of unprecedented espionage. It is oozing through us like water through lips. It is impossible to believe anyone. And salvation will not come from abroad...No, here a revolt is impossible. Even the thought of it is a warning. And to prepare for it is stupid. All that is water for their mill."[11]

One night as they were walking through the blizzard-choked city, waves of snow beating at their faces and their legs sinking deep into drifts, Gumilev suddenly stopped and said with obvious pain: "There really is still on earth a sun and a warm sea and blue, blue sky. Maybe we can't see them...And brave, strong people, who are not writhing in pain, like worms under the iron heel of that triumphant boor [Lenin]. And free song and the joy of life. And really Russia will be free, mighty, happy—only we won't see it."[12]

An eerie echo of Gumilev's words sounded two decades later from Akhmatova's *Requiem,* when she, too, raises her eyes from the ubiquitous terror and degradation to an imagined glimpse of that other, far away life. "Yet for someone fresh-sprung winds do blow and/Sunset revels in its own caress—/We don't know, we are the same all over,/ Hearing heavy footsteps of the soldiers/And the hateful grinding of their keys."[13]

Anna and Kolya would still meet on occasion. Once she had to go to his office at World Literature to apply for her membership card in the Writer's Union. Released from Shileiko's psychic, if not physical, imprisonment, poems flowed from Akhmatova's pen again, some twenty-seven in 1921. Akhmatova's fourth collection, *Plaintain (Podorozhnik)*, a tiny book containing poems written between 1917 and 1919, would soon be published.

She continued to work in the library of the Agronomy Institute. Early in 1921, she moved into a flat with her friends, Olga Glebova-Sudeikina and Arthur Lourie at number 18 Fontanka, a columned house not far from the Simeonev bridge. In spite of deprivations, she had recovered her health and spirits, as Kornei Chukovsky attested on meeting her in February at the House of Scholars: "She looked young, cheerful, and she had put on some weight. 'Come see me today and I'll give you a bottle of milk for your little girl.' I went that evening, and she gave it to me! Just imagine—in February of 1921, to offer someone a bottle of milk!"[14] The "little girl" was Lydia Chukovskaya, who would later become a close friend of Akhmatova's and whose journals have given us an invaluable insight into the poet's life.

When Akhmatova encountered Alexander Blok in the cafeteria of the Bolshoi Theater, she was taken aback: "I met an emaciated Blok with crazed eyes, who said to me: 'Everybody meets here as if they were in the other world.'"[15] At the House of Writers on February 10, 1921, she was in the audience at one of Blok's last public appearances in Petrograd, a celebration of the eighty-fourth anniversary of Pushkin's death. This haunting and memorable event in the cultural history of Petersburg was recorded by another writer: "That evening all the Petrograd literary and artistic intelligentsia arrived. They came by foot from everywhere—there were no trams. Everyone dressed poorly. They were hungry. Akhmatova sat with Khodasevich in a box."[16] We can only presume that Nikolai Gumilev was present as well.

Blok was suffering from a heart ailment and his face above the black frock coat and high-necked white sweater was pale and ghostly. Blok believed that his life as a poet, the only life he valued, had ended. As a poet he had nothing more to say—he was already dead. And those who had gathered to hear this poet who had personified Petersburg poetry for nearly two decades knew it as well. Harassed by hunger, want, and a hostile state espousing repugnant values, the hushed gathering of poets who had come to celebrate Pushkin and Blok hung upon every word he spoke. Erik Gollerbakh never forgot how "...in each word, in each sound of the cold, impassive voice, there was boundless weariness, wretchedness, waning..."[17]

Blok's lecture, "On the Purpose of the Poet," was based upon Pushkin's poem, "The Poet and the Crowd."[18] Nearly every listener in his audience could have recited that poem from memory, so there was no reference, no hint of meaning in Blok's words that was not profoundly understood. As the dour, self-important members of the Soviet literary bureaucracy sat listening impassively near-by, Blok spoke of the lofty and difficult life of the poet. Though his words may have referred to Pushkin, he was speaking to his friends and fellow poets of his life and of their lives at that moment in time. With a reckless courage, Blok spoke in the coded language of resistance in the very faces of his oppressors.

With a calmness that verged on indifference, Blok began: "From our earliest years our memories preserve the name—Pushkin. This name, this sound has filled many days of our lives. In twilit darkness are the names of the emperors, military leaders, inventors of the instruments of murder, torturers and martyrers of life. And opposite them—the bright name, Pushkin." Blok spoke of the unchanging essence of the poet and his work, however they might be judged by the surrounding society. The poet was the "son of harmony," who brought words and sounds out of a primordial anarchy into the ordered state of harmony. This was a continuous, dynamic process, for old forms were always dying and new forms coming into existence. This inevitable, ongoing change was frightening and difficult to comprehend. Human beings are swept along, playing an essentially passive role in this eternal change, growing up, growing old, dying.

The poet, "the son of harmony," had three tasks: "First, to liberate sounds from the native anarchic elements in which they reside. Second, to bring these sounds into harmony and give them form. Third, to carry this harmony out into the external world." The poet's words put the human heart to the test. Although simple people might not comprehend the poet's words, those who willfully refused to understand and prevented the poet from fulfilling his calling Pushkin designated as "the mob."

The poet must abandon "the cares of the everyday world," so as to lift the veil from life and reveal its depths. In an act that must spring from inspiration, as difficult and mysterious as birth, he must put what he discovered into sounds and words resonating in a single harmony. It was when the poet brought that harmony into the larger world that the clash came between the poet and the "mob." For Pushkin the "mob" was made of worldly people, but now: "These functionaries are our mob, the mob of yesterday and today. Not the elite and not the simple folk, not beasts, not lumps of earth, not wisps of mist, not splinters of the planet, not demons and not angels…[but] businessmen and the vulgar whose spiritual depths are hopelessly and firmly covered with 'the cares of the everyday world.'" This "mob" demanded that the poet serve the external world, as they did, that his work be pragmatic and positive, that he contribute constructively for the good of society. With censorship, "…they have placed obstacles on the the third path of the poet, the path of bringing harmony into the world."

Pushkin had demanded an even higher freedom for the poet when he wrote "'Love and a secret freedom/Instill in the heart a simple hymn.' This *secret freedom*…is not merely the freedom that allows the individual to exercise his own free will. It is a much greater freedom and is closely connected with the first two things that Apollo demands of the poet. What is ennumerated in the poems of Pushkin is the necessary condition for the liberation of harmony."

As more and more obstacles were piled in Pushkin's path, he grew weaker, as did the culture of his day. But it was not the bullets of Dantés that finally killed him. "He was killed by the absence of air…*Peace* and *freedom*. They are necessary to the poet for the liberating of harmony. But peace and freedom were taken away. Not outer peace, but creative peace. Not a childish freedom…but creative freedom—the secret freedom. And the poet dies, because he can no longer breathe. Life has lost its meaning."

Blok ended with a thinly veiled warning to those of the Soviet "mob" sitting on the stage not ten yards from where he stood. "Let those functionaries who intend to direct poetry along their own channels, infringing on its secret freedom and preventing it from fulfilling its mysterious purposes, be warned away from that vile name. We will die, but art will remain. Its final ends are unknown to us and cannot be known. It is one in essence and undivided."

Erik Gollerbakh recalled how the evening ended:

Blok had barely finished his last sentence; stormy applause resounded, an approving tumble of voices. Blok folded up the notebook from which he had read and sat down at the green table beside the other members of the presidium. His face was somewhat agitated. But always the same weariness, always the same indifference to his surroundings was in his gaze, gliding apathetically along the heads of the audience. Sometimes his bright blue eyes took on an unpleasant expression of alienation. The ovation didn't subside. Blok got up, his snowy sweater white above the green cloth of the table, his head thrown back slightly, as always. He got up, stood for half a minute. The applause became even more deafening. Everyone clapped. Blok looked somewhere into the depths of the auditorium, intently, coldy, not bowing, in no way responding to the noisy signs of approval. Then he sat down.[19]

As the crowd clamored for him to go on, Blok slipped backstage. Another in the audience that night witnessed Blok's last encounter with Akhmatova: "It was obvious how tired he was. 'If only they would leave him alone!' [Akhmatova] had whispered in Khodasevich's ear. They met in the wings. Blok raised his eyes to her and greeted her. 'But where is your Spanish shawl?'"[20] The

Frances Laird

shawl Blok had depicted Akhmatova wearing in his poem about her had never existed. In April, Kornei Chukovsky arranged an evening dedicated to Blok at the Bolshoi Theatre at which the poet was celebrated with ovations and bouquets of flowers, but Akhmatova was not present at that performance.

It was only by taking refuge in the world of the imagination that the poets of Petrograd could escape the trepidation and terror, hopelessness and despair that assailed them. Poems were more necessary to them than bread. They continued to meet in small groups where they knew and trusted one another, where they could read their poems and talk with some measure of freedom without fear of Cheka spies. Peter Ryss recalled of such an evening in an apartment near the Tuchkov bridge.

…In an enormous dining-room (ah, how cold it was there!) a small group had gathered. They were drinking tea without sugar and talking about politics "Let's read poems and forget about what is happening today!" This suggestion of Feodor Sologub was met with approval.

Nikolai Gumilev, so strange, so unlike a person of the twentieth century, read his new poems. It was as if he were no longer among the living; those such as he were not necessary to the Bolsheviks.

Then, having closed his eyes and crossed his arms over his chest, Sologub read his direct, powerful poems. He called them then "Poems about Russia."

And small, dark, impulsive Anna Nikolaevna Chebotarevskaya, screwing up her eyes, jerked her head up and sighed.

I stood at the window and gazed at the embankment, at Tuchkov bridge. It was as if out of the river rose lights, they twinkled and winked at one another.

It made me wonder:

Swan Songs
Akhmatova and Gumilev

"Do you think that Petrograd will become empty?"
Later that night we went our separate ways. The cold, damp wind grew stronger. Somewhere out in space a drunken mischief-maker was threatening somebody ...[21]

With Asya and the children in Slepnevo, Gumilev moved back into Makovsky's flat, which was smaller and easier to heat. But Asya was bored in the countryside, far from the excitement of the city, with only her aging mother-in-law for company. She begged Kolya to allow her to live in Petrograd with him, even threatening to kill herself if he did not agree. But there was no milk in the city for the baby, Lena, and she could not be left to his mother, who was growing too old to care for her as she had for Lev, now nearly nine years old. A brutal solution was found that left in question the maternal and paternal instincts of the couple: the baby was put into an orphanage, where she eventually died of starvation. Asya returned to Petrograd and would turn up occasionally at the meetings of the Guild of Poets.

Undoubtedly, one reason Gumilev wished to see his wife safely confined to Slepnevo was his desire to pursue his bachelor life without wifely interference. But undeterred by Asya's presence, Gumilev continued his love affairs with actresses and poetesses. But when even he, the Chairman of the Petrograd Union of Poets, could not find the wood to heat his flat, Gumilev moved into the House of the Arts, gaining by this the blissful comfort of central heating. Presumably Asya went back to the country.

In March of 1921, the Russian sailors based at Kronstadt, who had once been firm in their support of the Bolsheviks, had risen up against them and demanded that elections be held. Nikolai Otsup recalled that on the night of the Kronstadt rebellion, Gumilev had been with him at his flat on Serpukhovskaya Street.

> From far off the muffled gunshots flew to us...Gumilev was sitting on the carpet, lit by the flame of a candle, I was opposite him also on the carpet. In the building everyone was asleep. We were trying not to talk about what was going on—there was something tragically doom-like in the Kronstadt movement, as in the resistance of the Junkers in October, 1917.
> We were trying to talk and were speaking about art.
> "I spend a lot of time with young people who are not gifted," Gumilev answered me, "not because I want to make poets out of them. That is, of course, inconceivable—poets are born. I want to help them in a human way. Really poems don't make things easier, as if you could throw off something. It's necessary so that everyone can treat themselves [as with medicine] with the writing of poems..."[22]

One night not long after this, Otsup and Gumilev were walking down the street in Petrograd when military trucks drove past filled with hundreds of Kronstadt sailors guarded by armed students. From one of the trucks the soldiers shouted: "'Brothers, help us, they're taking us to be shot!'

> I seized Gumilev by the arm, Gumilev crossed himself. We sat down on logs on the English embankment and watched the chunks of ice slowly floating along the Neva. Gumilev was sad and preoccupied.
> "To kill unarmed men," he said, "is the greatest baseness." Then, as if rousing himself, he added: "But, in general, death is not so terrible. Death in battle is even ravishing."[23]

Swan Songs
Akhmatova and Gumilev

A piece of Gumilev's personal history disappeared when the Gumilev home was requisitioned by the Detskoe Selo Soviet. "Memory," written in April, 1921, may have been his attempt to retrieve and hold onto a past that was rapidly being obliterated. In this retrospective poem, as in "The Lost Streetcar," Gumilev looks back over the course of his life at the changing manifestations of the soul inhabiting his singular body. "Memory" again reveals the new, exceptionally promising level of expression, a final flowering of Gumilev's poetic gift.

Memory

Only snakes can shed, casting their skins off,
So that then the soul can age and grow.
We, alas, are not made as the snakes are,
We change not our bodies, but our souls.

Memory, with your giant's hand you lead on
Life, as if you led with reins a steed,
You can tell me of those earlier ones who
Lived in this my body before me.

The very first: the one, slender and homely,
Who loved only the twilight in the woods,
A fallen leaf, the magic-making child who

Frances Laird

      Stopped the falling rain with just a word.

      Those two that he took on as his friends were
      Just a reddish-brown dog and a tree.
      Memory, memory, you won't find the marker.
      You can't convince the world that it was me.

      The second…he loved southern winds' soft blowing.
      In every noise he heard the lyre's sounds.
      Life, he said, was his best friend and
      The carpet spread beneath his feet—the world.

      I really did not like at all the one who
      Wanted to become a god and tsar.
      He hung out the signboard of a poet
      On my silent house above the door.

      But I love the chosen one of freedom,
      The navigator and the rifleman.
      Ah, to him the waters sang so clearly
      And with envy clouds looked down on him.

      High and lofty was his tent erected,
      Strong and playful were the mules he led.
      As wine he drank up the sweet air

Swan Songs
Akhmatova and Gumilev

In wide spaces of an unknown land.

Memory, from year to year you weaken.
Is that the one or is it someone else
Who exchanged a gay and happy freedom
For the sacred, long-awaited fight.

He knew torments brought by thirst and hunger,
The anxious dream, the never-ending quest.
But upon a breast untouched by bullets
Saint George came to him and touched him twice.

I'm an architect, gloomy and stubborn,
Of a temple rising in the dark.
I was jealous of the Fathers' praises
Whether in the heavens or on the earth.

Scorched by fiery flames right to the bottom
Will my heart be when, arising, clear,
Stand the walls of a new Jerusalem
On my native country's open fields.

And a strange wind then will start to blow and
An awful light will spill down from the sky:
Unexpectedly, just like a garden

Frances Laird

      Of dazzling planets blooms the Milky Way.

      An unknown traveller will stand before me,
      Face hidden. But I'll understand it all,
      Seeing how the lion runs behind him
      And the eagle flies up at his call.

      I'll cry out…But really who will help me
      So my soul won't die and be no more.
      Only snakes can shed, casting their skins off.
      We change not our bodies, but our souls.

                                  Nikolai Gumilev
                                  April, 1921[24]

Gone is the willful, cocky, arrogant, bold, ceremoniously polite Mr. Know-it-all of Russian poetry. Here we are given a glimpse behind the mask Gumilev wore to face the world and into the very "I" of the poet's changing self. Inside the lifelong envelope of the body, he sees his soul in a continuous process of transformation. As the snake splits out of a skin too confining for its growing body, a person must shed the skin that constricts his spiritual growth and leaves unsatisfied his soul's yearning for wisdom. Gumilev imagines Memory, the pervasive power that urges the soul forward into its next manifestation, as a giant who leads his life by the hand like a horse by its reins. It is Memory that will allow him to resurrect, one after another, those souls that have occupied his body.

The first is the homely, solitary child of nature, befriended only by a dog and a tree, who loved the simplest things, a scarlet leaf, the light in a grove of trees at dusk. So intimate was his connection to the natural world that he believed he held a secret power over it. When he had ordered the rain to stop so that he could run out into the fields and woods to play, it had obeyed him. The second soul is that of the emerging poet whose love of words was aroused by the music of the natural world, the song of the wind sighing through the leafy boughs. All around him sounded the lyre, the ring of poetry. Then the earth was his and the possibilties of life and art had seemed limitless. But his youthful enthusiasm had turned into the desire "to become a god and tsar." Gumilev rejects this soul/self with its overweening self-confidence, its insatiable hunger for recognition and critical power over other poets.

Most of all Gumilev admires the soul of the adventurer he once was, the explorer, the man of action who roamed freely, so comfortable and at home anywhere on the earth's surface that even the clouds envied him. Far from the civilized world, guiding his pack mules over deserts and mountain passes, sleeping in a tent, Gumilev was the benevolent lord of his universe. In the vast reaches of a mysterious continent he drank in air as sweet and intoxicating as wine.

But as his soul's transformations approach the present, the power of memory has begun to wane. In his role as an officer in the army, Gumilev seems less certain of his identity. Was the adventurer who revelled in striding freely about the earth he who submitted himself to the iron discipline of the military life, trading his freedom for the chance to challenge himself in battle? It was with the testing of war—hunger, thirst, uneasy sleep, an endless road, the bombs and bullets of the battlefield—that he finally proved to himself and others his physical courage and was honored when the St. George Cross for bravery in battle was twice pinned to his breast.

Comparing himself to an architect, Mandelstam's favorite image of the poet as craftsman and builder, Gumilev understands the importance in the creative act of the workmanlike rules of construction. The cathedral of his poetic creation, spacious, sound, sacred, now rises in darkness, for his poetry will not be published and read in the new Soviet era. But he was too eager for adulation, yearning to named among the ranks of the "Fathers," whether in a literary or spiritual sense.

In an apocalyptic vision, Gumilev foresees the fiery purging of his heart when a new Jerusalem, founded on firm spiritual truths, rises on the open fields of Russia, a utopia of the spirit to replace the materialistic utopia of the Communists. Strange winds will sweep over the earth, fiery planets will bloom in the Milky Way as a mysterious stranger appears, accompanied by the lion and eagle, the reigning beasts of land and air. Perhaps it is Death, for the poet cries out in terror. Left with no assurance that his soul will not vanish along with his body, the poet comes to the realization in the closing lines, a repetition of the first, that death is merely another transformation of his ever-changing soul.

The darkness that enclosed the temple of his art was seeping into the corners of Gumilev's life. One by one the gates leading out of Russia were barred. Writers who now sat safely in the cafés of Paris and Berlin had few compunctions about attacking those left behind in Russia, even hurling criticism at them for their "co-operation" with the new regime. Merezhkovsky, in a letter to a Paris newspaper, condemned the editorial "colleagues" of World Literature for working in the government-run publishing house. Levinson wrote:

> Those called "colleagues" in the Soviet jargon were a group of writers and scholars, starving, poor, without rights, cut off from their readers, from their sources of knowledge, from the future, some of whom had already been touched by death, writers hunted down by informers, only feebly able to defend themselves from the strengthening onslaughts of those in power—yet unreservedly, to the end (whether brought by exhaustion or hunger or bullets), true to literature and scholarship. And there in that letter, for this effort, perhaps fantastic, perhaps hopeless, yet lofty and unselfish still, there were only two words, "Shameless speculation."[25]

Gumilev was outraged by Merezhkovsky's words, for he had thoughtlessly expressed opinions that could put his writer friends at home in a much worse position with Soviet officials. Gumilev, steadfastly defending the writers, wanted to respond immediately to the slurs of that foreign publication. But he was caught in a dilemma.

Levinson wrote: "...How could he prove the purity of his writerly feats, the whole measure of his spiritual independence from the regime? Didn't that mean he would doom to destruction both the enterprise and the people?"[26] The poets of Petersburg felt ever more crippled, isolated and abandoned.

Nikolai Gumilev and Alexander Blok attended a meeting held, by permission of the Commissariat of People's Education, in a freezing, vaulted room of a building near the Chernishev bridge. At the conclusion of business, each poet read a selection of his poems closest to his heart. As Rozhdestvensky recalled:

> When it came Blok's turn, he thought for a moment and began with his measured, hollow voice: "Why do you look down in confusion/ Gaze as you did before on me."
> As Blok recited no more than five or six poems, everyone was silent, bewitched by his voice. And when nobody expected that he would continue, Alexander Alexandrovich began the last: "Voice from the Choir." His face, calm until then, was distorted by a tormented fold at the mouth, his voice rang hollow as if it had cracked. He nearly fell forward in his armchair. Over his eyes fell heavy, half-closed eyelids. He pronounced the concluding lines almost in a whisper, with a tortured effort, as if mastering himself.
> And all of us were seized with a kind of dispirited feeling. No one wanted to recite anymore. But Blok smiled and said in his ordinary voice:
> "Very unpleasant poems. I don't know why I wrote them. It would have been better to have left these words unsaid. But I had to say them. One must overcome what is difficult. And after that the day will be clear. But you know," he added, seeing that no one wanted to break the silence, "let's all read something from Pushkin. Nikolai Stepanovich, it's your turn now."

Swan Songs
Akhmatova and Gumilev

Gumilev was in no way surprised at this suggestion and after a minute's pause began…The bright name of Pushkin relieved the general tension. It was as if the sun had peeped into the room.[27]

Chapter XV
Terror and Grief

In early July, 1921, Nikolai Gumilev left Petrograd for the Crimean peninsula aboard the *Nemitz*. Somehow Gumilev had managed to obtain a round-trip ticket to Sebastapol on this military train. Sergei Makovsky imagined that "on Nemitz's train the atmosphere was probably very amiable, the half-educated 'Reds' listened attentively and sympathetically to his 'African' poems. He played cards with them, joked, drank a lot..."[1] Gumilev's last book, *The Fiery Pillar,* was printed in Sebastapol, apparently paid for with money from admiring Crimean sailors.

Alexander Blok had suffered a heart attack soon after returning from Moscow and severe malnutrition and nervous exhaustion had complicated his condition. Besides his work as a director of World Literature and the Bolshoi Dramatic Theatre, he had been burdened by the manual labor needed to sustain his wife and mother, hauling cabbages back from the countryside, chopping ice-covered logs for the stove and taking his turn as night watch at the gate of his apartment building. He no longer wrote anything but reviews and critical articles. When Chukovsky asked him why he had stopped writing poetry, Blok answered, "All sounds have ceased. Can't you hear that there are no sounds?"[2] For a man whose world had been filled with the unending rhythms and harmonies of poetry, Blok's silence, both inner and outer, was deafening. To Yuri Annenkov, who was drawing illustratations for "The Twelve," he complained: "I'm suffocating, suffocating, suffocating! We're suffocating, we will all suffocate. The world revolution is turning into world angina pectoris!"[3] Like Pushkin, he was suffocating from a lack of that secret freedom, the very air the poet must breathe.

When it became clear that Blok badly needed medical treatment, Gorky and Lunacharsky tried to secure permission for him to go to Finland. But Lenin and the Politburo refused, fearing that once out of the country, Blok would speak out against the Soviet regime. Blok himself had resisted leaving Russia at first, citing Akhmatova's poem, "When in a suicidal anguish…" He told Chukovsky, "Akhmatova is right. They [the words encouraging her to emigrate] are unworthy. To run from the Russian revolution is shameful."[4]

At the end of July, Nikolai Gumilev, after a stop in Moscow and a reading at the Poet's Café, returned to Petrograd. It was clear to Nemirovich-Danchenko that he had lost all hope that the Communists could be removed from power. Gumilev told him:

"There is nothing to wait for. There will be no revolution, no Thermidor. These thugs have seized power with all their strength. They are directed into two armies: the Red Army and the army of spies. And the second is much more numerous than the first. I am surprised at who are drawn into conspiracies now…Blind men, they play into the hands of provocation. I'm no coward. Struggle is my element, but I wouldn't go to work now in secret organizations."[5]

From Akhmatova's family in Crimea, Gumilev had brought back the shattering news that her brother, Andrei Gorenko, had committed suicide in Greece. Anna, who as a child had been closest to her older brother, was devastated. Their conversation must have been strained, as Gumilev had brought along Georgy Ivanov, perhaps fearing that Shileiko might be there. When it was time to leave, Akhmatova led them down a dark, narrow, winding staircase to the street. She is said to have remarked: "You go down a staircase like this only to your execution."[6] Some time after this, Akhmatova recalled, she had her last glimpse of Kolya near "...Murazi's house on the corner of Liteiny...the day Yury Annenkov sketched me."[7]

As the summer neared its end, Vladislav Khodasevich was leaving for a vacation in the countryside. On the evening of August 2, he wandered through the House of the Arts saying good-bye to his friends. At about ten o'clock, he knocked on Gumilev's door. Just back after having given an evening lecture, Gumilev greeted him warmly. To Khodasevich's surprise, his usual pose of elaborate politeness had vanished and they chatted happily about many subjects. Khodasevich wrote:

...Then Gumilev began to assure me that it was his lot to live for a very long time. "At least to my nineties." He repeated it all. "Without question, to ninety years, no less." Until then he planned to write a pile of books.

He warned me: "Look, you and I are about the same age, but see: I am ten years younger than you, right? That's because I love young people. I even play blind-man's-bluff with my workshop students—I did today. And so there's no question but that I will live to be ninety and you'll go sour in five years."

Then, laughing, he demonstrated how in five years I would be bent over and shuffling my feet, while he would appear as "a young man."[8]

Khodasevich wanted to say good-bye to other friends, but every time he tried to get up, Gumilev would urge him to stay a bit longer. After asking if he could leave a few of his things with Gumilev to keep while he was away, Khodasevich said good-night. It was nearly two o'clock in the morning.

At the appointed time the next morning, he brought his things to Gumilev's door, but no one answered his knock. Khodasevich recalled that "...In the dining room, the worker Efim told me that in the night Gumilev had been arrested and taken away. So I was the last to see him free. In his exaggerated joy at my coming, it could have been that he had the presentiment that after me he would see no one else."[9]

Khodasevich was stunned by this news, but could hardly have taken it in when another unexpected blow fell. Back in his own room he found Nadezhda Pavlovich. "Red-faced from the heat, with her face swollen from tears, she had just run from the Blok's. She told me that Blok's death agony had begun. I began to comfort her and reassure her. Then, in her last despair, she ran to me and, stifled with tears, said: 'You don't know anything...don't tell anyone already for several days...he has been out of his mind!'"[10]

Nikolai Otsup, too, remembered running up the grand staircase of the House of the Arts to Gumilev's door that morning. He heard a constrained whisper behind his back and, turning around, saw Efim. "Don't go there, there is an ambush in Nikolai Stepanovich's room." Presumably, Cheka agents were at that moment pawing through Gumilev's papers for evidence of his "crimes."[11]

The literary world of Petrograd was stunned and incredulous at the news of Gumilev's arrest. At first, they were sure that there must have been a mistake, some silly misunderstanding which would be quickly cleared up and Gumilev released. Government officials would certainly remember his valuable work with the young proletarian poets. Although Gumilev had never concealed his scorn for the Soviet regime, that was no crime. And there couldn't have been anyone among his adoring circle of students who would make accusations against him. Nemirovich-Danchenko was tormented by the thought that, in trying to help Gumilev publish his poems abroad, he may have been responsible. The Bolsheviks considered any dealing with foreigners to be a criminal act.[12]

Because spies were busily at work everywhere, the writers spoke a coded language on the telephone. A call from World Literature alerted Georgy Adamovich of Gumilev's arrest:

"Did you know that *Kolchan* [*The Quiver*] has been held back in the printing...Probably it's some kind of misunderstanding."
Kolchan was the name of one of the earlier books of Gumilev. The second issue of it was then being printed. At first I didn't understand what I was being told. I thought that really it was some squabble about censorship or typography. And it was only by the intonation, by a kind of quaver in the voice, by the emphasis on the word "held back" that I guessed what it was about. Then in the city

everybody was accustomed to that conventional telephone language and caught the meaning of it at once. And these weren't conplicated conversations. Everybody spoke indifferently and as if by the way: "You know, it seems it will be warm soon." They meant that according to rumors changes were expected. If someone suddenly "fell ill," they understood that the hospital was located on Gorokovaya or Spalernaya streets [where the prisons were located].[13]

The arrest of a person so totally and single-mindedly devoted to the art of poetry aroused a flurry of rumours in the frightened and bewildered literary community of Petrograd. Alexander Amphiteatrov wrote: "...It was thought that Gumilev had gotten into trouble as a former officer who had concealed his rank. Others guessed that he was arrested as chairman of the Club [Guild] of Poets for not observing some formalities in the opening of that rather strange establishment which had too sharp a character."[14] Did Gumilev's downfall come about because of his sympathy for the monarchy? Gumilev didn't share Amphiteatrov's enthusiam for democratic republicanism. "Once, joking, I reminded him that Plato in his ideal utopian government advised that poets be chased out of the republic. 'The poets themselves wouldn't go into his republic,' Gumilev rejoined proudly. He was a monarchist and a strong one. He wasn't loud but he didn't hide it."[15]

But before his friends could discover what had happened to Gumilev and how they could help free him, they were struck by the news of the death on August 7, 1921, at the age of forty years, of Alexander Blok. Although the official cause of death was endocarditis complicated by malnutrition and nervous exhaustion,

Blok's friends believed that, with the end of his "secret freedom," he had suffered from a kind of "spiritual asthma," as Bely called it. The oxygen of creation had been sucked away and the spirit of the great poet had suffocated. On the following day, a terse announcement of the poet's death appeared on the front page of *Pravda,* the official newspaper of the Communist party.

The two leading poets of Petrograd, for years locked in a muted but stubborn literary quarrel, had suddenly vanished, one into prison, one into the grave. It was a terrible coincidence lost upon no one. Makovsky wrote: "For almost their whole lives Blok and Gumilev were enemies, although in my memory there was no personal antipathy between them. They 'didn't like' one another, but met at *Apollon,* sat on the committee of 'Poetic Academia,' never once openly displaying this dislike towards one another. And after the Revolution, they worked a great deal together, with the work of getting subsistence, and at the same time—how alien they were to one another in ideas, taste, disposition, relationship to Russia, all that creates the writer's personality."[16] That flow of passionate argument between two strong personalities was finally and tragically stilled.

On August 10, Blok's open coffin was carried through the streets of Petrograd to the Resurrection Chapel in the Smolensk cemetery by Nikolai Otsup and other poets and writers, followed by a crush of mourners. Evegeny Zamyatin wrote of that day:

A blue, hot day, the tenth of August. Blue incense smoke in the crowded room. An alien face, long, with prickly mustaches, with a pointed beard—resembling the face of Don Quixote...The full church of the Smolensk cemetery. A slanting ray above in the cupola, slowly descending lower and lower. An unknown girl makes her way through the crowd to the coffin, kisses the yellow hand, leaves.[17]

Blok was buried under an ancient maple tree, near the grave of his grandfather, with only a simple Orthodox cross as a marker. Wreathes and flowers were heaped over the gravesite. That day there were no speeches.

Because of her near legendary relationships to both Blok and Gumilev, Anna Akhmatova, dressed in black and veiled with black crepe, attracted the fascinated interest of the mourners. One remembered: "The choir sang. But everyone's eyes were directed not at the altar, or the coffin, but at where I was standing. I began looking around to see why, and I saw right behind me the tall, slender figure of Anna Akhmatova. Tears were streaming down her pale cheeks. She wasn't hiding them. Everyone wept and the choir sang."[18] Another mourner remembered how Akhmatova became faint at the service.[19] Yury Annenkov, as he helped to lower the coffin into the ground, remembered seeing Akhmatova weeping beside the grave.[20] She had good reason, for not only was she grieving a beloved poet; she had just heard of the arrest and imprisonment of Kolya Gumilev. She wrote this poem about that day:

> Today is the Smolensk Virgin's nameday,
> Over grass dark blue incense is drifting,
> And the panakhida singing is streaming.

> It is not sorrowful now, but dazzling.
>
> And the red-cheeked young widows are leading
>
> Their boys and girls to the cemetery
>
> To gaze on the graves of their fathers.
>
> But the cemetery—the nightengale thicket
>
> Stood dead still in the sun's radiance.
>
> We have brought to Smolensk's Patroness,
>
> We have brought to God's Holy Mother
>
> By hand in a silver coffin
>
> Our sun, extinguished in torment—
>
> We have brought our pure swan, Alexander.
>
> Anna Akhmatova
August, 1921[21]

For Nikolai Otsup, the events of the last rites of Blok and the disappearance of Gumilev ran together: "We carried the coffin of Alexander Alexandrovich Blok to the cemetery by hand. My shoulder ached from the heavy burden, my head swam from the incense and bitter thoughts, I had to act: they weren't releasing Gumilev."[22]

When the services were over, Akhmatova and Olga Glebova-Sudeikina searched the cemetery to find the grave of Vsevolod Knyazev, the young cadet who had shot himself for love of Olga in 1913. "'It's somewhere near the wall,' Olga said. But we couldn't find it." It was a moment Akhmatova would always remember.[23]

Swan Songs
Akhmatova and Gumilev

Since the night Gumilev had been arrested, there had been no news from prison except for a brief note written to his wife, Anna Englehardt: "Don't worry about me. I am feeling fine. I am reading Homer and writing poems."[24] But his friends were deeply concerned. At the cemetery Otsup and Kolya's other friends decided to go directly to the Cheka to petition for the release of Gumilev. They would offer the guarantee of the Academy of Sciences, World Literature Publishers, Proletkult and other organizations in which Gumilev had lectured. The frustrating and nightmarish search that Gumilev's friends were caught up in would become only too sickeningly ordinary in the years ahead. First they inquired at the central office of the Cheka about the charges laid against Gumilev. The Cheka official, obviously playing dumb, seemed not to understand why they were going to such trouble to free Gumilev: "'What is all this about Gumilevsky? And what are such poets to us when we have our own...'"[25] According to Amphiteatrov, when the official was asked why Gumilev was taken, he not only couldn't answer the question, he seemed to be unsure exactly who Gumilev was.

"So what was his business, your Gumilyevich?"
"Not Gumilyevich, but Gumilev..."
"Well?"
"He is a poet..."
"Oh? you mean, a writer...Never heard of him...Stop back in a week or so and we'll have information..."
"But what was he arrested for?"
He thought for a moment and explained:

"You see, as it is now, they are trading in freedom, the reason of speculation is ruled out, so probably citizen Gumilev was taken for some kind of malfeasance in office."[26]

Nikolai Otsup continued the story:

One of us answered that Gumilev didn't have any kind of official post. The President of the Petersburg Cheka was evidently unwilling to argue with him.
"At this point I can't say. Telephone on Wednesday. In any case, not one hair on Gumilev's head will fall."
On Wednesday, surrounded by friends of Gumilev, I telephoned the number given to our delegation by the Cheka official.
"Who is speaking?"
"From the delegation (I begin to name the institutions)."
"Oh, this is about Gumilev. You'll find out tomorrow."
On Wednesday, after the call to the Cheka, the young poet R. and I dashed off to all the prisons to search for Gumilev. We began at the Kresty Prison where, it turned out, no political prisoners were being held.
At the Shpalernaya Prison we succeeded in penetrating into the courtyard. We went up the staircase on one wing and asked a worker through the grating: where is the arrested Gumilev located?
Having taken us for someone in the administration, she checked a kind of book and answered from behind the grating:
"Last night he was taken to Gorokhovaya."
We went downstairs, more and more hastening our steps, because already behind us arose the shouting:
"Stop, stop, who are you?"
We hurried out onto the street.[27]

The young proletarian poets, who did not belong to the intelligentsia, might have had better success in saving their teacher if they had been able to muster the courage and will. Nemirovich-Danchenko was incensed at their behavior:

In their studies Gumilev taught them—half-illiterate, but greedily longing for art and knowledge—the laws of poetry, its history, giving them access to its beauty and power. He poured out on this young, still unblooming verdure the life-giving waters of our great literature, connecting and relating his students to the eternal creative works of the miraculous Russian language. They listened to him greedily, they loved him. But when it was necessary to gather as a whole audience and go to the Commissar of the Cheka, the man of their party who had attended their clubs and considered himself in sympathy with them, they turned cowardly and mean-spirited and basely repudiated Gumilev.[28]

At first, the fact that the charge against Gumilev had been "malfeasance in office" was cause for some amusement among those who knew the poet. But on the evening of August 31, frightening rumours began to circulate through the city. Otsup discovered that a secret meeting had been held that night, led by the Chairman of the Cheka, the very man who had received the delegation of poets. At that meeting, a report was read of the uncovering of the "Tagantsev conspiracy" and the execution by shooting of all the sixty-one "conspirators," including Nikolai Stepanovich Gumilev. Newspapers appeared the next morning, September 1, with accounts of the meeting and the liquidation of the conspirators.

The reporter for the *Red Gazette* set the scene of the meeting: "The Soviet opened in an overflowing hall...Perhaps not since the time of the Kronstadt events has a picture such as yesterday's appeared: all the aisles, the steps of the staircase, the seats were filled with members of the Petrosoviet and the chairmen of organizations."

Then the report was begun by Semenov, who attempted to construct the context for Gumilev's "crimes": "You understand that it threatens us and all of Russia when in the greatest toil of harvest, when pud [36 pounds] after pud is gathered and goes out into the regions where 20 millions of people howl for a crust of bread. The White Guard sought to disrupt the organization of the collection of the pronalog [tax] in order to profit from the dissatisfaction of the starving people and on their bones and blood erect the old building of the monarchy...In this the poet Gumilev, having recruited regular officers..."[29]

The Petrograd *Pravda* of the same day printed an official announcement of the execution by shooting, without a trial, of 61 people by the Cheka:

> At the present time, in view of the full liquidation of the White Guard organization in Petrograd, the publication of the full facts about the revolt that was being readied becomes possible...The White organizations, united by organizational connections and tactical association of centers located in Finland, presented a united conspiratorial front, readying an armed revolt in Petrograd at the moment of the collection of the pronalog. In the directives of the VCK is found a letter of the Paris chief of the Petrograd militant organzation, General Valdimirov. 'I earnestly beg you not to do it in an amateurish way. It is necessary to combine your purposes with any mass disorders.' From the time of the exposure in June of the first militant organization, the activity of the conspirators has not stopped for a moment. Across the Finland border agents for the ranks of the smashers continued to come...The struggle cost no little sacrifice to the organ of the Cheka. In the last two months, 7 were killed by White terrorists in Petrograd and 8 Communists were gravely wounded...The most significant was the Petrograd organization, "VOZSTANIYA." At the head of it stood a committee of three people; The head of the organization, Prof. V.N.Tagantsev,

former lieutenant-colonel V.G. Shvedov, and an agent of Finnish intelligence, former oficer Y.P. German...With the liquidation of the organization were discovered weapons, dynamite, typography, print, forms for many Soviet and military organizations, literature and leaflets. Measures were taken for the exploding of the Krasin train, in which, according to information of the PBO [Petrograd Military Organization], were gold and valuables, but the terrorists sent to the train station with the bombs were too late for the departure of the train...Explosions were prepared for the Nobel depots and arson of lumber mills...Two million rubles were received from the owner of a tannery, David Luries, for the organization of a revolt in Petrograd. The center of this organization in Paris consisted of General Vladimirov, cadets Kartashev, Struve, Kokovtsev, Ivanitsky and others...Tagantsev stood for the monarchy abroad...[30]

The Soviet authorities had developed an extremely effective technique for proving the "guilt" of the accused. They would hurl a multitude of charges at the accused, each one of which, considered separately, was not only false, but extremely improbable, if not preposterous. But the sheer volume of the accusations made it appear that there must be some guilt somewhere, according to the adage "Where there is smoke, there must be fire." Overwhelmed by the sheer number of charges, the defendant was unable to refute them all. Among the charges hurled at these 61 defendants were those of having a Germanophile orientation, negotiating with German social organizations and with the Ministry of Foreign Affairs, having links with the editorial board of the newspaper *Rul* (which was considered a crime) and with French intelligence, and many others, all difficult to refute.

Frances Laird

Half-way down the list of the "conspirators" who had been shot was Gumilev's name. "GUMILEV, N.S., 33 yrs., philologue, poet, member of the colleagues of the publishing house, 'World Literature,' partyless, former officer. He was active in putting together the leaflets. He promised to link a group of intellectuals with organizations at the moment of the rebellion. He received money from the organization for technical necessities."[31] The authorities couldn't even give Gumilev's correct age.

Although it is impossible to know exactly what happened to Nikolai Gumilev after he was swallowed up in the Cheka's capacious maw, there turned out to be witnesses, as there were to almost everything. Rumors about his last days were soon circulating. Knowing now the workings of the Soviet prison system, we can presume that torture was used in his interrogations—beatings, sleep deprivation, starving, threats against his family and brutal, manipulative questioning that continued uninterrupted day and night. Not only questioned about his own actions and convictions, he would have been pressured to implicate others in similar "crimes against the people." To encourage these denunciations, the Cheka may have extended their threats to his family, even to Anna Akhmatova.

Otsup concluded that Gumilev had been taken to the Gorokhovaya Prison, on the upper floors of a building that served as the center of the Petrograd Cheka, where Alexander Blok had been detained in 1919. Although Otsup theorized that Gumilev was killed late on that night of August 30 or early the next morning, his execution actually took place five days earlier, even as he and Gumilev's other friends were frantically trying to win his release. Under cover of darkness, crushed into a truck filled with other "conspirators," he was driven out of the city. Along a deserted roadway, the truck stopped beside a freshly-dug trench. The prisoners were roughly hauled out of the truck, forced to kneel beside the trench and shot with a pistol at point-blank range in the back of the head. As Nemirovich-Dancheko wrote: "...illiterate, stupid and foul people killed [him] like a stray dog, somewhere outside the city, so that it would be impossible to find the grave. Professors, artists and young girls barely out of childhood, as innocent as he was, lay with him in the brotherly grave."[32]

According to those shadowy witnesses, Gumilev faced death with that cool bravery one would expect of him. "Gumilev, who had not been guilty of anything, behaved...with his usual never-changing calmness and courage. As if in the trenches under the hellish attacks of the Germans. He met danger, never lowering his eyes and gazing contemptuously on that herd of executioners," Nemirovich-Danchenko believed.[33] As Otsup wrote: "Who those witnesses were I don't know, and even without their evidence to us, the friends of the deceased, it was clear that Gumilev died deserving of his reputation of a courageous and steadfast man."[34]

The rumor was that an official effort to free Nikolai Gumilev had been made when Maxim Gorky hurried to Moscow to arrange a pardon from Lenin. Supposedly Lenin assured Gorky that he would talk with Felix Derzhinsky, head of the All-Russian Cheka, about releasing Gumilev and promised him that none of the "conspirators" would be killed. But this was merely a ploy to distract Gorky, who learned upon his return to Petrograd that all sixty-one people, including Gumilev, had already been shot. Later Akhmatova doubted that Gorky would have risked his political position in their effort and was extremely skeptical of the truth of the rumor.

Anna knew little about the rescue attempts, for she was very ill and soon after Blok's funeral had left for Detskoe Selo to stay "...in something halfway between a hospital, and a sanatorium, and [she] was so weak that [she] did not go to the park even once."[35] In a letter from Shileiko, she heard of a rumour that Gumilev had been transferred to Moscow, a sign that he might be released. But with her usual prescience, Akhmatova seemed to have known that Kolya would never come out of the Chekist prisons alive. On August 16, while traveling on the train to Petrograd from Tsarskoe Selo, she went out onto the platform between the railroad cars. There, as approving Red Army soldiers looked on, she lit her cigarette from the sparks that flew back from the smokestack and landed on the railings. To the monotonous rumble of the wheels, this bleak and prophetic poem formed in her mind:[36]

> You are not with those who live,
> You don't rise from the snow.
> Twenty-eight from bayonets
> And five bullet holes.

Swan Songs
Akhmatova and Gumilev

> A new and bitter thing to wear
> I sewed for my friend.
> Drops of blood are loved, are loved
> By the Russian ground.
>
> Anna Akhmatova
August 16, 1921[37]

The same fearful foreboding emanates from a poem she wrote ten days later.

> A fence made out of wrought iron,
> A bed made out of pine.
> How sweet it is, no longer
> Need I feel jealousy.
>
> With sobs and supplications
> This bed was made for me.
> Stroll out about the world now,
> Go where you wish, Godspeed!
>
> Now your ears won't be wounded
> By raging, furious words.
> Now nobody till morning
> Will let the candle burn.

Frances Laird

> We have arrived at peace and
> Days so chaste and pure.
> You're crying—I am worthy
> Of not one of your tears.
>
> Anna Akhmatova
August 27, 1921[38]

Since this poem, dated four days before she learned of his death, refers so directly to her relationship with Kolya, Akhmatova may have altered this and the dates of some of the poems that follow to protect herself from official accusations of mourning an "enemy of the people."

With Kolya's death, an astonishing stream of passionate and anguished poems gushed from Akhmatova's pen. In the poem above, she sees Kolya, as she had seen Alexander Blok just days before, laid in a pine coffin inside the wrought-iron fence surrounding his grave. At last he rests from his wanderings and she is liberated from the jealousy aroused by his endless parade of paramours. Yet, with the inevitable guilt of the survivor, she feels that the grave/bed should have been hers. Kolya's adventurous spirit, freed from his body, can roam anywhere in the world it wishes. No wife will greet him with angry words or leave a candle burning all night in expectation of his return from exploits, amorous or otherwise. After a decade and a half of stubborn struggle, they have made peace with one another. The sexual tension wrought of passion and betrayal has vanished and all that remains is an eternal spiritual bond. If Kolya weeps for her in her grief and for her difficult life ahead, overcome with guilt for her own actions, she only feels unworthy of his tears.

If Lenin's aim was to paralyze the Petersburg intelligentsia with uncertainty, terror and grief, he succeeded. For Akhmatova, that terror took on mysterious, indefinable shapes:

> Terror, sorting through the things in darkness,
> Aims a beam of moonlight at the axe.
> Heard behind the wall sinister knocking—
> What is there, a thief, a ghost or rats?
>
> In the stifling kitchen it laps like water,
> Makes a count of rickety floor-boards,
> Flashes past outside the attic window
> With its lustrous black and glossy beard—
>
> It quiets down. How cunning and how evil,
> It hid the match, blew out the candle flame.
> Better if at my breast there were aimed
> A gleaming row of shiny rifle barrels.
>
> Better to lie down upon a scaffold
> Of bare wood in a green square, raised high,

> And beneath the groans and cries of gladness
> Let my red blood flow out till I die.
>
> To my heart I press the smooth cross tightly.
> God, give back to me my spirit's peace.
> The odor of decay, sweetish and sickly,
> Wafts up from the chilly linen sheets.
>
> Anna Akhmatova
August 27-28, 1921, Tsarskoe Selo[39]

Like a busy Cheka agent, Terror rummages through the house, invading the safe inner places of domestic life. It aims the moonlight like a spotlight on the executioner's axe and reveals itself in strange knocking, in lapping water, in a burst of air that blows out the candle's flame. As it flashes past the window, she glimpses the brutal masculinity of Terror with its gleaming black beard. Again rifles are raised in a firing line, but now it is the poet's own blood that flows out. Rather than having ubiquitous Terror haunting her, it would be better to surrender to the reality of annihilation. The poet resists that temptation only by clinging to the cross of her Orthodox Christian beliefs, as the smell of decay rising from the bedclothes suggests the intimate, even erotic presence of death.

On the following day, Akhmatova writes a poem filled with anguish, hate and remembered passion.

Swan Songs
Akhmatova and Gumilev

Oh, life without tomorrow's day!
In each word I pick out the treason.
And now for me the star is rising
Of a love that wanes away.

To fly off imperceptibly,
Almost not know one at a meeting.
But it's night again. And in moist languor
Are shoulders to be kissed again.

I was not dear to you. And you
Repelled me. But the torment dragged on
And, like a criminal, love languished,
Love with wickedness imbued.

You're like a brother, angry, mute.
But if our eyes meet one another—
I swear to you by skies above us,
That granite will melt in that heat.

Anna Akhmatova
August 29, 1921[40]

The poet struggles to reconcile irreconcilable opposites, an apt summary of the tortured history of their love. From its opening exclamation about life without continuation, the poem speaks in oxymorons—words that hold no meaning, love as a star that rises and dies at the same time, one who imperceptibly disappears, two who meet and almost don't know one another. It is as if Akhmatova's images are conflicted and choked out. These oppositions are cut short by a bold, unequivocally sensual image— "And in moist languour/Are shoulders to be kissed again" —that speaks of the powerful erotic pull between the poet and her lover. Yet this is expressed in an oddly impersonal way. Shadowing beneath passionate love is its opposite, hatred. The two lovers have tormented one another. He did not love her and she in turn looked upon him with repulsion. Akhmatova likens their love to a criminal, permeated with evil and guilty of terrible sins. As if to defuse the charged sexuality of the poem, the poet draws back to view Gumilev as her silent, angry brother. But her attempt fails and in some of the most self-revelatory of lines, Akhmatova speaks openly, almost brazenly, of the white-hot, sexual passion that would draw them to one another.

In a poem dated August 30, Akhmatova longs for a moment of mutual forgiveness which now will never come.

> Until I collapse at the fence and
> The wind comes to finish me off,
> The dream of salvation impending
> Will be burning in me like a curse.
>
> I stubbornly wait for what follows,

> As it happens for me with a song—
> As his everyday self, sure and cheerful,
> He will knock at the door as before.
>
> He'll enter and say, "That's enough, now.
> You see, I've forgiven you, too."
> It won't be too painful or awful…
> Neither roses nor archangels' hosts.
>
> So even in frenzied rebellion,
> I will take care of my heart,
> For without ever knowing this moment
> I cannot imagine death.
>
> Anna Akhmatova
August 30, 1921[41]

Until her dying hour comes, Akhmatova vows to wait for a reconciliation with Kolya, one raised to the level of a religious "salvation." She need only wait patiently, stubbornly for it to take form the way a new poem assumes its shape in her mind. A knock at the door and he will stride in, happy and confident, putting an end to the nightmare. It will be an ordinary moment, without pain or high drama. Even as this dream fades, she rebels against the reality of their fate and braces herself to endure what the future has in store for her.

Relinquishing the dream of Kolya's return has taught her of the absolute finality of death.

On the last day of August, Manya Rykova visited Akhmatova at the sanitorium, where, sitting on her balcony, they saw her father, who had just returned from Petrograd. He called to Manya and she ran down to speak with him. Akhmatova watched as Manya suddenly covered her face with her hands. To Akhmatova's worried question, she only answered "Nikolai" and Akhmatova knew at once what had happened.[42] On September 1, from the copy of *Pravda* posted at the train station in Detskoe Selo, Anna read the official account of Kolya's execution. She recalled: "That summer the forests near Petersburg burned—the streets were filled with overpowering yellow smoke…In the autumn the Field of Mars was an enormous, ravaged vegetable garden and there were clouds of ravens. After I arrived from Tsarskoe Selo, I set out on foot (everybody walked then) to Shileiko's at the Marble Palace—and he was crying."[43] It was as if nature had thrown a smoky shroud over the mourning city.

At the panakhida held for Nikolai Gumilev in the Kazan Cathedral, not in St. Isaac's as he had envisioned in "The Lost Streetcar," it was Akhmatova, not Asya, who was seen as the grieving widow. As the reports of the execution of the participants in the "Taganstev conspiracy" spread quickly throughout the country, Andrei Levinson struggled to articulate what had been lost with Gumilev's death:

Swan Songs
Akhmatova and Gumilev

Indignation and grief, the monstrosity of the crime overshadowed for a time his image in its intimate simplicity and his working ordinariness. The pathos and the solemnity of the making of poetry did not abandon him in everyday life. He didn't walk, but strode forth ardently, with a proud and slow importance. He didn't chat, but weighed out his words instructively, evenly, without a tremor of doubt in his voice. Poetry was the measure of things for him; the universe was material for the creation of images. The music of the spheres was the prototype of poetic rhythm...In "Red Petrograd," he became the tutor for a whole generation; the university and Proletkult equally sent prosletytes to him. However, it is not Gumilev's schemes, polished with pedanticism, not the formulae of creative work taught by him that won him such power over minds. Always in him could be sensed the even effort of a great will making beauty, but through the mask of a pedant...could be seen the youthful fire of the spirit, whole and without gaps, and in most cases, boyishly-simple.[44]

Frances Laird

Chapter XVI
An Unwed Widow

As Akhmatova lay in the sanitarium in Detskoe Selo, she tried to comprehend what had happened to Kolya, to herself, to her son, to all of Russia. This poem, dated two weeks after the announcement of his death, was published in a group entitled "The Voice of Memory," prefaced by an epigraph from Gumilev's "The Drunken Dervish." The epigraph reads: "The world is but a ray from the face of a friend, all else—its shadow." While there is no direct reference to Gumilev's death, apprehension resonates from the poem like the hollow clang of the church bell.

> The church gates have been thrown wide open.
> The lindens are beggaredly bare.
> And the dried-up gilding has darkened
> On the curving, inviolable wall.
>
> Rumbling fills the crypts and the altars,
> Past the broad Dnieper ringing soars.
> So the heavy bell of Mazepa
> Drones over St. Sophia square.
>
> More adamant, menacing, it rages,
> As if heretics were being killed here.

Swan Songs
Akhmatova and Gumilev

> But in woods past the river, placated,
> To the fluffy fox cubs it brings cheer.
>
> Anna Akhmatova
> September 15, 1921[1]

The church gates are gaping wide, not welcoming worshippers to the liturgy, but as evidence of a forced entry, a violation of that sacred space. Everything about the church has been impoverished and diminished, from the "beggaredly bare" branches of the churchyard trees to the fading gilt of the dome that no longer glitters in the candlelight. The meditative calm of prayer and singing is shattered by the heavy, relentless pealing of the bell of Mazepa. Ivan Mazepa, a Cossack leader who tried to bring independence to Ukraine, was defeated by Peter the Great at Poltava in 1709. Mazepa was considered a traitor, just as Gumilev was. The punishment for rejection of the political dogma, as for the religious dogma, was death. The ominous, funereal tolling echoes out over the countryside, arousing terror in the hearts of those who hear it. But when the sound reaches the unchanging, imperturbable peace of the natural world, where fox cubs romp in the woods, it has become only a distant, cheerful, musical chime.

In the Gumilev house in Tsarskoe Selo, Akhmatova's had long sensed a dark presence, perhaps some premonition of approaching disaster. In this unfinished poem, the "Sixth Elegy" from *Northern*

Frances Laird

Elegies, she asks Kolya, now "there" on the other side, who exactly it was that had been living with them then.

Sixth Elegy

In that house it was terrible to live,
And not the light of the patriarchal fireplace,
Nor the wooden cradle of my baby,
Nor the fact that both of us were young then,
And filled with projects and with plans.
[………………….And good fortune
From our threshold did not dare to take
A step away for all those seven years,—]
This feeling of terror did not diminish.
And I taught myself to laugh and to mock it
And left behind a droplet of my wine
And some crumbs of bread for one who nightly
Like a dog came scratching at the door
Or peered into the low-set little window,
At that time when we, silent now, had tried
Not to see what happened behind the mirror,
Under whose heavy weighing footsteps
Groaned the treads of the darkened staircase,
As if praying pitifully for mercy.
And you said to me, smiling strangely:

> "Who is it *they're* bringing down the stairs:
> Now you are there where all is known—so tell me:
> What lived in that house aside from us?
>
> Anna Akhmatova
1921, Tsarskoe Selo[2]

A poem dated September 15, 1921, expressed her state of mourning more directly:

> An autumn stained with tears, like a widow
> Dressed in black clothes, all hearts darkens...
> Sorting through the words of her husband
> She cannot bring an end to her sobbing.
> And so it will be till the quietest snowfall
> Takes pity on one grieving and exhausted...
> Oblivion of pain, oblivion of bliss—
> It's no small thing to give one's life for this.
>
> Anna Akhmatova
15 September 1921, Tsarskoe Selo[3]

She sees the dark, rain-lashed autumn as a widow dressed in mourning clothes. In an exhausted stupor of grief, she incessantly goes over her husband's words, written or remembered. Nature will take pity on her when winter comes with a silent, obliterating fall of snow that will cleanse and conceal both suffering and happiness, bringing with it a death-like oblivion.

As she grew stronger, Akhmatova occupied the long, sorrow-filled days walking in the park where she and Kolya had spent many tender hours of their youth. With its leaf-strewn paths and empty flowerbeds heaped with earth, it now looked more like a cemetery than a park.

> Like the fifth act of a drama
> The autumnal air is wafting.
> In the park each bed for flowers
> Seems like a grave freshly buried.
> With the pure funeral feast celebrated,
> There is nothing more that needs doing.
> So why is it here that I linger,
> As if a miracle would happen.
> In this way a boat heavy-laden
> Is held to the dock by a weak hand,
> Saying long good-byes to people
> Who'll be left behind on dry land.
>
> Anna Akhmatova
> Tsarskoe Selo, 1921[4]

As if caught in the final act of a Shakespeare play, Akhmatova senses a tragic end to the drama of her life. Although she has carried out the ceremonial rites due the dead, still she must linger, for it is there that the miraculous reappearance of the dead Kolya might take place.

The park of Tsarskoe Selo, with its evocations of her past life, also provides the setting for the next poem.

> All on the highest stars are those dear spirits.
> How good it is there's no one left to love
> And one can cry. The Tsarskoe Selo air was
> Created for repeating songs.
>
> Upon the lakeside bank the silvery willow
> Touches bright September waters' glass.
> Coming forth to meet me is my shadow,
> Silently roused up from the past.
>
> So many lyres are hung here on the branches
> But it's as if there were a place for mine.
> And to me the best of news and comfort
> Is this sparse and sunny shower of rain.
>
> Anna Akhmatova
1921[5]

In the Dante-esque image of those she has loved dwelling on distant stars, Akhmatova is thinking here not only of Gumilev and

Frances Laird

Alexander Blok, but of her brother, Andrei. With no one left to love, she is free to express her sorrow. But it is in the park at Tsarskoe Selo, the sacred territory of poets, where her own vocation is affirmed. She is met by the shadow of the young Anna, like Pushkin's shade she once imagined emerging from beneath the pine trees. On the willow beside the lake, hung with the lyres of the dead poets of Tsarskoe Selo, including Gumilev's, there will be a place for her lyre when she joins this eminent company. Finally, Akhmatova finds her ultimate consolation in the natural world where an unexpected sunny rain shower transforms the dying autumn landscape with a glittering radiance.

If at times Akhmatova can transcend her feelings of grief and loss, they always make a powerful return. She pores obsessively over her difficult love for Kolya and their life together in this poem written in late September of 1921.

> When exhausted by your long, fixed gazing,
> Then I learned how to torment, too.
> From a rib of your side created,
> How could I ever not love you?

> That I be your comforting sister
> Was willed to me by ancient fate,
> And I grew to be greedy and clever
> And the sweetest of all your slaves.

Swan Songs
Akhmatova and Gumilev

> But when, reconciled, I lay submissive
> On your breast that was whiter than snow,
> How triumphant, as if grown in wisdom,
> Was your heart—my nativeland's sun.
>
> Anna Akhmatova
> September 25, 1921[6]

Nikolai's infidelities shattered her illusions about love and he became her instructor in the arts of betrayal and the tortures of jealousy. Akhmatova acknowledges that, as the Eve created from his rib, she found her source in him, both as a poet and a woman. Marrying him was not an act of choice, but an act of fate, as she had written to von Shtein so many years ago. As one of Kolya's many "slaves," her submission to his sexual power was inevitable. With it, his "triumphant" heart, which Akhmatova likens to the sun warming the Russian earth, could only grow wiser. The sun image was one used in euglogies to Alexander Pushkin, in whose early death, like that of Gumilev, political motivations were suspected.

As winter drew in, Akhmatova returned to Petrograd to live with Olga Glebova-Sudeikina and Arthur Lourie at 18 Fontanka. Olga's artistic efforts now centered on the marionettes she was creating for a puppet theatre and the porcelain figurines she was designing for the Imperial Porcelain factory. Akhmatova had grown closer to Lourie, who as Commissar of Music had arranged concerts, organized music schools and even created a symphony orchestra as well as publishing his music and music criticism. However, in 1921, Lourie was removed from his position and was growing discontented with life in Russia.

A glimpse inside 18 Fontanka is given by Yuri Annenkov, who accompanied Olga home one night and, since it was raining and he had brought no umbrella, spent the night on the sofa. Next morning, Akhmatova, wearing an apron and bearing a tea tray, appeared, saying: "I've brought the children something to eat." Annenkov was moved by this homey scene and years later wrote: "I must admit the tea and sugar that day tasted better than the most elegant dish somewhere at the Tour d'Argent or Maxim's."[7]

Akhmatova returned to her job in the library of the Agronomy Institute, where a friend from the *Apollon* days, Mikhail Zenkevich, visited her: "...in a small, cold room. There was a cluster of people— evidently librarians. I asked where I could find Anna Akhmatova. Suddenly a tall woman came over out of the gloomy group of librarians, and with a smile, gave me her hand." The other librarians, who admired her poetry, did all they could to help her. One lit the stove and brought them hot cocoa as they sat bundled in their overcoats. Akhmatova talked with sad resignation about all those she had lost. When Zenkevich asked about the rumors that she would emigrate to the West, she answered: 'And what will I do there? They have all gone out of their minds there and don't understand anything.' Then the talk turned to Gumilev's death: 'It was so unexpected,' she said, 'He was so remote from politics. But he continued to maintain contacts with his old friends in the army, and they might have dragged him into some kind of plot...But let's read some poetry." When it was time to go, Zenkevich kissed her hand, thinking how much she had been changed by her suffering. Gone was the air of feminine vanity, now replaced by a calm wisdom.[8]

Akhmatova's reappearance in Petrograd relieved her friends, for rumors had been flying that she was mortally ill from a cold caught at Blok's funeral, that she had been poisoned, that she had committed suicide out of grief. According to a letter from Marina Tsvetaeva, these rumors had frightened even Mayakovsky: "...who, looking like a slaughtered bull, walked around the cardboard 'Poet's Café.' *Killed with despair*—really, that is what he looked like. He also sent, through friends, a cable asking about you, and it is *to him* that I am indebted for the joy of receiving news about you..."[9]

In November, Akhmatova read at a literary evening in the House of Writers. The tiny auditorium could accomodate only a fraction of those who crowded into the building to hear her. A journalist from Riga described how the audience "...nervously, excitedly, and...respectfully restrained, murmured—impatiently awaiting the entrance of the poetess."[10]

Even with the enthusiasm of her audiences, Akhmatova knew that her life as a poet was irremediably changed, now that she had become the former wife of an "enemy of the people." Her poetry was associated by Soviet officialdom with the hated pre-revolutionary past. Nor was she prepared to leap onto the literary bandwagon of the new Soviet state. But her isolation only deepened as a result of Chukovsky's lecture, "Akhmatova and Mayakovsky," read at the House of Arts in 1921.[11]

Comparing the two poets, Chukovsky saw Mayakovsky as a "poet of catastrophes and convulsions," of movement, storms, war and revolution, whose poems are written for the masses. "He is a cheeky poet, a shouting poet, a street, public poet...He needs not paper but a larynx. He is what a poet of the revolution ought to be. He is Isaiah in the guise of an Apache." Akhmatova, on the other hand, is "an assiduous inheritor of all the most valuable pre-revolutionary treasures of Russian literary culture...She has that elegance of spirit and the charm that one acquires through centuries of cultural tradition...Akhmatova has kept the old Russian faith in God, while Mayakovsky, like a true bard of the revolution, is a sacrilegious blasphemer. For her, the most sacred value is Russia, the motherland, 'our soil.' He...is an internationalist, a citizen of the world...She is a silent recluse, always in a hermitage, in stillness...He is in the street, at a mass meeting, in a crowd; he himself is a crowd..." Chukovsky concluded that "they are as different as two elements, two incarnations of gigantic historic forces, and let each man decide for himself which of these two poles he is to join, which to reject, and which to love." Chukovsky fervently admired both poets and advocated a synthesis of the differing elements they embodied. But

Chukovsky's last, crucial point was lost on the new Soviet man, whose choice was obvious.

In December of 1921, Akhmatova wrote a two-part poem entitled "Another's Voice," not in her own, but in the voice of Nikolai Gumilev.

<u>Another's Voice</u>

1

With you, I, my angel, was not clever.
How did it turn out that I have left you
Far behind me, taken and held hostage
By unremitting earthly pain and suffering?
Under bridges ice-bound pools are smoking,
Over bonfires sparks are turning golden,
Cursedly the massive northwinds howl out
And beyond the Neva a stray bullet
Searches for a way to your poor heart.
In a freezing house, you, solitary,
White, are lying down in a white radiance
Singing praises to my bitter name.

Anna Akhmatova
December 7, 1921[12]

Frances Laird

As Gumilev looks back from the other world to see her anguish and suffering over his death, he also understands the danger she is in, that there is a bullet meant for her, too. This image refers back to Gumilev's poem, "The Worker," written in April, 1916, in which an old man, standing at a red-hot furnace, pours the bullet that will kill him. "The bullet which was cast by him will search out/The way to my breast, for me it has come." Though intended as a prevision of his death on the battlefield, Gumilev's poem took on a new, heart-stopping significance in 1921.

The second poem of "Another's Voice" is more difficult to interpret. It begins with Gumilev's description, imagined by Akhmatova, of Anna Gorenko as a rapacious, hawk-like bird that tears with its claws at his breast.

2

In that year long ago, when love took fire,
Like an altar cross in a heart condemned to ruin,
Not clinging to my breast, a tender pigeon,
But like a kite you clawed with your sharp talons.
You gave to me to drink the accursed wine,
As a first betrayal offered to your friend.
But then came round the hour for you to gaze
Into green eyes, at stern and cruel lips,
To pray for that sweet gift, though all for nothing,
And for the vows which you had never heard,

> The vows which nobody as yet had spoken.
> Like someone poisoning water in a spring
> For one who follows after in the desert
> And getting lost himself and very thirsty
> In darkness does not recognize the spring.
> He drinks down death, having clung to the cool water,
> But can a thirst be satisfied by death?
>
> Anna Akhmatova
December 8, 1921, St. Petersburg[13]

If "Another's Voice 2" is Gumilev's, that voice is now accusatory, or rather self-accusatory, as Akhmatova is depicting herself as if from Gumilev's point of view. By speaking indirectly through his voice, she is able to admit that she had wounded him with her own betrayal, the "accursed wine" she offered him, an image from Gumilev's "Poisoned." The green eyes and cruel lips point to another, perhaps Shileiko, who, like Gumilev, was unable to make the "vows" of a lasting love. The poem ends with an extended metaphor about one who poisons a desert spring, intending to kill the person who follows him. But thirsty and lost in the desert, he mistakenly drinks from that very spring and poisons himself. Perhaps Akhmatova, intent on seeking revenge for his infidelities, had poisoned the well-spring of their love by her betrayal. But in her thirst for that love, she herself has been poisoned. The poem ends with the question: will that thirst ever be satisfied, even in death? "Another's Voice 2" can be read as

Akhmatova's confession of guilt in the breaking of their marriage vows and the dissolution of their marriage.

On December 24, 1921, Kornei Chukovsky visited Akhmatova at 18 Fontanka:

> The room was small; the large bed unmade. An icon of the Holy Mother in a silver frame was nailed to the left door of the cupboard. Next to the bed was a little table on which there was butter and rye bread. An old servant woman opened the door. Akhmatova had a blanket around her legs: "I have a cold and a cough."...She was lying on her bed in her coat. She put her hand under the blanket and pulled out some large sheets of paper rolled up into a scroll. "This is the ballet *Snow Mask*, based on Blok. Listen to it and tell me what you think of the style. I can't write prose." And she began to read the libretto she had written, which I thought was a wonderful and accurate commentary on *Snow Mask*. I don't know if it's a good ballet, but as a critique it's wonderful. "I've not come up with the death scene in the third act. I'm writing this for Artur Sergeyevich Lourie. He asked me to. Perhaps Diaghilev will stage it in Paris."
> Then she began to recite her poetry. But when she had finished reading about Blok, I let our a sob and ran out.[14]

Akhmatova returned to Slepnevo one last time to spend Christmas, 1921, with Lev. The gloom that hung over the house in this straitened, starving season, must have been almost unendurable. The shock of Gumilev's death, learned by his aging mother and ill brother through the newspaper account, had powerfully affected the family. They had been forced to accept that their Kolya had somehow betrayed his country—and them—by his participation in some kind of conspiracy. They puzzled endlessly, trying to ferret out the facts of the possible secret life of a Kolya other than the one they knew. If they were not to go mad, they had to believe that there was a rational explanation for his execution. There were so many agonizing, unanswered questions. But his mother suffered most from knowing that they would never find his body and could never give him a proper Russian Orthodox burial. Akhmatova evokes that last Christmas at Slepnevo in "Bezhetsk."

Bezhetsk

There white churches rise, there is clear-ringing, glittering ice.
And, cornflower blue, the eyes of my dearest son blossom.
Above the old city, the Russian nights shine out like diamonds
And a sky sickle even more yellow than honey from limes.
There up from the fields past the river the dry blizzards fly
And people like angels at God's own feastday are joyful.
They've cleaned up the front room and then lit the lamps by the icon
And out on the table of oak the Holy Book lies.
Now memory, strict and severe, is miserly there,
It opened its tower chamber to me, bowing deeply;
But I did not enter, I slammed the terrible door;
And filled with Christmas's gay, ringing sounds was the city.

         Anna Akhmatova
         December 26, 1921[15]

Frances Laird

And with this poem, Akhmatova slams shut the door on the horrific year 1921.

Chapter XVII
The Banks of the Neva

The oppressive machinery of Soviet censorship had not yet been brought to the state of awful perfection it was soon to attain. For early in 1922, a Petrograd theatre managed to stage Nikolai Gumilev's play, *Gondla*. At the conclusion of the dress rehearsal and at its first performance members of the audience, in the only open protest they dared mount, shouted "Author, author!" The piece was quickly pulled from the repertory.[1] Nikolai Gumilev, his life, and his poetry dropped out of sight and into apparent non-existence.

But Akhmatova's private mourning did not end. Though she spoke his name rarely and only among the closest friends—it was suicidal to show concern for an "enemy of the people" —thoughts of Kolya were never far from her mind. Although she had to keep an iron control over any expression of her feelings, she could relax with Osip Mandelstam and his wife, Nadezhda, when conversation often turned to Kolya, his extraordinary life and his terrible death. In a letter to Akhmatova dated August 25, 1928, the anniversary of Gumilev's execution, Mandelstam wrote: "You should know that I am able to conduct an imaginary conversation with only two people—Nikolai Stepanovich and you. My talks with Kolya have not been interrupted and never will be."[2]

It was not only their shared passion for the poetic word that bound Gumilev and Mandelstam, but very human ties as well. In the aftermath of the October Revolution, when poets depended on Maxim Gorky for rations and other handouts, Mandelstam put in a request for trousers and a sweater. As his wife wrote: "Gorky gave out the sweater, but with his own hand crossed out the trousers...Gumilev gave him his own—a spare pair. Mandelstam swore to me that strutting about in Gumilev's trousers, he felt unusually strong and manly."[3]

Akhmatova was haunted by the thought that Kolya's body had been thrown into a pit, an unknown, unmarked grave, that he was never to be properly interred as an Orthodox Christian. Secretly she tried to find out the location, a careful, clandestine search which was encoded in her essay "Pushkin and the Banks of the Neva." Written in the years when she was prevented from publishing her poetry and forced to take refuge in Pushkin studies, its subject is Pushkin's search for the graves of five executed Decembrists. After a failed uprising on December 26, 1825, these five young officers, leaders of a reform movement that would have established a freer, more representative political system in Russia, had been executed on orders of Tsar Nicholas I. Speculation was that their bodies had been buried in a wild and deserted part of St. Petersburg, on Golodai Island at the northernmost tip of Vasilevsky Island. According to Akhmatova, Pushkin maintained that "the grave of a just man is a national treasure and a blessing from the gods."[4] His preoccupation with a flat, dismal island, covered with tundra and washed with sea foam "allows us to suppose that he, too, had seached for the unmarked graves along the

Neva shore."[5] It is possible, judging from her first-hand description of the place, that Akhmatova, too, had searched those foam-laced shores of the Neva looking for Gumilev's grave: "There really are sea birds there...the fishing nets are hung out to dry, sometimes you pass a boat full of holes, the charred remains of campfires can be seen. At least that's how it was in the early twentieth century, when I often visited those places."[6]

It was only nine years after Gumilev's death that Akhmatova finally learned the exact location of the mass grave of the "Tagantsev conspirators":

> They were shot near Berngardovka, along the Irininskaya road. Some acquaintances had a laundress and her daughter was an investigator. She, that is the laundress, told them and even pointed out the place according to her daughter's words. They went there immediately and the ground was visibly stamped down with boots. But I found out after nine years and went there. A clearing, a small, crooked pine tree, next to it another more massive one with its roots twisted out of the ground. That was the wall. The earth had sunk down. It was lower because they didn't fill in the graves there. Holes. Two brotherly holes for sixty people. When I went there, tall white flowers were growing everywhere. I picked them and thought: 'Others bring flowers to the grave, but I pick them from the grave.'...[7]

With the miraculous appearance in 1945 of the British diplomat, Isaiah Berlin, who had been born in Riga and could converse fluently in Russian, Akhmatova felt free to reveal her feelings to someone from the outside world. He wrote: "She spoke of her first husband, the celebrated poet Gumilev…her eyes had tears in them when she described the harrowing circumstances of his death."[8] And this was twenty-four years later.

When the massive structure of Soviet rule fell apart like a house of straw in 1990 and before the next incarnation of the state security system could be locked into place, tons of ancient, dusty files in the KGB archives fell open. At last it was possible to penetrate beyond the spin of speculation to discover the truth about Nikolai Gumilev's last days. Vera and Sergei Luknitsky, whose father, Pavel Luknitsky, had led an effort to rescue Gumilev's name and work, visited the KGB offices in St. Petersburg to view File No.214224 PBO [Petrograd Military Organization], "the Gumilev file." They found an ordinary packet, like hundreds of thousands of others, yellowed documents covered with faded ink, often impossible to read. Along with the official forms and reports were receipts, orders for the search of Gumilev's room, tickets, lists of poems and poets, notes, including this touching one from his wife: "Dear Kotik, I didn't buy sweets or ham eat the kolbasa don't be angry. Eat more, in the kitchen is bread, kasha, drink all the milk, eat the rolls. You are not eating and all will have to be thrown away, it's terrible. I kiss you. Your Anya." Included was the futile appeal to the Presidium of the Petrograd

Municipal Emergency Commission for his release, as drawn up and signed by his literary colleagues, including Gorky, soon after Blok's funeral.[9]

It is only on page 68 of the file, with the confession of Vladimir Tagantsev, a young professor of geography at St. Petersburg University and the accused leader of the "conspiracy," that the case against Nikolai Gumilev is introduced. This turns out to be the most crucial document in the file.

Tagantsev claimed that in November, 1920, Gumilev had speculated in the presence of a man named German, that, in the event of an uprising in the streets against the Soviets, he might gather a group of intellectuals to join it. At the time of the Kronstadt uprising, March, 1921, he was approached by Svedov, who proposed that they draw up a proclamation. Gumilev agreed, but insisted that it reflect his views, which were not in support of the monarchy, but closer to the Soviet orientation. Svedov gave him 200,000 rubles for expenses [in the inflated Soviet currency it was enough to buy four loaves of bread] and a typewriter ribbon. But after the ruthless suppression of the Kronstadt rebellion, Gumilev had realized the futility of opposition, abandoned his counter-revolutionary views and did nothing further. Tagantsev's testimony could never be verified by either German nor Svedov, for, according to KGB files, Y.P. German, a naval officer, had been shot in May, 1921, by a border guard while trying to cross into Finland and V.G. Shvedov, a lieutenant-colonel, had been killed during his arrest by Chekists in March.

Gumilev underwent interrogation four times, to judge by the reports included in his file. In the first session, on August 9, six days after his arrest, he reported his encounters with a young man from Moscow who plied him with Russian emigré newspapers and then asked Gumilev if he knew anyone who wanted to work for the counter-revolution. Gumilev replied that he knew of no one and abruptly ended the conversation. Investigator Yakobson, the leading interrogator, was not satisfied. Gumilev was again brought in to be questioned on August 18. This time he admitted that at the time of the Kronstadt rebellion, "I indicated that in all probability I could at the moment of an uprising gather and bring with me a small group of passers-by using a general attitude of opposition." Later he admits that he had considered asking his comrades, former officers, which was thoughtless of him, because, as he had not been in touch with them, that would have been extremely difficult. He also had agreed to write counter-revolutionary poems. Offered 200,000 rubles and the typewriter ribbon, he had refused the ribbon but put the money in his desk drawer, afterwards intending to return it. After Kronstadt, he had "sharply changed [his relationship] with Soviet power," and thought no more about the matter.

The brief, matter-of-fact interrogation reports were most likely condensed from interminable hours of questioning. From the bland account of his testimony in the Cheka files it is impossible to say how long it took to extract Gumilev's admissions or how violent the means that were used on him. As so many others had, Gumilev easily may have been beaten, starved, and kept awake for days and nights on end. The lives of his wife, mother, son, or even Akhmatova may have been threatened. But knowing Gumilev's character, he would have been forthright and honest in his answers and, however brutal were the Cheka's methods, he would have carried himself honorably, never groveling, never begging for mercy, never implicating others in order to save himself.

The Cheka interrogators were relentless. Not satisfied with Gumilev's "confession," they wanted the names of others involved with him in the "Tagantsev conspiracy." So two days later, on August 20, Gumilev was brought for questioning a third time by Yakobson to extract the names of those "courageous and decisive people," that little band of heroic souls Gumilev had imagined would demonstrate their opposition to Soviet power. Gumilev could give no names, because he had none in mind when he had spoken of it.

In his final interrogation session three days later, on August 23, 1921, Yakobson was still trying to force from him an admission of his guilt and the names of other "conspirators." But Gumilev admitted no guilt in his acts, only in words and briefly-held intentions and he steadfastly refused to implicate anyone else, whatever means his interrogators had to use to break down his resistance. Alone in a dismal, cold interrogation room, lit by a single bulb hanging from the ceiling, with only the hard-eyed agents of the Cheka as witnesses, this poet/conquistador may have lived his most courageous, most heroic hours.

But non-confessions were irrelevant. He was charged with collaborating in the "crimes" of Taganstev's counter-revolutionary organization. Investigator Yakobson concluded his report:

On the basis of what is stated above, I consider it necessary to apply in relation to Cit. Gumilev, Nikolai Stanislavovich [corrected as above] as to an obvious enemy of the people and the worker-peasant revolution the highest measure of punishment—execution by shooting.
Investigator Yakobson

The corraborating signature on this document, necessary for a death sentence, is missing. With a nod from Lenin, the signature of one bureaucrat was all that was needed then to kill a man.

Gorky's signature on the letter to the Presidium asking for his release is the only trace of any attempt by him to rescue Gumilev. But there is no evidence that Gorky had dared to put himself at risk by taking on the perilous task of intervening with Lenin to save Gumilev's life. Gorky's relationship with Lenin, a friend from the earliest days of the Bolsheviks, had become increasingly strained. Lenin had even suggested that Gorky, who appeared lacking in enthusiasm for Lenin's unrestrained use of force against his fellow Russians, might be happier living abroad.

From the Presidium of the Petrograd Municipal Cheka, on August 24, 1921, the sentence came down:

Gumilev, Nikolai Stepanovich, 35 years, former aristocrat, philologue, member of the editorial board of "World Literature," married, party-less, former officer, member of Petrograd military counter-revolutionary organization, actively aided in the formulation of proclamations of counter-revolutionary content, promised to link a group of intellectuals and officers with the organization who at the moment of an uprising will take part in the uprising, received from the organization money for technical necessities.

Sentenced to the highest measure of punishment—execution by shooting.

So Gumilev's grandiose talk and idealistic notions were transformed by the clattering typewriters of the Cheka into hard, indisputable fact. He was shot almost immediately, either on the night of August 24 or in the early morning hours of August 25. While Otsup and the others were rushing about the city from Cheka offices to prisons searching for Gumilev, his lifeless body had already been dumped into one of the huge holes dug beside the Irininskaya road.

Nikolai Gumilev was not executed for his acts, but for his thoughts and words uttered in private conversations. The Cheka never dared accuse him of his real "crimes" —his staunchly independent voice, his lack of humility before his new Soviet masters, his determination to tell the truth as he saw it. Mandelstam was said to have observed that nowhere were poets more highly valued by their government than in Russia, for there they could be killed for their poetry. And his own life was a clear demonstration of that. Gumilev's name is only one of a long list of great Russian writers who were hounded into early graves under Soviet rule—Mandelstam, Babel, Klyuev, Esenin, Platonov, Pilnyak, Mayakovsky, Tsvetaeva, Bulgakov as well as hundreds of others less well-known.

Frances Laird

It was with the "Tagantsev conspiracy" that Lenin first put into practice the techniques to be used in decades to come to break down any opposition, real or imagined, to Soviet rule. First came the arrest of an individual or members of a group, then multiple accusations of treason against the state which were elaborately embroidered with details that had little or no basis in fact, then execution with a show trial or without. Not only was any real or potential resistance crushed, the terror, confusion and bewilderment sown in the population made control of it that much easier. In this case, the fractious and uncooperative intelligentsia of Petrograd, who up until then had exhibited little but distaste for their Bolshevik masters, were terrorized into silence. This savage technique would be perfected and taken to increasingly insane and murderous extremes under Lenin's successor, Joseph Stalin.

By 1921, Petersburg's two leading poets of the Silver Age, Alexander Blok and Nikolai Gumilev, had been erased from the literary landscape. Many of Gumilev's poet friends and disciples emigrated to Paris soon after his death, including Sergei Makovsky, Vladislav Khodasevich, Nikolai Otsup and Georgy Adamovich. Maximilian Voloshin retreated to the relative safety of Koktebel in Crimea and, although prevented from publishing after 1923, he provided a haven for other writers. Vyacheslav Ivanov descended from his "Tower" and headed to Italy, where he established himself as a professor of Russian.

Arthur Lourie and Olga Glebova-Sudeikina left Russia for Paris in 1922. At the invitation of conductor Serge Koussevitsky, Lourie eventually emigrated to the United States, but never realized success there. Olga, the enchanting "Columbine-Psyche," remained in Paris. Ever the free spirit, she collected parakeets, sparrows and doves which flew freely about her room under the eaves of her apartment building. In 1944, an exploding shell fell on the building, destroying her flat and killing her birds. Although Olga emerged unhurt, she fell ill and died a year later.

The old guard of Symbolist poets managed to survive by retreating into the shadows. After leaving Russia in 1923, Andrei Bely returned, living quietly and continuing to write novels, including his masterpiece, *Petersburg*, until his death in 1934. Fyodor Sologub, Konstantin Balmont and Mikhail Kuzmin had fallen out of favor and no longer were able to publish. Only Gumilev's old mentor, Valery Bryusov, turned his coat, joining the Communist party and organizing LITO, the literary branch of the Department of Education, which aimed to form correct literary tastes in Russians. Sergei Gorodetsky was another who adapted handily to the Soviet literary line and had the rare good fortune of living out a normal lifespan. But his success came at the expense of his fellow writers. Akhmatova wrote that he "uttered the following immortal phrase in the course of a public appearance somewhere: 'These are lines by the Akhmatova who has become a counter-revolutionary.'"[10] Alexei Tolstoy, who had left Russia at the outbreak of the October Revolution, returned in 1923 to become a popular novelist and the grand old man of Soviet letters, winning the Stalin prize for his historical novels about Peter the Great. Mikhail Lozinsky, despite his signature on the letter requesting Gumilev's release, was able to retain his artistic integrity as well as his life by concentrating on translation. His brilliant version of Dante's *Divine Comedy* was greatly admired by Anna Akhmatova. She wrote: "In the difficult and noble art of translation Lozinsky was for the twentieth century what Zhukovsky was for the nineteenth."[11] Despite serious illness, he worked on and remained a loyal friend to Akhmatova.

Maxim Gorky's fate was more complicated. In 1921, disillusioned by Lenin's iron-fisted methods and frustrated in his literary efforts, he left Russia for a villa in Sorrento, Italy. He soon grew sceptical of reports of the suffering at home and, with the bait of a town house in Moscow, dachas, money, and flattery, Stalin enticed him to return in 1931. Thoroughly entangled in spies and informers, Gorky was soon under the thumb of Yagoda, head of the OGPU, the Cheka's successor. Gorky, as the most eminent Soviet writer, established with his propagandistic novels about "life as it should be" what was the only acceptable literary style, "Socialist realism." By 1933, Gorky had been broken to the Stalinist bridle and was working hand in hand with the government to control his fellow writers. But Stalin was even then plotting his downfall. Yagoda arranged that Gorky's beloved son, Maxim, be poisoned, to hasten Gorky's death and free Maxim's wife, a fresh, young beauty who had caught

Yagoda's eye. A trapped and broken man, Gorky died under suspicious circumstances of pneumonia and other complications five years after his return to Russia.

The iconoclastic young Futurists also suffered varying but similarly unhappy fates. Velimir Khlebnikov, whose inventive mind had opened the door to innovations in modern verse, was driven from the city and died of typhus, destitute and alone, one year after Gumilev. Vladimir Mayakovsky, a fiery supporter of the Revolution, handed over his poetic gift to the state, devoting himself to the writing of patriotic and propagandistic verse. He was hailed as the foremost Soviet poet. But the inner tension between the free-thinking artist and the puppet manipulated by the State became so unbearable that, in 1930, he put a gun to his heart.

The "peasant poets," Nikolai Klyuev and Sergei Esenin, fared no better. After his brief marriage to the dancer Isadora Duncan, Esenin returned to Russia in 1924, a terminally bored and bitter alcoholic. Esenin could find no place for himself in a new society where neither the long-cherished peasant traditions nor the innovations of Imagism were valued. After writing a farewell poem in his own blood, he hung himself in a hotel room in Petrograd. Nikolai Klyuev's destruction came at the hands of the Soviet government. He openly condemned the campaigns of collectivization and industrialization for plunging his country into chaos and suffering and for destroying the rich culture of Russia. Klyuev was hounded out of the Writers' Union and forced to beg on the street to stay alive. When he was finally arrested in 1934, Klyuev had answered his interrogators as openly and honestly as Gumilev. First exiled to Siberia, he was re-arrested in 1937, accused of a plot to restore the monarchy and shot. Only recently unearthed from the KGB archives was the manuscript of *The Song of the Great Mother,* his mystical and prophetic masterpiece of more than 4,000 lines, long believed lost.[12]

As for two other Acmeist poets, Vladimir Narbut and Osip Mandelstam, though their paths initially diverged, they, too, ended in the gulag. After the Revolution, Narbut's poetry turned patriotic and he became an active literary bureaucrat. However, as one to whom Mandelstam had recited his damning poem about Stalin, he was arrested and died in a concentration camp in 1944. That "counter-revolutionary" poem by Mandelstam, only whispered within the circle of his friends and never committed to paper, led to Mandelstam's downfall as well. A copy in Mandelstam's delicate, precise handwriting was discovered in the KGB archives.

> We live without sensing the country beneath us,
> At ten paces, our speech has no sound
> And when there's the will to half-open our mouths
> The Kremlin crag-dweller bars the way.
> Fat fingers as oily as maggots,
> Words sure as forty-pound weights,
> With his leather-clad gleaming calves
> And his large laughing cockroach eyes.

> And around him a rabble of thin-necked bosses,
> He toys with the service of such semi-humans.
> They whistle, they meow, and they whine:
> He alone merely jabs with his finger and barks,
> Tossing out decree after decree like horseshoes—
> Right in the eye, in the face, the brow or the groin.
> Not one shooting but swells his gang's pleasure,
> And the broad breast of the Ossetian.[13]

It was this that the OGPU agents were after when they shoved their way into Mandelstam's apartment on a May evening in 1934. Akhmatova had just arrived from Leningrad to visit and sat with Nadezhda as agents rifled Mandelstam's papers, examining every book, manuscript, and letter, every drawer, crack and crevice of the apartment, dumping manuscripts on the floor and trampling them underfoot. As Nadezhda packed Osip's small suitcase with his toothbrush and razor, a clean shirt, his well-thumbed copy of Dante's *Divine Comedy,* Akhmatova insisted he eat the egg that they had borrowed from a neighbor especially for her. As she described it: "We all sat in one room. It was very quiet. You could hear someone playing a ukelele next door...He kissed me as he was leaving..."[14] In prison, when his interrogators thrust a copy of the "traitorous" poem in his face, Mandelstam admitted at once that it was his. He expected that this poem would earn him the death sentence. But Boris Pasternak intervened and Stalin for once changed his mind, deciding to "isolate but preserve" the poet. Badly damaged by physical and psychological torture, Mandelstam was sent into exile accompanied by his wife. In 1938, Mandelstam was arrested again and the frail and sickly poet died of typhus in transit to a Siberian prison camp.

No KGB file for Anna Akhmatova has ever been discovered. But if it had, probably written there would have been the same sentence—"isolate but preserve." Despite her constant, gnawing anxiety and the terrors that visited her in long, sleepless nights, even as she saw everyone around her taken away, Akhmatova was never arrested. But Stalin had other plans for tormenting her. Her son, Lev, was arrested in 1933, for no crime but being the child of Gumilev and Akhmatova. He was quickly released, then arrested again, along with Akhmatova's third husband, Nikolai Punin, in 1935. Akhmatova wrote a letter to Stalin begging for their release. By some miracle he let them go.

At the height of the Yezhov Terror, in March, 1938, Lev Gumilev was arrested for a third time and disappeared into the Soviet prison system. Akhmatova joined the thousands of other women who stood in lines outside the Kresty prison, waiting to hand in parcels for fathers, sons, brothers, and husbands. Lev was imprisoned for seventeen months in Leningrad, then shipped to Siberia. Out of this experience came her moving and magnificent poems of *Requiem (1935-1940)*. Lev was ultimately freed to fight in the Great Patriotic War (World War II) and returned to Leningrad in 1945. But Stalin could not keep his fat, itchy fingers from Akhmatova's only child. In 1949, both Lev and Nikolai Punin were arrested again. Punin died in

Swan Songs
Akhmatova and Gumilev

a prison camp. Seven years would pass and Stalin would die before the son of Akhmatova and Gumilev would return from Siberia.

Frances Laird

Conclusion
The Absent Hero

Anna Akhmatova devoted roughly the last twenty years of her life to writing and re-writing *Poem Without a Hero: a Triptych (1940-1962)*. In this long poem of nearly 750 lines, she gazes back with sadly experienced eyes at the heady days of pre-war, pre-revolutionary St. Petersburg and the frenzied, hedonistic, self-absorbed life that she and her friends then so complacently had led. The Introduction to *Poem Without a Hero* reads:

> From the year nineteen forty,
> As if from a tower I gaze on all
> As if once more I were saying
> Good-bye to those I took leave of
> Long ago, as if having crossed myself,
> I go down beneath the dark vaults.
>
> August 25, 1941
Beseiged Leningrad[1]

Poem Without a Hero is divided into three sections. Part One, entitled "The Year Nineteen Thirteen; A Petersburg Tale", takes place on New Year's Eve, 1913, in Fontanny Dom, the former Sheremetev palace in a remote wing of which Akhmatova had lived for many years. The poet, in anxious anticipation of her guests, has lit the sacred candles. But when the doorbell rings, it is not her friends, but a crowd of masked mummers who rush in. Their identities are hidden by disguises, among them Faust, Don Juan, John the Baptist, Dapertutto, the goat-legged nymph, and an elegantly dressed Demon. But the poet knows that concealed beneath the masks of these strange figures are the ghostly faces of her friends of long ago, all now dead.

A central motif in Part One is the suicide of Vsevelod Knyazev, the young soldier-poet who shot himself out of unrequited love on the doorstep of the actress, Olga Glebova-Sudeikina, a flaxen-haired charmer and close friend of Akhmatova. Akhmatova saw his tragic and senseless death, in which she feels a guilty complicity, as somehow paradigmatic of those times.

Part Two, "Intermezzo: The Other Side of the Coin," again takes place in Fontanny Dom, but in early January, 1941, at the Orthodox celebration of Christmas. The poet muses in this section of the *Poem* on the pain and difficulty of her creative work. "Epilogue", which makes up Part Three, is dated June 24, 1942, one day after Akhmatova's birthday, and is set in war-ravaged Leningrad (St. Petersburg). The poet is not present there. She has been evacuated by plane ("in the belly of a flying fish...") to distant Tashkent, carried high over the long roads to the prison camps down which her son and so many millions of others had travelled. From that city she turns back to gaze upon her beloved, beseiged Petersburg.

Although Akhmatova's language is deceptively clear and simple, the text of *Poem Without a Hero* is filled with mysterious allusions and packed with layers of meaning. As she rummages through her memories of the Silver Age of Russian poetry, she admits that this box of the *Poem* into which she has cast them "has a triple bottom," that her characters may have multiple identities, that the words of other poets bleed through onto her pages, that she dips her pen into invisible ink or uses cryptographic mirror-writing in order to simultaneously reveal and conceal the meanings of her poem.

To understand the context of the *Poem*, we must return to the year in which it is set, 1913. That was the year that Nikolai Gumilev set out for Africa on an expedition sponsored by the Academy of Sciences and in his absence Akhmatova came upon the letters that revealed the painful details of his latest infidelity. It was not only a year of raucous feuding between the Acmeists and Futurists, clamorous poetry readings, late-night hi-jinks at the Stray Dog cabaret and the suicide of Knyazev. It was in 1913 that Olga Vysotskaya became pregnant with Gumilev's child. After his affair with Tanya Adamovich, he began yet another adulterous relationship. In fact, 1913 marked the breaking point of the marriage of Akhmatova and Gumilev. Indisputably, Nikolai Gumilev then stood at the epicenter of Akhmatova's emotional and creative life. As an editor of the journal *Apollon* and a leading Acmeist and poet-theorist, Gumilev could be seen as one important axis around which the literary world of St. Petersburg revolved. Yet, surprisingly, there seems to be no trace of Gumilev in *Poem Without a Hero*. Akmatova makes no mention of his name, no reference to his work, no clear allusion to his

Frances Laird

existence either in a personal or literary context. At first reading he seems to appear nowhere in the text.

The dating of an Akhmatova poem, as we have seen, is crucially important in providing an insight into its meaning. The fact that Akhmatova dated the Introduction to *Poem Without a Hero* as August 25, 1941, the "memorial day" of the twentieth anniversary of Gumilev's death, conveys the unmistakable message that his life and death stand at the center of the *Poem* and are crucial to unravelling its riddles. With this clue, the poet is asking her readers to search for the evidence of his presence in the poem. And indeed, the hidden presence of Nikolai Gumilev can be discovered in four "layers" of *Poem Without a Hero*.

First, Gumilev can be seen as the striped milepost, a mysterious figure who slips in amongst the other maskers in the wild, Hoffmanesque revelry of New Year's Eve. Akhmatova identified him as the central character of the evening— "The main one was dressed as a striped milepost," crudely smeared with paint. He is an ancient, venerable character whom she describes as "the same age as the oak of Mamre," "the age-old one who chats with the moon" and a writer of "iron laws."

> This creature is of a strange nature,
>   He won't wait for gout or for glory
>   To set him down hurry-scurry
>   In rich anniversary armchairs,

Swan Songs
Akhmatova and Gumilev

> But along blooming heath, along deserts
> His magnificent triumph he bears.
> And he is found guilty of nothing,
> Not in this, not in that, nor the other,
> For poets and sin just don't fit.[2]

Akhmatova identifies the gaudily painted, striped milepost as "the Poet in general, the Poet with a capital 'P.'"[3] But why does she imagine the Poet as a striped milepost? The symbolism of the milepost may convey her sense of the Poet as a kind of ultimate measure. In a literary sense, he maintains the proper standards of poetry, the rules of Russian prosody and the high criteria of the Russian verse tradition. The Poet, endowed with the authoritative voice of the prophet, can trace his lineage back to the ancient prophets of the Biblical Genesis. In his role as prophet, with his unfailing courage and his insistence upon the truth, he must also be considered as a kind of moral measure.

The character of the milepost/Poet might conceivably apply to other poets, such as Mandelstam, Blok or Mayakovsky. But the references in this verse are fitting to Nikolai Gumilev in a powerful and particular way. Though Gumilev was the quintessential romantic, who could chat companionably with the moon, he was also a master of poetic theory. In his writing and teaching, he insisted upon the necessary role of the "iron laws" of metre and rhyme in the Russian poetic tradition.

Furthermore, we can recognize in Akhmatova's stanzas Gumilev's eccentricity, his African journeys over "heaths" and "deserts," his early death that struck him down before the coming of the ravages of age or the wider recognition of his poetic gift, and, most of all, his lack of guilt. "He is found guilty of nothing." This can refer not only to his innocence in the charges of the Tagantsev conspiracy that led to his execution in 1921, but Akhmatova's admission of his ultimate innocence in his behavior with respect to her.

The underlying generating force of the poem, what compelled Akhmatova to conceive of and tirelessly shape *Poem Without a Hero* for so many years, is her attempt to come to terms with the sins of the past, not only in a collective, historical sense, but in a deeply personal sense. In particular, she can be seen to be finally confronting and attempting to transform and redeem her broken relationship with Gumilev, a profound and painful rupture that had remained unhealed at his death. Akhmatova is struggling as well to come to terms with her feelings of guilt about her own behavior in their marriage and its subsequent dissolution. And beyond this is her sense of guilt at not only having survived Gumilev, but at being the only one to remain of that energetic, bumptious, high-spirited, immensely creative group of Silver Age poets.

The theme of guilt and retribution is repeatedly emphasized by the presence of the Don Juan theme which permeates the text of *Poem Without a Hero*. The title itself, it has been suggested, may have been taken from the opening stanza of Byron's narrative poem, *Don Juan*, a poem that Akhmatova knew well.[4] In a letter he wrote to Akhmatova, Gumilev mentioned that he was reading the poetry of Byron, perhaps this very work.[5] Chapter One of *Poem Without a Hero* is prefaced by an epigraph from Byron's poem: "In my hot youth—when George/the Third was king..." Lord Byron himself appears, holding the torch at Shelley's death, in stanza 22 of Part Two of *Poem Without a Hero*.

The epigraph to *Poem Without a Hero*, which appears on the title page is: *"Di rider finirai/Pria dell'aurora." ("You will stop laughing/before dawn")*. These are the words uttered by the statue of the Commendatore in Mozart's treatment of the Don Juan story, his opera, *Don Giovanni*. Amidst the masqueraders that swirl into Akhmatova's presence is one disguised as Don Juan. And in Chapter Two, the stage setting includes the portrait of Donna Anna from Alexander Blok's poem "The Steps of the Commendatore," that poet's version of the Don Juan story, as well as another reference further on in the text.

However, it is clear that Akhmatova's fascination with the Don Juan story stems from more than her preoccupation with the theme of guilt and retribution, one which scholars have pointed to as the rationale for its inclusion. For in her memoirs, Akhmatova referred more than once to Gumilev's betrayals of her in his extramarital romantic liaisons as his "Don Juanism." It may well be that, with her preoccupation with the Don Juan theme, Akhmatova was attempting to accomplish something quite different, namely, to retrieve, transform and redeem that person in her past who had been most important to her as poet and woman, Nikolai Gumilev. In envisioning him as an embodiment of the fictional Don Juan, Akhmatova may have sought to objectify, distance and aestheticize the person of Nikolai Gumilev and his puzzling and painful behavior toward her, which in the year 1913 threw her into such turbulent and confused feelings of hurt, bewilderment and disillusionment. In fact, there are striking parallels between Gumilev and Byron's hero. Byron's Don Juan, born with a thirst for glory, lived a life filled with adventures in exotic foreign lands, amatory pursuits, and heroic feats in battle, for which he was awarded from Empress Catherine the Great the St. George medal. This was the very medal that Gumilev himself had twice earned as a cavalry officer in World War I. By remaking Gumilev in her imagination as a poetic creation, a Byronic hero with all the weight and resonance such a character might embody, Akhmatova could not only resurrect the person who had caused her such suffering in his life and in his death. By transforming in her imagination the painful actualities of their relationship into a carefully defined and dramatic artistic conception, she could safely retrieve the idyll of their first love and rescue from oblivion the power and passion of their unique relationship. Finally, she could establish some control over the consuming feelings of sorrow, loss, guilt, and regret by casting Gumilev and his bitter acts of betrayal into the saving world of art.

Akhmatova's fascination with the Don Juan theme was further revealed in her study of Alexander Pushkin's version of the Don Juan story, *The Stone Guest*. In her study of Pushkin's text, she discovered that Pushkin had changed the tale in subtle and original ways which gave expression to deeply personal meanings. Pushkin made of Don Juan not only a society rake, but a repressed and exiled poet determinedly unafraid of death, but terrified by the loss of happiness. And he remained a hero to the end. The powerful resonance of Pushkin's hero with the life and person of Nikolai Gumilev is unmistakable.

In the tragic story of Vsevolod Knyazev yet another Gumilevian subtext can be uncovered. Akhmatova recalled that the first impetus in writing the *Poem Without a Hero* (which she concealed from herself for decades) was a note by Pushkin: "'Only the first lover leaves an impression on a woman, like the first casualty in a war!' Vsevolod was not the first casualty and never was my lover, but his suicide was so similar to another catastrophe that they have merged forever for me."[6] It seems safe to assume that Nikolai Gumilev was the first lover of the young Anna Gorenko. And if, as she assures us in *Poem Without a Hero*, Akhmatova saw Olga Glebova-Sudeikina as her double, one can conclude that she saw Olga's story as a parallel to her own. Gumilev, like Knyazev, was a poet and a soldier who was caught up in a life of amorous intrigues, and, although he did not die by his own hand, he had made four attempts at suicide for the love of Anna and had flirted with death throughout his life. Knyazev and

Gumilev were further forever linked in Akhmatova's memory on the traumatic day of Alexander Blok's funeral when she and Olga had searched for Knyazev's grave in the Smolensk cemetery and when she had first heard of Nikolai's arrest. Gumilev's violent death in 1921 by a gunshot to the head at a tragically young age, like Knyazev's, must be the "catastrophe" to which Akhmatova alluded.

But in *Poem Without a Hero* Akhmatova recalled not only the difficult years with Gumilev. She remembered their happier days as well, when as young lovers they strolled in the imperial gardens of Tsarskoe Selo. This stanza from Chapter Three of *Poem Without a Hero* she addresses directly to that young Kolya.

>
> But now let us go home quickly
> Through the Cameron gallery
> Into the icy, mysterious park,
> Where the waterfalls have gone silent,
> Where all nine will be happy to see me
> As once you were glad at heart.
> Past the island there, past the garden,
> Perhaps we will meet in the gazes
> Of our eyes as clear as before.
> And perhaps once more you will tell me
>   The word
>   That overcomes
>   Death

And the riddle of my life?[7]

So Nikolai Gumilev makes his appearance in four layers of *Poem Without a Hero*, assuming four manifestations—as the youthful Kolya in the park at Tsarskoe Selo, as the amorous adventurer, Don Juan, as the quintessential Poet disguised as a striped milepost, and as the soldier-poet, Knyazev, cut down tragically in his prime. Yet when we look again, as if into a blank mirror reflecting emptiness, Nikolai Gumilev has vanished. There is no one there.

The central, pervasive presence in *Poem Without a Hero* is, in actuality, a non-presence, the non-presence of Nikolai Gumilev. Akhmatova writes as much in her *Prose About the Poem:* "The one mentioned in the title, and the one whom I so desperately sought...is not actually in the *Poem*, but much is based on his absence."[8] This is a poem without a hero, not because there was no hero of sufficient stature to fill that role, as Byron ruefully observed in the first stanzas of his *Don Juan.* The poem is without a hero because its hero is not present. An enormous absence stands at the center of the poem like a gaping hole.

But clearly Akhmatova has in her mind a clear image of her missing hero when she says at the close of her ballet libretto for *Poem Without a Hero*: "The only one who is absent is the one who definitely should be there, and not just be there, but stand on the landing and greet the guests...But still: We must drink to him/Who is not yet with us."[9] Everything points to Nikolai Gumilev as

Akhmatova's absent hero, the host who, with his usual ceremonious politeness, would gaily, if ironically, greet his poet friends on the evening of that New Year's Eve celebration.

But if Nikolai Gumilev were so central in her life in 1913, why was it that Akhmatova, with her enigmatic references and cryptographic methods, so carefully concealed his presence when she wrote about him in the poem begun twenty years after his death? Obviously, in 1940, for political reasons Gumilev's name could not be uttered. Officially he remained a scorned, condemned, spat-upon traitor, an "enemy of the people," of whom it was highly dangerous for Akhmatova to speak, much less to write.

Another answer is offered by Nadezhda Mandelstam, who wrote revealingly about Akhmatova's tendency to conceal what she could not face. Once in Tashkent, the city to which both women had been evacuated by the Soviet government during the seige of Leningrad, Nadezhda had remarked to her that, unlike Mandelstam, Akhmatova could not bear muddle (presumably, those chaotic, confusing, unhappy circumstances of life over which she had little or no control). And that, in her opinion, was why Akhmatova spoke so little about her early years. "I said: 'You know you have that sense of the *raznochinets* that Mandelstam has.' [A term, coined in the nineteenth century, to denote an educated person who did not arise from the nobility, but entered the intelligentsia from a modest background.] She got terribly angry—in no way would she accept herself as a *raznochinets*. She was drawn into a higher circle where muddle is concealed with a noble shroud. It was as if she began her life with her return to Tsarskoe Selo as the wife of Gumilev, or even with her break with Gumilev. She had the tendency to smooth over the ruptures and mess of the past..."[10] It was only by first concealing, then transforming in *Poem Without a Hero* this problematic and emotionally messy chapter of her life with Kolya Gumilev that Akhmatova could carry on in the lofty and dignified role of the Prophet-Poet.

Poem Without a Hero, a title which rightly translated should read *Poem Without <u>the</u> Hero*, was Akhmatova's moving and masterful attempt to rescue a lost year, to remember lost friends and poets, to redeem a lost hero through her words, to bring a final reconciliation to a lost relationship with the person who had loved her most deeply. That was the "salvation" she had longed for in "Until I collapse at the fence...", the poem written in the days immediately following Gumilev's death. *Poem Without the Hero* is the "noble shroud" that she cast over the muddle of the past, not only over a year in the life of St. Petersburg, but over an excrutiatingly painful year of her own life. Clearly, "cryptographic writing" was nothing new for Akhmatova. As it had been for Nikolai Gumilev in his poetry, this had long been her tool for expressing the truth of her own experience. *Poem Without the Hero* was merely the culminating work of Akhmatova's lifelong effort of transforming the raw material of her life by means of the alchemy of art.

Frances Laird

The conclusion of this exploration of the passionate, complex, seminal and enduring relationship of Anna Akhmatova and Nikolai Gumilev through their poems comes with her own words. The poem, Akhmatova wrote, is nothing less than "a magic potion being poured into a vessel [that] suddenly thickens and turns into my biography..."[11] Though she was speaking then about *Poem Without the Hero*, the potion that hardened into her poems, and the poems of Nikolai Gumilev, from "The Rusalka" to "Bezhetsk," will continue to exert its magical and revelatory powers.

Abbreviations

AAC	*Anna Akhmatova and her Circle,* ed. Konstantin Polivanov, trans. Patricia Beriozkina, University of Arkansas Press, Fayetteville, Arkansas, 1994
AAP	*Anna Akhmatova, a Poetic Pilgrimage,* Amanda Haight, Oxford University Press, New York and London, 1976
AAPP	*Anna Akhmatova, Poet and Prophet,* Roberta Reeder, St. Martin's Press, New York, 1994
AB	*Alexander Blok,* Konstantin Mochulsky, Wayne State University Press, Detroit, 1983
ABD	*Dnevnik,* Alexander Blok, Russkie dnevniki, Sovietskaia Rossiia, Moskva, 1989
ABMP	*Alexander Blok as Man and Poet,* Kornei Chukovsky, trans. and ed. by Diana Burgin and Katherine O'Connor, Ardis, 1982
ABOL	*O literature,* Alexander Blok, Khudozhestvennaia Literatura, Moskva, 1989
AJ	*The Akhmatova Journals, Volume I, 1938-1941,* Lydia Chukovskaya, trans. Milena Micharski and Sylva Rubashova, Farrar, Straus & Giroux, New York, 1994
AV	*Arrested Voices; Resurrecting the Disappeared Writers of the Soviet Regime,* Vitaly Shentalinsky, Martin Kessler Books, The Free Press, New York, 1996

BN   *Black Night, White Snow; Russia's Revolutions (1905-1917),* Harrison E. Salisbury, Da Capo Press, New York, 1977

CPAA   *The Complete Poems of Anna Akhmatova,* Volumes I and II, trans. Judith Hemschemeyer, ed. Roberta Reeder, Zephyr Press, Somerville, Massachusetts, USA, 1990

HAH   *Hope Against Hope; a Memoir,* Nadezhda Mandelstam, trans. Max Hayward, Atheneum, New York, 1970

LM   *The Life of Mayakovsky,* Wiktor Woroszylski, trans. Boleslaw Taborski, The Orion Press, New York, 1970

MHC   *Anna Akhmatova, My Half Century; Selected Prose,* ed. Ronald Meyer, Ardis, Ann Arbor, 1992

NGOS   *V Ognenom stolpe,* Nikolai Gumilev, Russkie dnevniki, Sovietskaia Rossiia, Moscow, 1991

NGVS   *Nikolai Gumilev v vospominaniax sovremennikov,* ed. Vadim Kreid, Tretya Volna, Paris-New York, 1990

OM   *Osip Mandelstam; Stikhotvoreniia, perevody, ocherki, stati,* ed. G. G. Margvelashvili, Merani, Tbilisi, 1990

OMCPL   *Osip Mandelstam; Critical Prose and Letters,* ed. Jane Gary Harris, Ardis, Ann Arbor, 1979

PA   *Posviashchaetsia Akhmatovoi,* ed. P. Davidson and I. Tlasti, Hermitage, 1991

RAA   *Rasskazi o Anne Akhmatovoi,* Anatolii Naiman, Khudozhestvenaia Literatura, Moskva, 1989

RAAT *Remembering Anna Akhmatova,* Anatoly Naiman, trans. Wendy Rosslyn, Henry Holt and Co., New York, 1991

RTQ *Russian Literature Triquarterly,* "The World of Art," John E. Bowit, Number 4, Ardis, Ann Arbor, Michigan,1972

SP *St. Petersburg; a Cultural History,* Solomon Volkov, trans. Antonina W. Bouis, The Free Press, New York, London, 1995

SWNG *Selected Works of Nikolai Gumilev*, trans. Burton Raffel and Alla Burago, State University of New York Press, 1972

UM *The Unknown Modigliani; Drawings from the Collection of Paul Alexandre,* Noel Alexandre, Harry N. Abrams, New York, 1993

VA *Vospominania Akhmatovoi Iosif Brodskii-Solomon Volkov; Dialogi,* Nezavisimaia gazeta, Moskva, 1992

ZAA *Zapiski ob Anne Akhmatovoi, Tom II* (1952-1962), Lidia Chukovskaia, Paris; YMCA Press, 1980

Frances Laird

Notes

Introduction <u>The Swans of Tsarskoe Selo</u> (pp. 1-20)

1. The poems of Alexander Pushkin included in this text are from *A. S. Pushkin, Sochineniia v trex tomax,* Tom I, Stikhotvorenia 1814-1836, Khudozhestvennaia Literatura, Moskva, 1978.
   The Russian versions of poems of Anna Akhmatova can be found in *The Complete Poems of Anna Akhmatova,* Volumes I and II, trans. Judith Hemschemeyer, edited and introduced by Roberta Reeder, Zephyr Press, Somerville, Massachusetts, USA, 1990.
   Two books provided the poems of Nikolai Gumilev: *Nikolai Gumilev; Stikhotvoreniia i poemy,* "Sovremennik," Moskva, 1989, and *Nikolai Gumilev; Stikhotvoreniia i poemy,* Leningradskoe Otdelenie, 1988. All translations, unless otherwise noted, are my own.
2. *Tsarskoe Selo*
3. As cited in AAPP, p. 5
4. *"Smuglyi otrok brodil po alleiam..."*
5. MHC, p. 41
6. MHC, p. 117
7. CPAA, Vol. I, p. 261, *"On liubil..."*
8. CPAA, Vol. I, p. 239, *"Myzh khlestil menia uzorchatym..."*
9. *Pesnia poslednyi vstrechi*
10. As quoted in *A Sense of Place,* p. 245
11. MHC, p. 114
12. MHC, p.113
13. MHC, p. 117
14. AJ, p. 29

Chapter I <u>Under the Lime Trees</u> (pp. 21-35)

1. AAC, p. 53
2. AAC, p. 54
3. AAC, p. 58

Frances Laird

4. MHC, p. 25
5. AJ, p. 117
6. MHC, p. 4
7. MHC, p. 6
8. MHC, p. 3
9. AAPP, p. 5
10. AJ, p. 157
11. AJ, p. 171
12. MHC, p. 7
13. AJ, p. 145
14. MHC, p. 11
15. AJ, p. 93
16. AJ, p. 166
17. AAPP, p. 12
18. AJ, p. 166
19. AAC, p. 52
20. AAC, p. 52
21. AAC, p. 58
22. NGVS, p. 174
23. AJ, p. 120

Chapter II <u>The Rusalka</u> (pp. 36-68)

1. NGVS, p. 26
2. AAPP, p. 9
3. MHC, p. 41
4. *Pamiati Annenskovo*
5. MHC, p. 7
6. MHC, p. 1
7. AJ, p. 73
8. MHC, p. 2
9. *Rusalka*
10. MHC, p. 113
11. MHC, p. 118
12. MHC, p. 41
13. NGVS, p. 15-16
14. NGVS, p. 20
15. NGVS, p. 27

16. NGOS, see V. Bryusov's letters, p. 159-215
17. MHC, p. 271.
18. MHC, p. 272-3
19. MHC, p. 274
20. MHC, p. 275
21. MHC, p. 275-6
22. MHC, p. 276-7
23. NGOS, p. 162
24. NGOS, p. 162
25. NGOS, p. 161
26. AAPP, p. 18
27. NGVS, p. 33-34
28. NGOS, p. 165
29. AAPP, p. 18
30. NGOS, p. 169
31. MHC, p. 277
32. MHC, p. 278
33. MHC. p. 280
34. MHC, p. 113
35. *Beatriche*

Chapter III <u>Rejection</u> (pp. 69-93)

1. MHC, p. 281-2
2. NGOS, p. 355, n. 25
3. ZAA, p. 443
4. AAP, p. 13
5. *Otkaz*
6. *Severnye elegii*
7. AAC, p. 54
8. NGOS, p. 171
9. NGOS, p. 180
10. NGVS, p. 38
11. NGOS, p. 188
12. NGOS, p. 191
13. *Tsaritsa*
14. MHC, p.116
15. NGOS, p. 192

16. NGOS, p. 193
17. *Anna Komnena*
18. NGOS, p. 193
19. MHC, p. 116
20. *Ozera*
21. MHC, p. 113
22. NGOS, p. 198
23. NGOS, p. 227
24. *Ezbekie*

Chapter IV Ballad (pp. 94-120)

1. NGVS, p. 148
2. NGOS, p. 204
3. NGVS. p. 149
4. AJ, p. 61
5. NGVS, p. 40
6. *Son Adama*
7. AJ, p. 138
8. NGVS, p. 134
9. NGVS, p. 142-3
10. NGVS, p. 135
11. NGVS, p. 136
12. NGVS, p. 136
13. AJ, p. 140
14. NGVS, p. 146
15. NGVS, p. 146
16. NGVS, p. 147
17. *"I kogda drug druga proklinala..."*
18. *"Prishli i skazali: Umer tvoi brat..."*
19. NGOS, p. 206
20. NGOS, p. 230
21. *"Net tebia trevozhnei i kapriznei..."*
22. AJ, p. 97
23. MHC, p. 111
24. MHC, p. 110
25. NGOS, p. 207
26. *Ballada*

Chapter V <u>At the Fireside</u> (pp. 121-147)

1. NGVS, p. 83
2. MHC, p. 79
3. MHC, p. 81
4. MHC, p. 79
5. MHC, p. 76
6. NGVS, p. 83
7. MHC, p. 8
8. NGVS, p. 85
9. AAC, p. 55
10. MHC, p.117
11. *Margarita*
12. MHC, p. 112
13. *"Ty pomnish dvorets velikanov..."*
14. *U kamina*
15. NGSP, note #123, p. 565
16. MHC, p. 44
17. AJ, p. 109
18. MHC, p. 44
19. MHC. p. 44
20. AJ, p. 61
21. AAPP, p. 33
22. MHC, p. 46
23. AAPP, p. 35
24. NGVS, p. 83
25. RAAT, p. 200
26. AAP, p. 17
27. MHC, p. 47
28. AJ, p. 109
29. *Odnazhdy vecherom*
30. *Iz logova zmieva*—This poem offers an excellent example of why the original form should be retained in translation. The amphibrachs (~'~) and lines ending with double feminine rhymes convey a humorous, teasing quality. When translated into the free verse form, a severity and heaviness of tone

distorts the meaning of the poem. The wonderful playfulness of Gumilev's original is gone.
31. NGVS, p. 153
32. AJ, p. 168
33. UM, p. 164-5, plates 66-68
34. *Akrostik* The 'kh' sound in 'Akhmatova' is conveyed by the letter x in Russian. To retain the four-line stanza, I have omitted the h—and achieved the acrostic form.
35. MHC, p. 113
36. NGVS, p. 61
37. *"Eto byla ne raz..."*

Chapter VI Poisoned (pp. 148-175)

1. RAA, p. 107
2. MHC, p. 82
3. MHC, p. 76
4. MHC, p. 77
5. MHC, p. 77
6. See UM, Part One
7. MHC, p.78
8. MHC, p. 79
9, MHC, p. 79
10. MHC, p. 80
11. MHC. p. 76
12. MHC, p. 80
13. See *"Yevo Egiptianka, Anna Akhmatova i Amedeo Modiliani,"* Avgusta Dokukina-Bobel, p. 57, Lettre Internationale, No. 9,1996
14. UM, Plate 345
15. UM, Plates 243 and 244
16. MHC, p. 78
17. UM, Plates 91-93
18. UM, Plate 67
19. UM, Plate 104
20. UM, Plate 329
21. MHC, p. 77
22. Plates 172-186

23. AJ, p. 28
24. MHC, p. 76
25. VA, p. 35
26. VA, p. 35
27. MHC, p. 82
28. AAPP, p. 36
29. RAA, p. 106
30. *Otravlennyi*
31. MHC, p. 27
32. MHC, p.9
33. MHC, p. 9
34. MHC, p. 9
35. NGVS, p. 151
36. NGVS, p. 151
37. MHC, p. 115
38. AAPP, p. 38
39. NKVS, p. 122
40. NGOS, p. 210
41. NGVS, p. 90
42. *"Menia pokinul v novolune..."*
43. *Ukrotitel zverei*
44. MHC, p. 36
45. AAPP, p. 43
46. MHC, p. 43
47. AJ, p. 156
48. MHC, p. 86-88
49. AAPP, p.44
50. MHC, p. 85
51. MHC, p. 84
52. MHC, p. 85
53. See *Acmeism and the Legacy of Symbolism,* SWNG, p. 245
54. MHC, p. 115
55. See "Morning of Acmeism," OMCPL, p.61
56. MHC, p. 38

Chapter VII Evening (pp. 176-198)

1. OMCPL, p. 158

2. *Seroglazyi korol*
3. *"Ia prishli siuda, bezdelnitsa..."*
4. AAP, p. 20
5. AJ, p. 65
6. MHC, p. 8
7. NGOS, p. 248
8. *"V remeshkakh penal i knigi byli..."*
9. NGVS, p. 85-86
10. AAC, p. 55
11. *Ona*
12. *Zhestokoi*
13. *Tot drugoi*
14. MHC. p. 117
15. *Vechnoe*
16. NGVS, p. 92
17. MHC, p. 283

Chapter VIII <u>At the Stray Dog</u> (pp. 199-233)

1. NGOS, p. 249
2. NGOS, p. 230
3. NGOS, p. 230
4. NGOS, p. 53-79
5. NGOS, p. 346
6. *"Pokorno mne voobrazhene..."*
7. NGVS, p. 160
8. NGVS, p. 160
9. NGVS, p. 160
10. LM, p. 88
11. AAC, p. 65
12. NGVS, p. 161
13. MHC, p. 88
14. NGVS, p. 16
15. AAC. p. 64
16. APP, p. 29
17. AAC, p. 66
18. AAC, p. 66
19. ZAA, p. 269, (ll Dec 55)

20. LM, p. 140
21. AJ, p. 106
22. AAC, p. 122
23. AAC. p. 230
24. AAC, p. 232
25. AAPP, p. 65
26. AAPP, p. 25
27. AAC, p. 65
28. SP, 195
29. *"Vse my brazhniki zdes, bludnitsi..."*
30. AJ, p. 26
31. AAPP, p. 62
32. MHC, p. 69
33. MHC, p. 70
34. MHC, p. 69
35. AJ, p. 110
36. AJ, p. 147
37. MHC, p. 70
38. AJ, p. 174
39. *"Ia prishli k poetu v gosti..."*
40. AAC, p. 67
41. *"U menia est ulybka ogna..."*
42. *"Zdravstvui! Lekii shelest slyshish..."*
43. *"Stolko prosb u liubimoi vsegda..."*
44. MHC. p. 86
45. AJ, p. 192
46. *Akhmatova*
47. MHC, p. 73
48. AAPP, p. 65
49. MHC, p. 91
50. *"Ia ne liubvi tvoei proshu..."*

Chapter IX <u>The Real Twentieth Century Begins</u> (pp. 234-255)

1. MHC, p. 49
2. MHC, p. 12
3. MHC, p. 48
4. ZAA, p. 285, 7 December 1958

5. Reprinted in RAA, p.233
6. MHC, p. 26
7. NGOS. p. 251
8. MHC, p. 71
9. MHC, p. 285
10. MHC, p. 285
11. MHC, p. 8
12. MHC, p. 286
13. *Iiul 1914*
14. MHC, p. 71
15. AJ, p. 89
16. MHC, p. 115
17. NGOS, p. 252
18. NGOS, p. 252
19. NGOS, p. 241
20. *Uteshenie*

Chapter X <u>Love and War</u> (pp. 256-285)

1. AJ, p. 180
2. NGOS, p. 242
3. NGVS, p. 215
4. NGVS, p. 233
5. NGVs, p. 17
6. NGOS, pp. 94-154
7. NGOS, pp. 94-5
8. NGOS, pp. 108-110
9. *Piatistopnye iamby*. In Gumilev's *tour de force* of fourteen six-line stanzas, the aB rhyme scheme is never exactly repeated, an interesting challenge for the translator!
10. MHC, p. 24
11. SP, p. 184-6
12. AAPP, p. 40
13. AAC, p. 77
14. AAC, p. 77
15. *"Shirok i zhelt vechernii svet..."*
16. *"Est v blizosti liudei zavetnaia cherta..."*
17. *"Ved gde-to est prostaia zhizn i svet..."*

18. MHC, p. 113
19. *Detstvo*
20. NGVS, p. 173
21. AAC, p. 80
22. PA, p.14
23. AAC, p. 53
24. AAC, p. 79
25. AAC, p. 80
26. *"A! Eto snova ty..."*
27. *"Kogda v mrachneishei iz stolits..."*
28. *Tsarskoe Selo statuia*
29. *"Vnov podaren mne dpermotoi..."*
30. AJ, p. 62
31. MHC, p. 9
32. MHC, p. 9

Chapter XI <u>Revolutions</u> (pp. 286-314)

1. AAC, p.60
2. *"Tam ten moia ostalas i toskuet..."*
3. MHC, p. 127
4. AAC, p. 84
5. MHC p. 94
6. AAC, p. 113
7. *Akrostik*
8. *"Ty pozhalela, ty prostila..."*
9. NGVS, p. 170
10. AAPP, p. 109
11. MHC, p. 9
12. *"Prosypatsia na passvete..."*
13. *"Ty—otstupnik: za ostrov zelenyi..."*
14. AAPP, p. 190
15. MHC, p. 52
16. *"Kogda v toske samoubiistva..."*
17. AAP, p. 55
18. *"Teper nikto ne stanet slyshat pesen..."*
19. *Molitva*
20. OM, p. 112, *Kassandre*

21. *Angel boli*
22. AAC, p. 86

Chapter XII Dying Petersburg (pp. 315-336)

1. AJ, p. 165
2. PA, p. 43
3. *"Ty vsegda tainstbennyi i novyi..."*
4. AAPP, p. 119
5. AAC, p. 59
6. AJ, p. 148
7. NGVS, p. 201
8. NGVS, p. 128
9. NGVS, p. 204
10. NGOS, p. 277
11. AJ, p. 106
12. AJ, p. 110
13. NGVS, p. 223
14. NGVS, p. 223
15. NGVS, p. 19
16. NGVS, p. 203
17. NGVS, p. 167
18. NGVS, p. 206
19. NGVS, p. 225
20. NGVS, p. 225
21. NGVS, p. 206
22. NGOS, p. 310; SWNG, 234 (in English)
23. ABOL, p. 307
24. LM, p. 190r

Chapter XIII The Lost Streetcar (pp. 337-368)

1. *"Ot liubvi tvoei zagadochnoi..."*
2. MHC, p. 91
3. *Tretii Zachatevskii*
4. *"Chem xuzhe etot bek predshestruiuschix..."*
5. NGVS, p. 176
6. NGVS, p. 231

7. NGVS, p. 231
8. NGVS, p. 265
9. S. Lipkin, *Vzglyad: Kritika, Polemika, Publikatsii*, No. 3, Sovietskii pisatel, Moscow, 1991, p. 379
10. NGVS, p. 176
11. NGVS, p. 176
12. NGVS, p. 176
13. ABMP, p. 25
14. ABMP, p. 25
15. *Petrograd, 1919*
16. MHC, p. 91
17. NGVS, p. 178
18. MHC, p. 91
19. *"Ia gorkaia i staraia..."*
20. NGVS, p. 197
21. *Zabludivshiisia tramvai*
22. Dead Souls, Nikolai Gogol, W.W.Norton & Company, New York, London, 1985, p. 270
23. AAC, p. 92
24. HAH, p. 110
25. AJ, p. 62
26. AAC, p. 93
27. MHC, p. 96
28. NGVS, p. 216
29. NGVS, p. 204
30. NGVS, p. 216
31. NGVS, p. 216
32. NGVS, p. 216
33. NGVS, p. 238
34. NGVS, p. 21
35. NGVS. p. 197
36. NGVS, p. 197
37. NGVS, p. 198
38. NGVS, p. 17
39. NGVS, p. 216
40. NGVS, p. 178
41. NGVS, p. 301, n.9r

Frances Laird

Chapter XIV <u>The Silver Age Tarnishes</u> (pp. 369-395)

1. NGVS, p. 21
2. NGVS, p. 22
3. NGVS, p. 23
4. ABD, p. 304
5. NGVS, p. 209
6. ABOL, p. 372
7. NGVS, p. 205
8. NGVS, p. 129
9. NGVS, p. 221
10. NGVS, p. 228
11. NGVS, p. 228
12. NGVS, p. 229
13. *Rekviem 1935-1940, Posviaschenie*
14. AAC, p. 93
15. MHC, p. 71
16. AAPP, p. 139
17. AB, p. 427
18. ABOL, p. 381
19. AB, p. 427
20. AAPP, p. 139
21. NGVS, p. 221
22. NGVS, p. 177
23. NGVS, p. 177
24. *Pamiat*
25. NGVS, p. 219
26. NGVS, p. 220
27. NGVS, p. 226

Chapter XV <u>Terror and Grief</u> (pp. 396-421)

1. NGVS, p. 102
2. ABMP, p. 226.
3. SP, p. 231
4. ABMP, p. 32
5. NGVS, p. 232
6. AAPP, p. 141

7. SP, p. 238
8. NGVS, p. 210-211
9. NGVS, p. 210-211
10. NGVS, p. 210-211
11. NGVS, p. 179
12. NGVS, p. 232
13. NGVS, p. 243
14. NGVS, p. 240
15. NGVS, p. 241
16. NGVS, p. 100
17. AB, p. 433
18. SP, p. 238
19. SP, p. 238
20. SP, p. 233
21. *"A Smolenskaia nynche imeninnitsa..."*
22. NGVS, p. 179
23. MHC, p. 128
24. NGVS, p. 325, n. 2
25. NGVS, p. 235
26. NGVS, p. 241
27. NGVS, p. 180
28. NGVS, p. 234
29. NGVS, p. 288, n. 9
30. NGVS, p. 288, n. 9
31. NGVS, p. 288, n. 9
32. NGVS, p. 234
33. NGVS, p. 235
34. NGVS, p. 181
35. MHC, p. 35
36. RAAT, p. 129
37. *"Ne byvat tebe v zhivyx..."*
38. *"Chugunaia ograda..."*
39. *"Strax, v tme perebiraia veschi..."*
40. *"O zhizn bez zavtrashnevo dnia..."*
41. *"Poka ne svalius pod zaborom..."*
42. AAPP, p. 145
43. MHC, p. 35
44. NGVS, p. 213

Chapter XVI An Unwed Widow (pp. 422-438)

1. *"Shiroko raspaxnuty vorota..."*
2. *Severnie elegii,* *"V tom dome bylo ochen strashno zhit..."*
3. *"Zaplakannaia osen, kak vdova..."*
4. *"Piatym deistviem dramy..."*
5. *"Vse dushi milyx na vysokix zvezdax..."*
6. *"Dolgim vzgliadom tvoim istomlennaia..."*
7. AAPP, p. 150
8. AAPP, p. 151
9. LM, p. 277
10. AAPP, p. 151
11. LM, p. 271
12, *Drugoi golos 1*
13. *Drugoi golos 2*
14. AAC, p. 93
15. *Bezhetsk*

Chapter XVII The Banks of the Neva (pp. 439-456)

1. NGVS, p. 212
2. MHC, p. 97
3. *Vtoraya kniga,* Nadezhda Mandelstam, Moskovskii Rabochii, 1990, p. 59
4. MHC. p. 250
5. MHC, p. 250
6. MHC, p. 400, n.5
7. ZAA, p. 432
8. *A Guest from the Future; Anna Akhmatova and Isaiah Berlin,* Gyorgy Dalos, trans. Antony Wood, John Murray, London, 1996, p. 34
9. "Shagreneie Pereplety," Oleg Khlebnikov, *Ogonek,* No. 18 (1990), p. 13-16.
10. MHC, p. 102
11. MHC, p. 74
12. AV, p. 205
13. AV, p. 173

14. MHC, p. 101

Conclusion The Absent Hero (pp. 457-470)

1. *Poem Without a Hero,* Introduction, *"Iz sorokovo..."*
2. *PWH,* Chapter I, lines 105-125
3. MHC, p. 128
4. MHC, p. 198
5. NGOX, "Pisma N. C. Gumileva k A.A.Axmatovoji"
6. MHC, p. 128
7. *PWH,* Chapter III, lines 385-398
8. MHC, p. 133
9. MHC, pp. 142-143
10. *Vtoraya kniga,* p. 351
11. MHC, p. 135

Frances Laird

Bibliography

Akhmatova, Anna, *The Complete Poems of Anna Akhmatova, Volumes I and II,* trans. Judith Hemschemeyer and ed. Roberta Reeder, Zephyr Press, Somerville, Massachusetts, USA, 1990
———*Anna Akhmatova, My Half Century; Selected Prose,* ed. Ronald Meyer, Ardis, Ann Arbor, 1992

Alexandre, Noel, *The Unknown Modigliani; Drawings from the Collection of Paul Alexandre,* Harry N. Abrams, New York, 1993

Billington, James H., *The Icon and the Axe; An Interpretive History of the Russian Culture,* Alfred A. Knopf, New York, 1966

Blok, Alexander, *Dnevnik,* Russkie Dnevniki, Sovietskaia Rossiia, Moskva, 1989
———*O literature,* Khudozhestvenaia Literatura, Moskva, 1989

Bowit, John, E. "The World of Art," *Russian Literature Triquarterly,* Number 4, Ardis, Ann Arbor, Michigan,1972

Brodsky, Joseph and Solomon Volkov, *Vospominaia Akhmatovu; Iosif Brodskii-Solomon Volkov; Dialogi,* Nezavisimaia gazeta, Moskva, 1992
——— "The Keening Muse," *Less Than One; Selected Essays*, Farrar Straus & Giroux, New York, 1983

Brown, Edward J., *Mayakovsky; A Poet in the Revolution,* Paragon House Publishers, New York, 1973

Chukovskaya, Lydia, *The Akhmatova Journals, Volume I, 1938-1941,* trans. Milena Micharski and Sylva Rubashova, Farrar Straus & Giroux, New York, 1994
———*Zapiski ob Anne Akhmatovoi, Tom II* (1952-1962), Paris; YMCA Press, 1980

Chukovsky, Kornei, *Alexander Blok as Man and Poet,* trans. and ed. Diana Burgin and Katherine O'Connor, Ardis, 1982

Dalos, Gyorgy, *A Guest from the Future; Anna Akhmatova and Isaiah Berlin,* trans. Antony Wood, John Murray, London, 1998

Davidson, P. and I. Tlasti, ed. *Posviashchaetsia Akhmatovoi,* Hermitage, 1991

Dokukina-Bobel, "Yevo Egiptyanka, Anna Akhmatova i Amedeo Modilyani," *Lettre Internationale,* No. 9, 1996, p. 57

Gumilev, Nikolai S., *Nikolai Gumilev; stikhotvoreniia i poemy;* Biblioteka Poeta, ed. Yu. A. Andreev, Leningradskoe Otdelenie, 1988
———*Nikolai Gumilev; Stikhotvoreniia i poemy;* Sovremennik, Moskva, 1989
———*V Ognenom stolpe,* Russkie dnevniki, Sovietskaia Rossiia, Moskva, 1991
———*Selected Works of Nikolai Gumilev,* trans. Burton Raffel and Alla Burago, State University of New York Press, 1972

Haight, Amanda, *Anna Akhmatova, a Poetic Pilgrimage,* Oxford University Press, New York and London, 1976

Kreid, Vadim, ed. *Nikolai Gumilev v vospominaniax sovremennikov,* Tretia Volna, Paris-New York, 1990

Larousse Encyclopedia of Mythology, Paul Hamlyn, London, 1959

Lipkin, S. "Besedy s Akhmatovoi," *Vzglyad: Kritika, Polemika, Publikatsii,* No. 3, Sovietskii pisatel, Moskva, 1991

Loseff, Lev and Barry Scherr, ed. *A Sense of Place; Tsarskoe Selo and its Poets,* Slavica Publishers, Columbus, Ohio, 1993

Mandelstam, Nadezhda, *Hope Against Hope; a Memoir,* trans. Max Hayward, Atheneum, New York, 1970

———*Vtoraya kniga,* Moskovskii Rabochii, 1990

Mandelstam, Osip, *Osip Mandelstam; Stikhotvoreniia, perevody, ocherki, stati,* Merani, Tbilisi, 1990
———*Osip Mandelstam; Critical Prose and Letters,* ed. Jane Gary Harris, Ardis, Ann Arbor, 1979

Massie, Robert K., *Nicholas and Alexandra,* Dell, 1967
———*The Romanovs; the Final Chapter,* Ballantine Books, New York, 1995

McVay, Gordon, *Esenin: a Life,* Paragon House, New York, 1976

Mochulsky, Konstantin, *Alexander Blok,* Wayne State University Press, Detroit, 1983

Moorhead, Alan, *The Russian Revolution,* Carroll and Graf, New York, 1958

Nicholas and Alexandra; The Last Imperial Family of Tsarist Russia, State Hermitage Museum and the State Archive of the Russian Federation, Booth-Cliburn Editions, London, 1998

Naiman, Anatolii, *Rasskazi o Anne Akhmatovoi,* Khudozhestvenaia Literatura, Moskva, 1989
———*Remembering Anna Akhmatova,* trans. Wendy Rosslyn, Henry Holt and Co., New York, 1991

Polivanov, Konstantin, ed. *Anna Akhmatova and her Circle,* ed. trans. Patricia Beriozkina, University of Arkansas Press, Fayetteville, Arkansas, 1994

Pushkin, Alexander, *A. S. Pushkin, Sochineniia v trex tomax,* Tom I, Stikhotvoreniia 1814-1836, Khudozhestvennaia Literatura, Moskva, 1978

Reeder, Roberta, *Anna Akhmatova, Poet and Prophet,* St. Martin's Press, New York, 1994

Riasanovsky, Nicholas V., *The History of Russia*, Oxford University Press, New York and Oxford, 1993

Salisbury, Harrison E., *Black Night, White Snow; Russia's Revolutions 1905-1917,* Da Capo Press, New York, 1977

Shentalinsky, Vitaly, *Arrested Voices; Resurrecting the Disappeared Writers of the Soviet Regime,* trans. John Crowfoot, The Free Press, New York and London, 1993

Volkov, Solomon, *St. Petersburg; a Cultural History,* trans. Antonina W. Bouis, The Free Press, New York, London, 1995

Terras, Victor, ed. *Handbook of Russian Literature,* Yale University Press, New Haven and London, 1983
———*A History of Russian Literature,* Yale University Press, New Haven and London, 1991

Woroszylski, Wiktor, *The Life of Mayakovsky,* trans. Boleslaw Taborski, The Orion Press, New York, 1970

About the Author

Even before learning the Russian language, the author *of Swan Songs: Akhmatova and Gumilev* had been fascinated by the life of Anna Akhmatova and her poetry in English translations. While studying Russian at Bryn Mawr College, Frances Laird began to attempt her own translations of Akhmatova's poems. She went on to study Russian literature and the translation of Russian poetry under Prof. George Kline, the first translator of the poetry of Nobel prize winner, Joseph Brodsky, and Anatoly Naiman, a poet and close friend of Akhmatova. Naiman called Laird's translation of *Requiem* (1935-1940) the best he had read and an "echo in English" of the Russian original. Frances Laird has traveled and studied in Russia and, since receiving a Master's Degree in Russian Literature from Bryn Mawr College, has published her translations of contemporary Russian poets as well as those of Anna Akhmatova and Nikolai Gumilev.

LaVergne, TN USA
03 September 2009

156874LV00001B/76/A